TRAVELER

rome

NATIONAL GEOGRAPHIC
TRAVELER

rome

Sari Gilbert and Michael Brouse

National Geographic
Washington, D.C.

CONTENTS

Pages 2–3: The Colosseum
Left: Picturesque courtyard on one of the city's quieter backstreets

TRAVELING WITH EYES OPEN

Alert travelers go with a purpose and leave with a benefit. If you travel responsibly, you can help support wildlife conservation, historic preservation, and cultural enrichment in the places you visit. You can enrich your own travel experience as well.

To be a geo-savvy traveler:

- Recognize that your presence has an impact on the places you visit.

- Spend your time and money in ways that sustain local character. (Besides, it's more interesting that way.)

- Value the destination's natural and cultural heritage.

- Respect the local customs and traditions.

- Express appreciation to local people about things you find interesting and unique to the place: its nature, scenery, music or food, historic villages, and buildings.

- Vote with your wallet: Support the people who support the place, patronizing businesses that make an effort to celebrate and protect what's special about the place. Seek out shops, local restaurants, inns, and tour operators who love the place—who love taking care of it and showing it off. Avoid businesses that detract from the character of the place.

- Enrich yourself, taking home more memories and stories to tell, knowing that you have contributed to the preservation and enhancement of the destination.

That is the type of travel now called geotourism, defined as "tourism that sustains or enhances the geographical character of a place—its environment, culture, aesthetics, heritage, and the well-being of its residents." To learn more, visit National Geographic's Center for Sustainable Destinations at *www .nationalgeographic.com/travel/sustainable.*

rome

ABOUT THE AUTHORS

Sari Gilbert was born and bred in New York City and became interested in things Mediterranean while still attending Hunter High School there. She spent part of her junior year in Italy, at Syracuse University's semester abroad program in Florence. After receiving her B.A. in political science from Syracuse, Sari returned to Italy to attend the Johns Hopkins Bologna Center, and subsequently received an M.A. and a Ph.D. in international relations from the School of Advanced International Studies in Washington, D.C. Her doctoral dissertation was on Italian foreign policy. After concluding her studies, Sari returned again to Rome, where she lives in the heart of the ancient Trastevere district and, for almost 20 years, worked as a correspondent for important U.S. newspapers and magazines. She speaks Italian and French and is currently a full-time reporter for a major Italian daily.

Michael Brouse is a native San Franciscan who spent much of his childhood in Hawaii. After graduating from high school in Marin County, Michael attended the University of Santa Clara, where he received a B.A. in history, but only after spending his junior year abroad, in Rome. Like Sari, Michael returned to Rome in 1972 where, after a stint of teaching English, he worked for many years in men's fashion. His ongoing passion for history and art history found an outlet in popular walking tours he conducts for visitors to the city. Michael is fluent in Italian, French, and German and is an accomplished translator. He returned to his first love (teaching) several years ago and is now a history instructor at St. Stephen's School, an American international high school. Most mornings on his way to work he walks through the Roman Forum.

Charting Your Trip

Lucian, the second-century Greek rhetorician, described Rome as "a bit of Paradise." Fifteenth-century Tuscan scholar Gian Francesco Poggio Bracciolini praised the city as "the most beautiful and magnificent of all those that either have been or shall be."

These opinions survive and may have helped convince you to visit what has long been described as the Eternal City. And why not? Almost three thousand years of history, layer upon layer of it, testify not only to the genius, perseverance, and adaptability of the peoples who founded Rome and developed it through the ages, but also to that of those who followed. A large number of archaeological sites, ancient monuments, and early structures still exists today, attesting to the glory that was Rome, all ready for you to discover.

Like many other great cities, there's no better way to explore Rome than by using your own two feet. (Unless you're planning on making a lot of trips out of the city, a car in central Rome is more of a hindrance than a help.) The city also has two subway lines (A and B), which service limited parts of the city. The A line goes to Piazza di Spagna and Piazza Barberini, to near the Vatican Museums (Cipro station), and out to Cinecittà. The B line is useful for trips to the Colosseum and the Circus Maximus. The integrated network of buses, trams, and local trains also comes in very handy.

Most visitors come to Rome for only three or four days. If that's your plan, we suggest you concentrate on the two things for which Rome is still best known: the former capital of the Roman Empire and the seat of the Roman Catholic Church. If you have more time, there's plenty to add.

A gold coin bearing the name and image of the first-century emperor Nero

Ancient Rome

Fortunately for tourists, the visible remains of the Roman Empire are for the most part located in a fairly manageable area in the city center.

The first thing you should see is the **Colosseo** (Colosseum), also known as the Flavian Amphitheater after the first-century emperors who sponsored its construction. It took ten years to build and could house 50,000 spectators, and it has survived miraculously through the centuries. In front of the imposing structure—where gladiators once killed lions, tigers, and one another—sprawls the **Foro Roman** (Roman Forum), which includes the remains of the Roman Senate, the most important temples and basilicas of the ancient city, and several imposing triumphal arches.

A short walk to one side of the Roman Forum lie the remains of the **Fori Imperiali** (Imperial Forums) built by a variety of emperors. The most important is that of Trajan, positioned just below Trajan's Markets (now a museum dedicated to the Forums). Here you will see **Colonna Traiana** (Trajan's Column), celebrating Trajan's victory over the Dacian armies. On the other side of the Forum is the **Monte Palatino** (Palatine Hill), where Augustus and other emperors and dignitaries lived and where, in a far earlier era, the city's legendary twin founders, Romulus and Remus, are said to have been born. From here you can see the broad expanse of the **Circo Massimo** (Circus Maximus), where once chariots raced before massive, cheering crowds.

Other important monuments in the area include the underground **Domus Aurea,** otherwise known as Nero's Golden House; the **Case Romane del Celio** (Roman Houses), an ancient villa and apartment block under the church of Santi Giovanni e Paolo; and the **Basilica di San Clemente**, a short walk away where intriguing first- and fourth-century structures are layered underground. From here it is an easy half-mile (0.9 km) walk to the **Terme di Caracalla** (Baths of Caracalla), which once served as a health club and spa for the elites of Rome.

NOT TO BE MISSED:

The evocative Roman Forum and Palatine Hill **44–51**

Glorious St. Peter's Basilica **164–170**

The magnificent Sistine Chapel and the Raphael Rooms in the Vatican Museums **172–177**

Trevi Fountain's ornate baroque brilliance **96–97**

The impressive 2nd-century Pantheon **128–131**

Michelangelo's Campidoglio on the Capitoline Hill **40–42**

Piazza di Spagna and the beautiful Spanish Steps **110–111**

Roma Pass

Visiting Rome has now become easier with the city's three-day tourist card, Roma Pass, offering discounts for museums combined with full free access to the public transport system. For 20 euros, you get free admission to the first two museums or archaeological sites visited, discounts on other participating sites and museums, and the public transport ticket. You'll also receive a city map, a guidebook detailing the complete list of eligible museums and sites, and "Roma News," a list of events and services where discounts are also available. You can buy the pass at any participating museum or at a tourist information kiosk (see sidebar p. 11).

The Vatican

A short taxi or subway ride across the Tiber from the ancient sites brings you to **Citta del Vaticano** (Vatican City), a tiny walled city-state, the smallest in the world. Shortly after the death of Jesus, the apostle Peter arrived in Rome to help spread the new Christian faith. **Basilica di San Pietro** (Saint Peter's Basilica) supposedly stands on the spot where the saint was buried after his crucifixion by the Romans. The basilica you see today was constructed centuries later, its foundation stone laid in 1506. The church and square, designed by Michelangelo, Bernini, and a host of others, may well be one of the most imposing landmarks in the world as well as an inspiring place of worship. No one should come to Rome

A Few Etiquette Tips

Say *"buon giorno"* (*"buona sera"* after lunch) and *"arrivederci"* when entering and leaving shops, restaurants, and bars. Although nobody expects you to speak Italian, an attempt to utter a few words, no matter how basic, is greatly appreciated. In general Italians use "please" and "thank you" (*per favore* and *grazie*) less than English-speakers do, so don't be offended if people seem brusque. If you are giving flowers, avoid chrysanthemums; here they are only put on graves.

without making a visit to the top of Michelangelo's magnificent dome.

But there is much more to the Vatican. Just around the corner from St. Peter's lie the **Musei Vaticani** (Vatican Museums), one of the finest museum complexes anywhere. Foremost is the **Cappella Sistina** (Sistine Chapel), built in the late 1400s and once the private chapel of the popes, where for centuries the cardinals of the Roman Catholic Church have met to elect the next pontiff. On the **ceiling**, Michelangelo produced his masterpiece, 20 years later adding the glorious **"Last Judgement"** on the wall behind the altar. You don't want to miss **Raphael's Rooms** or the other museums either.

If You Have More Time

What next after the Colosseum and Forums, St. Peter's, and the Vatican Museums? Only about another thousand years of history. You will find Rome rich with medieval, Renaissance, and baroque reminders of the past, as well as other museums and a few contemporary sites.

Since time immemorial, the **Campidoglio** on the Capitoline Hill (just across from the Colosseum) has been—and still is—the center of the city. All the roads that led to Rome led here, so it's a must on your list. The design for the piazza can be attributed to Michelangelo, who decided to place the second-century equestrian statue of Marcus Aurelius in the center of the square and to renovate the existing buildings that framed it. The three are now, respectively, Rome's City Hall and the two wings of the **Musei Capitolini** (Capitoline Museums).

A mile (1.6 km) northwest of the Capitoline Museum, and a must see, is **Piazza Navona,** in the shape of a horseshoe. Originally the site of the first-century emperor Domitian's stadium, the square is encircled by Renaissance and baroque buildings constructed on the foundations of the ancient structure. By day, Piazza Navona buzzes with activity: street-artists, outdoor cafés, and culture vultures studying the details of Bernini's **Fontana di Quattro Fiumi** (Fountain of the Four Rivers) or of Borromini's imposing facade on the church of **Sant'Agnese in Agone.** From here you can easily walk over to the **Pantheon**, one of the world's sublime examples of classical architecture, and the lovely church of **Santa Maria sopra Minerva.**

If you can't get enough of the baroque, the **Galleria Borghese** (1.5 miles/2.5 km northeast of Piazza Navona) in beautiful Villa Borghese park is the place to visit. This former *casino*, or suburban estate, was built to house the family's magnificent sculpture collection. It now also displays a fine collection of paintings, with masterpieces by the likes of Raphael, Caravaggio, Rubens, Titian, and more. The building alone, with its sumptuous decor, is well worth the visit.

Above: Michelangelo's statue of Jesus in Santa Maria sopra Minerva

Not far is the **Piazza di Spagna,** Rome's dining and shopping center, with the famous **Spanish Steps,** a magnet for visitors from all over.

Roman Neighborhoods

Several *rioni* (neighborhoods) in Rome still maintain a colorful local character and allow you to savor the city without throngs of other tourists. The **rione Monti,** region number 1 in Augustus' city reorganization in the first century A.D., is tucked in to the north and east of the Colosseum and Piazza Venezia. It includes two of Rome's patriarchal basilicas, **San Giovanni in Laterno** and **Santa Maria Maggiore,** and some of the best mosaics in the city (in the churches of the two sister saints **Prassede** and **Pudenziana,** for example).

Two thousand years ago, foreigners (including tens of thousands of Jews) settled in **Trastevere,** on the west side of the Tiber to the south of Vatican City. Today's *Trasteverini* proudly bill themselves as the *veraci* (true) Romans. By day, the neighborhood's warren of picturesque alleys and lanes provide the perfect setting for wandering while slowly making your way to the **Villa Farnesina** (decorated by Raphael and Sebastiano del Piombo) or the churches dedicated to **Santa Cecilia** or **S. Maria in Trastevere.** Trastevere swarms with restaurants, pubs, and wine bars.

In recent years, the area around **Campo dei Fiori** has grown to rival Trastevere as the hot spot for nightlife, at least for the under-25 set. Here, too, there is lots to see during the day. **Via Giulia** is perhaps the most beautiful street in town, and the **Palazzo Farnese** (designed by Antonio Sangallo, Michelangelo, and others) is considered to be the epitome of high Renaissance architecture. All lie between Piazza Navona and the Tiber. ■

When to Visit

The peak tourist seasons in Rome are May to June and September to October, when temperatures are perfect for sightseeing. Easter is also busy, with pilgrims flocking to the city for Holy Week. Christmas, on the other hand, attracts fewer visitors. January and February are definitely the quietest months for tourists. (See also p. 236.)

Info Made Easy

There is a new dedicated tourism information phone number, 060608, where English-speaking operators can provide details about museums, monuments, places of worship, libraries, sports facilities, parks, hotels and restaurants, as well as theater, concert, and dance performances. They can help you purchase tickets and even tell you the best route for city transport from one point to another. Visit their website at www.060608.it.

Other recent improvements include the information kiosks (PIT for *punto di informazione turistica*) located in various parts of the city :

Castel S. Angelo *(Lungotevere Vaticano, 9:30 a.m.–7:00 p.m.)*
Piazza delle Cinque Lune *(Piazza Navona, 9:30 a.m.–7:00 p.m.)*
Aeroporto Leonardo Da Vinci *(Arrivals, Terminal C, 9:00 a.m.–6:30 p.m.)*
Via Marco Minghetti *(corner Via del Corso, 9:30 a.m.–7:00 p.m.)*
Via Nazionale *(Palazzo delle Esposizioni, 9:30 a.m.–7:00 p.m.)*
S. Maria Maggiore *(Via dell'Olmata, 9:30 a.m.–7:00 p.m.)*
Stazione Termini *(Via Giovanni Giolitti 34, 8:00 a.m.–8:00 p.m.)*
Trastevere *(Piazza Sidney Sonnino, 9:30 a.m.–7:00 p.m.)*

History & Culture

St. Peter with the keys to the Kingdom of Heaven
Opposite: St. Peter's Basilica is said to stand over the apostle's first-century grave.

Rome Today

Known to the ancients as *caput mundi*, the center of the world, Rome was a crossroads of power, wealth, and culture for centuries—far beyond the decline of the Roman Empire. Today the city wields less international influence, but the beauty and fascination of its attractions and allure survive, despite the difficulties of modern life.

You can visit this city countless times, or live here for years, and its magnificent light, its colors (soft reds, ochers, and oranges mixed with the off-white and gray of marble and travertine), its harmonies of marble bridges across a curving river, its tree-shaded Renaissance villas and parks, its skyline of domes and *campanili*, will still take your breath away. The Pantheon, the Colosseum, the Campidoglio at sunset,

Rome today presents the visitor a vivid mix of past and present.

the Roman Forum in the flattening afternoon light—these are timeless wonders that over past centuries have make this city a destination for anyone who loves history and admires the artistic capacities of man. While the rampant building speculation that took place after World War II has turned the city's outskirts into prosaic concrete canyons, the area within the still resistant Aurelian walls, particularly the *centro storico* (historic center), has lost little of its magic.

Rome, of course, has always had its critics. Scan the centuries for the reports of travelers, or talk to some of today's inhabitants, and words such as decay, dirt, noise, and traffic jump off the page. Even Poggio Bracciolini, writing in the early 1400s, told in dismay of a city "stripped of beauty, lying prostrate like a giant corpse, decayed and everywhere eaten away." At that time the popes had recently returned to Rome from self-imposed exile in Avignon, France, to find a city that plague and factional strife had reduced to severe filth and disarray. Other low points in Rome's history

You can visit this city countless times, or live here for years, and its magnificent light, its colors...its harmonies... its skyline...will still take your breath away.

include the Visigoth invasion in 410; the bloody aftermath of the sack of Rome in 1527 by the French and German troops of the Holy Roman Emperor, Charles V; and, centuries later, the brutal German occupation, which ended with the Allied liberation in 1944.

Italy's capital since 1870, Rome gradually recovered after World War II, thanks largely to the Marshall Plan and to the Italians' natural resilience. The new, democratic party system that was grafted onto the roots of pre-Fascist liberalism, grew quickly, if chaotically. And despite all the problems that have ensued—corruption, government instability, strikes, and terrorism—Rome is now the flourishing capital of a major, and wealthy, European power.

Largely a service and administrative center as well as a tourist destination, Rome has elegant (and expensive) stores and boutiques, and busy restaurants. Its lovely parks provide bikers, strollers, and families with some 21,000 acres (8,400 ha) of green. Its middle-class families are well enough off to give their teenagers motorbikes that often go for as much as $3,000 a throw, and it's hard to find a Roman who doesn't have a *telefonino* or *cellulare* (cell phone).

A City in Transition

Rome today is a city of almost three million people, most of whom have come from the surrounding Lazio region or from southern Italy. Drawn to the capital by the possibility of work and useful political contacts, they have helped the city to expand far beyond its original perimeters. This was never an industrial capital, and for decades Rome's 20-odd government ministries were swollen repositories of political patronage. The headquarters of most major banks are located here, as are those of airlines, labor unions, and the unbelievable, and still expanding, plethora of Italian political parties. Many young Italians have poured into Rome to attend its three open-admission public universities and some newer private ones. And, of course, Rome is the capital of *Alta Moda* (High Fashion or couture) as well as the home of the Vatican and the pope. It thus attracts hundreds of thousands of tourists and pilgrims each year. According to City Hall, in 2006 the number of tourists reached almost 18 million, two-thirds of whom were foreigners, with the three biggest groups being Americans, Japanese, and British, followed by Germans, French, and Spanish. And in April 2005 alone, more than four million pilgrims came here to honor the memory of Pope John Paul II.

> **Rome appears to be on the brink of recapturing the multiracial and polyglot atmosphere it surely had during the imperial period.**

Despite this constant influx, for decades Rome strongly resisted most foreign influences, boasting a society that was almost stiflingly homogeneous: Almost everyone was white and Catholic (at least nominally). As recently as the mid-1970s, you could count the number of foreign restaurants on two hands. Now all this has changed, and Rome appears to be on the brink of recapturing the multiracial and polyglot atmosphere it surely had during the imperial period, when people from all corners of the Roman Empire came here, albeit—especially in the case of slaves—not always voluntarily.

The arrival of tens of thousands of immigrants from Africa, Asia, and the Middle East has set in motion an ethnic revolution that is bound to have profound social and cultural implications. Many immigrants are illegal, but many others have succeeded, thanks to Italy's frequent amnesties, in getting work papers. At present, the city's foreign-born population is approaching 10 percent. The largest foreign group is from the Philippines followed, in order, by Romanians, Poles, Peruvians, Bangladeshis, and Egyptians. People from developing countries work as domestic help, construction workers, housepainters, or home aides for the elderly. Many Senegalese are street peddlers. Chinese run scores of Chinese restaurants and carry-outs, while Egyptians work in restaurant kitchens and may have cooked that luscious *all'amatriciana* that you are eating.

La Dolce Vita, Roman Style

Most of the new arrivals have come to Rome for very clear, work-related reasons. They are part of a huge south-north, east-west migration toward Europe that reflects the sharp differences in living standards that afflict our world. In contrast, foreigners who have come to Rome from developed countries such as the United States and the United Kingdom are generally motivated by different considerations. First, they know that this city is an open-air museum where the ruins of the near and more distant past can be found at almost every turn in the road and under nearly every step.

Furthermore, Rome would also appear to have an inside track on sensuality, relaxation, and overall hedonism. And how could it be otherwise in a society that puts beauty and pleasure first and foremost? Although they frequently lose their tempers in traffic, Romans have turned being laid-back into an art form. More than two thousand years

The Spanish Steps are used as a meeting place and for pageants and other special events.

of history, with all its vagaries, have left the average Roman with one major conviction: Nothing is more important than the here and now. And Romans do their best to live up to that conviction.

How do you know when it's spring in Rome? Because at the first warming of the sun's rays, everyone is outdoors, chatting on street corners, filling sidewalk cafés, or taking prolonged and possibly undeserved coffee breaks. How do you know when it's summer? Because everyone has left the city for the nearby beaches to soak up the sun, hoping to become even more beautiful in the process. During other seasons, they opt for the *gita in campagna*, a country jaunt, or a short trip to some nearby lovely village, especially if there's a good restaurant in the area. In the evenings, except when it's raining or when a soccer match is being telecast, Romans pour into the streets, particularly in neighborhoods such as Trastevere, Testaccio, and the area around the Pantheon. Many head for the local trattorias, since eating is definitely the number-one Roman sport. An after-dinner *caffè* or *gelato*, a bit of people-watching, and some gossip are other favorite pastimes of the average Roman, especially since his *telefonino* allows him to keep in touch with his friends and, if necessary, reschedule. ∎

History of Rome

Rome is one of the few cities in the world to have been continuously inhabited for the last 2,700 years, which is why so few traces of early settlement have been found. Although centuries may have passed, the influence of Rome's ancient heritage remains paramount and holds the key to understanding its later development.

The Founding of Rome

From a literary point of view it sounds great: Aeneas flees Troy by boat, carrying his aged father Anchises on his back and leading his small son Ascanius by the hand. He lands in Italy and founds the city of Lavinium on the coast. When Ascanius grows up, he founds Alba Longa in the Alban Hills, but because of family squabbles over the throne in the succeeding generation, Romulus and Remus are thrown into the Tiber River and wash up on the slopes of the Palatine Hill where they are, in

Eight massive columns are all that remain of the Temple of Saturn in the Roman Forum.

short order, suckled by a she-wolf and rescued by a shepherd. The boys grow up, and set about founding their own city. In the process they quarrel; Romulus kills Remus and becomes the first king of Rome.

Unfortunately, very little of this may be true. The Romans, in fact, were just one of the many various peoples to inhabit the central portion of the peninsula in the late Iron Age, sharing the land with Etruscans, Latins, and Samnites. The original population of the area occupied by the future city of Rome was therefore probably composed of an aggregation of local tribes. In this context, the legend of the Sabine women makes perfect sense. The women were probably kidnapped by Romulus's men because of a real shortage of females.

The traces of Rome's early Iron Age dwellings found on the Palatine Hill indicate that whoever settled this area had good instincts. Easy to defend and close to a major river with natural port facilities, the Palatine was, after all, the most strategic location for a primitive settlement. Furthermore, the hill was not too distant from the most fordable spot on the river, where the existence of Tiber Island made crossing considerably easier.

Royal & Republican Rome

Legend tells us that Romulus was the first of seven kings, the others being Numa

Pompilius, Tullus Hostilius, Ancus Marcius, Tarquinius Priscus, Servius Tullius, and Tarquinius Superbus ("the proud"). The existence of the first four cannot be proved, but indications are that the last three did exist. Their Etruscan names testify to possible tribal intermingling. Another clue is that the Etruscans had highly developed engineering skills—and it was precisely then, in the sixth century B.C., that the marshy area between the Palatine and Capitoline Hills, the future Roman Forum, was drained.

After Tarquinius Superbus was deposed in 509 B.C., the monarchy was replaced by a republic with two consuls elected annually by the men of the city. The consuls appointed the members of an advisory council that eventually became known as the Senate. Formally at least, this system lasted until the advent of imperial rule under Octavius, or Augustus, as he preferred to be called after 27 B.C. But over the centuries it evolved and changed. At first, the government was dominated by a patrician elite whose influence derived largely from the wealth that allowed them to lead the republic's armies and, later, to dominate the Senate. During the fourth century B.C., after years of conflict and skillful manipulation of public opinion in the Forum's open-air assemblies, the dispossessed finally won the right to equal representation. In fact, say historians, Rome's first expansionist forays may have been designed to acquire territory for the newly enfranchised.

The Roman Empire, Its Rise & Its Decline

Rome had an empire long before it had an emperor. In fact, despite the on-going conflict between plebeians and patricians (or perhaps because of it!), the Roman Republic gradually gained control of the city's hinterland. According to Roman mythology, the twin deities, Castor and Pollux, lent a hand during the Battle of Lake Regillus in 496 B.C., when the Romans defeated the Latin League. Be that as it may, the victory proved to be the start of an almost unbroken series of military successes, ending with the complete conquest of Latium, the area surrounding Rome). And if the invasion of central Italy by the Gauls in 390 B.C. looked like it was about to become a major setback, it didn't. The young republic was saved when the Veneti attacked the Gauls on their northern flank, forcing them to head back home.

By the middle of the third century B.C., Rome's armies had conquered most of southern Italy. During this period the Romans built the major consular roads, beginning with the Via Appia to the south and the Via Aurelia and Via Flaminia to the north, to facilitate troop movement and trade. Expansion almost to the shores of Sicily brought Rome into open conflict with the North African stronghold, Carthage. The three Punic wars, lasting on and off for 118 years (264–146 B.C.), ended with the destruction of what was then Rome's only major rival for power in the western Mediterranean and witnessed the first Roman expansion outside the Italian peninsula. Sardinia, Corsica, and Illyria (today's Dalmatian coast) then fell, soon followed by Macedonia, Greece, and parts of Asia Minor.

When Julius Caesar appeared on the scene in the first century B.C., Rome's attention had for almost a century been focused on political and social problems at home rather than on further expansion. During his reign, however, Caesar did manage to defeat and annex Gaul. The social unrest of the era allowed him increasingly to concentrate power in his own hands, a trend that continued and was further reinforced by Augustus. Under Augustus, who defeated Mark Antony and Cleopatra, Egypt became a Roman province, Spain was completely subjugated, and the empire's borders were extended as far as the Rhine and the Danube. The next hundred years saw more of the same. The Romans conquered Britain and annexed Palestine. Under Trajan (A.D. 98–117), the empire reached its maximum limits, stretching from the British Isles to Asia Minor.

The Empire's Legacy

Despite its unhappy end, the achievements of the Roman Empire cannot be minimized. Military prowess, combined with an ability to incorporate conquered peoples into its social and political system, brought unparalleled success. The proof? Five Latin-based Romance languages (Italian, French, Spanish, Portuguese, and Romanian), the 26-letter Western alphabet, the continued use of Roman numerals, and a calendar of 12 months and 365 days.

By the late second century A.D., however, barbarian tribes had begun to pose a real threat. Hadrian's decision to build his famous defensive wall in England, completed in A.D. 136, was significant. As Roman competence on the battlefield declined, partly attributable to the empire's overextension, barbarian encroachments increased. In A.D. 330, Constantine inaugurated Constantinople, which soon became the administrative capital of the empire. Not many years after Constantine's death in A.D. 337, the empire was divided in half.

Governed from Constantinople, the Eastern Empire was strong enough to survive for another thousand years. Disaster loomed in the west, however, where repeated barbarian invasions took place. In 410, the Visigoths, led by Alaric, descended on Rome, pillaging for three days and putting an end to the city's reputation of invincibility. In 476, the Germanic warrior, Odovacar, deposed the last emperor, Romulus Augustulus, then but a teenager. The western Roman Empire had come to an end.

Christianity & the Papacy

The history of Christianity is inextricably intertwined with that of the Roman Empire. Indeed, in the Middle Ages many believed that the Roman Empire had been part of a divine plan to provide a stable geographical area and a fertile terrain for the spread of Christianity. Having achieved its purpose, the pagan Roman Empire could decline and disappear, to be replaced by the new universal, but Christian, empire. Unfortunately, things were not quite so cut and dried.

Peter and Paul both died in Rome, probably during Nero's persecutions between A.D. 64 and 67. For centuries, however, Christianity remained only one of many cults exported to Rome from the East. And even after it had become the favored sect of the imperial family under Constantine, there were problems. Much of the Roman elite remained fiercely pagan. It was only in the fifth century that Christianity became strong enough to step, definitively, out of the closet. It was in this period that the first grandiose churches, such as Santa Sabina (see pp. 210–211), were built.

As the papacy began to reign supreme

The pontiff performs ceremonial rites at his altar under Bernini's bronze canopy in St. Peter's Basilica.

in spiritual matters it also gradually assumed responsibility for the temporal welfare of Rome's population, filling in increasingly for the absentee rulers in Constantinople. In the aftermath of the disastrous sixth-century Gothic wars, Pope St. Gregory the Great (590–604) had to provide food and shelter for a population swollen with impoverished refugees. Newly created *diaconates* supervised the distribution of food, and in the ninth century, Leo IV had defensive structures erected around the Vatican to protect it from marauding Saracens. Greater power meant a larger bureaucracy and, particularly after the reign of Gregory VII (1073–1085), an increased determination to remain independent of any temporal authority, be it king or emperor. This led to the conflict over who had the authority to appoint (or invest) bishops, the so-called Investiture Controversy, between the Holy Roman Emperor Henry IV and Pope Gregory VII, which continued to rankle even after the compromise solution of the Concordat of Worms (1122).

If the 12th and 13th centuries witnessed the papacy's transformation into a first-rate European political power, a gradual decline in status and effective political clout was inevitable. By the beginning of the 1300s, other European nations, as well as the increasingly prosperous Italian city-states, were emerging as independent power brokers.

In Rome, rampant factionalism and bitter rivalries among the city's noble families led the popes to move the Holy See to Avignon in France (the so-called Babylonian Captivity), where they were to remain for much of the 14th century. During this period a vast reorganization of Church agencies and administration was begun, as were reform measures for the clergy. The close connection to the French court, and the consequent tensions with England and Germany, ended by damaging the papacy's prestige.

Renaissance

Historians have been discussing the true significance of the Renaissance (literally "rebirth") almost since its inception. What is not questioned, however, is its outcome (the birth of modern Europe) and its place of origin (Italy). The upsurge

The Swiss Guard was instituted in the 16th century to protect the pope.

of renewed interest in the learning and values of classicism was probably inevitable in Italy with its abundance of classical ruins. The result was humanism, a philosophy propounded by secular men of letters, as well as Church scholars whose primary emphasis was on the intellectual and artistic capacities of man. This period of heightened artistic expression really took off when the prosperous and ambitious princes of the burgeoning Italian city-states, such as the Medici in Florence, summoned to their courts some of the era's most prestigious painters, sculptors, architects, and draftsmen.

The papacy, always resilient, reached new heights in the rarefied atmosphere of the Renaissance, and again in the 1500s, in response to the birth of Protestantism, becoming an incomparable patron of the arts. By the middle of the 15th century, the pontiffs had reasserted their authority over the Eternal City and, applying their vast resources to the city's embellishment, shifted the center of the Renaissance from Florence to Rome.

Starting about 1450, a series of ambitious, wily, and, occasionally, erudite popes dedicated much of their attention to beautifying their city. They brought to Rome Tuscan and Umbrian artists such as Fra Angelico, Pinturicchio, and Michelangelo to decorate Vatican interiors such as Nicholas V's chapel, the Borgia apartments, and, of course, the Sistine Chapel, which for close to 60 years kept many famous artists occupied. In architecture, too, the Renaissance left its mark on Rome and here, as well, the Church proved a major patron. An eloquent example, Donato Bramante—considered the creator of High Renaissance architecture—designed the classically inspired Tempietto at San Pietro in Montorio (see p. 191) and then, appointed Papal Architect by Julius II (1503–1513), produced the first designs for the new, gigantic St. Peter's.

Counter-Reformation & the Baroque

The religious movement identified as the Counter-Reformation had a profound effect on its capital, Rome, as well as on the psychology of its governing elite. At its inception, it was a reaction to the Protestant Reformation begun by Martin Luther in the early part of the 16th century. The reaction and reforms set off by the challenge of that breakaway movement (see also sidebar p. 24) stimulated an era of intense religious fervor, bringing to the fore zealot saints such as St. Philip Neri, St. Theresa of Ávila, and St. Ignatius of Loyola. The latter's soldier mentality (he was once quoted as declaring that he had "never left the army") left its mark on the quasi-military structure of his newly created order, the Society of Jesus (the Jesuits), who were often referred to as the "pope's legions."

Il Risorgimento & National Unification

Il Risorgimento (from the Italian verb, risorgere, to rise again) was the prime force in 19th-century Italy. The ideological and bureaucratic groundwork laid by the French Revolution and the Napoleonic Wars had set in motion a desire for national unification. Three great men were on hand to make it happen: Giuseppe Mazzini, a democratic nationalist; Giuseppe Garibaldi, a firebrand general; and Count Camillo Cavour, a Piedmontese aristocrat and skilled politician-diplomat. Their combined efforts resulted in the proclamation of the Kingdom of Italy in March 1861. Only two pieces were missing: Venice (to be conquered from Austria in 1866) and Rome, which, thanks to French acquiescence, was taken from the pope by Italian armies on September 20, 1870.

The papacy, always resilient, reached new heights in the rarefied atmosphere of the Renaissance.

Papal rule and the overweening influence of the fractious Roman nobility had not done much for the city. At the end of the 18th century, Rome, with a population of under 200,000, was still a backwater provincial capital. But intellectual currents were running swift. Occupation by Napoleon's armies had infected many with the virus of liberalism and republicanism, and in 1848 Pope Pius IX was forced to grant a constitution. This didn't satisfy Mazzini and his supporters, who, in 1849, proclaimed the short-lived Roman Republic. Despite a valiant defense by the "Garibaldini" and others, the French, acting for the pope, retook the city. But time was running out for the papacy.

Before 1859, as Austria's Metternich had put it, Italy was only "a geographical expression." Divided into eight separate states, it was subject to the domination of foreign powers, mainly France, Spain, and Austria, while the popes still controlled a broad swathe of central Italy. The desire for unification snowballed, however, particularly after Cavour became prime minister of Piedmont in 1852. Allied with the French, in 1859 the Piedmontese took Lombardy from the Austrians and the next year annexed Umbria and the Marches. In the south, Garibaldi and his Thousand defeated the Bourbon armies, conquering Sicily and then Naples. The remaining Italian states chose union with Piedmont. Rome remained in papal hands, but not for long, although attempts by Garibaldi to capture the city in 1862 and 1867 were unsuccessful. In 1870, with France weakened by its war with Prussia, Italy had its chance. On September 20, Italian troops opened a breach in the city walls (at Porta Pia) and entered Rome. After a plebiscite, Rome became Italy's capital.

The Counter-Reformation & the Council of Trent

The Counter-Reformation lasted from the mid-16th to the 17th century and represented a period of serious self-analysis on the part of the Roman Catholic Church. The three-part Council of Trent (1545–1563) established the doctrinal foundations and institutional structures that helped the Church survive the Protestant challenge. It also outlined the basic tenets that governed the life of ordinary Catholics until the Second Vatican Council (1962–1965). Primarily conservative in nature, it confirmed that the Church alone could interpret Scripture, reformed monastic and religious orders, created a new catechism, and adopted the Tridentine Latin Mass.

The renewed vigor brought to the papacy by the Counter-Reformation and the Council of Trent also gave it a new lease on political life and two more centuries as a truly important player on the European stage. The emergence of a new world of young nation-states changed things, however, gradually pushing a reluctant Holy See to the political sidelines.

Fascism, War, & Democracy

Rome's population grew rapidly after 1870. By the onset of World War I it had hit 500,000. Neutral when the war began, Italy joined up in hopes of territorial gains. The war was unpopular, however, and the loss of 600,000 men made it particularly hard to swallow the Triple Entente's refusal to give Italy Dalmatia and Fiume, now part of Croatia, leading nationalists to bemoan a "mutilated victory." Serious postwar economic problems—including galloping inflation and soaring unemployment—increased the social unrest that led to the growing popularity of the Left as well as to the rise of the Right. Fascist Benito Mussolini's October 1922 march on Rome won him the government, but within two years he had already eliminated democracy, disbanding most of Italy's constitutional system, banning free speech and association, bridling the press, and, in the late 1930s, introducing anti-Semitic laws. Nevertheless, many aspects of the regime were genuinely popular.

At this point, the city had expanded well beyond the old Roman walls built by Aurelian (by 1930 there were more than one million inhabitants). Given the imperial ambitions of Mussolini, it is not surprising that the Fascist regime undertook important archaeological excavations that brought to light or restored many of the monuments of ancient Rome. It was at that time, too, that a major impetus was given to the transformation of the city into a modern capital. The then avant-garde EUR section was built, as were new, grandiose avenues such as Fori Imperiali and Conciliazione, although the latter two cost the city two important medieval neighborhoods.

Following Italy's censure by the League of Nations for invading Ethiopia, Mussolini moved closer to Hitler. The military alliance with Germany had disastrous economic and military consequences. In July 1943, following the Allied invasion of Sicily, Mussolini was dismissed and arrested and an armistice signed. The Germans immediately occupied Rome and the Italian army disintegrated. Despite the valiant efforts of the Resistance, more active farther north, the Allies were not able to liberate Rome until June 1944. After World War II, which had left the country devastated and Rome demoralized, the foundations were laid for a democratic system. In 1946 Italians voted to end the monarchy and found a republic. The new 1948 constitution established a multiparty, parliamentary system which, although chaotic and confusing, has allowed Italy to regain a place of respect within the family of nations.

This was a favorite pose of Benito Mussolini, the fascist dictator.

To the Present

The Marshall Plan provided the catalyst for a postwar economic boom and a remarkable national transformation. The country's emergence into the European mainstream was symbolized by the 1957 Treaty of Rome, laying the foundations of the European Union, of which Italy was a founding member.

Italy's transformation was not without problems. By the 1960s, coalition governments became weaker, and the economy faltered, leading to violent social tensions. Unrest exploded in the *autunno caldo* (literally, "hot fall") of 1968, when worker and student demonstrations swept Rome and the country. And then during the next couple of decades, Italy was ravaged by political terrorism, left-wing and right-wing alike.

No sooner had the terrorist menace abated in the early 1990s, however, than corruption scandals wracked Italy's moribund political system, causing the demise of several major political parties. What at the time appeared to be a genuine desire for change led to the so-called Second Republic, more rhetoric than significant institutional change, although the birth of new parties such as Silvio Berlusconi's Forza Italia, and the transformation of the "mainline" communists into social democrats has reduced the number of parties and brought Italy closer to a bipartite system.

In general, change has been hard to come by, although the activism of the European Union has produced a degree of modernization by default. Government in Italy and in its capital, Rome, continues to be hamstrung by sharp political divisions. And yet the country has prospered, generally overcoming circumstance and politics in the same inspired manner it has for much of its checkered history ∎

The Arts

The beauty of the Eternal City is not contemporary. The two major influences on Rome's artistic heritage were, without a doubt, the Roman Empire and the papacy, both of which have left their indelible marks on the city.

Architecture & Art

The Emperor Augustus reportedly claimed that he had found a city made of brick and left one made of marble. In a sense this is true. Like his adoptive father, Julius Caesar, Augustus learned early on that public works constituted an effective way not just to embellish an imperial city and heighten its prestige, but to gain the good will, or at least the tolerance, of the public. From the Colosseum and the Arch of Titus to the refurbished Temple of Vesta and the Baths of Caracalla, the political significance of monumental architecture was fundamental. The concept

A craftsman helps restore Michelangelo's "Last Judgment" in the Sistine Chapel.

that "art is the handmaiden of politics" has been around for a long time. Perhaps no other country has so benefited from the ambitions and, yes, megalomania of its rulers, be they emperors, popes, or princes. The final result is layer upon layer of artistic and architectural glory. Look around you at the ruins of so many past regimes. The stratification is such that if you observe carefully, you can usually identify the successive layers of Rome's past majesty, often in the very same structure.

Architecture had its first real boom with the advent of Imperial Rome. Some emperors built for their own enjoyment alone: Nero and his Golden House come to mind. But in most instances, their major building projects were destined for public use. The architects remain largely unknown, but some of their constructions—the Pantheon, the Colosseum, Trajan's Markets, the Arches of Titus, Septimius Severus, and Constantine—still stand, mute witnesses of past glories, silent embellishments even today of man's all too brief existence.

The construction of Santa Sabina in the early fifth century in the midst of an elegant, and until then largely pagan, aristocratic quarter, affirmed Christianity's march toward primacy. In fact, the Church's decision to convert many ancient Roman structures into churches was hardly made on practical grounds alone. The symbolic and psychological significance of certain gestures, for example moving the doors of Julius Caesar's Senate to the Basilica of San Giovanni in Laterano, appears obvious.

> **Perhaps no other country has so benefited from the ambitions...of its rulers, be they emperors, popes, or princes.**

Naturally, some Christian buildings were largely idealistic in inspiration. In some of the earliest churches, built near or over the shrines of early martyrs, or like Santa Maria in Cosmedin, on the site of an early diaconate, you can almost sense the aura of Christian faith. Later, vigorous building campaigns by the papacy, especially in the 9th and 13th centuries, served a dual purpose. New structures were needed not only to welcome the faithful but also to glorify the mother institution. The building of St. Peter's basilica in the 16th and 17th centuries may have been the most blatant example of architectural self-glorification.

The papacy also used interior decoration to effectively reaffirm its precepts, and the examples of decorative work with an explicit political quality are numerous. One of the most eloquent examples from the Middle Ages is the series of 13th-century frescoes in the St. Sylvester chapel in the church of the Quattro Coronati near the Colosseum. The decision to depict events in the life of the Emperor Constantine in such a way as to make him appear subservient to Pope Sylvester is propaganda at its best. How else to explain the final scene, in which Constantine, on foot, humbly holds the reins of the pope's donkey!

Starting in the Renaissance, mosaic work—for centuries the most widely used decorative medium in the classical world—was replaced gradually by sculpture and painting, perfect tools for the expression of political concepts and conceits. For centuries, most statues represented gods and rulers. One thinks, for example, of the equestrian statue of Marcus Aurelius (long believed to be Constantine) or the statue of Augustus from Livia's villa at Prima Porta. In the 13th century, the popes, too, began to commission statues of themselves—as rulers rather than religious leaders—to be displayed in public. So only a few feet away from Arnolfo di Cambio's statue of Charles of Anjou (dressed as a Roman senator) in the Capitoline Museum are Bernini's statue of Pope Urban VIII, a Barberini, and Algardi's statue of Innocent X, a Pamphili. And you can't miss the political overtones of Raphael's paintings in the so-called Rooms of Raphael in the Vatican Museums. The "Expulsion of Heliodorus from the Temple," for example, was a clear allusion to Pope Julius II's military campaign to expel usurpers from Church lands.

The Baroque: Gian Lorenzo Bernini, "sovereign of the arts, to whom popes, princes and peoples reverently bowed" (see the plaque on his house on Via della Mercede, near the corner with Propaganda Fide), was undoubtedly a genius. The baroque style, of which Bernini is indisputably one of the major creative protagonists, is perhaps the maximum example of art used to convey concepts—primarily faith in the Church and in its doctrines—that transcend the purely ornamental. Designed to combat the rapidly spreading Protestant Reformation and, at the same time, to emphasize the importance of Catholicism, the baroque was blatantly propagandistic. All the plastic arts (architecture, painting, sculpture) were used to make an appeal to the faithful that was both sensory and emotional. The magnificence of Rome's baroque churches, such as Il Gesù (the mother Jesuit church) or Santa Maria della Vittoria, intended to underscore the splendor and importance of the papacy, to convince the viewer that the Roman Catholic Church was the only institution qualified to decipher Divine Will and scripture, a sharp contrast to Martin Luther's reforms, which stressed the necessity for individual interpretation of scripture.

Great Baroque Artists

The three great baroque geniuses—Bernini, Francesco Borromini, and Pietro da Cortona—were contemporaries and spent most of their creative lives in Rome. Utilized in complex compositions, their extravagant styles, were characterized by rich colors, gold decoration, unlimited movement, endless depth, diagonal lines, dramatic lighting, and theatricality. Impressive and dramatic, their works stimulated piety and devotion in viewers, and helped underline the importance of the clergy and the Church as an institution. The overall effect—marked by dynamism and movement in sharp contrast to the stability and unambiguous definition of Renaissance painting and sculpture—is often overwhelming.

The Church also encouraged and utilized musicians. Palestrina, from the nearby town of the same name, was a major innovator of contrapuntal composition. He composed at least 105 Masses while in Rome, many of which he dedicated to Pope Julius III, for a while his patron.

In the 17th century, secular rulers elsewhere adopted the Italian baroque. The situations may have been different, but the message was the same: I am powerful, I am to be admired, feared, and—above all—respected.

Rulers paid homage to the pope in the Sala Regia room in the Apostolic Palace.

In the 20th century, the Fascist government continued (albeit less successfully) to use art and architecture to reinforce its own power and prestige. In the 1920s and 1930s, Mussolini's regime fostered a style that used many ancient Roman motifs in modern guise in order to bolster its legitimacy as the true heir to the grandeur of Rome. At its inauguration, the present-day Via dei Fori Imperiali was called the Via dell'Impero (Avenue of the Empire). Perhaps a reference to the empire that Italy sought to create with the annexation of territory in North Africa, the name also evokes the "Impero" that, with far greater success, had existed two thousand years before.

Literature

Although Greek was initially popular, Latin had asserted itself as the written language of choice by the first century B.C. Plautus, a comic poet, used colloquial Latin for his plays, as did Ennius in his epics and tragedies. By the second half of the first century B.C., there were many Roman writers of distinction, including Julius Caesar, but it was the complex, abstract thought of Cicero—philosopher, orator, and poet—that stood out. Although Virgil, the author of the *Aeneid,* was not a Roman, he became part of an elite circle of poets close to the Emperor Augustus. The poet Horace was lauded for the perfection of form of his *Odes* and *Epistles.* Ovid wrote witty and elegiac poetry. Whereas Livy and Tacitus excelled in history, Seneca chose tragedy, and Juvenal, satire. The post-Augustan period, while subject to political repression, still produced writers as skillful as Petronius, Statius, Martial, and

Suetonius. Later, some scholars again wrote in Greek; the greatest work by a Roman in the first centuries A.D., Marcus Aurelius's *Meditations*, was composed in Greek.

In the intervening centuries, most writing in Latin was done by prelates or people trained in church schools. The 13th century, however, brought the first examples of literature in the vernacular and the emergence of major Italian writers such as Dante, Petrarch, and Boccaccio, none of whom were Roman, although Petrarch was crowned with laurel at the Campidoglio in 1341. Torquato Tasso was also supposed to be made Poet Laureate of Rome but died shortly after arriving (1595) and is buried in the Church of Sant'Onofrio. Papal rule was probably not conducive to the development of secular literature and poetry. It was not until the 19th century, in fact, that a major Roman poet appeared. Composed for the most part around 1830, Giovanni Gioacchino Belli's 2,000 sonnets in Roman dialect present a vivid and satirical picture of contemporary Rome.

By the late Renaissance, however, Rome had become a magnet for many foreign writers. Well-known early visitors include the French essayist Montaigne and the English poet John Milton. In the 18th and 19th centuries, inspired visitors included the German poet Goethe, the French writer Stendhal, the American writers Nathaniel Hawthorne, Mark Twain, and later Theodore Dreiser, and the English poets Percy Bysshe Shel-

The Foro Italico sports complex was begun under Mussolini.

ley, George Gordon Byron, and John Keats as well as Robert and Elizabeth Browning. George Eliot sent her *Middlemarch* protagonist, Dorothea Brooke, on an eye-opening trip to Rome with her parson husband, and much of Henry James's *Daisy Miller* is set here.

In the 20th century, several major writers emerged in Rome. Alberto Moravia, who died in 1990, started out as a journalist and wrote of alienation in modern society. His first novel, *Gli Indifferenti (Time of Indifference)*, was published when he was only 21. Other major works, most of which have been translated into English, include *Agostino (Two Adolescents, 1944)*, *La Romana (The Woman of Rome, 1947)*, *Il Conformista (The Conformist, 1951)*, and *La Ciociara (Two Women, 1957)*, which became a prize-winning movie with Sophia Loren. Moravia was married for a while to the writer Elsa Morante, who died in 1985. Her best-known work, remarkable for its epic quality, is the 1974 *La Storia*, published in English as *History: A Novel*.

Born in northern Italy in 1922, Pier Paolo Pasolini, a well-known writer, poet, and movie director, came to Rome after World War II and used the material from his contacts among the city's down-and-outs for two novels: *Ragazzi di Vita* (*The Ragazzi*, 1955) and *Una Vita Violenta* (*A Violent Life*, 1959). Like his first film, *Accattone*, the novels deal with the lives of thieves, prostitutes, and other denizens of the Roman underworld. Other major postwar writers include Italo Calvino, Primo Levi, and Umberto Eco (*The Name of the Rose, Foucault's Pendulum*). More recently, Susana Tamaro, Alessandro Baricco, and Sicilian detective writer Andrea Camilleri have been translated and published abroad.

The Museum Revolution

In classical terms, Rome is not a cultural center. It is not a city you would visit specifically for a chance to see opera or ballet. The theater, such as it is, is limited to Italian speakers, and with a few exceptions, classical music programs leave much to be desired. Nor are the city's art galleries generally on the international circuit. However, the city has incomparable riches to offer any art lover.

The 13th century... brought the...emergence of major Italian writers such as Dante, Petrarch, and Boccaccio.

Itself an open-air museum full of temples, palaces, and fountains designed by master sculptors, Rome also has a large number of well-endowed museums. Many of them have been renovated, reorganized, and reopened to become far more user-friendly. A case in point is the Borghese Gallery. Now on everyone's A list (and justly so), it was closed for over a decade while its poorly displayed masterpieces stood alone and ignored. Now, after a glorious restoration (although the internal organization is still far from perfect), it has a modern museum structure to show off its incomparable collections.

The Museo Nazionale Romano (National Museum of Rome), originally housed in the Baths of Diocletian, has also been drastically reorganized; its works, long hidden from view in storerooms and cellars, have been brilliantly distributed among four separate sites. The baths now house the excellently reorganized Epigraphy Museum, while other sections are devoted to pre-Roman history; Palazzo Massimo alle Terme, a former high school right across Esedra Square, harbors magnificent Greek and Roman statuary, mosaics, and frescoes; treasures such as the Ludovisi throne are on display at a former Renaissance cardinal's palace, Palazzo Altemps, near Piazza Navona; and the Crypta Balbi, just a short walk from Largo Argentina, presents relics of the city's history from the end of the ancient Roman period through the later Middle Ages.

Located in a former power plant in the Ostiense neighborhood, and originally established to host many artworks from the Capitoline Museums (then under restoration), the Montemartini has become a permanent structure that displays alternating parts of the Capitoline's overflow collection. The Villa Giulia (the Etruscan Museum) has been refurbished, although too many labels are still in Latin. The National Gallery in the Barberini Palace, though still inefficiently organized, is being renovated and will expand now that the Army Officer's Club is giving up part of its space.

And it doesn't end there. In 1827, Stendhal complained in his *Promenades dans Rome* that "the small-minded brains which currently hold power permit us to visit these museums [the Capitoline and the Pio Clementino at the Vatican] only once a week." Of course, that was a long time ago, but until only recently the visiting hours at Rome's museums were frustratingly short (most closed at 1 or 2 p.m.) and differed notably one from the other. Now all this has changed. Except for Mondays, when most public museums are still closed (the Vatican Museums and the Roman Houses under the church of Sts. John and Paul on the Celio Hill are exceptions), museums are open all day and, in summer and during other holiday periods, until late in the evening. Services have become far more efficient, better qualified personnel have been hired, and centralized reservation systems and information offices established, representing the creativity, flare, and style at which the Italians are so good—when they wish to be.

"Hollywood on the Tiber" & After

Determined to make Italian film production into a source of national prestige, Mussolini founded the giant studio Cinecittà in 1937. Ironically, his project bore its best fruit only after the Fascist regime had been soundly defeated in World War II and superseded by a young democratic republic. As early as the 1950s, neorealism and post-neorealism had put the Italian film industry on the map, and the names of the best directors, actors, and actresses were known throughout the intellectual world. The success of Cinecittà was brought home to all in 1963 on the set of *Cleopatra*, which also became the setting for a love story between the film's two principal stars, Elizabeth Taylor and Richard Burton. By the end of the 1960s, "Hollywood on the Tiber" was churning out between 200 and 250 films a year, some of which, over 40 years later, are still considered masterpieces.

Today, all this has changed. Most of the major directors who made their names in that period—Roberto Rossellini *(Roma Citta' Aperta)*, Lucchino Visconti *(Obsession, Senso, The Earth Trembles)*, Vittorio De Sica *(The Bicycle Thief* and *Sciuscià)*, Pietro Germi *(Divorce Italian Style, Seduced and Abandoned)*, Federico Fellini *(La Strada, La Dolce Vita, Roma, Amarcord, etc.)*, and others—have died or, like Michelangelo Antonioni *(Blowup, L'Avventura)* and Gillo Pontecorvo *(The Battle of Algiers)*, are over 80. Pier Paolo Pasolini *(The Gospel According to St. Matthew, The Decameron)* was murdered in 1975. Major actors such as Marcello Mastroianni and Ugo Tognazzi have passed away or, like Sophia Loren, make few films. Producer Dino De Laurentiis has been in Hollywood since the 1970s, and Cinecittà's only major recent films are *Oceans 12* and Martin Scorsese's 2002 hit, *Gangs of New York*.

Today, Cinecittà Holding rents out the once bustling studios primarily to RAI (Italian state television) and Mediaset (Silvio Berlusconi's film production company). Well-known directors like the Taviani brothers work largely for television, while others, such as Bernardo Bertolucci *(Last Tango in Paris)*, have been working abroad. Nowadays, Italy produces only 80 to 100 films annually, and no more than 25 get first-run distribution.

A Few Smaller Museums

Rome also has a series of lesser known museums that are also worth a visit. The Museo di Roma has artifacts and art related to Rome's history from the Middle Ages on. The Baracco Museum, with its collection of ancient sculpture, has recently reopened. A new, expanded museum in the Rome synagogue opened in Fall 2005. The Museum of the Imperial Forums, in Trajan's markets, opened in 2007. And itinerant exhibitions are housed in spaces such as the Palazzo Ruspoli and the Museo del Corso, on different ends of Via del Corso; the newly popular Complesso del Vittoriano round the back of the Victor Emanuel Monument; Trajan's Markets on Via IV Novembre; and the magnificently restored Scuderie, or stables, across the piazza from the Quirinal Palace.

Marcello Mastroianni is a frustrated journalist in Federico Fellini's 1960 masterpiece, La Dolce Vita.

Decidedly, American films are among the most popular in Italy, although European and Asian films have a following among Roman intellectuals. There are, however, a few native bright stars on the horizon. Giuseppe Tornatore (Nuovo Cinema Paradiso) and iconoclast Nanni Moretti are popular with many. In March 1999, the Tuscan comedian Roberto Benigni won three Oscars for the touching Life is Beautiful, about an Italian Jew in a German concentration camp, who convinces his young son to believe it is all a game. And in 2002, new director Gabriele Muccino's l'Ultimo Bacio (The Last Kiss) won a prize at the Sundance Film Festival.

L'Estate Romano
(The Roman Summer)

The concept of L'Estate Romano was first set in motion in the mid-1970s, when city culture commissioner Renato Nicolini turned the city into an outdoor festival with a something-for-everyone flavor. Every year, parks become ballets stages, piazzas are turned into concert halls, basilicas into auditoriums, and riverbanks into bookstalls. Film showings are held at intriguing venues such as the Basilica di Massenzio, the Circus Maximus, and Tiber Island, as well as the area facing the Arch of Constantine where, in September 1981, thousands turned up for the historic screening of Abel Gance's Napoleon.

Parks are co-opted, too, with ballet in Villa Ada, concerts in Villa Pamphili, jazz at Villa Celimontana and in the Testaccio neighborhood, and prose near what remains of Tasso's Oak. Concerts, classical to rock, are also held in different downtown sites, while mimes, poets, Sicilian puppet troupes, majorettes, and other performers fan out through less central neighborhoods. In recent summers, events have attracted as many as five million spectators. Critics contend the quality is not what it once was. But there is no doubt that the Roman "Kulturmarket" is alive and well, making sure that tourists and non-vacationers alike have no excuse to be bored (see pp. 260–263). ■

Food

The ancients may have liked honey-glazed dormouse (a favorite of Trimalchio, Petronius' intemperate gourmet in *Satyricon*), crushed boiled brains, fish sauce made from fermented fish intestines, and roast pig stuffed with live quail, but don't worry. Although food is as important today, some things have changed, and happily dormice and fish sauce are off the menu.

Other things, too, have changed for the better. In fact, if you look through Apicius's *De Re Coquinaria*, the first thing you'll realize is that many of the staple products that we associate with Italian cuisine today were unknown in ancient Rome. Tomatoes, eggplant, and zucchini to name just a few, arrived later from the New World. Instead of durum wheat—not used to make pasta in Naples until the 17th century—the Romans imported a type of grain called *faro adoreum*, and this was used to make *puls*, a boiled cereal that may have been similar to polenta.

A Roman maestro prepares a healthy serving of tortellini.

The unleavened bread of those days was sometimes cut into strips but it was far different from ours. What the two eras have in common, however, is gastronomic enthusiasm. Although the crowded sandwich bars and the proliferation of fast-food outlets confirm that the three-hour lunch has more or less disappeared (and multicourse dinners are, also, increasingly infrequent), food is still a top priority. In fact, if there is anything a Roman likes to do more than eat, it is to regale his dinner companions with tales of what he ate yesterday, or on some more remote occasion.

Rome has never been cited for the delicacy or the refinement of its cuisine, which is instead hearty and robust, a collection of dishes, often washed down with a bottle of Castelli white, that represent real comfort food but which the wise will ingest only infrequently. Among the best vegetable dishes are artichokes, either Roman style *(carciofi alla romana)* or fried, Jewish style *(carciofi alla giudea)*. Also typical are *punturelle in salsa d'alici* (raw chicory with anchovy sauce), *peperoni alla Romana* (red and green peppers sautéed with onion), lima beans with pancetta, or wild chicory with oil and lemon.

> **If there is anything a Roman likes to do more than eat, it is to regale his dinner companions with tales of what he ate yesterday.**

Another favorite is fried zucchini flowers, often part of a *misto fritto* (mixed fry) of mozzarella, artichokes, olives, and sometimes brains. As far as meat goes, the most characteristic dishes are roast pork *(maialino arrosto),* baby lamb *(abbacchio),* and tripe. In fact, innards are an important part of the city's traditional *cucina povera,* roughly translated as "poor man's cuisine." In the old days *rigatoni alla pajata* (lamb's intestine) was popular, and some people still swear by lamb heart *(coratella),* served with artichokes, and *coda alla vaccinara* (oxtail stew).

Pasta

Of course, no discussion of Italian food is complete without a few hearty paragraphs about pasta. As with most great creations, there is a lot of confusion and controversy about where pasta came from and just who invented it. Despite the legend, it certainly pre-existed the travels of Marco Polo, is definitely Mediterranean in origin, and it appears almost certain that dried pasta—of which today there may be as many as 350 different shapes—may have been brought to Sicily by that island's Arab invaders and from there headed north...and then west, east, and south. But never mind. Like everyone, you adore pasta, and the question is what are you going to do about it while you are in Rome.

Romans love pasta just as much as any other Italians do and, indeed, in the city's thousands of restaurants you can certainly find pasta dishes of every type. But Romans do put their own spin on it. They generally don't go in for using cream sauces as happens in some parts of the Italian north. Nor do they specialize in serving pasta made with vegetables, as in much of the Italian south. Rome's pastas reflect the area's general culinary background of cucina povera, in which primary importance is given to simple ingredients within everyone's reach, like oil, garlic, pancetta or guanciale (the preferred meat is a long-smoldering dispute), eggs, and one of the Lazio region's best known products, pecorino cheese. So it's important that you know what to order when you go out to eat while you are here. Here are the main "Roman" choices.

A viable alternative to a pasta meal can be a plate of starters or *antipasti* followed by a second meat or fish course.

1. The very basic aglio, olio pepperoncino, which the true Romans refer to as **spaghetti ajo e ojo,** is simply spaghetti that has been seasoned with oil in which garlic and red pepper (some add parsley) have been fried.

2. For spaghetti **alla carbonara** (the origins of the name are unclear), the spaghetti is "dressed" with fried guanciale or pancetta (there are heated disputes about which is better) and then raw egg yolk mixed with pecorino cheese.

3. Spaghetti **cacio e pepe** results from mixing freshly drained spaghetti with pecorino, plus a bit of the water in which the spaghetti was cooked. The dish is then amply sprinkled with black pepper.

4. Said to have originated in Amatrice, in the Rieti province of Lazio, bucatini (or rigatoni) **all'amatriciana,** or **la matriciana** as some call it, is now considered a typical Roman pasta dish. Never mind that there are bitter arguments between those who add onion to the sauce of guanciale, tomato, and red chili pepper and those who shudder at the thought. At the end it is amply dusted with pecorino, or pecorino and parmigiano mixed. It is a real favorite.

5. Spaghetti or pasta **alla gricia** is basically the matriciana without tomato sauce.

6. Penne **all'arrabbiata** is a spicier pasta dish, again with the same basic ingredients—tomato, garlic, red chili pepper, parsley, and pecorino (again, some use onion rather than garlic).

7. Fettuccine **alla romana** are fresh noodles served with a tomato sauce with mushrooms and bits of ham.

8. Spaghetti **alla carrettiera** includes lard, tuna, mushrooms, garlic, and tomato sauce.

....and, for the truly courageous, there is

9. Rigatoni **alla pajata,** in which the pasta sauce is made from the intestines of a milk-fed or unweaned calf, along with tomato sauce, celery, garlic and onion, pancetta, parsley, white wine, and a touch of vinegar.

Of course, if you are staying in an apartment, you can also make these dishes for yourself. If you want to learn how while you are here, you can even take a one-day cooking class (see sidebar p. 185). ■

The heart of ancient Rome, where splendid ruins testify loudly to the magnificent past when the city was *caput mundi,* center of the world

Ancient Rome

Emperor Marcus Aurelius astride his mount at the Campidoglio

Ancient Rome

From the back of the Capitoline Hill, the Roman Forum stretches for almost half a mile. Alongside it lie excavated portions of the later imperial *fora*, built to enlarge and beautify an increasingly cramped downtown area. This small valley, tucked among several hills, is the heart of ancient Rome, in effect its birthplace.

The first settlements on Rome's hilltops date to the ninth and eighth centuries B.C. Below them, in a somewhat marshy enclave, lay an open space that was soon used for everything from town meetings to commerce. As the city grew, this space, known as the Forum, gradually transformed into a bona fide civic and religious center, a site for everything from protests and funerals to gladiatorial fights and theatrical presentations.

The Forum's first monuments were erected during the monarchy. The Comitium, the circular open space in front of the Senate building, quickly became institutionalized as a place for discussion and debate. As Rome's wealth and power grew, and as conquering rulers returned victorious from their first encounters with the more advanced Hellenistic world, the Forum was further transformed, and increasingly embellished, to represent the grandeur of what was rapidly becoming a far-flung empire.

The importance of the Forum began to decline in the fifth century A.D. Until the excavations of the 1800s, it held little interest for most Romans, who called the area Campo Vaccino, the cow pasture.

From your vantage point on the Capitoline Hill, the smallest of the city's seven hills, you can easily identify the Forum's major sites. In the foreground stands the Arch of Septimius Severus and, to its left, Diocletian's massive brick Curia, or Senate building. The large open space in front of the arch is the original Roman Forum, for centuries kept cleared of anything but Rome's three traditional food staples: the olive, the fig, and the grape. Farther to the right, the eight large columns belonged to the portico of the Temple of Saturn. The long rectangle beyond is all that remains of the Basilica Julia courthouse. Winding its way toward the Arch of Titus is the famous Via Sacra, once a major thoroughfare with room for two carts to drive abreast. Opposite you, toward the right, is the Palatine Hill, and farther away, to the left, you can just make out the top of the Colosseum.

Here on the hill, just to your right, you can see the gray blocks of peperino marble that were once part of the Tabularium, the archives of ancient Rome. Nearby, atop a column, is a copy of the Capitoline wolf suckling Romulus and Remus. In front of the Palazzo Senatorio is the Campidoglio, the magnificent Renaissance complex designed by Michelangelo to bring renewed glory to a site that for kings, tribunes, tyrants, and emperors was the heart of political and religious Rome. The Capitoline Museums are also here, with famed statues such as the "Dying Gaul" and the "Boy with a Thorn." ∎

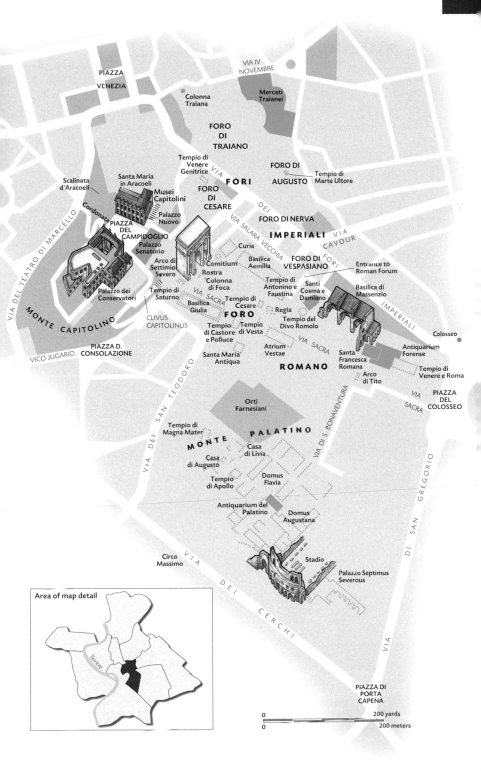

PIAZZA VENEZIA

VIA IV NOVEMBRE

Colonna Traiana

Mercati Traianei

FORO DI TRAIANO

Tempio di Venere Genitrice

FORO DI AUGUSTO

Tempio di Marte Ultore

Scalinata d'Aracoeli

Santa Maria in Aracoeli

F O R I

Cordonata

Musei Capitolini

FORO DI CESARE

Palazzo Nuovo

VIA DEI

FORO DI NERVA

PIAZZA DEL CAMPIDOGLIO

VIA SALARA VECCHIA

I M P E R I A L I

VIA CAVOUR

Palazzo Senatorio

Curia

FORO DI VESPASIANO

VIA DEI FORI

Arco di Settimio Severo

Comitium

Basilica Aemilia

Entrance to Roman Forum

VIA DEL TEATRO DI MARCELLO

Palazzo dei Conservatori

Tempio di Saturno

Rostra

Colonna di Foca

Tempio di Antonino e Faustina

Santi Cosma e Damiano

Basilica di Massenzio

VIA SACRA

Basilica Giulia

Tempio di Cesare

F O R O

Regla

Tempio del Divo Romolo

IMPERIALI

MONTE CAPITOLINO

CLIVUS CAPITOLINUS

Tempio di Castore e Polluce

Tempio di Vesta

VIA SACRA

Colosseo

PIAZZA D. CONSOLAZIONE

VICO JUGARIO

Santa Maria Antiqua

Atrium Vestae

R O M A N O

Santa Francesca Romana

Antiquarium Forense

Arco di Tito

Tempio di Venere e Roma

VIA SACRA

PIAZZA DEL COLOSSEO

VIA DEI SAN TEODORO

Orti Farnesiani

VIA DI S. BONAVENTURA

Tempio di Magna Mater

P A L A T I N O

MONTE

Casa di Livia

Casa di Augusto

DI SAN GREGORIO

Tempio di Apollo

Domus Flavia

Antiquarium del Palatino

Domus Augustana

Circo Massimo

VIA DEI CERCHI

Stadio

Palazzo Septimus Severous

VIA

Area of map detail

Tevere

PIAZZA DI PORTA CAPENA

0   200 yards
0   200 meters

Campidoglio

Its architecture and history make the Campidoglio, or Capitol (Capitoline Hill), an absolute must for every visitor. Come during the day, preferably in the late afternoon, for an astonishing view of the sun-kissed Roman Forum below, and again at night, when marvelous lighting turns the piazza, designed by Michelangelo, and the Roman ruins below into pure magic.

Every April 21 an evening candlelit concert is performed in the piazza to celebrate Rome's founding.

The Cordonata

The best way to reach the piazza is from the gradually ascending flight of stairs, called the Cordonata, designed by Michelangelo in 1536 and flanked at the bottom by two black, basalt Egyptian lions. At the top of the staircase stand giant, ancient marble statues of Castor and Pollux. Before you lies **Piazza del Campidoglio,** set in a hollow between two hill crests.

Commissioned by Pope Paul III for a planned visit by the Holy Roman Emperor, Charles V, the piazza features statues of the Emperor Constantine and his son, Constantius, as well as two Roman milestones from the Appian Way. The modern statue halfway up the hill, to the left of the Cordonata, marks the spot where Cola di Rienzo, the 14th-century tribune who dreamed of restoring the Roman Republic, was executed.

Exploring the Piazza

The two identical buildings on your left and right are, respectively, the **Palazzo Nuovo** (built from scratch in 1655 to Michelangelo's design) and the older

Palazzo dei Conservatori, the facade of which was redesigned by the Florentine sculptor and further modified by later Renaissance and baroque architects. Today, the two buildings house different sections of the Musei Capitolini (see p. 43).

The back portion of the Palazzo dei Conservatori (originally called Palazzo Caffarelli) stands on the site of what in ancient times was the temple of Jupiter Maximus Capitolinus, built in the sixth century B.C. and reputed to be the largest of its kind ever constructed. A circular, glass-enclosed structure, recently inaugurated, was built over the gardens of the palazzo specifically to showcase the excavated portions (the podium and *cella,* or cell) of the temple of Jupiter and to dramatically display the ancient bronze equestrian statue of Marcus Aurelius.

Palazzo Senatorio: Facing you from the bottom of the Cordonata is the Palazzo Senatorio. Built in the 13th and 14th centuries on the remains of the Roman Tabularium, it is today the seat of Rome's municipal government.

Michelangelo designed the double ramp of stairs at the front, which is embellished by a fountain sporting two enormous reclining river gods, the Tiber on the right and the Nile on the left. In the niche in between is the "Dea Roma," a red-and-white stone composite of two earlier statues of Minerva, the goddess of wisdom and war. The bell tower, designed by Martin Longhi the Elder, was built between 1578 and 1582. The rest of the facade was added a bit later by architects Giacomo della Porta and Girolamo Rainaldi.

In Center Square: At this point, you'll probably only have eyes for the equestrian **statue of the emperor Marcus Aurelius** that stands in the center of the square. Actually, what you are looking at is a copy (the original, removed in 1981 for restoration, is now in the Palazzo dei Conservatori). But the copy manages to convey the same sense of history and drama.

The original sculpture is one of the rare surviving equestrian statues from classical Rome, possibly because for centuries

it was believed to be a statue of Constantine, the emperor who converted to Christianity. It was brought to the Campidoglio in 1538 on the recommendation of Michelangelo, who created the pedestal.

The statue shows the bearded emperor with his right

Campidoglio
- Map p. 39
- Bus: C3, H, 46, 62, 63, 64, 70, 81, 84, 85, 87, 95, 119, 170, 175, 492, 628, 715, 716, 780

INSIDER TIP:

In early September Rome celebrates *Notte Bianca,* or "white night." The city comes to life as piazzas fill with live entertainment and museums are open and free throughout the night.

—MAURO PALELLA
National Geographic researcher

hand raised in a gesture of clemency. But don't be fooled! Historians tell us that the horse's raised hoof originally rested on the head of a vanquished barbarian. The bronze statue was once covered in gold, and Romans used to say that if the gilt coating ever reappeared it would signal that the day of judgment had arrived.

Santa Maria d'Aracoeli: As you walked up the Cordonata, you will have noticed a second, much steeper flight of stairs on the left, leading to **Santa Maria d'Aracoeli** (pronounced A-ra-CHEY-li; see p. 138), which translates into "St. Mary of the Altar of Heaven." Don't miss the partly concealed remains of a multistory, second-century *insula*, or apartment building, on the far side of the steeper staircase.

Said to have been built in 1348 in gratitude for God's deliverance from the plague, the 122 steps up to the church (not to worry, you can also get in from Piazza del Campidoglio) provide a telling contrast to the Cordonata and reflect the medieval view that to achieve salvation life must be painful and arduous. Michelangelo's design, conceived 200 years later, embodied the concepts of Renaissance humanism; life's final destination is the same—death and salvation—but why not make the intervening voyage more enjoyable?

The Palazzo Senatorio rests on the ancient Tabularium and, if you take the road to the left of the building—which leads to a lovely lookout point over the Roman Forum—you will see the blocks of peperino marble from the Tabularium that have been incorporated into the sides of the newer building, as well as the medieval corner towers added later. ■

EXPERIENCE: Crossing the Street

While it may be reasonably safe to cross the street at home, in Rome it can be hazardous and even downright frightening. Throughout the city, black and white zebra stripes clearly mark pedestrian crosswalks, called *strisce*, and motorists are supposed to give you the right-of-way. Nevertheless, you will inevitably find yourself unable to cross as cars, motorcycles, and motor scooters whiz past with no signs of stopping.

The worst thing you can do is look undecided when trying to cross the street. Try to make eye contact with a driver. Optimally, you should just stride ahead. Don't run, and certainly don't stop short in the middle of the road or you risk confusing the *automobilisti*. Holding up the palm of your hand in a "stop, please" position may help—although this will surely mark you for a foreigner.

Try to cross at intersections where there are other people crossing or, better yet, where there is a traffic light. But, importantly, remember that when there is a traffic light and it is red for you, you do NOT have the right-of-way even if there is a crosswalk painted on the ground. Strange as it seems, the Italians use the same stripes to denote a regular street crossing as they do for the *strisce* that give pedestrians precedence.

Musei Capitolini

Together, the two buildings on either side of the Piazza del Campidoglio constitute the Capitoline Museums—the city's sculpture and painting gallery and one of the world's oldest public museums. An underground passageway linking the two buildings runs under the Palazzo Senatorio and through the ancient Tabularium, affording a splendid view of the Forum.

Start in the delightful courtyard of the building on the right, the **Palazzo dei Conservatori.** The marble body parts on view here come from the colossal statue of Constantine that originally stood in the huge basilica of Constantine (or Maxentius) in the Forum. The marble fragments embedded on the upper portion of the opposite wall are also interesting. Look for the word "brit" on one of the larger pieces, a relic of the triumphal arch celebrating the Emperor Claudius's military campaigns in Britain. The large marble reliefs below probably come from Hadrian's temple in the Piazza di Pietra (see p. 136).

The first floor of the palazzo contains magnificent statuary, including several celebrated pieces such as the "Boy with a Thorn," the Capitoline wolf, and Bernini's statue of Pope Urban VIII. The latter is in the Horatii and Curatii room, which contains frescoes depicting episodes from the days of the earliest Roman kings. This floor also displays the equestrian statue of Marcus Aurelius and a few other giant bronzes next to the extant remains of Jupiter's temple.

The **Pinacoteca** (painting gallery) on the second floor includes works by Velázquez, Dosso Dossi, Titian, Antonio Van Dyck, Reni, Annibale Caracci, and Caravaggio.

The remaining marble pieces of a giant statue of Constantine

On the staircase landings you will find reliefs showing Marcus Aurelius making sacrifices to the gods. They may be part of the same series that Constantine "borrowed" to decorate the upper portion of the Arch of Constantine.

Built in 1655, and opened to the public in 1734, the **Palazzo Nuovo** (on the left) includes much of the city's best-known statuary. "Marforio," one of Rome's famous talking statues (see p. 147), reclines in the courtyard. The **Sala dei Filosofi** (Philosophers' Room) and the **Sala degli Imperatori** (Emperors' Room) contain innumerable Roman busts and heads. Upstairs is the poignant "Dying Gaul," a marble copy of the bronze original and a superb example of classical sculpture. ∎

Musei Capitolini

 Map p. 39

✉ Piazza del Campidoglio 1

☎ 060608. For disabled access: 06 6710 2071

🕐 Closed Mon.

💲 $$. Audio guide: $

 Bus: C3, H, 46, 62, 63, 64, 70, 81, 84, 85, 87, 95, 119, 170, 175, 492, 628, 715, 716, 780

en.museicapitolini .org

Foro Romano

For almost a thousand years, the Foro Romano (Roman Forum) was the heart of ancient Rome and the nerve center of an empire. Altered and rebuilt over many centuries, its monuments— one superimposed on another—are often confusing. Today, all that remains is a jumble of romantic ruins, although its wistful, gentle beauty and myriad historical echoes still make the Forum the most important archaeological site in Europe.

Foro Romano

- Map p. 39
- Largo della Salara Vecchia 5/6 (off Via dei Fori Imperiali) & Via San Gregorio 30
- 060608 or 06 3996 7700
- $$ (valid 2 days, includes entry to Colosseum and Palatine). Daily tours in English: $ (Colosseum entrance)
- Bus: 60, 75, 81, 84, 85, 87, 175, 673 Metro: Linea B (Colosseo)

www.pierreci.it

Enter the Forum from Via dei Fori Imperiali, and when you get to the end of the ramp, turn right. To your left lies the Forum proper, a rectangular open space surrounded by a low iron railing. The remains of basilicas flank both of the Forum's long sides. On its short west side, you will see the high Rostra, or speaker's platform, which faces the Temple of the Divine Julius Caesar on the east. In front of you stands the Arch of Septimius Severus and, to its right, the surviving columns of the portico of the Temple of Saturn.

Western Section

Originally built in 179 B.C., the **Basilica Aemilia** once stood to the right of the Forum proper. Like all basilicas—which the Romans used primarily as tribunals or meeting halls, not churches— it had one wide central nave and two narrower side aisles.

At the far end of the basilica you'll find the **Curia,** or Senate. Built by Julius Caesar, and reconstructed by Diocletian after a fire in A.D. 283, the building was converted into a church in the seventh century. The original doors still survive and are on display at St. John Lateran.

The Curia's marble pavement is a stunning example of *opus sectile,* a repetitive geometric pattern of different colors. The wide, marble-faced steps on the right and left sides are the platforms where the senators sat in their portable *curile* chairs, moving to the "aye" or "nay" side as necessity dictated. The two marble reliefs, or *plutei* (note the Roman buildings in the background), probably came from the **Rostra** or speakers' platform outside. The holes on the base of the Rostra once held the iron "beaks" of captured warships.

The triple **Arco di Settimio Severo** (Arch of Septimius Severus) was erected in A.D. 203 to mark the tenth anniversary of Septimius' reign and to honor his and his sons' military victories. The "barbarians" carved on the column pedestals appear to support the weight of the entire arch. Nearby, the **Lapis Niger** (literally, the black stone) marked the location of an important early grave, possibly that of Romulus himself.

On the other side of the Forum, and just across the Via Sacra, stood the **Basilica Giulia,** another courthouse. On the steps leading

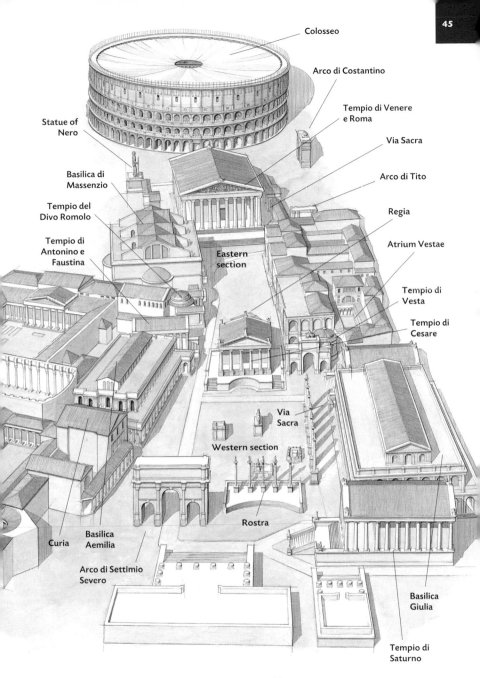

Colosseo

Arco di Costantino

Tempio di Venere e Roma

Via Sacra

Statue of Nero

Arco di Tito

Basilica di Massenzio

Regia

Tempio del Divo Romolo

Atrium Vestae

Tempio di Antonino e Faustina

Eastern section

Tempio di Vesta

Tempio di Cesare

Via Sacra

Western section

Rostra

Curia

Basilica Aemilia

Arco di Settimio Severo

Basilica Giulia

Tempio di Saturno

up to the ground floor you can still see some stone game boards that may have provided diversion to those waiting patiently outside.

Farther ahead, toward the Capitoline, only eight towering

Ionic columns remain of the *pronaos,* or porch, of the **Tempio di Saturno** (Temple of Saturn). Saturnus was originally the god of seed or sowing, and the Saturnalia festival was the Romans' favorite

Foro Romano Reconstruction

Built in A.D. 81, the Arch of Titus spans the Via Sacra, which leads from the Forum to the Colosseum.

holiday. A mix of Christmas and Mardi Gras, it lasted seven days. The temple also served as the state treasury. The top line of the inscription on the architrave reads "Senatus Populusque Romanus" (the Senate and People of Rome). Today you can see the famous acronym, SPQR, mainly on manhole covers and buses.

The **Forum** proper measures about 394 feet (120 m) by 164 feet (50 m). Paved in travertine under Augustus, this area was deliberately left clear and unencumbered to symbolize the openness of democracy. For centuries its only "occupants" were the three Mediterranean plants par excellence, the fig, the olive, and the grape. Only under the emperors were structures erected.

Julius Caesar rebuilt the Rostra and the Basilica Giulia, and after his death the Romans erected a monument over the site of his funeral pyre, effectively closing

off the Forum on the eastern side. From then on, the Forum grew increasingly crowded, with commemorative columns and triumphal arches springing up everywhere. The **Colonna di Foca** (Column of Phocas), put up in 608 to honor the Byzantine emperor of the same name, was the last monument erected here.

Looking eastward toward the Palatine, you will see three lovely Corinthian columns on the right that once belonged to the **Temple of Castor and Pollux,** twin brothers and semi-gods. Legend has it that, in the early fifth century B.C., the brothers helped the Romans defeat the Latins in the battle of Lake Regillus.

After his assassination in 44 B.C., Julius Caesar's body lay in state in a gilded shrine on the Rostra. Mark Antony's funeral oration so moved the crowd that the Romans decided to forgo the traditional funeral on the Campus

Martius and cremate Julius Caesar in front of the **Regia** instead. Little more than a pile of rubble today, the Regia was the headquarters of the chief priest, or Pontifex Maximus, a title still used by the Roman Catholic Church for the Pope.

Although controversial, Caesar's deification soon followed his funeral, initiating a practice adopted by many later emperors, some of whom actually became divine even before death! The **Tempio de Cesare** (Temple of Deified Julius Caesar) was built in 29 B.C. on the spot where he was cremated. Sadly, the remains of the temple are rather insignificant. But stand in front of it for a nice view of the western Forum. Note, too, the imposing size of the **Tabularium,** which forms the base of the Campidoglio's **Palazzo Senatorio.**

Eastern Section

Return to where you entered the Forum, and walk up the Via Sacra in the direction of the Arch of Titus. On your left stands the **Tempio de**

Antonio e Faustina (Temple of Deified Antoninus Pius and his wife Faustina). Erected by the Emperor Antoninus in 141 upon the death of his beloved wife, Faustina, the temple was rededicated after the emperor's own death 20 years later. On the entablature above the columns, you can see "Divo Antonino" ("Divine Antoninus"), which was added above the original inscription. The temple was later converted into a church.

On your right, on the other side of the jumble of ruins that once formed the Regia, you'll find the intriguing complex of the Vestal Virgins. Composed of the circular **Tempio di Vesta** (Temple to Vesta, goddess of the sacred fire) and the **Atrium Vestae,** the complex housed the Vestal Virgins (see sidebar), six priestesses who lived in isolation and safeguarded the sacred fire. The size of this second century residence gives you an idea of the vital role the Vestal Virgins played in Roman life. In fact, they were probably the most important women after members

Vestal Virgins

Chosen from Rome's grandest patrician families when they were between the ages of six and ten, the Vestal Virgins tended the city's sacred flame for 30 years. Housed in the Tempio di Vesta, the flame burned perpetually, a symbol of Rome's eternal nature.

In return for their services, the Vestals enjoyed high esteem and special rights, among them the power of mercy over condemned criminals, permission to drive in carriages (a right usually granted only to

empresses), and the safekeeping of wills, including that of the emperor.

Once the 30 years had expired, those who had successfully performed their duties received a pension and could finally marry. However, any Vestal who lost her virginity before then was buried alive since the Vestals could not be killed. If a virgin allowed the flame to die out, she was whipped by Rome's highest priest and forced to rekindle the fire with sacred pieces of wood.

**Church of
Santi Cosma e
Damiano**

▲ Map p. 39

☎ 06 692 0441

🕒 Closed 1–3 p.m.

**Santa Francesca
Romana**

▲ Map p. 39

☎ 06 679 5528

🕒 Closed
noon–3:30 p.m.

of the royal family. A cornerstone of Roman life, the cult survived until the end of the fourth century, when Christianity had practically become the state religion.

Located on the left, a short way up the Via Sacra, the small, round **Tempio del Divo Romolo**—whose original bronze doors still operate perfectly—may have served as a vestibule to Vespasian's Forum of Peace. Today the temple is occupied in part by the church of **Santi Cosma e Damiano** (Sts. Cosmas and Damian), whose entrance lies outside the Forum on Via dei Fori Imperiali.

In its apse, the church boasts a magnificent sixth-century mosaic,

INSIDER TIP:

The Roman Forum has little shade and no cafés or concession stands, so take a sun hat and something to drink—and avoid the heat of midsummer afternoons.

—TIM JEPSON
National Geographic author

whose stylized design shows Jesus raising his arm in benediction with saints flanking him. Below, 12 sheep, representing the apostles, stand between the holy cities of Bethlehem and Jerusalem. One of few surviving mosaics in the late classical Roman style, it was used as a model for later mosaics in many Roman churches.

Continue along the road to the huge **Basilica di Massenzio**

(or di Costantino; the Basilica of Maxentius or Constantine). The building was begun by Maxentius (A.D. 306–312), who was killed by his brother-in-law, Constantine, in the Battle of the Milvian Bridge before he could finish it. The giant statue of Constantine, now on display in pieces in the Palazzo dei Conservatori, once stood here.

Follow the Via Sacra uphill to a wide flight of steps leading to a large open space. The steps are all that remain of the western entrance to the enormous double temple complex designed by the Emperor Hadrian in the second century A.D. and rebuilt later, after a fire, by Maxentius. Joined at their apses, the **Tempio di Roma** (Temple of Rome) faced the Forum and the **Tempio di Venere** (Temple of Venus) faced the Colosseum. Built on the site of the Tempio di Roma, **Santa Francesca Romana,** also called Santa Maria Nova, is also accessible from Via dei Fori Imperiali.

Farther up the Via Sacra, you'll find yourself at the **Arco di Tito** (Arch of Titus). Completed in A.D. 81, this triumphal arch commemorated a victory against the Jews and the destruction of the Jerusalem Temple in A.D. 70. The reliefs inside the archway are particularly interesting. The one on the south side, closest to the Palatine, depicts the triumphal procession on its return from the campaign. Jewish slaves, money, and the trumpets and menorah from the Temple are depicted as campaign booty—one reason why, until the foundation of Israel in 1948, no Roman Jew would walk under the arch. ■

Palatino

One of the loveliest spots in the city, the Palatino (or Palatine Hill) was the site of Rome's original Paleolithic settlements and, later, of many of its ancient imperial palaces. Lush and green, often breezy, and featuring a reasonable number of park benches, this hill, one of Rome's seven, is a place tailor-made for dreaming and contemplation.

The Palatine Hill was turned into a cardinal's private park in the Renaissance.

None of the structures erected atop the Palatine are intact today, and the average visitor will find most of the ruins hard to identify. Nevertheless, because of their extent and intricacy (there are massive substructures beneath these buildings, many of which housed workshops, warehouses, and underground passages), the ruins are still imposing. So arm yourself with imagination, and keep in mind that this is where it all started!

This area has always been associated with Rome's founder, Romulus, and his twin, Remus.

Supposedly, the two brothers were brought up somewhere on this hill by Faustulus, the shepherd, who had found them after they washed up onto the river bank.

Paradoxically, then, this area was the site of both humble, early Iron Age settlements and—as time went by—a residential neighborhood reserved for the elite. During the late Republican period (the second and first centuries B.C.), notables such as Cicero, the politicians Crassus and Catullus, and the orator Hortensius lived here. Once Octavius (later Augustus) chose to forsake his residence near the

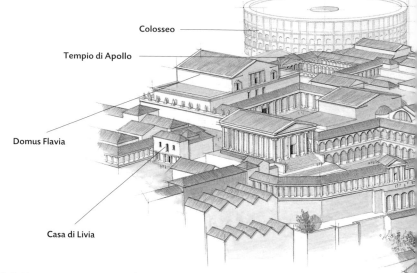

Colosseo

Tempio di Apollo

Domus Flavia

Casa di Livia

Palatino

Map p. 39

✉ Via San Gregorio 30 & Largo della Salara Vecchia 5/6 (off Via dei Fori Imperiali)

☎ 060608 or 06 3996 7700

💲 $$ (valid 2 days, includes entry to Colosseum and Foro Romano). Daily tours in English: $$ (San Gregorio entrance)

🚌 Bus: C3, 60, 75, 81, 84, 85, 87, 175, 673. Tram: 3. Metro: Linea B (Colosseo)

www.pierreci.it

Forum for the Palatine house he had bought (from Hortensius), it became the "in" place to live, especially if you were a Roman emperor. It remained the site of the imperial residences until Constantine moved to his new capital in the fourth century in what is today Turkey. But if Octavius's lifestyle was fairly austere, he found few imitators among his successors (in particular Nero, Domitian, and Septimius Severus), whose unchecked taste for opulence made the Palatine synonymous with luxury. No wonder it is the root of our word "palace."

What Remains Today

Although much of it remains to be excavated today, the Palatine can be divided into three sections. The first includes the ruins from the imperial residences, particularly that of the Emperor Domitian (A.D. 81–96), which includes a private area (Domus Augustana) and a public, or ceremonial, area (Domus Flavia). From the Arch of Titus, walk through the turnstile and follow

the path (Via di San Bonaventura) as it turns left, skirting past the ruins of the **Domus Flavia.** Dedicated to official business, this part of Domitian's palace includes the audience hall, or *aula regia,* a basilica for court cases that required the emperor's personal attention, and the enormous *triclinium* for state dining. This last structure—decorated in different colored marbles and flanked by courtyards, each containing a fountain—must have been impressive.

Domitian and his architect, Rabirius, erected the Domus Flavia over earlier buildings constructed by the emperors Tiberius and Nero, among others. Furthermore, despite all the greenery, the ground level has been artificially pumped up (some scholars say by as much as 50 feet/15 m) by layers and layers of used and discarded building materials. Located in an ex-convent near the Domus Flavia, the small **Antiquarium del Palatino** displays archaeological finds from the area.

Palatino

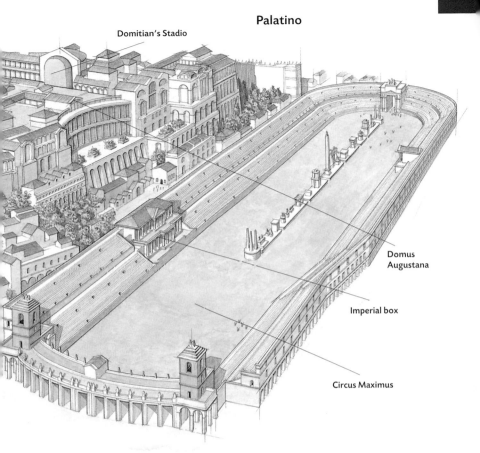

Domitian's Stadio

Domus
Augustana

Imperial box

Circus Maximus

Keep walking until you reach **Domitian's Stadio** (or hippodrome), an impressive, large sunken area generally assumed to have been a racecourse or stadium. The ruins directly to the right of the stadium once comprised the **Domus Augustana,** a sprawling complex of archways, sunken rooms, some of which may have been pools or fountains, and courtyards that you can explore, even if they are not easily identifiable. Gradually work your way toward the terrace, where there is a fantastic view of the **Circus Maximus** below.

At the southwestern end of the hill lie the sites of those Iron Age settlements from the time of Romulus and Remus. There is also a temple to Apollo and another to a goddess known as Magna Mater, or Great Mother. Two houses in the area from the late Republican period, the so-called **Casa di Livia** and **Casa di Augusto,** both recently opened to the public.

The **Orti Farnesiani,** a Renaissance garden once full of rare botanical species, was created in the 16th century. Two pavilions afford a fine view of the Forum below. Steps to the right and the left lead down to another landing with a stupendous, fern-draped nymphaeum, or monument dedicated to the nymphs. ■

The Emperors: the Good, the Bad, & the Ugly

The Roman emperors personified the best and the worst of Roman culture. One of the best was Octavius (27 B.C.–A.D. 14), who assumed the title of Augustus in 27 B.C. and is generally considered to be the first true emperor in the Julio-Claudian dynasty started by Julius Caesar.

This French painting shows the Sibyl interpreting Augustus's vision of the Virgin and Child.

Augustus

Born in 63 B.C. to Julius Caesar's niece, and later adopted by his great-uncle, Octavius (Octavian in English) was only 19 when Caesar was assassinated in 44 B.C. He joined with Mark Antony to punish the assassins then divided the empire with him. The alliance ended in 31 B.C., when Octavian trounced Antony and the Egyptian queen, Cleopatra, at the naval Battle of Actium (Greece). Although he always made sure to maintain a facade of republicanism, Octavian dedicated the rest of his life to the process, begun by his uncle, of concentrating power in the hands of one person: himself.

Shrewd, astute, and an able administrator, Octavian (soon to become Augustus) reformed the Roman bureaucracy, overhauled the fiscal system, and reorganized the military. Above all, he extended and secured the empire's borders, giving rise to what was known as the Pax Romana, a 200-year period of stability and security. Under this same stable and secure regime the new Christian religion was born. Furthermore, the solidity of Augustan Rome proved conducive to the new cult's rapid expansion.

Hadrian & Other Good Emperors

Several other "good" emperors left important legacies. Vespasian (A.D. 69–79) restored stability after the Neronian chaos, and Trajan (A.D. 98–117) extended the empire to its greatest limits. His successor, Hadrian (A.D. 117–138), is often referred to as the philosopher-emperor because of his devotion to the arts, literature, and architecture. Hadrian enormously embellished the city of Rome. He built a magnificent mausoleum that today we call Castel Sant'Angelo (see pp. 179–180), the sprawling villa in Tivoli that bears his name (see pp. 232–233), and he rebuilt the Pantheon (see pp. 128–131).

Hadrian also put into effect a policy of containment that had far-reaching impact. Military contingents became fixed rather than mobile. Civilian settlements near military installations thus grew in size, and commerce exploded. Fortification became increasingly important, with defensive architecture reaching new heights with the construction of Hadrian's Wall in Britain. Hadrian traveled widely during his reign, both for pleasure and because of his unusual view of the Roman Empire as a single political entity rather than a series of subject states.

Nero & Other Bad Emperors

You probably already know the names of Rome's bad emperors: Caligula, tall, pale, ungainly, with a wide but sinister forehead and clearly mentally unstable, or Caracalla, who had his younger brother, Geta, killed. But it is Nero who most frequently personifies the worst in Roman imperial rule.

Born into the imperial family in A.D. 37, Nero was adopted by Claudius after the emperor had married Nero's mother, Agrippina the Younger (Caligula's sister). He became

A bust of Julius Caesar in the Vatican Museum

emperor in A.D. 54. During the first ten years of his reign, Nero had a good record. He promoted legal and bureaucratic reform and demonstrated interest in the well-being of his population. All of this changed with the raging, nine-day fire of A.D. 64 during which the emperor did not actually fiddle, as the story goes, but did take his time in leaving his villa to come to Rome. Later, he blamed the new Christian religious sect, setting off a series of persecutions during which both Peter and Paul were probably martyred.

Although Nero rebuilt much of the city after the fire, he gave precedence to his own personal interests, expropriating large tracts of terrain to build the vast and sumptuous Domus Aurea (see p. 68). The populace seethed in response and threatened rebellion. In A.D. 68, Nero committed suicide, thus bringing the Julio-Claudian dynasty to a premature and inglorious end.

Fori Imperiali

Rome's highest leaders built the Fori Imperiali, Imperial Forums, between the first century B.C. and the start of the second century A.D., in order to glorify themselves and to create additional space for the political, religious, and institutional needs of the expanding Roman Empire. Although they appear to be separate today, the forums of Augustus, Nerva, Vespasian, and Trajan once formed an integral part of the Roman Forum.

Detail of the relief sculptures on the towering column in Trajan's Forum

You may find it difficult to comprehend the layout of the five Imperial Forums because the Via dei Fori Imperiali, built for military parades by the Fascist regime in the early 1930s, cuts directly through them and covers over much of the area. The long-term plan is to narrow the avenue significantly.

Earlier Imperial Forums

Begun in 54 B.C. by Julius Caesar, the **Foro di Cesare—** the first forum constructed by an emperor—stands between the Curia, or Senate building, and Via dei Fori Imperiali. Measuring 147 by 406 feet (45 by 124 m), it was surrounded by a double portico, a small portion of which is still visible, as is the base of the Tempio di Venere Genitrix, the goddess from whom the Julio-Claudian dynasty traced its descent.

Augustus, Caesar's political heir, followed suit. The **Foro di Augusto,** near that of his adoptive father, ends at the high fire wall he erected to protect the civic center from the frequent fires in the densely populated residential Suburra area on the other side. The forum took 20 years to complete and was dominated by the Tempio di Marte Ultore, which the young emperor built after killing Caesar's assassins at the battle of Philippi in 42 B.C. Three of its 24 tall Corinthian marble columns are more or less all that remain, but try to imagine it as it was. Statuary dotted the porticoes; floors and walls were constructed in colored marbles—pure white, Phrygian purple, Numidian yellow, Lucullan red or black; there was even a separate room for a colossus in precious metal, possibly Caesar or Augustus himself, presumably some 33 feet (10 m) tall.

Most of the **Foro di Vespasiano** (built between A.D. 71 and 75 to mark the defeat of the Jews) lies hidden beneath the intersection of Via dei Fori Imperiali and Via Cavour. What remains of the Temple of Peace, as it was called, is incorporated into the monastery and church of **Santi Cosma e Damiano.**

In between Augustus's and Vespasian's forums is Nerva's Forum **(Foro di Nerva)**, which actually was built by Domitian, Nerva's predecessor. Long and narrow, and flanked by colonnades, it was often called the Forum Transitorium and transformed the Argiletum, the route from the Suburra to the Roman Forum, into a decorated passageway. All that remains are two massive Corinthian columns (the Italians call them the *colonnacce,* the ugly

columns) in the corner near Via dei Fori Imperiali and the podium of a temple dedicated to Minerva. The entablature between the columns has a lovely frieze depicting domestic scenes like spinning and weaving, while a statue, until recently identified as Minerva, keeps watch. Archaeologists have now found a second statue, leading them to wonder if they might instead have represented two imperial provinces.

Trajan's Column

Colonna Traiana (Trajan's Column) stands in a small courtyard beyond the Basilica Ulpia. Made of 29 cylindrical blocks, and spiraling up for about 100 feet (30 m), the column features magnificent carved reliefs—2,600 figures in all—that tell the story of the emperor's military campaigns against the Dacians. Forty small windows light the staircase inside. Trajan's remains were placed inside the hollow base after his unexpected death in A.D. 117. In the 16th century, the statue of St. Peter replaced the original one of Trajan.

Fori Imperiali

- Map p. 39
- Information Centre Via dei Fori Imperiali
- 06 679 7702
- At present not open to the public, but the ruins are all readily visible from surrounding streets and vantage points
- Bus: C3, 60, 75, 84, 85, 87, 175, 673. Tram: 3. Metro: Linea B (Colosseo)

Foro Traiano

The major attraction of the Imperial Forums is the magnificent forum and markets built by the Emperor Trajan and dedicated in A.D. 112. This was the last of the forums to be built and undoubtedly was the grandest and the most splendid.

**Museo dei Fori
Imperiali &
Trajan's Markets**

🅰 Map p. 39

✉ Via IV
Novembre 94

☎ 060608

🕐 Closed Mon.

💲 $$$. Audio
guide: $

🚌 Bus: H, 40, 60,
64, 70, 170

en.mercatiditraiano
.it

The entrance to Trajan's Forum is a large, rectangular courtyard flanked by two long porticoes, 367 feet (112 m) in length, and closed off at the northern end by the gigantic two-story **Basilica Ulpia**. The latter, richly decorated in sumptuous colors, marble work, and precious metals, had five aisles separated by columns, with a semi-circular apse at each end.

To make space for his forum, Trajan and his court architect, Apollodorus of Damascus, hollowed out much of the high ridge that links the Capitoline and the Quirinal Hills, a technological miracle for the time.

Museo dei Fori Imperiali

Don't miss the Museo dei Fori Imperiali in Trajan's Markets. This three- or four-story semicircular structure was also built by Apollodorus and was essentially a reconstruction of the neighborhood removed by the forum's construction.

An ancient Roman street (Via Biberatica) runs through it, and wandering from shop to shop (there are about 150) will give you an idea of what life was like in the second century A.D. The alcove-like shops on the ground floor probably sold dry goods (flour and sugar), flowers, and vegetables. Those off the gallery were probably storehouses for wine and oil. There were also fishponds as well as special shops for Eastern spices. The world's first mall, with its impressive vaulting, now hosts the Museo dei Fori Imperiali, where each room is dedicated to one of the imperial forums. ∎

EXPERIENCE: Bike Around Town

When in Rome, why not travel the way the Romans do? These days, more Romans are discovering that cycling is healthy, fun, and a time-efficient means of transportation. They increasingly use bikes to go to work, run errands, and even transport their children from place to place.

Visitors unused to the vagaries of Roman drivers should not attempt to ride a bike through Rome's traffic. However, the city, which is now setting up share-a-bike stands in some parts of the *centro storico*, has created some bike paths, including a long, picturesque stretch along the lower banks of the Tiber River.

On Sundays, when both are closed to traffic, you can bike up the Via dei Fori Imperiali, past the Forum and the Colosseum, and along the Via Appia Antica (Appian Way), where you will join scores of bikers pedaling past ancient monuments and the haunting remains of Roman aqueducts. The initial stretch, outside Porta San Sebastiano, is now a bike-friendly park *(www. parcoappiaantica.it)*, where 2.5-hour guided bicycle tours in English are available daily for groups of 12 *(fax 06 513 5316, email: puntoappia@parcoappiaantica.it, €12 per person including rental)*.

Conveniently located bike-rental shops include: Bici & Baci *(Via del Viminale 5, tel 06 482 8443, www.bicibaci.com)*, near the Stazione Termini; Spagna Rent, near the Spanish Steps metro stop *(Vicolo del Bottino 8/E, tel 339 427 7773)*; and Bici Pincio *(Viale della Pineta, tel 06 678 4374)*, in the Borghese Gardens. Prices range from €3 an hour to €12 a day.

The massive Colosseum, imperial monuments, and the glorious
frescoes and mosaics of early Christian churches

Colosseo to San Clemente

Detail from the 12th-century apse
mosaic in San Clemente

Colosseo to San Clemente

Set in a valley between the Palatine, Esquiline, and Caelian Hills, the Colosseo (Colosseum) is the Roman world's largest surviving structure, its majestic impact undimmed either by the passage of time or the blight of encircling traffic. It is also, undoubtedly, the landmark most closely identified with the city itself.

Two thousand years after it was built by the Emperor Vespasian, on the site of the artificial lake that Nero had built for his magnificent pleasure house, the Domus Aurea, the Colosseum is still standing. It looms over one of the most extensive archaeological areas in the world, a reminder of man's achievements and his cruelty. It cannot be forgotten, after all, that while this was a place of celebration it was also a site of unchecked (human and animal) slaughter.

Not far away is the Arch of Constantine, built in A.D. 315 to celebrate the emperor's victory at Ponte Milvio over his brother-in-law and predecessor, Maxentius. But for all its size (it is the largest surviving triumphal arch) and apparent splendor, the arch, decorated mostly with derivative art, is generally considered to be an indication of Rome's incipient decline.

On the other side of the Colosseum are the remains of the first-century Domus Aurea (Golden House) which, with the exception of Diocletian's Palace in Split (Croatia), is the only floor-to-ceiling Roman imperial structure to have survived. Nero's extensive pleasure palace, which reflects the vast wealth and architectural prowess of imperial Rome, was built in the aftermath of the terrible fire of A.D. 64 which totally destroyed 3 of Rome's 14 neighborhoods. Its exact dimensions are as yet unknown. The Domus is closed for restoration but "works in progress" visits are offered.

The surrounding area has many important early churches. San Pietro in Vincoli, the location of Michelangelo's imposing "Moses," was originally named the Basilica Eudoxiana, after the empress who built it to hold St. Peter's Chains. The multilevel San Clemente, which lies between the Colosseum and San Giovanni in Laterano, was built in the fourth century to commemorate Clement, martyred in the Crimea sometime during the reign of Trajan (A.D. 98–117). In the 11th century invading Norman armies destroyed the original church, but important treasures from the new church survive, such as the wonderful 12th-century apse mosaic. San Clemente is also a prime example of Rome's architectural stratification, concealing the remains of a fourth-century church as well as older, first-century structures.

The quiet Caelian Hill, facing the Palatine on the opposite side of Via di San Gregorio, offers other jewels of both early Christian culture and Renaissance design. St. Gregory (San Gregorio Magno) built his church and monastery here in the sixth century, although both the church and the three frescoed chapels near it were rebuilt in the 17th century. The Basilica of Santi Giovanni

---

NOT TO BE MISSED:

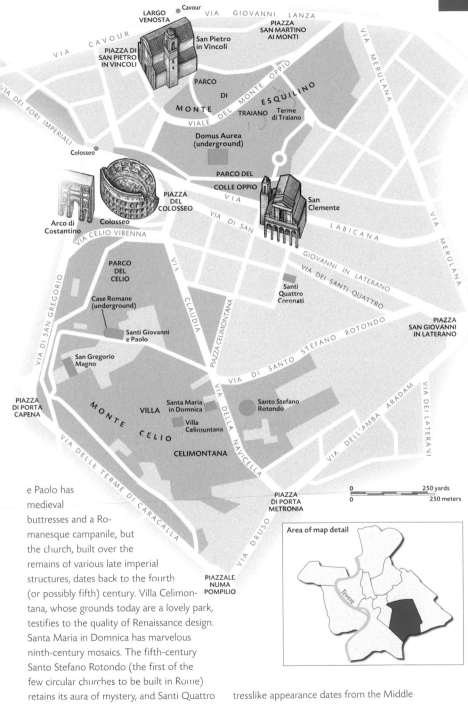

e Paolo has
medieval
buttresses and a Ro-
manesque campanile, but
the church, built over the
remains of various late imperial
structures, dates back to the fourth
(or possibly fifth) century. Villa Celimontana, whose grounds today are a lovely park,
testifies to the quality of Renaissance design.
Santa Maria in Domnica has marvelous
ninth-century mosaics. The fifth-century
Santo Stefano Rotondo (the first of the
few circular churches to be built in Rome)
retains its aura of mystery, and Santi Quattro
Coronati has interesting frescoes and one of
Rome's oldest, and loveliest cloisters. Its for-

tresslike appearance dates from the Middle
Ages when the monastery was fortified to
serve as a refuge for the popes. ■

Area of map detail

Colosseo

Properly called the Flavian Amphitheater, the Colosseo, or Colosseum, was built by the three Flavian emperors to promote a good public image. Construction began under Vespasian (A.D. 69–79), who drained the artificial lake that had formed part of Nero's extravagant Domus Aurea complex to transform the site into a place for public entertainment.

Most of the holes in the Colosseum, the largest Roman amphitheater anywhere, held the iron grapples that were plundered and reused during the Middle Ages.

Inaugurated in A.D. 80, the Colosseum was probably built with the spoils brought back from the Temple of Jerusalem at the end of the so-called Jewish campaign, a war waged and won by Vespasian's son Titus in A.D. 70. It was made from travertine hewn from quarries near Tivoli and hauled to Rome along a specially built road. The largest amphitheater in the Roman world, this stone oval measures 620 feet (189 m) long, 512 feet (156 m) wide, and 157 feet (48 m) high. Some 300 tons of iron are believed to have been used for the grapples that held the stones together.

Many historians believe that the name, Colosseum, derives not from the structure's super size but from the giant, or colossal, bronze statue that stood nearby. You can still see its base, today planted with five trees, between the arena and the Temple of Venus and Rome. The original statue depicted Nero, but later the Flavians very pragmatically added sunbeams around the statue's head, changed the inscription, and dedicated the image to the sun god instead. The statue remained standing until sometime in the early Middle Ages, when it was removed and probably melted down.

The Colosseum itself is composed of a series of three **arcades,** topped by a fourth story, or attic. The columns are disposed on three levels—from the ground up, Doric, Ionic, and Corinthian—according to classical canons. Running below the fourth story cornice, 240 small ledges once held the long wooden poles that supported the *velarium,* the canvas awning that sailors from the imperial fleet raised to protect spectators from the heat, rain, and winter cold.

Inside the Arena

Estimates of crowd capacity in the Colosseum range from 50,000 to almost 90,000. There were three tiers of seats: the *ima* (lowest), the *media,* and the *summa,* each arranged according to social status and profession. Members of the imperial family and the Vestal Virgins had special boxes. The senators, in their red-bordered white togas, sat on the same level, in the "orchestra" section. Then came the knights *(equites)* followed by the *plebs* (ordinary citizens). Other sections were set aside for soldiers, scribes, students with tutors, and foreign dignitaries. A standing-room-only balcony at the top of the arena was reserved for the least important members of society: women, slaves, and the poor.

Spectators poured into the Colosseum through the 80 arched entrances on the ground level. They poured in and out through the 160 exits, called *vomitoria,* distributed throughout the tiers on various levels

INSIDER TIP:

In order to avoid waiting in line for tickets to the Colosseum, first visit the much less crowded Forum, where you can purchase a combination ticket for both sites.

—BRIDGET A. ENGLISH
National Geographic contributor

and allowing for quick exit by often unruly and rambunctious crowds. Some say the Colosseum could empty in as few as 10 minutes.

Animal Hunts & Gladiator Games

The Colosseum's program included animal hunts *(venationes)* in the morning, public executions at noon, and gladiatorial contests in the afternoon. The arena's wood floor, which has been partially reconstructed, was covered with sand to absorb the blood and stench of the spectacles. Today, the uncovered portion reveals

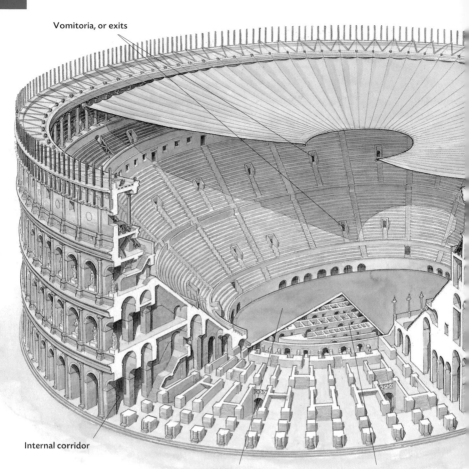

Vomitoria, or exits

Internal corridor

Colosseum

Wood floor of arena,
covered in sand

Understage corridors
and tunnels

the **corridors and tunnels** underneath that celebrities used to avoid the crowds and animals and gladiators used to enter the arena. Vertical shafts held caged animals, which were brought up to the arena level along ramps or in pulley-system elevators.

A tunnel connected the understage section with the Ludus Magnus, the gladiatorial barracks and training area located between the Colosseum and San Clemente. The gladiators—who were chosen from among condemned crimi-

nals, slaves, and prisoners of war—were divided into three categories: those who fought heavily armed, with sword and shield; those lightly armed with dagger and arm buckler; and those armed only with nets and tridents as you can see in the Roman floor mosaics in the Galleria Borghese.

"Ave, Imperator, morituri te salutant" ("Hail, Emperor, we who are about to die, salute you"), the gladiators scheduled to fight that day would intone during the pre-games parade. Naturally, they

Velarium, a canvas awning for all-weather protection

early fifth century; animal hunts lasted another hundred years.

After the Heyday

After the decline of Rome, the Colosseum was utilized for a variety of purposes. However, time, natural calamity, and the Romans themselves led to its deterioration. The southern side of the arena collapsed in a major earthquake in 1349. Afterward, for about 400 years, it served as a quarry for marble and travertine building blocks used in other city structures, such as the Palazzo Venezia and even the new St. Peter's.

This practice ended when Pope Benedict XIV (1740–1758) declared the Colosseum a sacred place because of the Christian

Colosseo

🅰 Map p. 59

✉ Piazza del Colosseo

☎ 060608 or 06 3996 7700

💲 $$ (valid 2 days, includes entry to Colosseum & Palatine). Daily tours in English: $ (Colosseum entrance)

🚌 Bus: C3, 60, 75, 81, 85, 87, 175, 628. Tram: 3. Metro: Linea B (Colosseo)

www.picrreci.lt

all hoped to survive and enjoy the booty that came with victory. Except in rare cases, however, survival (or the thumbs-up sign from the crowd) generally meant only having to fight again. The lucky few were awarded the laurel crown and allowed to retire.

The thousands of animals killed in the festivities, which on special occasions could last for three to four months, included lions, tigers, hyenas, elephants, hippopotamuses, giraffes, and zebras.

As Christian influence grew, the importance of the Colosseum declined. The last recorded gladiatorial games were held in the

INSIDER TIP:

Many Roman sights repay a late-night visit when they are floodlit. The Colosseum, St. Peter's, the Piazza del Campidoglio, and the Trevi Fountain are four of the best.

—TIM JEPSON
National Geographic author

martyrs' blood that reportedly had been shed there. Since the 19th century, a Way of the Cross ceremony involving the direct participation of the pope has been held in the Colosseum every year on the evening of Good Friday before Easter. ∎

Arco di Costantino

Constantine is often referred to as the first Christian emperor, but you won't find any Christian images on the arch built in his honor in A.D. 315. His baptism, such as it was, only took place on his deathbed 22 years later. And, impressive as it seems, the Arch of Constantine is atypical.

Arco di Costantino

 Map p. 59

✉ Between Via di San Gregorio & Piazza del Colosseo

🚌 Bus: C3, 60, 75, 81, 85, 87, 175, 628. Tram: 3. Metro: Linea B (Colosseo)

Most of the Arch's decorative work was, in fact, taken from structures built by previous emperors, suggesting that Roman art had entered a phase of decline. Thus, the eight **rectangular reliefs** on both sides of the upper portion (the attic) originally adorned a structure dedicated to Marcus Aurelius (A.D. 161–180) and the portrait of the emperor was recut with Constantine's likeness. (The narrative content of three other reliefs from the same series, now in the Capitoline Museums, clearly shows the Emperor Marcus Aurelius.)

Also plundered from other monuments were the **round medallions** over the lateral arches (four on each side). These hunting and sacrificial scenes date from the first half of the second century, a period coinciding not with the reign of Constantine but with that of Hadrian. Eight **statues of barbarians** (the ones wearing trousers, of course!) on top of the columns were also derivative. Naturally, some of the work was original but, even to the untrained eye, it appears clearly inferior workmanship.

By way of example, the four **panel friezes** below the above-mentioned medallions, on both sides, were sculpted specifically for the arch. Note the one on the south side (toward the Circus Maximus), over the leftmost arch, showing Constantine and his army besieging the city of Verona: The figure of the centurion who is scaling the walls appears dwarfish, and there is a general lack of perspective. Compare the body proportions in this relief with the ones directly above, sculpted about 180 years earlier, and the difference in artistic skill becomes quite apparent. ■

Constantine built this arch, near the end of the Via Triumphalis, to mark his tenth year in power.

San Pietro in Vincoli

Try to schedule your visit to San Pietro in Vincoli (also known as the Basilica Eudoxiana) early in the day, in the hopes that you can beat the crush of tourists coming here to see Michelangelo's "Moses." Situated at the end of the right transept, this is the pièce de résistance of the unfinished tomb of Pope Julius II (1503–1513), the pontiff who built the Sistine Chapel.

A gash on Moses' knee is said to have been caused when Michelangelo threw a tool at it.

The Empress Eudoxia built San Pietro in Vincoli to house the chains worn by St. Peter during his imprisonments in Jerusalem and Rome. According to the story, when the chains were placed side by side they miraculously fused. Today they are displayed under the church's altar.

Michelangelo's incredibly powerful **statue of Moses** shows Moses returning from Mount Sinai carrying God's Commandments under his arm and scowling, clearly annoyed with his idolatrous brethren for flirting with the Golden Calf. The striking statues of Jacob's two wives, Leah and Rachel—symbols of active and contemplative life—were probably finished by one of Michelangelo's pupils, Raffaele da Montelupo.

Ignore the baroque ceiling to get a good idea of the stark and simple basilica structure that so appealed to the ancient Romans and which was later adopted by many churches. Despite repeated reconstruction, the brickwork above the windows of the Renaissance facade, best seen inside, still reveals the outline of the five arches of the church's original fifth-century entrances.

The lovely 15th-century fresco to the left of the main entrance depicts a 1476 procession against the plague. ∎

San Pietro in Vincoli

 Map p. 59

✉ Piazza di San Pietro in Vincoli 4

☎ 06 488 2865

🕐 Closed 12:30–3:30 p.m.

🚌 Bus: 75, 84. Metro: Linea B (Cavour)

Monks, Mosaics, & Martyrs Walk

Only a short distance from the hue and cry of the Colosseum, the Caelian (Celio) Hill has always been one of the quieter and less populated areas of Rome. Right from the earliest centuries of Christian Rome it was therefore a perfect setting for monastic life and spiritual contemplation.

Like many Roman parks, Villa Celimontana was once the home and gardens of a nobleman.

NOT TO BE MISSED:

Chapel of Santa Barbara • Santa Maria in Domnica • Case Romane del Celio • Santi Quattro Coronati

From the Colosseum, follow Via di San Gregorio on the left-hand sidewalk. The brick arch across the street once formed part of an aqueduct built by the Emperor Nero to supply water to the imperial residences on the Palatine. Just past the arch, the steps on your left lead up to the imposing facade of **San Gregorio Magno ❶**. (Be careful crossing the tram tracks!) Pope Gregory the Great (A.D. 590–604)—later St. Gregory—built the church *(tel 06 700 8227, closed 12:30 p.m.–3 p.m. and when celebrating Mass)* on the grounds of his family home.

The church's baroque facade was added in the 17th century, but its atrium is typical of Rome's early churches, especially those built in sparsely inhabited areas like the Caelian Hill. The fresco in the rightmost lunette shows Gregory at the head of a procession to St. Peter's in 590 to pray for deliverance from the plague. Along the way he sees the archangel Michael above Hadrian's Mausoleum. The angel is sheathing his sword, a clear sign that the Roman plague has ended (and the reason a statue of the archangel stands atop Castel Sant'Angelo.) To see the interior, ring the bell on the wall of the atrium's right portico.

By the way, it was from here that Pope Gregory, himself a monk, dispatched St. Augustine of Canterbury and 40 Benedictine monks to the British Isles to convert the Angles and Saxons to Christianity and bring that distant land back into contact with the classical world. All ties with Rome had been cut in the early fifth century, when the last Roman garrisons were withdrawn.

Leaving the church, an iron gate on the left leads to three small chapels *(tel 06 7049 4966, open 9:30 a.m.–12:30 p.m. Tues., Thurs., & Sat.–Sun.).* The **chapel of Santa Barbara,** farthest to the left, is frescoed with scenes from the life of St. Gregory, including one showing the pope sending Augustine off on his mission. In it is the stone table at which Gregory usually served meals to 12 paupers. Once, a 13th diner turned out to be an angel.

The other two chapels, dedicated to St. Andrew and St. Sylvia (Gregory's mother),

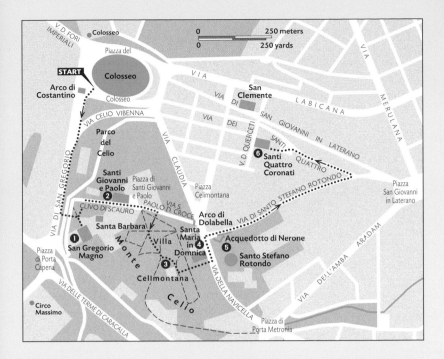

contain frescoes by Domenichino and Guido Reni. Behind the chapels stands the so-called **Library of Agapetus,** originally part of a late Roman mansion.

From San Gregorio, walk up the steep Clivo di Scauro on the left, from where you will have a fine view of the apse of the church of **Santi Giovanni e Paolo ❷,** dedicated to John and Paul, two Roman soldiers who suffered martyrdom after refusing to worship pagan idols. Walk under the church's medieval flying buttresses, unusual for this city, to find the **Piazza dei Santi Giovanni e Paolo.** Here you can visit the underground ruins, accessed from beneath the buttresses, and the fine small museum in the **Case Romane del Celio** (see p. 74).

Directly ahead, you will see the back entrance to the **Villa Celimontana ❸,** once the gardens to the Renaissance Villa Mattei. After a pleasant stroll past the fountains and ferns, leave the park from its main entrance. You'll find yourself on **Via della Navicella,** named for a Roman votive boat now placed

🅰	Also see area map, p. 59
►	Colosseo
↔	1.5 miles (2.5 km)
⏱	2.5 hours
►	Santi Quattro Coronati

atop a fountain in the middle of the street to your left as you exit. The fountain stands in front of the church of **Santa Maria in Domnica ❹,** with its superb ninth-century apse mosaic of the "Virgin Enthroned with the Christ Child."

Across the street (beyond more remnants of Nero's aqueduct) begins Via di Santo Stefano Rotondo. At No. 7 is the round church of **Santo Stefano Rotondo ❺** (see p. 73). Continue along Via di Santo Stefano Rotondo to a Romanesque portico made with recycled Roman columns.

Turn left onto Via dei Santi Quattro, which leads to the medieval fortress that encloses **Santi Quattro Coronati ❻** (Four Crowned Saints church and its monastery, see p. 74).

Domus Aurea

Built by Emperor Nero on the lower slopes of the Colle Oppio, the Domus Aurea (Golden House)—which got its name from the ample use of gold leaf in its decorations—was a vast estate that included a pleasure palace, reception and banquet halls, gardens, and an artificial lake. Today it is closed for restoration, but guided "works-in-progress" visits are available.

Domus Aurea

- 🅐 Map p. 59
- ✉ Via della Domus Aurea (inside park)
- ☎ 06 3996 7700
- 🕒 Closed for restoration. Visit to the works in progress on frescoes closed Sat.–Mon. Reservation mandatory
- 💲 $
- 🚍 Bus: 60, 75, 81, 85, 87, 117, 175. Tram: 3. Metro: Linea B (Colosseo)

www.pierreci.it

Soon after Vespasian, the first of the Flavian emperors, began his reign in A.D. 69, he drained the lake and demolished part of the Domus Aurea to make room for the Colosseum. Half a century later, Trajan systematically removed all the statuary and precious materials, including the marble on the walls, to make way for his imperial baths. In the process, however, he unwittingly, created the conditions for the Domus Aurea's preservation through the centuries.

INSIDER TIP:

The Virgin Mary icons you see everywhere in Rome do not display art taste, but are crime deterrents. Robbers often avoid plying their trade in front of them.

—RAFAEL SANDOR
National Geographic International Channel

Covered over and long forgotten, the Domus Aurea was rediscovered during the Renaissance, when parts of the structure above collapsed. Artists like Michelangelo, Raphael, and Pinturicchio visited the site, eager to examine the unusual decoration revealed on the upper portion of what turned out to be very high-ceilinged rooms. This type of decoration, often called *grotteschi,* is similar to that used on the walls and ceilings of many buildings in Pompeii.

Several 18th-century artists, such as Piranesi, also visited the ruins, then erroneously identified as the Baths of Titus, and made engravings that today are essential for our understanding of first-century imperial art. Only later did archaeologists identify the underground structure as part of Nero's famous estate.

Today the Domus Aurea—once a riot of colored marble, stucco, and gold leaf—is a mere shadow of its former self. We can only imagine its full glory, because another of Trajan's projects closed in all the terraces that looked out over the lake toward the Palatine.

Of the 150 rooms excavated, only a few underground are currently open to the public. "Works-in-progress" *(Aperto per restauro)* tours are scheduled from 10:00 a.m. to 4:00 p.m., Tuesday through Friday, and last about 30 minutes. They begin in the Gallery of the Baths of Trajan and meander through various rooms as far as the Room of the Gilded Vault *(closed to the public).* In summer, bring a sweater because the temperature is very cool. ∎

San Clemente

This multilevel church, founded in the fourth century to commemorate the martyr Clement, the Church's fourth pope, is one of the most fascinating in the city. Destroyed by the invading Norman armies in 1084, the church was rebuilt over the rubble of the preexisting church by Pope Paschal II in the early 12th century.

Much of San Clemente is baroque in style, but this hasn't altered its 12th-century essence.

San Clemente may have a baroque veneer—primarily the out-of-place gilded ceiling and the pilasters that encase several of the original columns—but fortunately it does not overwhelm the church's older treasures, such as the reconstructed sixth-century *schola cantorum*, the marble barrier defining the monks' choir stall, the colorful pre-cosmatesque (see p. 206) pavement, and the porticoed atrium, which is conceptually part of the main entrance from Piazza San Clemente.

The wonderful 12th-century **apse mosaic** has a triumphal cross in the center (with twelve doves symbolizing the Twelve Apostles) between Mary and St. John. From the base of the cross, a luxuriant Tree of Life sends out spirals of foliage, each of which encloses images of the learned Doctors of the Church, exotic birds, flowers, and other Christian symbols.

The waters of life flow at the base of the mosaic, and if you've brought your binoculars, be sure to note the tiny figures performing daily farmyard activities, a return to the classical style that, by the fifth century, had largely disappeared. Farther below is

San Clemente
- Map p. 59
- Via di San Giovanni in Laterano 108
- 06 7045 1018
- Underground: $. Audio guide: $.
- Church and underground closed daily 12:30–3 p.m. Underground closed Sun. until noon.
- Bus: C3, 60, 75, 81, 85, 87, 673. Tram: 3. Metro: Linea B (Colosseo)

The unusual apse mosaic represents a tree of life, growing out of an acanthus plant at the base of the Crucifix.

the Lamb of God, *Agnus Dei,* standing in the center with six sheep on either side.

The external arch around the apse is just as interestingly decorated. Jesus is center top, flanked by symbols of the Four Evangelists. Just below, Paul and St. Lawrence are shown on the left while Peter and Clement are shown in the corresponding spot on the right.

The Chapel of St. Catherine

Located immediately to the right of the Via di San Giovanni in Laterano entrance, the **Chapel of St. Catherine of Alexandria** contains a series of celebrated frescoes dating from about 1430 and painted by Masolino da Panicale, who was probably helped by his assistant, Masaccio. A Crucifixion scene completely covers the far wall, while the ceiling vaults show the Four Evangelists and their symbols, as well as the Doctors of the

Church. The most interesting frescoes, however, are on the side walls. Those on the right depict scenes from the life of St. Ambrose. Those on the left are scenes from the life of St. Catherine, including, in the middle scene in the lower order, the unsuccessful attempt to murder her on a spiked wheel.

Note the 15th-century St. Christopher painted on the outside left wall of the chapel (protected by a glass panel) with some ancient graffiti etched into its lower right-hand section.

An Odyssey Through Time

San Clemente is a microcosm of the architectural stratification that is a prime characteristic of Rome. You enter the 12th-century church at street level, descend to the excavated fourth-century church below, and eventually go down a

INSIDER TIP:

San Clemente is a lesser known gem with literally layers of history. Deep below the current basilica is a second-century temple dedicated to the Persian god Mithras.

—NATASHA SCRIPTURE
National Geographic contributor

further level to the remains of several first-century structures. Access (for a small fee) is from the sacristy, and there are gener-

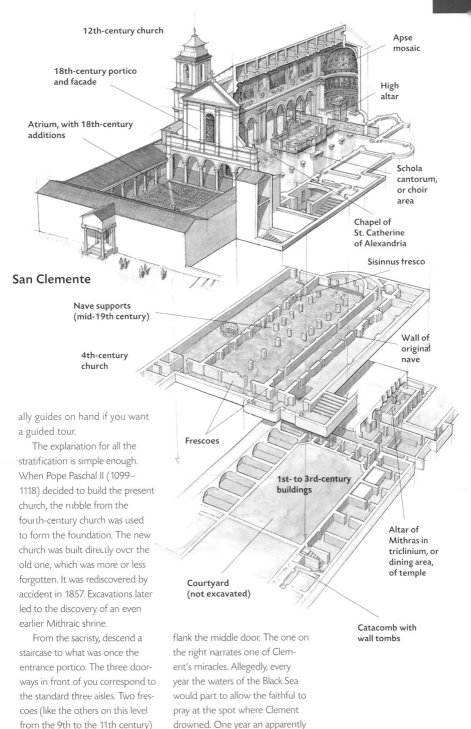

12th-century church

18th-century portico and facade

Atrium, with 18th-century additions

San Clemente

Apse mosaic

High altar

Schola cantorum, or choir area

Chapel of St. Catherine of Alexandria

Sisinnus fresco

Nave supports (mid-19th century)

4th-century church

Wall of original nave

Frescoes

1st- to 3rd-century buildings

Altar of Mithras in triclinium, or dining area, of temple

Courtyard (not excavated)

Catacomb with wall tombs

ally guides on hand if you want a guided tour.

The explanation for all the stratification is simple enough. When Pope Paschal II (1099–1118) decided to build the present church, the rubble from the fourth-century church was used to form the foundation. The new church was built directly over the old one, which was more or less forgotten. It was rediscovered by accident in 1857. Excavations later led to the discovery of an even earlier Mithraic shrine.

From the sacristy, descend a staircase to what was once the entrance portico. The three doorways in front of you correspond to the standard three aisles. Two frescoes (like the others on this level from the 9th to the 11th century)

flank the middle door. The one on the right narrates one of Clement's miracles. Allegedly, every year the waters of the Black Sea would part to allow the faithful to pray at the spot where Clement drowned. One year an apparently absentminded mother forgot her child and he was submerged. When she returned the next year, she found him safe and sound; the fish painted around the border represent the encroaching sea.

Step through the doorway and walk until you are almost parallel with a door leading off to the right aisle. To get an idea of the dimensions of this church, look

the language that eventually evolved into Italian.

The Mithraeum

Reach the third and **lowest level** of the site by descending another staircase at the far end of the left aisle. At the bottom, you'll hear the gurgling of an underground spring. Follow the path until you reach the ancient **Mithraeum,**

Saints & their Symbols

In Roman Catholic iconography, many saints—especially those who were martyred—have a symbol that represents them, often the instrument of their death. Thus Bartholomew is represented by a knife because he was skinned alive. Cecilia's symbol is a musical instrument because she sang while her persecutors tried to steam her to death. And Jerome— who was not martyred, but exiled himself in the desert to resist temptation and translate the holy scriptures—is shown as a scantily clad old man with a lion.

The church of San Clemente is notable because you can find the symbols of three saints here. First, of course, is Clement himself, whose symbol, the anchor, appears on the canopy over the main altar in both the upper and lower church.

The frescoes in the Chapel of St. Catherine show the torture wheel on which she was martyred. And on the arch outside the apse, St. Lawrence is shown with his foot over a flame and grill, his symbol because he was slowly roasted to death.

through the door at a column embedded in a retaining wall. Now look, to your left, at the wall where other columns are embedded. The distance between the columns indicates the width of the central nave of the fourth-century church (which was bigger than the present one), laid out in a typical basilica plan.

There are other interesting frescoes here. One (on the left wall of the nave, just before the altar) tells the story of a Roman prefect named Sisinnus. Scholars believe that the inscription on the bottom half is one of the earliest written examples of the vernacular,

a temple to the Eastern god, Mithras. Dating from around the end of the second century, or the beginning of the third, it has an altar and a ceiling decorated to simulate a grotto (Mithras was reportedly born in one). The barrel-vaulted room opposite, with traces of stucco work on the ceiling, was probably a vestibule of the temple. The Mithraeum stood opposite the original first-century Christian place of worship, possibly Clement's own house.

Amazing as it may seem, the labyrinthine way to the exit takes you through a series of first-century rooms. ■

Santo Stefano Rotondo

Modeled on the Church of the Holy Sepulchre in Jerusalem, and unusual because of its spherical shape, this extremely picturesque building is the oldest circular church in Rome. Gruesome 16th-century frescoes depicting the various methods of persecution and torture suffered by early Christian martyrs adorn the interior.

Enter the church grounds through the sustaining wall of Nero's aqueduct. The church itself, which probably dates to the fifth century, is dedicated to St. Stephen, the first Christian martyr, whose feast day, December 26th, is an official holiday in most Catholic countries.

The original structure consisted of a circular center space surrounded by two concentric rings, or ambulatories, which in turn were intersected by the four "arms" of a virtual Greek cross (one with arms that are all the same length). Two circles of granite columns, 22 in all, still stand between the central space and the first ambulatory. The 34 marble columns embedded in the frescoed walls once divided the second ambulatory from a third, which is no longer extant. This outer ambulatory, and the walls of three of the cross's four arms, were eliminated in the 1450s. Today a single portico encircles the central space, which includes the main altar.

Three arches, supported by two giant Corinthian columns added in the 12th century, dissect the central space. To enter the church, you must walk from an external portico, also added in the 12th century, through the vestibule, or entrance hall, and past the remains of the fourth arm of the cross.

Visit in mid-morning, when sunlight streams in through the church's 22 clerestory windows. Once inside, however, you may find your reverent serenity disrupted by more than 30 extremely realistic frescoes that depict the various torture methods used by Rome's authorities on the empire's early Christians.

To the left of the entrance, the marble bishop's throne may have belonged to Pope

INSIDER TIP:

Most public buildings, churches, and museums close between 1:00 and 4:00 p.m. or so. Don't fret: Do as the locals do and enjoy a nice long lunch and a nap or saunter around town.

—CHRISTOPHER SOMMERVILLE
National Geographic author

St. Gregory the Great (R. A.D. 590–604). The chapel to the left of the throne, dedicated to Saints Primo and Feliciano, features a magnificent seventh-century mosaic of Christ and a jeweled cross. Archeologists have also discovered a Mithraic temple *(not usually open to the public)* beneath this church. ∎

Santo Stefano Rotondo

- ▲ Map p. 59
- ✉ Via di Santo Stefano Rotondo 7
- ☎ 06 3996 7700
- 🕐 Closed 12:30– 3:00 p.m., Tues.– Sat. Closed Sun. p.m. to Mon.
- 🚌 Bus: 81, 117, 673 (from downtown and Circus Maximus) Metro: Linea B (Colosseum)

More Places to Visit

Santi Quattro Coronati

The Church of the Four Crowned Saints commemorates nine martyred saints. The four soldiers and five sculptors were killed for refusing either to pray to the Greek god Aesculapius or to sculpt his image. The early 17th-century apse fresco shows the story of their demise.

Partially damaged during the 1084 Norman invasion, the church was rebuilt by Pope Paschal II (1099–1118); the second of the two outdoor courtyards was once part of the interior. Ring the bell near the door in the left aisle and a nun will admit you to the beautiful, tiny 13th-century cloister, one of the first in Rome. A small offering is expected.

To see the frescoes in the **chapel of St. Sylvester** (*closed noon–3:30 p.m. Mon.–Sat., 10:45 a.m.–3:30 p.m. Sun., $*), head for the vestibule marked Suore Agostiniane, ring the bell, and get the key from the nun who answers. The chapel's frescoes seek to explain Constantine's supposed "donation" to Sylvester of the western Roman Empire.

🅜 Map p. 59 ✉ Via dei Santi Quattro 20 ☎ 06 7047 5427 🚌 Bus: C3, 60, 75, 81, 85, 87, 175, 673. Tram: 3. Metro: Linea B (Colosseo)

Case Romane del Celio

Joined in the third century A.D. to form a single luxurious dwelling, this former apartment block and villa were later dedicated to the soldier saints Giovanni and Paolo. More than 20 rooms on various levels, some of them frescoed, are viewable. In the futuristic Antiquarium you can see artifacts from excavations plus a collection of Muslim ceramics. www.caseromane.it

🅜 Map p. 59 ✉ Clivo di Scauro ☎ 06 7045 4544 🕐 Closed 1–3 p.m., Tues.–Wed. 🚌 Bus: 60, 75, 87. Metro: Linea B (Colosseo). ∎

EXPERIENCE: Get Underneath and See It All

Over the past 3,000 years, Romans have continued to use old buildings as the foundations for new. This means, of course, that there is another, older city underground, that includes not only the catacombs but also other early Christian structures, pagan temples dedicated to Roman gods and pre-Roman deities such as Mithras and Dionysius, secular Roman structures such as *insulae*—Roman apartment houses—sewers, and aqueducts, and even more exotic remains, like the vestiges of Augustus' huge *Horologium solarium*, or sundial.

You can see many of these places on your own by visiting sights like San Clemente (see pp. 69–71) with its layers of civilization, the Roman houses underneath the Church of Saints Giovanni and Paolo, and the excavations under the churches of S. Nicola in Carcere, Ste. Cecilia, and S. Bartolomeo on Tiber Island, as well as the Tabularium (archive) underneath the Capitoline Museum. The Vatican allows tourists to visit the excavations taking place underneath St. Peter's, but you must book at least a month ahead, either by email (*scavi@fsp.va*) or by fax (*06 6987 3017*).

You can also take an organized walk of Rome's best—and perhaps most forgotten—underground places. The co-author of this book, **Michael Brouse** (*brouse.m@gmail.com*) leads a walk of this type, as does **Contexttravel** (*www.contexttravel.com/rome/tours*).

Another option, should you speak or understand Italian, is to sign up with **Roma Subterranea** (*www.sotterraneidiroma.it*) and check if they have any interesting excursions scheduled during your visit.

Byzantine mosaics, relics from the Holy Land, and a treasure trove of antiquities in a major museum complex

Laterano to Terme di Diocleziano

An angel in Santa Maria Maggiore

Laterano to Terme di Diocleziano

After St. Peter's, San Giovanni in Laterano is the most important Roman Catholic church in the world; along with the Baptistery and Santa Croce, it was one of few Christian structures built by the Emperor Constantine inside the walls of Rome. Today it is the episcopal seat of the bishop of Rome, the pope.

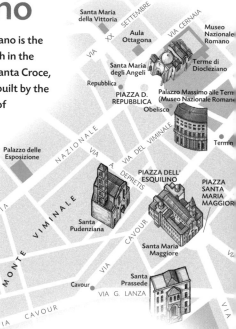

The term "in Laterano" means that the Basilica is part of a loosely knit complex of structures that includes some of Christianity's most important monuments: the Scala Santa, the Sancta Sanctorum, the Baptistery, and the Lateran Palace. The area takes its name from the Laterani, a Roman family whose *pater familias,* Plautius, participated in a plot against Nero, thus losing both his life and

NOT TO BE MISSED:

the family estate. The land was confiscated by the emperor, and later Constantine chose the location for San Giovanni.

For centuries, the original Lateran Palace was the official residence of the popes, who moved to St. Peter's only after their return from self-imposed exile in Avignon in 1377. Today the area is traditionally the site of the annual May Day rally organized by Italy's unions and of demonstrations by left-wing political parties.

The area that lies between the Lateran and the Esquiline and Viminale Hills contains other important Christian churches, most notably Santa Pudenziana and Santa Prassede, both known for their mosaics. Here, too, you will find the imposing Basilica of Santa Maria Maggiore, one of Rome's seven pilgrim churches, dedicated to the Virgin Mary and filled with mosaics celebrating her life. Several popes lie buried in this church, which, unusually, has two imposing domes. Also buried here, is the baroque sculptor and architect Gian Lorenzo Bernini. The most famous of Bernini's three "Ecstasies," the "Ecstasy of St. Theresa," is nearby in the church of Santa Maria della Vittoria.

In recent years the Museo Nazionale Romano (National Museum of Rome) has been renovated, refurbished, and decentralized. One of several new branch sites, the Palazzo Massimo alle Terme, across the street from the baths and near bustling Termini train station, may well be the best organized museum in the city, with a unique exhibition of ancient Roman frescoes and mosaics. The museum's collection of Greek and Roman statues is equally magnificent.

Facing Diocletian's Baths, Piazza della Repubblica, also illustrates the architectural stratification of Rome. Built shortly before World War I, the piazza's design follows the outlines of the external perimeter and the *exhedra* (a hemicycle enclosure) of the ancient baths. This busy traffic circle, which the Romans call Piazza Esedra, coincides with what was once the open-air *palestra* or gym of Diocletian's complex. At the break in the exhedra is the onset of Via Nazionale, a major thoroughfare and shopping street which passes by the Palazzo delle Esposizioni, a giant exhibition space, as well as Trajan's Market, to end in Piazza Venezia. The modern fountain in the center of the piazza (Fountain of the Naiads) raised eyebrows when it was unveiled at the beginning of the 20th century because of the generously endowed female statues. ■

Stazione Centrale Roma-Termini

VIA

MARSALA

VIA

GIOVANNI

ALBERTO

PIAZZA VITTORIO
Vittorio Emanuele
EMANUELE II

GIOLITTI

VIA PR. EUGENIO

VIA CONTE VERDE

EMANUELE

MANZONI

VIA S CROCE

VIA PORTA MAGGIORE

PIAZZA DI PORTA MAGGIORE

MERULANA

Manzoni

VIALE

FILIBERTO

VIA

STATILIA

IN GERUSALEMME

ELENIANA

VIA

VIA CASILINA

Santa Croce in Gerusalemme

PIAZZA DI S. CROCE IN GERUSALEMME

VIALE CASTRENSE

PIAZZA S. GIOVANNI IN LATERANO
Palazzo Lateranense
Obelisco Lateranense
Battistero

Scala Santa e Sancta Sanctorum

VIALE CARLO FELICE

PIAZZA DI PORTA SAN GIOVANNI

VIA LA SPEZIA

San Giovanni

VIA SANNIO

San Giovanni in Laterano

0   400 yards
0   400 meters

Area of map detail

Tevere

San Giovanni in Laterano & Around

Founded by Constantine in the fourth century A.D., San Giovanni in Laterano (St. John Lateran) has been rebuilt several times. In fact, the pope's church only assumed its modern appearance in the 17th century, after major overhauls of the interior and the facade.

The Gothic canopy at the end of the nave contains a wooden table that St. Peter may have used to celebrate Mass.

Alessandro Galilei designed the church's travertine **facade** in 1735. Divided into a ground-floor portico with a loggia above, it is crowned by 15 statues, each about 23 feet (7 m) tall and visible from miles away. The three central statues—Jesus, St. John the Baptist, and St. John the Evangelist—are flanked, six on each side, by 12 Doctors of the Church, men and women recognized for the profundity of their theological thinking.

Five doors lead into the barrel-vaulted portico, one for each of the aisles within. The central bronze doors open onto the wide central nave. Brought here in 1600, they originally stood in the Curia (or Senate) in the Roman Forum. Like that in St. Peter's, the door farthest to the right—the Holy Door—is only opened during the Holy Years, generally every 25 years.

The Interior

The interior, in some ways rather cold and unwelcoming (although this is less true of the warmly hued transept), betrays nothing of the church's ancient past. But there is significant grandeur, not surprising since the popes were crowned here until 1870, the year pontifical Rome—until then an independent state—fell to the armies of the Savoy monarchy. But the basilica's monumental magnificence reflects, above all, the creative genius of Francesco Borromini, commissioned by Pope Innocent X in 1646 to do a total renovation for the 1650 Holy Year.

Borromini created the 12 niches flanking the central nave, later transformed into a parade of giant baroque **statues of the Apostles.** If you are not well versed in Apostolic lore, not to worry, the statues are labeled. If you are, you'll be able to identify them by their trademarks: for example, St. Matthew's bag of money (he had been a tax collector) or St. Bartholomew's knife, the symbol of his martyrdom. Artistically, however, the most interesting are the four statues sculpted by Camillo Rusconi: Matthew, James the Elder, Andrew, and John.

Borromini's contribution did not end with the statues. To preserve something (but not too much) of the church's former style, he selected pieces of medieval monuments or artworks housed in the church, enclosed them in elaborate baroque frames, and created the **funerary monuments** against the pilasters in the outer aisles. The cosmatesque-style pavement (see p. 208) in the central aisle was made during the reign of Pope Martin V (1417–1431), whose bronze floor tomb is in the sunken *confessio.*

The Transept: The transept of the church was renovated in the late 16th century by Giacomo della Porta, and the frescoes (the "Baptism of Constantine," the "Foundation of the Basilica") were painted under the direction of Cavalier d'Arpino, who was responsible for the "Ascension" over the altar at the end of the left transept. The beautiful frescoed Gothic canopy over the main altar (where only the pope is allowed to say Mass) dates from 1367. Above the frescoes, a grill safeguards two silver bust-shaped reliquaries that contain the **heads of St. Peter and St. Paul,** the two founders of the Church of Rome.

INSIDER TIP:

See the church of San Giovanni in Laterano in the morning. That way you can also visit the morning market in nearby Via Sannio, one of Rome's best.

—TIM JEPSON
National Geographic author

Although reconstructed, the **apse mosaic,** portions of which may date from the original fourth-century basilica, is striking. It depicts a panoply of figures of varying sizes depending on their importance. The tiny figure kneeling at the feet of the Virgin is Pope Nicholas IV (1288–1292), who commissioned the mosaic's restoration. The even smaller kneeling figures inserted into the row of Apostles on the bottom are the mosaicists, Jacopo Torriti and Jacopo da Camerino.

San Giovanni in Laterano

🅰 Map pp. 76–77
✉ Piazza di Porta San Giovanni 4
☎ 06 7720 7991
🕐 Open daily
💲 Basilica: Free. Cloister: $. Audio guide: $
🚌 Bus: 16, 81, 85, 87, 218, 360, 665, 714. Tram: 3. Metro: Linea A (San Giovanni)

Via Sannio

🅰 Map pp. 76–77

Battistero

☎ 06 6988 6452

🕐 Closed 12:30–4 p.m.

A door in the left-hand wall, just before the transept, leads to the **cloister** and its accompanying mini-museum. Fashioned between 1215 and 1223 by Cosmati Maestro Pietro Vassalletto and his son, the cloister has a lovely mosaic frieze running around the garden side of the portico and a number of attractive cosmatesque colonettes. Monuments from the original basilica decorate the walls, including what may be one of the oldest surviving papal thrones.

Leaving the church by the side door (in the right transept), you will be in Piazza San Giovanni in Laterano, with the tallest and oldest obelisk in Rome facing you (see p. 86), the Battistero on your left and, to the right, the Lateran Palace. Note the double brick arch on the other side of the piazza. It was part of the Claudian aqueduct lengthened by Nero to furnish his Domus Aurea with water. If you cross the street, you get an excel-

INSIDER TIP:

The inscription SPQR (a Latin abbreviation of "the Senate and Roman People") on many road grates are a quick reminder of Rome's enduring past.

—ADAM THEILER
National Geographic International Channel

lent look at the Lateran complex. The basilica's side facade has a portico, surmounted by a loggia designed by Domenico Fontana in 1586. The twin, triangle-topped bell towers of an older 13th-century version of the church are visible above it.

The **Battistero** (Baptistery) also dates back to Constantine and was built into a previous structure that formed part of an imperial residence. In the

---

EXPERIENCE: Learning Italian

You can get through and around this city with just a couple of phrases, a map, and a lot of finger-pointing. But you'll enjoy your stay in Rome so much more if you know a bit of Italian. Romans are very patient and don't mind if you make mistakes, although they may answer in English if they know any.

So why not choose to combine sightseeing with an Italian language course? If this is the route you choose to follow, you may find yourself pleasantly surprised by the number of choices available. A quick search on the Internet for *"scuole di italiano roma"* or "Italian language schools

in Rome" will yield a remarkably long list.

If you are looking to learn something specific, however, a few schools do offer a bit more. The Torre di Babele school (*www.torredibabele.com/it*), for example, features cultural classes and cooking courses. Percorsi d'italiano (*www.percorsiditaliano.it*) combines morning language classes with discovery walks through the city. It also offers monthly Sunday guided tours. And the program at the Dilit school (*www.dilit.it*) also includes courses in art history, cooking, and archaeology. A more extensive list can be found at *www.inromenow.com*.

Emperor Constantine was baptized on his deathbed in A.D. 337. He built this baptistery earlier, and it quickly became a model for future churches.

earliest days of Christianity, only the pope could baptize new converts, usually on Easter, and this was where it was done. With the spread of the new religion, however, this became impractical and parish priests were authorized to perform baptisms.

Restored many times, the Baptistery has retained its fourth-century octagonal shape. The circular center space is surrounded by eight porphyry columns surmounted by an architrave with eight smaller white marble columns above. A green basalt urn (for baptisms) stands in the center. The 17th-century frescoes on the outer walls depict scenes from the life of Constantine, and the medallions encompass views of Roman churches somehow connected to him. The chapel to St. Venantius, on the left, has magnificent seventh-century Byzantine-style mosaics,

although the altar partially obstructs them.

Perhaps the most interesting mosaics are in the chapel opposite the door, which until the 12th century was the narthex (entrance) into the Baptistery. Their classical motifs—acanthus or vine leaves on a blue background—confirm that in the fifth century a real Christian iconography had not yet emerged.

The Palazzo Lateranense:
The Palazzo Lateranense (Lateran Palace), also built by Fontana, replaced the original papal residence (the Patriarchate), which after a thousand years had been reduced to a pitiful state. Fontana salvaged the **Sancta Sanctorum,** the private chapel of the early pontiffs, by moving it to a new though somewhat uninspiring structure across the street. Because of the many relics accumulated there, this

Santa Croce in Gerusalemme

- △ Map pp. 76–77
- ✉ Piazza di Santa Croce in Gerusalemme 12
- ☎ 06 7014 779
- ⏱ Closed 12:45– 2 p.m.
- 🚍 Bus: 649. Tram: 3. Metro: Linea A (San Giovanni)

Scala Santa

- ☎ 06 772 6641
- ⏱ Closed winter noon–3 p.m., summer noon–3:30 p.m.

chapel was known in the Middle Ages as the holiest site on earth. Renovated in the 13th century, it, too, is a cosmatesque marvel. Above the altar is an *acheiropoieton* image of the Redeemer, meaning it was (supposedly) not painted by human hands.

Scala Santa

The Scala Santa was the ceremonial staircase believed to have been the one ascended by Jesus in Pontius Pilate's Jerusalem palace. Composed of 28 marble steps sheltered by a wooden covering, the staircase leads up to the Sancta Sanctorum. Even today the highly religious climb it on their knees. Lateral staircases are available for non-believers and the less energetic. Along with the Sancta Sanctorum, the Scala Santa was also moved across the street.

Santa Croce in Gerusalemme

Santa Croce, a short walk from San Giovanni down Viale Carlo Felice, was originally part of the palace of St. Helena, Constantine's mother. Its baroque appearance belies its classical origins. Redecorated in the 18th century, the facade's concave and convex movement reveals a strong Borromini influence.

It is topped by an array of statues, including St. Helen (holding the cross) on the left and her son, Constantine, on the right. The name (Holy Cross in Jerusalem)

INSIDER TIP:

The San Lorenzo district around Piazza dei Sanniti (north of Santa Croce in Gerusalemme) is a lively new hot spot for cafés, restaurants, and music clubs.

—RUTH ELLEN GRUBER
National Geographic author

derives from the church's foundation as a home for the important relics Helen brought back from the Holy Land. Around the back of the church to the right, just through the arches in the Aurelian Wall you can see the outlines of the Castrense amphitheater, used for court performances.

It's hard to discern the original basilica's layout. Only eight of the original granite columns remain; the others are encased in concrete piers. Fortunately, the marvelous cosmatesque pavement (see p. 208) has survived, as has the wonderful fresco in the apse, sometimes attributed to Antoniazzo Romano (circa 1492), showing Jesus and scenes relating to the discovery of the cross.

Downstairs, the chapel of St. Helen is built over soil that she brought back from the Holy Land. From the left aisle in the church, stairs lead up to the Chapel of the Relics. Here you'll find what are said to be parts of the True Cross, parts of its inscription, two thorns from the Crown of Thorns, a nail from the Cross, and the finger of (the Doubting) St. Thomas. ∎

Santa Maria Maggiore & Around

Legend has it that in A.D. 352 Pope Liberius had a vision: The Virgin Mary commanded him to build a church dedicated to her on a snow-covered spot. It hardly ever snows in Rome, much less in the summer. Nonetheless, on August 5 it supposedly snowed on the Esquiline Hill, the place where Liberius built what was to become one of the four major basilicas of Rome.

Ferdinando Fuga's 17th-century facade belies the early Christian origins of Santa Maria Maggiore.

Every August a ceremony is held inside Santa Maria Maggiore to re-enact that miracle, with thousands of white flower petals (the snow) fluttering down from the ceiling. Naturally, the church you see is a later version, built by Pope Sixtus III in the early fifth century, at the tail end of a raging battle among Christian dogmatists over Mary's status: Was she only the mother of Christ the human being *(Christokos)*? Or was she the mother of Christ in both his human and divine natures *(Theotokos)?*

The second view prevailed at the Council of Ephesus in 431, so it shouldn't surprise you that Jacopo Torriti's 13th-century **mosaic** in the apse depicts Mary as a Byzantine princess being crowned by Jesus. By the way, if you have binoculars, you will need them here. The 36 **fifth-century mosaic panels** in the nave, illustrating scenes from the Old and New Testaments, have recently been cleaned, but they are high up and hard to see.

Many additions have been made to this church throughout the centuries, but its basic form—a basilica with three wide aisles divided by 40 massive Ionic columns—faithfully reflects

Santa Maria Maggiore

🅰 Map pp. 76–77

✉ Piazza Santa Maria Maggiore

☎ 06 488 1094 (Sacristy), 06 483 195 (Chapel)

🕐 Basilica: open all day. Sistine Chapel: Closed Sun. 9:30 a.m.–1:30 p.m.

💲 Museum: $$ Audio guide: $

🚌 Bus: C3, 16, 70, 71, 75, 105, 360, 590, 649, 714. Metro: Linea A or B (Repubblica)

fifth-century canons. The beautiful coffered ceiling was gilded with gold from the New World donated by Ferdinand and Isabella of Spain. The sunken *confessio* holds an 1802 gold and silver relic case said to contain pieces of Jesus' cradle. The giant statue is of Pope Pius IX (1846–1878), who enlarged the confessio.

The two richly decorated, domed chapels on the ends of the transept were added in the 16th and 17th centuries. The one on the left was built by Pope Paul V, who is buried in the Borghese family crypt below. The other, commissioned by Pope Sixtus V is, like its cousin in St. Peter's, called the **Sistine Chapel.** It is decorated with colored marbles from the Septizodium (a pagan structure which stood below the Palatine Hill) and contains Sixtus's tomb. Near the chapel entrance,

in front of the side presbytery banister, a marble slab on the floor marks the **grave of sculptor Gian Lorenzo Bernini** and his ancestors. How peculiar so lavishly baroque an artist should have such a simple, nondescript tomb!

A new small museum has been inaugurated to display a nearly complete set of magnificent manger figures from the 13th century, some by Arnolfo di Cambio, as well as sketches of the basilica's facade before renovation in the 18th century.

The 18th-century front facade partially covers the early 14th-century mosaics in the loggia. These are worth a visit anyway since they tell the story of that miraculous August snowfall. Stop by the piazza at night when, thanks to the Italian genius for artificial lighting, the mosaics glow much as they must have by candlelight.

EXPERIENCE: Staying in a Convent

The pilgrims who visited Rome in ancient times stayed in humble inns and hostels or, if they were particularly devout, put up in one of the city's hundreds of religious orders. Monks and nuns were, after all, well-schooled in the Gospel teachings of kindness and generosity and, along with providing meals and a bed, encouraged participation in religious services and contemplation.

If you want to get a taste of this tradition and see the Eternal City from a different vantage point, consider staying in a convent or a guest house run by a religious order or confraternity. The furnishings may be simple, but you will find comfortable beds, newly renovated private bathrooms, and, in many cases, a hearty breakfast or even the possibility,

for an additional modest fee, of a filling lunch or dinner. Your housekeeping staff may be motherly nuns who continue to practice the long-standing tradition of Christian hospitality and, on occasion, spiritual comfort or even guidance. You might not find a TV in your room, and some convents or religious guest houses have curfews, but after hours of walking around Rome you may be too tired to care. During your stay, you may also meet fellow travellers with whom you can share a glass of wine and exchange stories and information about your visit.

Rooms are available all over the city. The following websites will be of help: www.santasusanna.org www.monasterystays.com www.hospites.it

The Seven Pilgrim Churches

The relics of Santa Croce, all of which relate to Jesus' Passion, made it one of Rome's seven pilgrim churches, Christian places of worship notable because of their association with important saints or their relics. In medieval and Renaissance times, pilgrims who managed to visit all seven were granted a special indulgence known as a plenary indulgence. A formal itinerary helped them better navigate the distances. The grand tour included the four patriarchal basilicas (St. Peter's, San Giovanni in Laterano, Santa Maria Maggiore, and San Paolo fuori le Mura), plus San Lorenzo fuori le Mura, Santa Croce, and San Sebastiano on the Appian Way.

The 14th-century bell tower is the tallest in Rome. The giant marble column in front of the church comes from the Roman Forum.

Santa Prassede

The present church was built by Pope Paschal I (817–824) and later restored several times, most recently in the 19th century. A typical basilica structure with a restored cosmatesque pavement (see p. 208), this church is known for the ninth-century Byzantine mosaics in its apse.

The Redeemer is flanked on the right by St. Peter, Santa Pudenziana (see below), and St. Zeno, and on the left by St. Paul, Santa Prassede, and Pope Paschal, who holds a model of the church and whose square halo shows he was alive at the time. These mosaics are Byzantine in character (the two sisters are dressed like Byzantine princesses). A second mosaic, one of the most important Byzantine monuments in Rome, is the decoration in the Chapel of St. Zeno. The figures are placed against a gold background, which in Eastern iconography symbolized heaven.

Santa Pudenziana

It is unclear whether Santa Pudenziana, supposedly Santa Prassede's sister (see above), really existed. The name may stem from a semantic error. Her father was a senator and early Christian named Pudens who had welcomed St. Peter into the family home. Centuries later, the church built on the site was referred to as Ecclesia Pudenziana. In any event, this is believed to be one of the oldest churches in Rome, although frequent restorations have undermined much of its charm.

A notable exception is the fourth-century apse mosaic. Classical in style, it shows Jesus seated on a jeweled throne surrounded by ten Apostles; the two others were cut off during a 16th-century restoration. The women standing behind the Apostles hold crowns in their hands and have been variously identified as Prassede and Pudenziana, or as symbols of the early church. What is significant is that they are all dressed as Romans. Furthermore, the architectural background, with temples and basilicas, is unmistakably classical in nature. ∎

Santa Prassede

⬛ Map pp. 76–77

✉ Via S. Prassede 9A

☎ 06 488 2456

🕐 Closed noon–4 p.m.

🚌 Bus: C3, 16, 70 71, 75, 105, 360, 590, 649, 714. Metro: Linea B (Cavour)

Santa Pudenziana

⬛ Map pp. 76–77

✉ Via Urbana 160

☎ 06 481 4622

🕐 Closed noon–3 p.m.

🚌 Bus: C3, 16, 70 71, 75, 105, 360, 590, 649, 714. Metro: Linea B (Cavour)

Obelisks

One of the most popular trophies for a victorious Roman leader from an Egyptian campaign was an authentic obelisk (*obelisco*). Symbols of divinity and immortality for the pharaohs, obelisks were brought to Rome and used to decorate temples, circuses, and mausoleums. After the fall of Rome they lay buried for centuries until the Renaissance, when they were unearthed and given over to the glory of the popes.

Part of the Landscape

Today, you can find 13 of these stone giants in modern Rome. They embellish some of the city's most beautiful squares and are now as much a part of the Romans' cultural heritage as triumphal columns or arches.

In fact, obelisks have been so well integrated into Rome's decor that you may almost miss them. Bernini incorporated the Agonale Obelisk into his imposing baroque Fountain of the Four Rivers (see pp. 98, 147) in Piazza Navona, and the Minerva Obelisk, a relative dwarf at only 17 feet (5 m), rides on the back of the whimsical marble elephant in front of Santa Maria sopra Minerva (see pp. 134–135). Renaissance nobleman Ciriaco Mattei placed his in the gardens of Villa Celimontana. And the Macuteo Obelisk stands atop Giacomo della Porta's fountain in Piazza della Rotonda.

Converting Pagan Monuments to Christian Use

Pope Sixtus V (1585–1590), known for his urban planning schemes, obviously had a thing about obelisks: He converted four of them to Christian usage. The Vatican Obelisk in St. Peter's Square was brought to Rome by either Caligula or Nero, and from A.D. 40 on it beautified a nearby circus. It was, amazingly, still standing in 1585, when Sixtus ordered architect Domenico Fortuna to move it to its current location, a feat requiring 900 men and 140 horses

The pontiff's campaign to Christianize Rome's pagan monuments proceeded with the installation on the Esquiline Hill (behind Santa Maria Maggiore and, incidentally, in front of Sixtus's private villa) of the almost 50-foot (15 m) tall Esquiline Obelisk. Once, it had graced the entrance to the Emperor Augustus's Mausoleum but now, says the inscription, it is "serving the Lord Christ."

The Lateran Obelisk (see p. 80) was retrieved from the Circus Maximus, along with another now in Piazza del Popolo, and the Flaminio Obelisk was now "prouder and happier" to be dedicated to Mary.

Sixtus V was not the only obelisk-minded pontiff. Two centuries later, Pope Pius VI (1775–1799) also had a go at relocating a few. He put the red granite Quirinal Obelisk in between Castor and Pollux in front of the Quirinal Palace. A similar monument was erected at the top of the Spanish Steps. And in 1792, the obelisk Augustus had used as the needle for his giant Campus Martius sundial was raised in Piazza Montecitorio.

Two other obelisks were repositioned in the 19th century. The Antinous Obelisk, originally erected by Emperor Hadrian to honor the memory of his dazzlingly handsome friend and lover, Antinous, was put on the Pincian Hill by Pius VII in 1822. The Termini Obelisk dates from the reign of Rameses II. Excavated in 1883, it has been relegated to a small, somewhat neglected park near the Termini train station.

Rome's only modern obelisk was erected during Mussolini's rule. The 118-foot (36 m) monument stands on the grounds of the Foro Italico sports complex and still reads "Mussolini Dux." After his demise, any and all references to "Il Duce" were ordered deleted, but the inscription on the obelisk was too large to be removed and now stands as testament to the man's ego.

Pope Pius VI placed this obelisk before the Italian parliament. He gave it a pointer like the one it had when it was the needle in Augustus' giant sundial.

Palazzo Massimo alle Terme

Linchpin of the National Museum of Rome's four sites scattered around the city, the Palazzo Massimo alle Terme plays host to some of the museum's finest pieces of Greek and Roman sculpture. Here you'll also find mosaics, frescoes, paintings, and jewelry, as well as the world's premier coin collection. The building, constructed in 1883–1887 to house a Jesuit college, copies the style of early Roman baroque noble residences.

The "Reclining Hermaphrodite," a popular statue found in the ruins of a private garden in Pompeii

Palazzo Massimo alle Terme

🅰 Map pp. 76–77

✉ Largo di Villa Peretti 1

☎ 060608 or 06 3996 7700

🚫 Closed Mon.

💲 $$. Audio guide: $. Guided tours in Italian: Sun.; in English on request: $$$$$

🚌 Bus: H, 16, 38, 40, 64, 75, 86, 90, 92, 170, 175, 217, 310, 360, 649, 714. Metro: Linea A or B (Repubblica)

www.pierreci.it

The museum has four display floors including the **basement**, where the massive coin collection dating back to Roman times is enhanced by a charming audio-visual presentation in several languages. Automated magnifying glasses allow you to study any coin in detail.

How to Visit

When you arrive at the museum ticket office, sign up for the next available accompanied visit to the top floor (the second floor, Italian style), which is dedicated to ancient Roman interior decoration, primarily wall frescoes and wall and floor mosaics. Entire rooms from first-century to late-Roman Empire villas have been reconstructed with their original parietal decoration. While the museum's own guidebook will tell you that the frescoes here do not compare in number with those from Pompeii, "nonetheless, Rome and its suburbs preserved pictorial cycles of exceptional importance and quality."

To avoid any security risks, the National Museum of Rome's authorities have decided not to allow visitors to wander freely on this floor. To make sure everyone gets a chance to visit, they have, unfortunately, set a rather draconian time limit: 45 minutes on weekdays, 30 minutes on Sundays and holidays.

These are not exactly guided visits as we know them, and there is no extra charge. But the *accompagnatori*, all of whom speak English, lead you through the area, stopping at the major points of interest to give a brief description of what you are to see. They are knowledgeable and courteous and will also answer questions.

Top Floor

Whether you've been to Pompeii or not, you probably won't be prepared for the beauty of the summer triclinium (dining room) with the garden wall frescoes from the **House of Livia.** Married to Augustus and the mother of the future emperor, Tiberius, Livia also had taste. The walls of this room, transported here from a site on the Via Flaminia outside Rome, were frescoed to create an imaginary walled garden with trees, plants, flowers, exotic birds and animals, and fruits of all types. Incredibly, experts were able to remove the frescoes from each of the long side walls in a single piece. Take notice of the stucco work on the ceiling, as well as the grotesques, smallish painted decorations on walls and ceilings in which leaves, spirals, and mythological figures generally alternate.

Another set of staggeringly beautiful **frescoes** comes from a first-century villa discovered in 1879 on the grounds of the Villa Farnesina in Trastevere (see pp. 188–189). These frescoes have black backgrounds with friezes and decorative motifs.

The **mosaics** are equally enthralling. The four charioteers from a third-century villa belonging to the imperial Severi family show the delicacy of pictorial design. The marble inlay decorations from the Basilica of Junius Bassus are disturbingly modern.

Ground Floor & First Floor

Whether it's before your accompanied tour or after, you won't want to miss the other two floors, dedicated to the sculpture and statuary that make up the bulk of the Museo Nazionale Romano's ancient art section. The museum has sought, quite successfully, to organize the sculptures thematically and by historical periods.

It is impossible to mention all the pieces, but the ground floor, which deals primarily with the images and accoutrements of power, mainly from the second and first centuries B.C., contains a variety of treasures, some of which are Greek or bear clear Hellenistic influences. Most notable are the multicolored giant cult **statue of Minerva** (the head is a modern plaster cast of another statue) and the various **portraits of Augustus** in Room V, which also contains the beautiful **Ostia altar,** dedicated to Mars.

The **frescoes** from the Esquiline colombarium, or dovecote tomb, and the mosaic floor from a suburban villa (Galleria I) are also particularly lovely.

INSIDER TIP:

One of Rome's newest museums, Palazzo Massimo is a hidden treasure. Don't miss Empress Livia's magic frescoed garden.

—DENNIS CIGLER
*Tour coordinator & guide,
In Italy's Companions*

One flight up, on the first floor, there's more. Much more. Here the emphasis is on the iconographic trends in official Roman art, again many with considerable Greek input. The collection is extremely rich. **Room V,** for example, contains marvelous pieces from suburban imperial villas (Anzio, Tivoli, Subiaco) and includes the "Anzio Apollo" and the magnificent "Crouching Aphrodite." The Lancellotti "Discobolus" **(Room VI),** the bronze "Dionysus," the amazingly beautiful "Reclining Hermaphrodite," the "Wounded Niobid" (all in **Room VII),** and the not-to-be-missed Portonaccio Sarcophagus **(Room XII),** with its battle scenes between Roman and barbarian soldiers, are all simply thrilling.

You'll be amused to note the juxtaposition of the statues in **Room II.** The busts of the Emperor Hadrian, his wife Sabina, and Hadrian's lover, Antinous (the one to whom he dedicated an obelisk), are grouped together. The busts of the emperors will give you a good idea of what these men looked like. Another gallery is dedicated to women's head portraits.

Room XIV is also memorable. Grouped under the title "Iconography and celebration from the Severi to the Constantine," the pieces here include several commemorative sarcophagi. The artwork on some of the sarcophagi—for example that of Marcus Claudianus, with its scenes from the Old and New Testaments—indicates that influential Romans were beginning to forsake paganism for Christianity. In general, however, there is only one word for the carved reliefs on these stone coffins: breathtaking. ∎

EXPERIENCE: Join an Italian Family for Dinner

Look around you the next time you're out to dinner in a downtown Roman trattoria, and you'll likely notice that most of the tables around you are occupied by other foreigners. Instead of eating in a crowded restaurant with dozens of other tourists like yourself, consider joining an Italian family for dinner.

Picture yourself sitting down to dinner with Mario Rossi (the Italian John Doe) and his wife to eat not in a restaurant but *in famiglia,* in the living room of their middle-class Roman home. While you are eating your antipasti, perhaps a selection of salamis and sausage, tasting the home-made fettuccine, and savoring Signora Rossi's saltimbocca—the same recipe her mother used when she was growing up—you are also being treated to some interesting conversation. The Rossis' two children have practiced some of the English they have learned in school and have told you which soccer teams they root for, and about their grandfather, who lives around the corner.

After dinner, the children leave the table to do homework or, if it is a weekend, to grab their scooters and head out to the corner café or the local discotheque. Meanwhile, the Rossis, like folks everywhere, talk about recent events, the day at work, problems at the children's high school, and the worrisome economy.

If this appeals to you, one local agency gives you a chance to have a good meal and, at the same time, see a slice of real Italian life: **A Casa Loro** (At Their House), *www.liveromelikearoman.com.*

Terme di Diocleziano

The Baths of Diocletian (A.D. 284–305), inaugurated in A.D. 306, could accommodate about 3,000 bathers. They were built so well that much of the complex's outer structure is still standing. As in Trajan's and Caracalla's baths, the *natatio, frigidarium, tepidarium,* and *calidarium* were laid out along a central axis.

The Great Cloister of Santa Maria degli Angeli was built into a portion of Diocletian's baths.

In 1561, Pope Pius IV (1559 1565) commissioned Michelangelo (age 86) to design a church utilizing part of the Baths of Diocletian. The result was **Santa Maria degli Angeli** *(Piazza de la Repubblica, tel 06 488 0812, closed noon–4 p.m., Bus: 60, 61, 62, 64, 115, 492, 640, Metro: Linea A/Repubblica),* the imposing entrance to which was built into an apse of the *calidarium* (the hot room), while the vestibule corresponded to the ancient *tepidarium.*

In the 18th century, architect Luigi Vanvitelli changed the axis of the church by creating a new main altar opposite the entryway and transforming Michelangelo's nave into a somewhat oversized transept. The proportions are awe inspiring. The eight massive

granite columns are 45 feet (14 m) high. The overwhelming transept is 298 feet (90 m) long, 88 feet (26 m) wide, and more than 90 feet (27 m) high.

In 1889, another portion of the baths was transformed into the **Museo Nazionale Romano** (National Museum of Rome), which has since been decentralized into four different sites (see p. 31). This branch, recently renovated, now holds the **Epigraphic Museum,** where 10,000 inscriptions and funerary monuments, along with mosaics and frescoes, illustrate aspects of ancient Roman daily life such as religion, education, and professions.

And don't miss the **Great Cloister,** built in 1565 and attributed to Michelangelo. ∎

Terme di Diocleziano

- Map pp. 76–77
- Viale E. De Nicola 78
- 060608 or 06 3996 7700
- Closed Mon.
- $$. Audio guide: $. Guided tours in Italian: Sun.; in English on request: $$$$$
- Bus: H, 16, 38, 40, 60, 61, 64, 75, 86, 90, 92, 170, 175, 217, 310, 360, 492, 649. Metro: Linea A or B (Repubblica)

www.pierreci.it

More Places to Visit

The opulent Santa Maria della Vittoria contains sculptures by Bernini.

Aula Ottagona

This octagonal structure between Via Cernaia and Via Parigi was originally the western corner of the central baths complex. Its concrete dome has remained intact, and for this reason it was turned into a planetarium in the 1920s. Since 1986 it has been an annex of the Museo Nazionale Romano (see pp. 88–90) and houses statuary from the Baths of Diocletian, the Baths of Caracalla, and the remains of Constantine's baths on the Quirinal Hill. The marble statue of Aphrodite, a copy of a Greek original dating back to the second or third century and the fatigued expression on the first-century bronze statue of a boxer are both worth seeing.

Map pp. 76–77 Via G. Romita 8 06 4870690 Open 9 a.m.–7:45 p.m., subject to staff availability; closed Mon. Bus: H, 40, 60, 61, 62, 64, 70, 84, 170, 175, 492, 590, 910. Metro: Linea A (Repubblica)

Santa Maria della Vittoria

Built between 1608 and 1620, this church is designed by Carlo Maderno was originally dedicated to St. Paul. But in 1622, in commemoration of a victory over Protestant forces in the Battle of the White Mountain, near Prague, it was renamed Santa Maria della Vittoria (St. Mary of Victory). The image of the Madonna displayed in the giant sunburst over the altar is a copy of one found near the scene of the battle and to which the victory was attributed.

The church's decoration is the epitome of baroque opulence. Marble, gilded stucco work, sculptures, and paintings abound. Despite the works of artists such as Guercino and Domenichino, the main attraction is Gian Lorenzo Bernini's **"Ecstasy of St. Theresa"** in the Cornaro Chapel at the left end of the transept. St. Theresa, enveloped in folds of marble drapery, wounded by an arrow shot by the cherubic angel to her left, lies in the throes of a mystical ecstasy. Members of the Cornaro family are sculpted into what appear to be theater boxes on the right and left walls of the chapel. This emphasizes the dramatic, theatrical effect so often achieved by Bernini and is enhanced by the indirect lighting, in this case from above, favored by the artist.

Map pp. 76–77 Via XX Settembre 17 06 4274 0571 Closed noon–3:30 p.m. daily & Sun. a.m. Bus: H, 16, 60, 61, 62, 84, 90, 175, 492. Metro: Linea A (Repubblica) ■

The Trevi Fountain, other Renaissance and baroque masterpieces, a major museum, and once glamorous Via Veneto with its luxurious hotels and cafés

Fontana di Trevi to Via Veneto

Detail from the Fontana del Moro in Piazza Navona

Fontana di Trevi to Via Veneto

Instantly recognizable, the giant Fontana di Trevi (Trevi Fountain) lies tucked away among narrow side streets. Even in a city like Rome, where fountains abound, you will find it hard not to be impressed by Nicola Salvi's dramatic, late-baroque masterpiece, cunningly built into the side of a (contemporary) princely palace.

Even though it is right downtown, the area around the Trevi Fountain—where simple artisans' shops and boutiques mix with baroque masterpieces—has retained much of its traditional character. Nearby is the Colonna Palace, with its private art gallery open only on Saturday mornings. Walk uphill along Via della Dataria to reach the Quirinal Hill and, on top of it, the Quirinal Palace. Once the summer residence of the popes, the palace is now the home of the president of the Italian Republic, where most afternoons you can see the changing of the guard.

After the late Renaissance popes made this their summer getaway (today's pontiffs head instead to Castelgandolfo on Lake Albano),

the surrounding neighborhood became more desirable and several important churches, such as the Jesuit Sant'Andrea al Quirinale and San Carlo alle Quattro Fontane, were built here by architects such as Bernini and Borromini.

In fact, these two masters of Italian architecture were thrown together repeatedly, and in the beginning, Borromini worked for the older Bernini as a draftsman. They had already collaborated on Palazzo Barberini, the huge baroque palace that Maffeo Barberini, recently elected Urban VIII, had decided to refurbish and expand to make worthy of the Barberinis' newly exalted status. Decorated by some of the major artists of the 17th century—the ceiling of the great hall of the palace bears the remarkable frescoes of Pietro da Cortona—it is now one of the two sites of the National Gallery (the other is Palazzo Corsini). Its collection includes a series of masterpiece paintings ranging from a Fra Filippo Lippi "Annunciation" to Caravaggio's "Judith Beheading Holofernes."

Near the Palazzo lies Piazza Barberini, which is today both a busy traffic circle and the center of a major shopping area. Because of all the activity, and despite the repaved traffic island, most passersby probably don't even notice Bernini's charming Triton Fountain, one of the first he designed.

The Fontana delle Api, which enshrines the Barberini family's bee symbol, is now located across the street. Today, Romans don't pay much attention to it either, but when it was erected in the 17th century things were different. An inscription stated that the fountain had been put up in the 22nd year of the

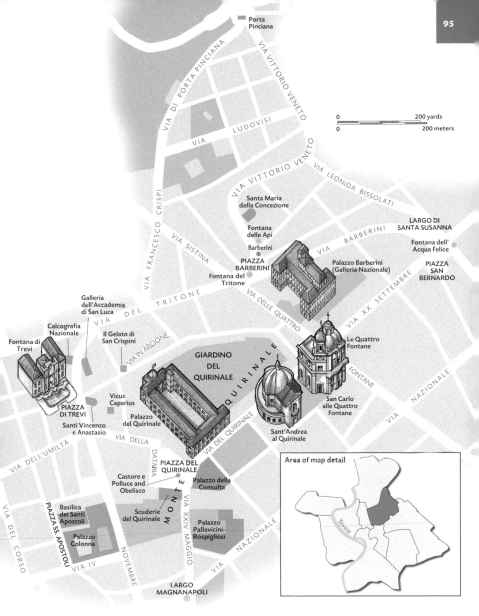

Porta
Pinciana

VIA DI PORTA PINCIANA

VIA VITTORIO VENETO

VIA LUDOVISI

VIA

0   200 yards
0   200 meters

VIA VITTORIO VENETO

VIA LEONIDA BISSOLATI

VIA FRANCESCO CRISPI

VIA SISTINA

Santa Maria
della Concezione

Fontana
delle Api

Barberini

PIAZZA
BARBERINI

Fontana del
Tritone

VIA BARBERINI

Palazzo Barberini
(Galleria Nazionale)

LARGO DI
SANTA SUSANNA

Fontana dell'
Acqua Felice

PIAZZA
SAN
BERNARDO

Galleria
dell'Accademia
di San Luca

VIA DEL TRITONE

VIA DELLE QUATTRO

VIA XX SETTEMBRE

Calcografia
Nazionale

Fontana di
Trevi

PIAZZA
DI TREVI

Il Gelato di
San Crispini

VIA IN ARCIONE

GIARDINO
DEL
QUIRINALE

QUIRINALE

Le Quattro
Fontane

FONTANE

VIA NAZIONALE

VIA

San Carlo
alle Quattro
Fontane

Vicus
Caparius

Santi Vincenzo
e Anastasio

Palazzo
del Quirinale

VIA DEL QUIRINALE

Sant'Andrea
al Quirinale

VIA DELLA

VIA DELL'UMILTÀ

DATARIA

PIAZZA DEL
QUIRINALE

Castore e
Polluce and
Obelisco

Palazzo della
Consulta

MONTE

Area of map detail

Tevere

VIA DEL CORSO

PIAZZA SS. APOSTOLI

Basilica
dei Santi
Apostoli

Palazzo
Colonna

VIA IV

NOVEMBRE

Scuderie
del Quirinale

VIA XXIV MAGGIO

Palazzo
Pallavicini-
Rospigliosi

VIA NAZIONALE

LARGO
MAGNANAPOLI

papacy of the Barberini pope, Urban VIII.
Unfortunately, it was unveiled a few weeks
before the anniversary, making the supersti-
tious Romans nervous. Rightly so, it would
seem. Urban died eight days before his 22nd
year would have begun.

The Bee Fountain sits at the start of Via
Veneto, the long winding avenue that for
decades was this city's "great white way" as well
as the location of the most elegant hotels and

cafés. Once (both in Roman times as well as
much later, in the 16th and 17th centuries) a
neighborhood of sprawling residential villas, this
area was wantonly subdivided in a frenzy of real
estate speculation after 1870. Following World
War II, the Via Veneto became known for the
dolce vita, an era of glamour and glitter, now
vanished, that was depicted in many movies of
the time, in particular, Federico Fellini's movie
La Dolce Vita (1960). ■

Fontana di Trevi

By Roman standards the Fontana di Trevi, or Trevi Fountain, is almost new; it was, after all, built only some 240 years ago. However, the water that flows through it was brought to Rome by the Aqua Virgo, a largely underground aqueduct originally built by Marcus Agrippa (Augustus's right-hand man) in 19 B.C. to supply water to baths in the Campus Martius.

The Acqua Vergine spring (Italian for "Aqua Virgo") is reputed to have the best water in Rome.

The Aqua Virgo got its name because the spring from which it comes was reputedly revealed to Agrippa's soldiers by a young virgin. You can see her in the relief on the right side of the fountain's upper portion (the *attic*) as she points to the spring.

A succession of popes thought about building a monumental fountain on this spot, and various projects, including one by Bernini, were presented. In 1732, Pope Clement XII—whose papal crest you can see at the top of the fountain—approved a design submitted by Nicola Salvi.

The project, which took 30 years to complete, emphasizes the central portion of the fountain, dominated by Neptune. Below, among the rocks, two Tritons struggle with two horses (one calm, one bucking to represent the sea in its various moods), while the bubbling and gushing water re-creates the ocean's power and turbulence. These central figures were begun by little-known Giovanbattista Maini but were finished by Pietro Bracci. Created by Filippo Valle, the figures in the niches represent Abundance (left) and Health (right). The four figures set against the attic, all by different sculptors, represent the beneficial and fertilizing effects of water in the different seasons.

As the terminus of the Aqua Virgo aqueduct, the Trevi Fountain is also one of Rome's several *mostre d'acqua*, a term meant to denote a monumental fountain with enough pressure to push water on to other outlets.

INSIDER TIP:

Near Trevi is Vicus Caprarius, ancient apartments discovered during construction of a movie theater. Listen closely to hear water from Aqua Virgo, the last functioning aqueduct in Rome.

—PAUL BENNETT
National Geographic writer and founder of Context Travel

Where and when the custom began of throwing a coin (over your shoulder, if you please!) into the Trevi Fountain in order to guarantee a return trip to Rome is not really known. But to judge from the amount and type of coins pitched in here daily, the practice has become generally accepted by tourists and was, of course, immortalized in the 1954 film *Three Coins in the Fountain.*

Don't miss the beautiful late 18th-century *aedicola* (niche) on the building at the corner of the piazza with Via del Lavatore. Facing it is the high baroque church of **Santi Vincenzo e Anastasio,** parish church for the popes while they lived on the Quirinal. In the crypt are the hearts of almost all the popes of the 17th, 18th, and 19th centuries. The surrounding streets, Via del Lavatore (where there is a morning food market), Via Panetteria, and Via in Arcione, have grocery and artisans' shops. ∎

Fontana di Trevi
- Map pp. 94–95
- Piazza Fontana di Trevi
- Bus: C3, 52, 61, 62, 63, 71, 80, 81, 85, 95, 116, 119, 175, 492, 590, 628. Metro: Linea A (Barberini)

Vicus Caprarius
- Map pp. 94–95
- Vicolo del Puttarello 25; entrance is at the back of the Cinema Trevi movie theater
- Open daily 11 a.m.–3 p.m.

EXPERIENCE: Doin' the Gelato Crawl

What is it that makes "gelato" so special and different from the ice cream you eat at home? In part, despite its name (which means "frozen" in Italian), gelato is kept frozen at a lower temperature for a shorter period of time than ice cream. It also has less butterfat, which intensifies the flavor.

And flavor you certainly will find. Varieties of fresh fruit gelato include melon, raspberry, strawberry, kiwi, banana, watermelon, lemon, orange, and others. The amazing array of cream gelatos includes everything from vanilla *(crema),* panna or fior di latte *(cream),* to yogurt, hazelnut, walnut, almond, pistachio, and nougat. And then there's the chocolate family, which runs a remarkable range of subtle tastes and combinations from *stracciatella* (vanilla with chocolate stripes) and milk chocolate to dark chocolate, darker chocolate, *bacio, gianduia,* and many more.

You will find *gelaterie* everywhere in Rome. It's hard to go wrong, but there is a difference between those who sell *gelato artigianale,* made on the premises, and those who sell *gelato industriale,* which only looks like it's made on the premises. Some of the best are **San Crispino,** near the Trevi Fountain *(Via della Panetteria 42);* **Giolitti** *(Via Uffici del Vicario 40)* and **Pasqualetti** *(Piazza della Maddalena 3a),* both near the Pantheon; **Palazzo del Freddo** *(Via Principe Eugenio 65-67),* near the Termini station; **Al Settimo Gelo** *(Via Vodice 21a)* and **Gelateria dei Gracchi** *(Via dei Gracchi 272),* both in the Prati area; and, adjacent to the Vatican museum, **Old Bridge** *(Via Bastioni di Michelangelo 5).* Also good are **Alberto Pica** *(12 Via della Seggiola),* near Campo dei Fiori, and, in Trastevere, **La Fonte della Salute** *(Via Cardinale Marmaggi 2)* and the nameless gelateria in Via Benedetta at the back of the Piazza Trilussa fountain. (See also Ice Cream, p. 263)

Fountains & Aqueducts

Immortalized in two films, *Three Coins in the Fountain* (1954) and Fellini's *La Dolce Vita* (1960), the Trevi Fountain is certainly the best known fountain in Rome. But it is hardly alone. Water spouts from fountains *(fontane)*—small and large, sculpted and plain—everywhere in the Eternal City. It trickles, too, from the small neighborhood *fontanelle* from which many Romans once drew their drinking water.

The Acqua Marcia aqueduct, off the Via Appia Antica, still stands after more than 2,000 years.

Romans swear by their fontanelle, learning early that a finger placed over the spigot opening turns a small hole in the top into a drinking spout. It gushes from the *mostre d'acqua* (monumental fonts) that help circulate water throughout the fountain network.

"Nothing can be more agreeable to the eyes of a stranger, especially in the heats of summer, than the great number of public fountains that appear in every part of Rome, embellished with all the ornaments of sculpture, and pouring forth prodigious quantities of cool, delicious water," wrote British writer Tobias Smollett in 1765. In fact, the fountains are omnipresent, testifying both to the grandiosity of the city's ruling class, and to the special relationship that Romans have always had with this life-giving liquid. Historically, Rome had few nearby sources of water, and its engineers

built aqueducts *(aquedotti)* to bring enough of it into the urban area, from as far as 31 miles (50 km) away.

For a fountain lover, Rome is a dream. In the Trident area, on the same aqueduct line as the Trevi, are the Barcaccia, (the "old boat" fountain at the foot of the Spanish Steps), the Pantheon Fountain, and the magnificent 16th-century fountains of Piazza Navona, designed by Gian Lorenzo Bernini. The star attraction in Piazza Navona is Bernini's Fontana dei Quattro Fiumi (Fountain of the Four Rivers), inaugurated in 1651 and financed to the tune of 29,000 scudi by a highly unpopular bread tax. Its four stone giants represent the great rivers of the then known world: the Ganges, the Plate, the Danube, and the Nile, whose veiled countenance stood for the mystery of its (then) uncharted source.

Bernini also designed Il Tritone (the Triton
Fountain) and the Fountain of the Bees in
downtown Piazza Barberini (see p. 105). These
fountains are fed by another mostra d'acqua,
the oversize fountain in Piazza San Bernardo
near the Grand Hotel. Commonly called the
Moses Fountain because of its large central
figure, its real name is the Fontana dell'Acqua
Felice, after the modern aqueduct built in 1586
by Pope Sixtus V to bring running water to that
area. It also sends water to the four charming
corner fountains on the intersection of Via
delle Quattro Fontane with Via Venti Settembre, and to another beautiful Bernini Triton
Fountain in the courtyard at Via della Panetteria
15 (near the Trevi).

A third mostra d'acqua is Fontana dell'Acqua
Paola (see p. 191) on the Janiculum Hill, which
commemorates the reopening in 1612 of Trajan's aqueduct, built in A.D. 109 to bring water
from Lake Bracciano. Probably one of the most
beautiful fountains in Rome is the Fontana delle

This Neptune group was added to a Piazza
Navona fountain in 1878.

Tartarughe (Tortoises) in tiny Piazza Mattei, a
small square tucked away behind the Ghetto
(see p. 204). In 1581 Giacomo della Porta's
design was executed by Taddeo Landini, who
sculpted the four boys and dolphins that
make up this lyrical bronze composition. The
tortoises, by an unknown artist, were added a
century later.

EXPERIENCE: Tours of the Fountains

Enjoying the beauty of Rome's
celebrated fountains is one of the best
parts of visiting the Eternal City. A
guided tour will give you an opportunity
to learn how the aqueduct system has
served the city practically and aestheti-
cally for generations.
Avventure Bellissime (*tel 41 97 04 99,
www.tours-italy.com*) offers a tour that
highlights the most famous fountains,

as well as some lesser-known ones, with
fascinating bits of history intertwined.
Argiletum Tour Operators (*via Madonna dei Monti 49, tel 06 454 38 378 or
06 47 825 706, www.argiletumtour.com*),
organizes a 3-hour walking tour (*Wed.
& Fri., 9:30 a.m.*) starting at Quirinal Hill
and continuing through piazzas and
past fountains before ending the day at
Campo dei Fiori.

Quirinale & Around

The Quirinal Hill (Monte Quirinale), the highest of Rome's seven famous hills, is just up the street from the Trevi Fountain and offers a magnificent view over the city. Probably named after the ancient Temple of Quirinus, which once stood here, it houses a fine piazza as well as two outstanding churches, of contrasting design, created by rivals Bernini and Borromini.

This obelisk once embellished the entrance to Emperor Augustus' mausoleum.

Palazzo del Quirinale

- 🅰 Map pp. 94–95
- ✉ Piazza del Quirinale
- ☎ 06 46991
- 🕐 Open (unless there is an official reception) 8:30 a.m.–noon. Sun. Sept.–June. Changing of the Guard: 3:15 p.m. Mon.–Sat., 4 p.m. Sun. (summer 6 p.m.)
- 💲 $
- 🚌 Bus: 40, 60, 64, 70, 170

As far back as the first century B.C., this area had a particular residential cachet. The writer Martial lived here, as did Cicero's good friend, Pomponius Atticus. In the late 1500s, Pope Gregory XIII decided to build a summer residence here, where it was somewhat cooler than at the Vatican. Over the decades many important artists—Ponzio, Fontana, Bernini, Maderno, Fuga—worked on the **palazzo,** which has a Renaissance facade facing onto the piazza and a secondary entrance on the wing known as the *manica lunga*

(the long sleeve) on the Via del Quirinale.

Other Quirinale Palazzi

Also on the piazza are several other important palazzi. The **Consulta,** on the far side looking toward St. Peter's, was built by Pope Clement XII in the 1730s to house a papal tribunal. Today it is the site of Italy's Constitutional Court.

Next door stands the **Palazzo Pallavicini-Rospigliosi,** constructed in 1603 for the Borghese family. While across from the Quirinale you will find the renovated **Scuderie del Quirinale,** or stables, now used for temporary exhibits.

After Italian unification in 1870, Italy's Savoy kings moved into the Quirinale. Since 1947, it has been the residence of the president of Italy.

Sant'Andrea al Quirinale

In 1658, the Jesuits decided to build a new church to serve its novices. They chose the "Strada Pia" (today's XX Settembre), the road designed a century earlier by Michelangelo to connect the Quirinal Palace—which in the time being had become the summer residence of the popes—to the Porta Pia gate. The man in charge was Cardinal Camillo Pamphili, and his choice of designer fell on Gian Lorenzo Bernini, who had already created the Piazza Navona fountains for the Pamphili family.

Oval in shape, the church is generally considered Bernini's masterpiece in ecclesiastical architecture. The interior embodies his theory that the visual arts, combined with effective lighting and color, should aim at the creation of an intensely emotional, even theatrical, experience. For Bernini lovers, this is a site not to be missed. Note the colored marbles, the gilded ceiling, and the stucco cherubs tumbling down from the small, elliptical dome in a swirl of frenetic activity.

San Carlo alle Quattro Fontane

How fitting that the architect of San Carlo alle Quattro Fontane,

located down the street, should be none other than Bernini's archrival, Carlo Borromini. In his first solo commission, Borromini seems to have knowingly created an antithesis to Bernini's opulence. Take note especially of the church's monochromatic off-white interior. Completed in 1667, the church is so small

INSIDER TIP:

Try the gelato at Il Gelato di San Crispino. Favorites include the wild honey and *crema al whisky* flavors; the latter features a 32-year-old Highland malt.

—IAN D'AGATA
National Geographic contributor & Director of the International Wine Academy of Roma

that it could fit into one of the four supporting pilasters of St. Peter's Basilica.

Borromini's genius is exemplified by his sublimely beautiful dome, as well as a beehive of geometric design—crosses, octagons, and hexagons in relief. Stucco decorations ingeniously hide the church's windows.

Outside, note the four late 16th-century fountains (two river gods and two virtues, Fidelity and Strength) at the intersection with **Via delle Quattro Fontane.** From the intersection's center you can see three of Rome's obelisks—but be careful! ∎

Sant'Andrea al Quirinale
- ⓜ Map pp. 94–95
- ✉ Via del Quirinale 29
- ☎ 06 474 4872
- 🕐 Closed noon–3:30 p.m. & Sun. noon–4 p.m.
- 🚌 Bus: H, 40, 60, 64, 70, 170

Il Gelato di San Crispino
- ⓜ Map pp. 94–95
- ✉ Via della Panetteria 42
- **www.ilgelato disancrispino.it**

San Carlo alle Quattro Fontane
- ⓜ Map pp. 92–93
- ✉ Via del Quirinale 23
- ☎ 06 488 3261
- 🕐 Closed daily 1–3 p.m. & Sat. p.m.
- 🚌 Bus: C3, H, 40, 52, 61, 62, 63, 64, 70, 71, 80, 95, 116, 170, 175, 492, 590. Metro: Linea A (Barberini)

Palazzo Barberini & Galleria Nazionale d'Arte Antica

An architectural masterpiece, the Palazzo Barberini was the home of Maffeo Barberini, who was elected Pope Urban VIII in 1623. A wealthy art patron, the pope spared no expense, hiring some of the major artists of the 17th century—Pietro da Cortona among them—to decorate the palazzo, which now houses the priceless masterpieces of the National Gallery.

Eighteenth-century paintings adorn the Sala de Battaglie, part of Cornelia Barberini's apartments.

Visiting the Museum

Ongoing renovations promise to reorganize the collection in a manner worthy of its art. Different sections of the museum will be closed for various periods, and the display is subject to change. Currently, the only working entrance is located in Via delle Quattro Fontane.

The permanent collection is currently displayed on two floors. On the first floor (Italian-style), the first rooms to your left contain some lovely primitives (mostly on wood). Paintings from the 15th and 16th centuries are in the next rooms, among them Fra Filippo Lippi's "Annunciation" and a "Madonna and Child" and "Mary Maddalena" by Piero di Cosimo, all in **Room 3.**

In **Room 4** you will find several important works by Antioniazzo Romano and Perugino. **Room 6** contains Raphael's famous "La Fornarina" (the "Baker's Daughter"), although some art historians attribute it to his pupil, Giulio Romano. Note Raphael's name on her bracelet. Also here are Giovan Antonio (Il Sodoma) Bazzi's "Rape of the Sabine Women" and Andrea del Sarto's "Sacred Family" and "Madonna and Child." The ceiling vault displays Andrea Camassei's "Creation of the Angels." In contrast, the vast ceiling of **Room 7** is a "Divine Providence" painted by Andrea Sacchi.

In **Room 8,** there are several masterpieces: Tintoretto's "St. Jerome," Titian's "Venus and Adonis," Lorenzo Lotto's "Sacred Conversation," and Bronzino's striking "Portrait of Stefano Colonna." **Room 9** features an interesting "Pietà" by a follower of Michelangelo, as well as Jacopo Zucchi's "Bath of Bathsheba."

But the pièce de résistance is without a doubt Pietro da Cortona's magnificent ceiling in the **Salone,** the "Triumph of Divine Providence over Time." The room also includes several of Da Cortona's cartoons. Unfortunately, if a special exhibit is on, you may have to buy an exhibit ticket to see this exceptional masterpiece.

Up Bernini's Staircase: The rest of the collection continues up the staircase designed by Bernini. In the first room you will find several paintings by Guido Reni, including his "Beatrice Cenci," and a "Pietà" by Giovan Battista Gaulli (Il Baccicia). The room down a few steps on the left has Hans Holbein's "Henry VIII" and leads to yet another chamber, where you will find three Caravaggios ("Judith Beheading Holofernes,"

"Narcissus," and "St. Francis"). Wander back to the other side of the first room, where you can join a tour of the small but lovely 18th-century apartment designed for Princess Cornelia Costanza Barberini.

The Palazzo: Bernini and Borromini both contributed greatly to the impressive palazzo. However, the original design is attributed to Carlo Maderno, Borromini's uncle, who died a year after construction began. Commissioned by the Barberini family in 1625—shortly after Maffeo Barberini became Pope Urban VIII—it epitomizes noble

INSIDER TIP:

Metro tickets are sold at street kiosks near the subway stations. Count your change; the kiosk vendors routinely try to short-change you. Keep your temper and think of it as a game.

—CHRISTOPHER SOMMERVILLE
National Geographic author

life in 17th-century Rome. Borromini is believed to have designed the oval staircase in the right wing viewed from Via delle Quattro Fontane. At some point you'll want to walk outside to the garden to get a good look at Bernini's impressive central portico and what was built as the original main facade. ■

Via Veneto

In ancient times, this was a residential suburb where the wealthy had their landscaped villas. Today, there are next to no traces of those first-century buildings or of the extensive gardens that surrounded most of them.

In the 1950s and '60s, Roman paparazzi would stalk the famous habitués of the Via Veneto cafés.

Via Veneto

 Map pp. 94–95

Bus: C3, 52, 63, 80, 95, 116. Metro: Linea A (Barberini)

The best known of the first-century gardens were the Horti Sallustiani. They surrounded the magnificent home of Sallust, a Roman general and scholar who was a contemporary of Julius Caesar. After the turmoil of the fifth and sixth centuries A.D., a period marked by barbarian invasions and a series of wars that interrupted the water supply into the city, the area was abandoned in favor of more central zones.

The suburban tradition was reborn in the 17th century, when the Villa Ludovisi occupied much of this area. The villa was sold in the late 19th century, when real estate speculation opened the way for modern urban development.

The Sweet Life

By the early 20th century, the Via Veneto (officially the Via Vittorio Veneto) had become Rome's most elegant street, the site of the city's best hotels and restaurants. In the 1950s, its upper portion became the undisputed hub of la dolce vita (the sweet life), a term used during Italy's economic boom of the 1950s and '60s to describe the gossip and glitter of Roman night life, the comings and goings of the Eternal City's international galaxy of stars, and the unrelenting assault of its tabloid photographers on the city's beautiful people.

The era was depicted in many movies of the time, in particular La Dolce Vita (1960), one of the finest works of Federico Fellini. The movie includes the unforgettable scene of a voluptuous Anita Ekberg, the prey of the cynical reporter Paolo Rubini (Marcello Mastroianni), immersing herself in the waters of the Trevi Fountain (see pp. 94–95). The most memorable character was Paparazzo, Rubini's photographer sidekick.

By then the street's most famous bars and cafés—Doney's, Café de Paris, and Harry's Bar—had become hangouts for actors and directors such as Sophia Loren, Gina Lollobrigida, Vittorio De Sica, Roberto Rossellini, Ingrid Bergman, Liz Taylor, Richard Burton, Burt Lancaster, and many more who went there to see and to be seen.

Today, however, Via Veneto is simply one of Rome's broader avenues, pleasingly lined with charming (and very expensive) sidewalk cafés, elegant shops, and luxury hotels such as the Excelsior and the Marriott Grand Hotel Flora. At the upper end is **Porta Pinciana,** the fortified gateway built into the Aurelian walls in 403 by the Emperor Honorius, leading to Villa Borghese and the Galleria Borghese.

Its lower end, where you'll find banks, ministries, and more hotels, ends in **Piazza Barberini,** one of downtown Rome's major traffic junctions and the site of two famous Bernini statues (see p. 99). ■

Thwarting Pickpockets & Other Thieves

The crime rate in Italy is lower than in many other countries. But, as in any big city, Rome has its share of extremely talented pickpockets and purse snatchers. It also has a large population of gypsies, some of whom, including small children, survive by petty stealing and often prey on foreigners.

As a result, it is a good idea to learn how to protect yourself from thieves and also how to file a police report, should the worst happen. Ensure a smooth trip by following a few simple rules, many of which you probably follow at home.

- Leave your passport, valuables, money, and credit cards you don't need immediately in a hotel safe—but keep a photocopy of your passport with you.
- Try not to bring out tempting wads of cash when you're paying for anything.
- Cameras and purses should be worn across the chest.
- If you wear a backpack, take it off when you are on a subway or bus.

- Do not keep your wallet in an outside jacket or pants pocket.
- If you are sitting at an outdoor café, do not hang your purse or backpack on a chair near the street or leave it sitting on the ground.
- Do not wear expensive watches or jewelry while touring.
- If you are surrounded by a small group of children carrying pieces of cardboard or newspaper, don't be intimidated. Yell "*via, via*" loudly and, if you're comfortable doing so, swat at them.
- Be especially alert on crowded public transport, especially bus no. 64.

In the unfortunate event you are the victim of a robbery, head for the nearest police station (*commissariato*) or Carabinieri post (*stazione dei carabinieri*). The stations most used to dealing with foreigners downtown are those at Piazza Collegio Romano (police) and Piazza Venezia (carabinieri), and, in Trastevere, Via Francesco a Ripa (police) and Via Morosini (carabinieri).

More Places to Visit

Galleria Colonna

Although only open on Saturday mornings, the art gallery of the magnificent 15th-century Palazzo Colonna is well worth a visit. Built between 1650 and 1700 to house the Colonna family's art collection, the gallery is a masterpiece of baroque architecture with colored marbles, ornate mirrors, and frescoed ceilings. You'll find works by such masters as Bronzino, Ghirlandaio, Jacopo e Domenico Tintoretto, and Rubens. Walk around the corner to Piazza S.S. Apostoli 66 to look at the facade. Across the street is the **Basilica dei Santi Apostoli** with its 15th-century portico and an 18th-century facade designed by Carlo Fontana.

🅼 Map pp. 94–95 ✉ Via della Pilotta 17 ☎ 06 678 4350 🕑 Open 9 a.m.–1:00 p.m. Sat.; closed Aug. 🚍 Bus: H, C3, 40, 46, 60, 62, 63, 64, 70, 81, 84, 85, 87, 95, 119, 170, 175, 628, 715, 716, 780.

Galleria dell'Accademia di San Luca

Since the 1930s, when its former neighborhood near the Roman Forum was razed by Mussolini, the Academy of St. Luke has been housed in Palazzo Carpegna, around the corner from the Trevi Fountain. The late 16th-century building, originally designed by Giacomo della Porta, was later modified by Borromini, who built the spiral staircase. This was one of the little optical diversions that Borromini and his rival Bernini liked to create to trick the eye of the beholder. The staircase is beyond the tiny open garden on the right, which is decorated with 19th- and 20th-century sculptures.

The academy was founded in the late 16th century by a group of artists whose gifts, along with bequests by nonmembers, make up the interesting collection. It was named for St. Luke because the Apostle was supposed to have had artistic inclinations. The collection includes works by such masters as Raphael, Titian, Bronzino, Rubens, Van Dyck, and Canova, as well as some of the few female artists of the time, including Lavinia Fontana, Angelika Kauffmann, and Élisabeth Vigée-Lebrun.

Nearby, at Via della Stamperia 6, is the **Calcografia Nazionale,** with what may be the largest collection of copperplate engravings in the world. It has more than 20,000 plates including more than 1,400 by G.B. Piranesi and is generally open to the public. Two blocks away in Vicolo di Scanderbeg 117 is the amusing **Museum of Pasta** (closed for restoration; tel 06 699 1120).

🅼 Map pp. 92–93 ✉ Piazza dell'Accademia di San Luca 77 ☎ 06 679 8850 🕑 Closed for restoration 🚍 Bus: C3, 52, 61, 62, 63, 71, 80, 81, 85, 95, 116, 119, 175, 492, 590, 628. Metro: Linea A (Barberini)

Santa Maria della Concezione (dell'Immacolata)

From an architectural point of view, the Church of the Cappuccini, as it is generally called after the Franciscan monks that run it, is simple and unprepossessing, an attempt by its founder, Cardinal Antonio Barberini (the younger brother of Pope Urban VIII—he is buried there), to run counter to the then (1626) baroque tide. Inside, however, there is rich decoration. The first chapel on the right has Guido Reni's "St. Michael Trampling on the Devil" and was decorated by Pietro da Cortona; the second has works by Lanfranco; the third by Domenichino; and the fifth by Andrea Sacchi. Most of the church's visitors, however, have something else in mind. In fact, the church conceals several somewhat macabre but nonetheless fascinating underground burial chapels lined with the skeletons (or loose bones) of some 4,000 Capuchins. Take a sweater.

🅼 Map pp. 92–93 ✉ Via Veneto 27 ☎ 06 487 1185 🕑 Church and Crypt closed noon–3 p.m. 🚍 Bus: C3, 52, 61, 62, 63, 80, 95, 116, 175, 492, 590. Metro: Linea A (Barberini) ∎

The magnificent Spanish Steps, elegant shops, the impressive Piazza del Popolo, and shady Villa Borghese park

Piazza di Spagna to Villa Borghese

Pauline, Napoleon Bonaparte's sister, posed for Casanova's "Venus Victrix."

Piazza di Spagna to Villa Borghese

The Italian word *salotto*, living room, describes an area that is both central and welcoming. In that sense the Trident, and in particular Piazza di Spagna, is the salotto of Rome, the neighborhood that best plays host to the city's myriad visitors, who come to dine, shop, and revisit Rome's architectural, artistic, and archaeological past.

The area begins just inside the Porta del Popolo, the gateway in the Aurelian walls (once called Porta Flaminia) that was the terminus of the Via Flaminia, the Roman road built to connect the capital to Rimini on the Adriatic Sea. It includes important archaeological monuments such as Augustus's Mausoleum and the Ara Pacis, Renaissance palaces such as Villa Medici, and innumerable churches, including Trinità dei Monti, with its splendid view of the city.

The name, "il Tridente," literally something with three teeth, takes its cue from the street plan developed by the popes of the 1500s, then the city's temporal rulers. Three major streets fan out from Piazza del Popolo: Via Ripetta, which ran to the ancient river port; Via del Babuino, which runs through Piazza di Spagna and on to the Quirinal Hill; and Via del Corso, which cuts straight through downtown Rome before ending at Piazza Venezia. The side streets in the "Tridente," such as the evocative Via Margotta, are interesting and much quieter than the big three.

For centuries, the area stretching from the Pincio Hill (see p. 114) to the Tiber had been uninhabited. Rumored to be haunted by evil spirits, this was a weak point in the city's defenses. With the construction of Santa Maria del Popolo and the other churches of Piazza del Popolo all this was to change, and Via del Babuino's route through Piazza di Spagna would transform the latter into an all-important tourist and shopping center, which it remains today. The Spanish Steps linked the area to the Pincio Hill and, through the latter to the Villa Borghese, a magnificent and expansive park that embraces several major museums such as Villa Giulia and, in particular, the beautifully renovated Galleria Borghese. ∎

NOT TO BE MISSED:

Bustling Piazza di Spagna & the Spanish Steps 110–111

Window shopping on Via dei Condotti 111

Having a coffee at the historic Caffè Greco 111

S. Maria del Popolo's Caravaggio and Raphael paintings cum Bernini chapel 116–117

Augustus' Ara Pacis, in its new, controversial modern setting, designed by Richard Meier 118

Villa Giulia, the one and only Etruscan Museum 119

Biking at Villa Borghese park 121

The sculpture and paintings in the magnificently decorated Galleria Borghese 122–124

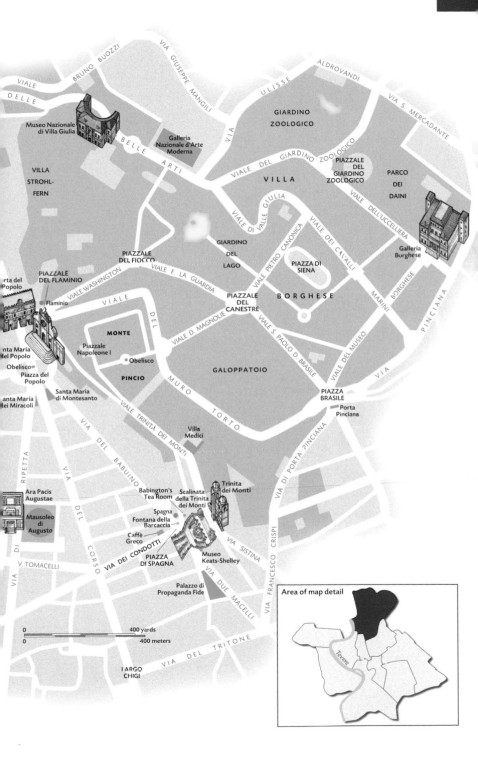

VIALE BRUNO BUOZZI

VIA GIUSEPPE MANGILI

ALDROVANDI

VIA S. MERCADANTE

VIALE DELLE BELLE ARTI

Museo Nazionale di Villa Giulia

Galleria Nazionale d'Arte Moderna

GIARDINO ZOOLOGICO

ULISSE

VILLA STROHL-FERN

VIALE DEL GIARDINO ZOOLOGICO

VILLA

VIA

GIARDINO ZOOLOGICO

PIAZZALE DEL GIARDINO ZOOLOGICO

PARCO DEI DAINI

VIALE DI VALLE GIULIA

VIALE DELL'UCCELLIERA

VIALE DELLA VALLE GIULIA

GIARDINO DEL LAGO

VIALE PIETRO CANONICA

VIALE DEI CAVALLI

Galleria Borghese

PIAZZALE DEL FIOCCO

VIALE F. LA GUARDIA

PIAZZA DI SIENA

BORGHESE

VIA BORGHESE

PINCIANA

rta del Popolo

PIAZZALE DEL FLAMINIO

VIALE WASHINGTON

VIALE

PIAZZALE DEL CANESTRE

VIALE DEI MARINI

Flaminio

VIALE

DEL

VIALE D. MAGNOLIE

VIALE S. PAOLO D. BRASILE

VIALE DEL MUSEO

nta Maria del Popolo

MONTE

Piazzale Napoleone I

VIA

Obelisco

Obelisco

Piazza del Popolo

Santa Maria di Montesanto

PINCIO

MURO

GALOPPATOIO

TORTO

PIAZZA BRASILE

nta Maria ei Miracoli

Porta Pinciana

VIALE TRINITÀ DEI MONTI

Villa Medici

RIPETTA

VIA DEL BABUINO

Trinità dei Monti

VIA DI PORTA PINCIANA

Ara Pacis Augustae

VIA DEL CORSO

Babington's Tea Room

Scalinata della Trinità dei Monti

Mausoleo di Augusto

Spagna Fontana della Barcaccia

VIA SISTINA

Caffè Greco

VIA DEI CONDOTTI

PIAZZA DI SPAGNA

Museo Keats-Shelley

VIA FRANCESCO CRISPI

V. TOMACELLI

VIA DI

Palazzo di Propaganda Fide

VIA DUE MACELLI

0   400 yards
0   400 meters

VIA DEL TRITONE

LARGO CHIGI

Area of map detail

Tevere

Piazza di Spagna

For at least four centuries, this long, irregularly shaped piazza with its un-Italian palm trees has been the heart of nonarchaeological Rome. The elongated square boasts one of the city's major monumental attractions, the Scalinata (Spanish Steps).

In Charles Dickens's day, the Scalinata (Spanish Steps) was a meeting place for artists' models.

Piazza di Spagna

 Map pp. 108–109

🚌 Bus: 116, 119, 590. Metro: Linea A (Spagna)

Spanish Steps

Designed by Francesco de Sanctis, the Scalinata della Trinità dei Monti, or Spanish Steps, were built in the 1720s to replace the footpath linking the piazza to the lovely French church of **Trinità dei Monti,** with its double bell towers and the double flight of front stairs. The money to build the 138 travertine steps (24,000 scudi) was bequeathed by a 17th-century French diplomat in his will and then augmented by a

contribution from the then king of France, Louis XV.

The steps, today a popular meeting place for young tourists, are particularly lovely in the spring, when they are adorned with a magnificent display of flowering azaleas. At Christmastime, a life-size nativity scene is erected there, and every December 8 the pope pays a visit to the narrower, southern end of the piazza where a wreath is placed on the statue of the Virgin Mary atop a Roman column, erected in the 19th century to mark the 1854 dogma of the Immaculate Conception.

Fontana della Barcaccia

Attributed to Pietro Bernini (Gian Lorenzo's father), the fountain at the foot of the Spanish Steps (see p. 98) was commissioned by Pope Urban VIII in the 1620s, almost a century before the staircase was built. The pope was a Bernini, and his family's symbol, the bee, adorns the fountain.

Because of low pressure, the water does not spout forcefully from the top of the fountain but rather trickles from nozzles located on the prow, stern, and sides of this marble version of an old, leaky boat. Was this a reference to St. Peter's role as a fisher of men? Or a commemoration of the 1598 flood? It's not clear.

Other Sites around the Piazza

The street facing the steps is **Via dei Condotti,** *the* shopping street in Rome. It is named for the underground conduits that Pope Gregory XIII (1572–1585) had

(see p. 98)

INSIDER TIP:

Visit the top of the Spanish Steps at the end of the day to catch a spectacular sunset over the city.

—RUTH ELLEN GRUBER
National Geographic author

built to supply the neighborhood with running water.

Beyond the Roman column you'll see, wedged between two streets, the 17th-century **Palazzo di Propaganda Fide,** which houses the Vatican's Congregation for the Propagation of the Faith.

Considered an architectural masterpiece, the building combines the work of the two rival geniuses of the era, Gian Lorenzo Bernini and Francesco Borromini. Bernini designed the facade facing the piazza. Note that it features yet more bees, like those found on the fountain. His artistic nemesis, Borromini, was commissioned to create the side facade fronting Via Propaganda Fide. ■

The English Quarter

In the 18th century, the foreign presence in the Piazza di Spagna area escalated, with intellectuals and artists of many nationalities taking up residence in the surrounding streets. But there were so many English visitors that Italians began using the word *"inglesi"* to mean foreigners in general. The major hotels had names like Hotel de Londres and the Hotel des Anglais (even today, a favorite in the area is the Hotel d'Inghilterra). Tennyson and Thackeray had lodgings on Via dei Condotti across the street from the Caffè Greco, a famed meeting place for intellectuals. The young English poet, John Keats, was living at Piazza di Spagna 26 (the rose-colored building to the right of the steps) when he died in 1821, and his apartment now houses the small but interesting Museo Keats-Shelley (Keats and Shelley Museum and library). Babington's Tea Rooms, on the other side of the Steps (great scones!), is an expensive but charming Victorian institution opened to cater to Rome's English-speaking community.

Shopping & Fashion

Piazza di Spagna and adjoining Via dei Condotti are at the heart of Rome's major shopping district and the city's fashion world. Armani, Fendi, Ferragamo, Gucci, MaxMara, Prada, Valentino, Versace—all the signature stores are here, as are countless other shops that sell elegant clothing, jewelry, housewares, and objets d'art.

Shoppers find premier fashion retailer in the streets around the Spanish Steps.

The prices are not low, bargaining is rare, *saldi* (sales) are very often misleading, and tax rebates, while enticing, generally require enormous patience at the airport on your day of departure. Nevertheless, the clothes are beautiful, eye-catching, and well made and, with some products, particularly leather goods—clothing, shoes, and bags—you may find a real bargain, a trophy to show off at home.

Naturally, there are also apparel stores with lower prices. On tiny **Via del Gambero** you can find bargain blouses and sweaters. On **Via del Corso,** the long street connecting Piazza del Popolo and Piazza Venezia

(adored by writers such as Stendhal for its now vanished 18th-century elegance), there are many shoe stores and casualwear outlets. And the same goes for **Via della Croce,** which in addition has some nice food stores.

Department Stores

Recently refurbished, Rinascente at Largo Chigi, one of Rome's few department stores, does a brisk trade in attractive clothing and accessories for both men and women. Like many stores in the center, including those in the newly renovated Alberto Sordi Galleria across the street, it now stays open all day. Rinascente is open every single day, including

Sundays and Monday mornings when clothing stores are generally closed.

Specialty Shops

A few of the many specialty shops that once filled the center still survive. Some sell items for a specific clientele. The many shops clustered in the streets behind the Pantheon, for example, satisfy the haberdashery needs of ecclesiastics. Others make articles requiring a great deal of time and qualified workmanship, like those that sell handmade knotted silk fringes, the tassels for keys to antique armoires, and drapery pull-ropes. You can find one of these *passamanerie* shops on the **Via d'Aracoeli,** up the street from Il Gesù; another operates near the Parliament.

Despite the overflow of clothing stores, **Via del Babuino** retains something of its former character as a center for antiques. Shops along here sell everything from silver spoons to marble-topped tables and credenzas.

Other Districts

The streets around the Spanish Steps are not the only important shopping district. One alternative is **Via Nazionale,** the broad cobblestone avenue that runs from Largo

INSIDER TIP:

For men, there is nothing more Roman than Battistoni, a historic shop at Via dei Condotti 61/a, just down from Piazza di Spagna. Their tailoring provides the typical Roman look you can take home with you.

—BARBARA LESSONA
*National Geographic Traveler contributor
and personal shopper*

Magnanapoli to Piazza della Repubblica (or Esedra), where clothing and leather goods stores abound. Another is **Via Cola di Rienzo,** across the river in Prati, which offers similar prices. If you are in this neighborhood, check out Franchi (pronounced FRANCK-ee), known for its expensive-but-worth-it takeout food. If you have a craving for something from home, Castroni, the specialty food shop next door, may well have it. In addition, the area around Campo dei Fiori and Piazza Navona is filled with interesting boutiques and specialty shops.

Rome, 2008: A model wears a creation of designer Abed Mahfouz's Haute-Couture collection.

Pincio

Historians disagree about the origins of the Pincio (pronounced Pin-CHO) Hill. Was it the location of an imperial residence? The site of the Emperor Nero's tomb? Or simply a suburban residential area inhabited by ancient Rome's patrician families, including the Pinci, to whom the hill owes its name? Whatever. At the beginning of the 19th century, the area was transformed into a charming park and promenade called the Bois de Boulogne of Rome.

Pincio

🗺 Map pp. 108–109

🚌 Bus: C3, 88, 95, 119, 490, 495, 590, 628, 926. Tram: 2. Metro: Linea A (Flaminio)

The French influence in the layout was inevitable since it was landscaped during a brief period of French administration (1800–1815). Architect Giuseppe Valadier designed circular ramps and terraced landings that lead from the Piazza del Popolo to a lookout with a magnificent view.

The paths are lined with the busts of Italian patriots added several decades later at the instigation of Giuseppe Mazzini, the 19th-century Italian nationalist. The Egyptian **obelisk** (see p. 86), brought to Rome by the Emperor Hadrian, was placed on the Pincio in 1822 by Pope Pius VII.

A Magnificent View

The ramps and landings lead to the lookout. The view from here is spectacular (especially at sunset—as guidebooks never fail to point out). The cupolas of Rome, including that of St. Peter's, loom up at you through the gathering dusk, as does the impressive dome of the Pantheon and the all-too-white monument to Victor Emanuel II.

Like the **Piazza del Popolo** below, a century ago the Pincio was considered to be the in place for a stroll. Today, however, on weekends there are far more children than lords and ladies, but the view is certainly worth a visit. For those in the mood for a long walk, remember that from the Pincio you can walk to Villa Medici, Trinità dei Monti, and the Spanish Steps or, in the other direction, to the Villa Borghese park (see pp. 120–121). ■

Domes, bell towers, and terraces form the skyline view.

Piazza & Porta del Popolo

This large, open space echoes the monumental architectonic style of Paris and is probably one of the most impressive piazzas in the city, especially now that Rome's municipal government has banned all traffic. Piazza del Popolo takes its name from the church of Santa Maria del Popolo (see pp. 116–117), but it has always been a major landmark. Since Roman times, the Porta has been one of the principal entrances into the city.

Blood once ran in this piazza, which was formerly used for public executions.

In 1589, Pope Sixtus V moved the Egyptian **obelisk** that stood in the Circus Maximus (see p. 209) to the center of the piazza. The foundations for the two churches, whose presence dramatically enhances the theatrical effect of the square for those entering the city by the Porta del Popolo, were laid in the 17th century. Although apparently identical, **Santa Maria di Montesanto,** on the left, has an oval dome, whereas **Santa Maria dei Miracoli's** dome is round.

In 1655, Pope Alexander VII commissioned Bernini to redecorate the inside facade of the Porta to honor the arrival of Queen Christina of Sweden, whose conversion to Catholicism was regarded as a great propaganda coup for the Counter-Reformation. *"Felice faustoque ingressui"* reads the inscription, "For a happy and blessed entrance."

Credit for the piazza's final neoclassic layout, however, goes to Valadier, who created the semicircular structures that enclose the piazza, as well as the fountains and the lions. Since the early 19th century, **Piazza del Popolo** has been considered a chic place to enjoy a coffee or an aperitivo. ■

Piazza & Porta del Popolo

 Map pp. 108–109

Bus: C3, 81, 88, 95, 119, 490, 495, 590, 628, 926. Tram: 2. Metro: Linea A (Flaminio)

Santa Maria del Popolo

The remains of the Emperor Nero were said to have been buried on the site of this church, and as part of the medieval penchant for exorcising the remnants of paganism, Pope Paschal II (1099–1118) dug up the supposed gravesite, burned the remains he found there, and threw them into the Tiber. He then built a chapel and dedicated it to the Virgin Mary.

Santa Maria del Popolo

⚠ Map pp. 108–109

✉ Piazza del Popolo 12

☎ 06 361 0836

🕐 Closed Mon.–Sat. noon–4 p.m., Sun. 1:30–4:30 p.m.

🚌 Bus: C3, 81, 88, 95, 119, 490, 495, 590, 628, 926. Tram: 2. Metro: Linea A (Flaminio)

Santa Maria del Popolo has been rebuilt several times, and what we see today—a church with three aisles and many side chapels—is basically the 15th-century Renaissance version. Subsequently, there were some other modifications. Bramante enlarged the apse, and Bernini redecorated the interior and added some baroque touches to the facade.

They Knew Him When...

In the early 1500s, Martin Luther boarded in the monastery that adjoined Santa Maria del Popolo. It was only a few years later that the Augustinian monk triggered the Protestant Reformation when he posted his 95 theses on the church door in Wittenberg (in today's Germany). The monastery no longer exists.

Interior Adornments

The enormous artistic value of the church lies in its interior decoration, to which some of the most talented artists of the 1500s and 1600s contributed. The Della Rovere Chapel, the first on the right, has frescoes by Pinturicchio, who also painted the "Adoration of the Child" located above the altar and the magnificent biblical scenes that adorn the vaulted ceiling of the presbytery.

The painting of the "Madonna del Popolo," set into the main altar, which is baroque in style, for centuries was believed to have been painted by St. Luke, until art experts attributed it to the 13th-century Sienese school. The original marble altar designed by Andrea Bregno in 1473 now stands in the sacristy. To see it, go through the door at the end of the right transept and down the corridor within.

The magnificent tombs of Cardinal Ascanio Sforza and Cardinal Girolamo Basso della Rovere, both by Andrea Sansovino, lie behind the main altar.

Cerasi & Chigi Chapels

The star attraction of the church is the **Cerasi Chapel,** which lies to the left of the main altar. Here you will find two of Caravaggio's paintings, the "Conversion of St. Paul" and the "Crucifixion of St. Peter."

Also not to be missed is the **Chigi Chapel** by Raphael Sanzio. The chapel's unusual pyramid-shaped marble tombs of the banker, Agostino Chigi, and his brother on the left and

Bernini designed the marble floor and hanging bronze lamp in the Chigi Chapel.

right walls of the chapel, may have been inspired by the Roman pyramid of Cestius.

The mosaic decoration in the dome of the chapel is based on designs (generally known as cartoons) of Raphael. Two of the four corner statues, "Habakkuk" (who in the Old Testament brought food to Daniel in the lion's den) and "Daniel and the Lion," are by Bernini. The "Birth of the Virgin," above the altar, was created by Sebastiano del Piombo. Unusual in Rome to begin with, the two stained-glass windows in the apse (behind the main altar) were surely among the first in the city.

Before you leave, note the somewhat gruesome skeleton sharing a cage with a butterfly (symbolizing rebirth or resurrection) to the right of the rightmost door. ■

Ara Pacis Augustae

One of the most famous monuments in ancient Rome, the Ara Pacis was a ceremonial altar inaugurated in 9 B.C. to commemorate the Pax Romana that followed Augustus' conquest of Spain and Gaul (as France was then known). Recovered in 1568 near Piazza San Lorenzo in Lucina, the altar was reassembled (with missing segments reconstructed) in the 1930s.

Ara Pacis Augustae

- 🅜 Map pp. 108–109
- ✉ Lungotevere in Augusta
- ☎ 060608
- 🕐 Closed Mon.
- 💲 $$. Audio guide: $
- 🚌 Bus: C3, 81, 119, 224, 590, 628, 926

en.arapacis.it

Made of white Italian (Luna) marble, the altar is set on a rectangular platform and surrounded by four walls with entrances on two sides. The reliefs are a stunning example of the highest quality classical sculpture and are also of great historical interest. The procession represented on the outside of the longer, lateral walls actually took place (on July 4, 13 B.C.). The half-figure on the side facing the nearby mausoleum is Augustus. He is followed by several priests (*flavins*) and family members, including his son-in-law Agrippa, whose place as the second nobleman in the procession indicates he is the heir apparent. An inscription on the outer modern structure reads "*Res gestae Divi Augusti*," the title of the Emperor's own account of his accomplishments.

The Ara Pacis has been the focal point of the grandiose (and controversial) renovation project directed by well-known American architect Richard Meier that also houses a conference center, a bookshop, libraries, offices, and new exhibition space.

The overgrown and sorely neglected **Mausoleo di Augusto** next door was once a major monument of ancient Rome, the first of the city's two large circular tombs (the other is Castel Sant'Angelo). The Rome city government is preparing a competition for the mausoleum's long-overdue restoration. ■

EXPERIENCE: Learn More About Wine

Archaeologists tell us that wine has been with us in some form since almost the beginning of civilized life, and that it has been produced on a large scale since about 3000 B.C. The ancient Romans drank wine daily, although theirs was a syrupy brew that they diluted with water. They then added honey and spices to improve the taste. Today, wine continues to be an essential part of Italian life.

In Rome's smaller *trattorie*, you may want to save money and try the house white or red, asking simply for *il vino della casa*. Elsewhere, you'll want bottled wine.

But how will you know what to ask for? The best place to take a short course in Italian wines, or in wine and food pairing, is the **International Wine Academy of Roma** (*Vicolo del Bottino 8, tel 06 699 0878, www.wineacademyroma.com*). Established in 2002 by Robert Wirth, the owner of the prestigious Hassler Hotel, the academy is located on the far end of Piazza di Spagna in the lovely Il Palazzetto building, which also houses the restaurant of the same name, a nice wine bar, and a terrace overlooking the top of the Spanish Steps and the piazza below.

Villa Giulia

Since 1889, the 16th-century Villa Giulia—a superb example of Renaissance architecture—has housed one of the most important collections of Etruscan and pre-Roman antiquities in the world. The building is a consummate expression of the Renaissance architectural concept of exterior–interior "interpenetration" that began with the Villa Farnesina 40 years earlier.

The Villa Giulia was built between 1551 and 1553 by Pope Julius III (1550–1555), who commissioned some of the most important architects of the time, including Michelangelo, to enlarge and ennoble an earlier structure.

Once past the entrance vestibule, you find yourself in a semicircular portico, its ceiling frescoed to create a pergola effect that is in perfect harmony with the courtyard and gardens. At the other end of the courtyard follow the loggia down to a shady, sunken *nymphaeum*.

The two-floor museum (**Museo Nazionale di Villa Giulia**) is housed in the villa's right and left wings, access to which is from the far left-hand side of the portico. The first six rooms display artifacts primarily from the necropolis of Vulci and other sites. There is even a reconstruction of a tomb from Cerveteri, a town in the heart of what was once Etruria.

Not all of this will have general appeal, but who would want to miss **Room 7** with its compelling, life-size terra-cotta polychrome statues of Hercules, Apollo, and a goddess holding a young child, dating from the late sixth century B.C. They were probably created by Vulca, the master sculptor of Veio, who may also have decorated the giant temple to Jupiter that stood on the Capitoline Hill.

The mysterious Etruscans dominated central Italy until the sixth century B.C., when power shifted to the Romans.

Room 9 on the left-hand side of the ground floor houses the magnificent world-famous sarcophagus (also sixth century B.C.) of a young husband and wife reclining on a couch. Upstairs are countless objects—domestic implements, bronze utensils, armor, jewelry, and ceramics.

The other wing of the museum exhibits additional material from tombs or temples. The partially reconstructed pediment of the Temple of Apollo allo Scasato is intriguing, and the bust of Apollo is superb. His face, in deep concentration, is turned slightly to the right as if he were listening to a prophetic phrase. ■

Villa Giulia

🅰 Map pp. 108–109

✉ Piazzale di Villa Giulia 9

☎ 06 32 26 571

🕐 Closed Mon.

💲 $. Audio guide: $

🚃 Tram: 2, 3, 19

Villas & Parks

One of Europe's greenest cities, Rome has vast areas of rolling grassland, normally open from dawn to dusk and ideal for joggers, pensioners, and idlers of all types. The city owes its unusual number of parks to the aristocracy and—it must be said— to the financial difficulties that forced them, in modern times, to sell their suburban villas to the State. The word *villa* indicates that a park was once a private estate.

The Villa Borghese park is a place to relax for Romans and visitors to the city.

The first villas were called *casinas* or *casinos*, literally little houses, but the word "little" should be used advisedly. Starting in the Renaissance and continuing into the baroque era, as the nobility rushed to build elegant pleasure palaces steeped in verdant and contemplative surroundings, the houses grew ever greater and grander. They used these buildings as refuge from the summer heat, a place to picnic or party, or, as in the case of Villa Borghese, to house and display a magnificent art collection.

Not all have survived. Villa Ludovisi, which once occupied much of the Via Veneto area, has totally disappeared. The gardens of Villa Giulia, today the Etruscan Museum, have been swallowed up by urban encroachment, as have those of Villa Giustiniani near the Lateran. But

fortunately for today's Romans, dozens remain. Villa Ada, Villa Torlonia, and Villa Sciarra are only some of the parks providing a fresh-air outlet for families, lovers, and fitness freaks.

Naturally, there are other parks, including those built around ancient monuments, such as the Parco di Traiano (the Colle Oppio) around Trajan's Baths and the Parco degli Scipioni, near the Appian Way, extending around the remains of the tomb of the Cornelii Scipiones, built by that powerful family around the third or second century B.C.

Villa Borghese

Villa Borghese (pronounced Bor-GAY-zi) is the Roman equivalent of Central Park in New York or St. James's Park in London. Its 198 acres (80 ha) offer the city's residents a downtown escape for strolling, biking, horse-back riding, and jogging among extensive greenery, statuary, neoclassic temples, and fountains. There is an artificial lake, a zoo, and a grassy amphitheater (Piazza di Siena) shaded by graceful umbrella pines, where a horse show is held every May.

You can access the Villa Borghese from various points including Porta Pinciana, at the top end of Via Veneto, Piazzale Flaminio, just beyond Piazza del Popolo, and from the Galleria Borghese. Several major museums (Galleria Borghese, see pp. 122–124, the Modern Art Museum and Villa Giulia, see p. 119) are located in the park.

Other Villas, Casinos, & Gardens

Heading south from Villa Borghese, between the Pincio (see p. 114) and the Spanish Steps, is Villa Medici. Built for a Tuscan cardinal on the site of the gardens of Lucullus, the famed Roman gourmet and high-liver,

this late Renaissance building's gardens were described by Henry James as "a fabled, haunted place." Today it houses the French Academy, which is used for temporary art exhibitions (tel 06 67611). In summer, outdoor concerts offer a rare chance to see the spectacular gardens.

Among the city's other parks, Villa Doria Pamphili on the Janiculum Hill was laid out in the 17th century for Prince Camillo Pamphili and has a beautiful casino, unfortunately not generally open to the public. With 445 acres (180 ha) and a 5.5-mile (9 km) perimeter, it is the city's largest park, a haven for joggers and fresh-air enthusiasts. Villa Celimontana (see pp. 67–68), originally Villa Mattei after the family that built it in the 16th century, is on the Caelian Hill. It is a lovely place for a stroll amid pieces of ancient sculpture, and one of Rome's 13 obelisks (see pp. 86–87). A popular jazz festival is held here in summer.

EXPERIENCE: Sunday in the Park

Find yourself in Rome on a lazy Sunday? Why not relax like the Romans do and head for **Villa Doria Pamphili,** a public park located in the Monteverde neighborhood on the Janiculum Hill above Trastevere. It certainly offers something for everyone.

Here you will find joggers and cyclists enjoying the paths that wind through the park, whole families crowded around the pond throwing bread to the ducks and swans, and kids of all ages scrambling up the steps of the 17th-century villa, Il Casino del Bel Respiro. You may even run across a yoga class in full swing or a group of amateur artists sketching the 18th-century Palazzino Corsini. Sit back and enjoy the activity, but be sure not to miss the museum, which draws lines of people. Located in the Villa Vecchia, it traces the history of the park, much of which was once a farm.

If you get hungry while in the park, follow the power walkers speeding toward the café at the park's farthest end. Or, should you decide to eat lunch at one of the picnic tables or even spread out luxuriously on the grass, pick up a readymade meal on the way.

Depending on where you are staying, there are other open-air choices. **Villa Sciarra,** also in the Monteverde area, **Villa Ada** between the Parioli and Salario neighborhoods, and of course, **Villa Borghese,** where, if you can walk far enough, you also have the option of visiting major museums like Villa Giulia, Il Museo dell'Arte Moderna, the Galleria Borghese (reservations required), the children's movie house, the Cinema dei Piccoli, and the newer Casa del Cinema. **Gina's** restaurant (Via San Sebastianello 7, tel 06 687 0251, www.ginaroma.com) offers yummy picnic baskets.

Galleria Borghese

The Galleria Borghese was originally built in the early 1600s as a *casino* (a suburban estate or summerhouse) on the vast estate of Cardinal Scipione Borghese in what was then the outskirts of the city. Today it is owned by the State but still exhibits the family painting collection as well as many pieces from its collection of sculpture.

Bernini's "Rape of Proserpine" is one of the magnificent sculptures housed in the Galleria Borghese.

Modified in the 18th century and restored again in recent years, the gleaming white, three-story building today has a facade composed of twin towers flanking a recessed central core or portico. A double ramped staircase (that deliberately imitates Michelangelo's entrance to the Palazzo del Senatore in the Campidoglio) leads up to the main entrance, a mezzanine which is nevertheless considered the ground floor. Stucco work and decorative niches embellish parts of the facade.

Inside the Villa

The remarkable interior decoration of the villa also dates from the 18th century. Frescoed ceilings, sumptuous wall coverings, faux marble wall decoration, porphyry mantelpieces, gilded moldings, and marble inlay all vie for attention. Remember that every room has a theme, that the ceiling decorations (you mustn't forget to look up) and sculptures are displayed in tandem, and that wherever possible an attempt has been made to extend this thematic link to the paintings on the walls. You'll want to buy a book in the basement bookshop or rent an audio guide.

Sculptures & Mosaics: The fourth-century Roman floor mosaics in the entrance room on what passes for the ground floor, or *pianterreno*, depict gladiatorial combat scenes. Excavated from a family estate, they are real portraits of gladiators, whose names appear near them in the mosaic. Those marked with a θ, the first letter in the Greek word *thanatos* (death), got the thumbs-down sign and were no more. The frescoed vault depicts a Roman victory over the invading Gauls.

The sculpture collection contains some of the most famous pieces in the world. In **Room I** is Canova's marble **statue of Paolina Borghese,** also known as Pauline Bonaparte, Napoleon's sister. She is reclining, seminude, on a sort of chaise longue, and legend has it that the sculpture was kept under lock and key for years by her husband, Prince Camillo, who was scandalized by her lack of modesty.

There are also three extraordinary **sculptures by Bernini,** all completed while he was still in his mid-20s. In **Room II** you'll find his "David" (circa 1624), in which the young hero is preparing to hurl a stone at his adversary. The face, with its intense and concentrated expression, is a self-portrait of the sculptor. In **Room III,** "Apollo and Daphne" (1622–1625) depicts the young nymph's vain attempts to escape the god (the same scene is painted on the ceiling). Daphne's hands and feet are in the process of being transformed into a laurel tree. The swirling and sensual movement of the two intertwined bodies shows Bernini's amazing ability to capture the surface texture of skin and hair, as does his other work, in the next room, the

Galleria Borghese

 Map pp. 108–109

✉ Piazzale Scipione Borghese 5

☎ 06 32810 (for reservations)

⊖ Closed Mon. Advanced booking required.

$ $$. Audio guide: $. Daily tours in English: $

🚌 Bus: 38, 52, 63, 80, 86, 88, 92, 116, 217, 360, 495, 910

www.ticketeria.it

Galleria Borghese Access

Access to Galleria Borghese is more complicated than other museums. First, you only have two hours to see the museum. Second, if you are carrying anything (including handbags), head straight to the basement check room, otherwise you'll be sent straight there from the entrance. (Strangely, coats cannot be checked.) After seeing the ground floor (sculptures), you may not be able to go directly upstairs without returning first to the basement level. Never mind. What's displayed more than makes up for any organizational defects.

"Rape of Proserpine" (circa 1622). Notice the way Pluto's fingers sink into Proserpine's thigh.

The last room **(VIII)** on this floor is exceptional more for its paintings than its sculptures. There are six incredible **Caravaggios** here, including "St. Jerome" (1605), "David with the Head

of Goliath" (1609–1610), and the "Madonna dei Palafrenieri," sometimes called the "Madonna del Serpente," which was removed from an important altar in St. Peter's almost immediately as sacrilegious. The "Bacchino Malato" ("Sick Bacchus") from 1593 is a self-portrait.

The Treasures Upstairs: Upstairs (a good place to peek out at the gardens in the back) is the painting gallery, or **Pinacoteca,** where one marvelous painting succeeds another and where astounding works by some of the best-known painters in Western history—Bellini, Bronzino, Correggio, Cranach, Domenichino, Fra Bartolomeo, Lanfranco, Lorenzo Lotto, Pinturicchio, Raphael, Reni, Rubens, Titian, and Veronese—are represented.

Room IX is particularly thrilling, with Botticelli's richly colored "Madonna con Bambino S. Giovanino e Angeli" (ca 1488) and Raphael's "Ritratto di Giovane Donna con Unicorno" ("Young Woman with a Unicorn"), dated 1506, as well as his very well-known "Deposition" (1507) and many other treasures. In the next room **(X)** is Bronzino's intriguing "Young San Giovanni Battista" (1525). Note the ceiling. Its theme is Hercules but along with the mythological scenes is a sumptuous prune-colored geometric design. The gilded eagles and dragons are the two symbols of the Borghese family.

You might want to pay special attention to **Room XIV,** where there are several more works by Bernini, including two self-portraits, the busts of his patron, Scipione Borghese, and the majestic terra-cotta model of a statue of the Sun King, Louis XIV of France, which was never made. **Room XIX** contains Domenichino's famous painting of the "Cumana Sibyl," in all her turbaned glory, as well as his "Diana" (1616–1617). Federico Barocci's painting of "Aeneas Fleeing the Burning Troy" (1598) inspired Scipione Borghese to commission Bernini to produce the large marble group you saw on the ground floor **(Room VI).** The gloriously beautiful "Sacred and Profane Love" is among several Titians in **Room XX.** ∎

The heart of modern Rome, where massive monuments of yesterday brush against major modern political institutions

Pantheon to Piazza Venezia

Detail from the marble elephant in front of Santa Maria sopra Minerva

Pantheon to Piazza Venezia

The downtown area stretching from the Pantheon to Piazza Venezia is an unusual melange of ancient, medieval, and Renaissance history. Along the Via del Corso and on Piazza Venezia, major Italian banks and insurance companies are ensconced in magnificent stone palaces once owned by Roman princes and noblemen.

In Piazza Colonna, the Italian prime minister's office (the 16th-century Palazzo Chigi) looks out on the Marcus Aurelius column, which dates to A.D. 193. In nearby Palazzo del Montecitorio, the view from the Chamber of Deputies, with a facade by Bernini, includes one of the city's 13 Egyptian obelisks (see p. 86). And only in this neighborhood, can you sip a cappuccino against the thrilling backdrop of the Pantheon. Built, 1,900 years ago, this pagan temple subsequently became a church and is today a national monument and the burial place of kings, a queen, and several painters.

The rulers of Rome have always found it difficult to keep order in Piazza della Rotonda.

Recently repaved and today lined with cafés, it is now closed to traffic. But the trying task of keeping out the mopeds resembles the problems of the 19th century, when authorities tried desperately to close down the fish market and other food stands that continued to spring up. Ironically, at least in the view of many Romans, the plaque erected by Pope Pius VII, who tried to rid the area of what he called "disgraceful shops" and "things of unbelievable ugliness," adorns the wall of a building that houses one of the square's newest arrivals, a McDonald's.

Only a short distance away stands Santa Maria sopra Minerva. Steeped in history, the church belongs to the prestigious Dominican religious order, a major protagonist of both the Inquisition and the Counter-Reformation. The charming small stone elephant in the piazza, designed (but not sculpted) by Gian Lorenzo Bernini, symbolized intelligence. The overhead bridge spanning Via di Sant'Ignazio (behind the Minerva church) gave 16th-century Dominican prelates access to their Jesuit counterparts and to the Jesuit church of Sant'Ignazio.

Across the street from the Collegio Romano—once a Jesuit college—is Palazzo Doria Pamphili. That noble Roman family, which boasts both popes and princes among its ancestors, has now turned its imposing block-wide palace, with its magnificent private art collection, into a very modern museum. A short distance away at the Jesuit mother church, Il Gesù, baroque opulence has been unstintingly employed to the glory of God.

The Via del Corso terminates at Piazza Venezia which, since several major streets converge there, today seems less a city square

NOT TO BE MISSED:

Sublime classical architecture—the Pantheon   128–131

The best cappuccinos in town at Tazza D'Oro   133

A coffee and a cold treat of gelato from Giolitti   133

A Gothic *rarità* in Rome, Santa Maria sopra Minerva   134–135

The 360-degree panoramic view of Rome from the Victor Emanuel II monument   138

One of the largest private painting collections in the world, Palazzo Doria Pamphili   139–140

The over-the-top baroque interior of Il Gesù   140–141

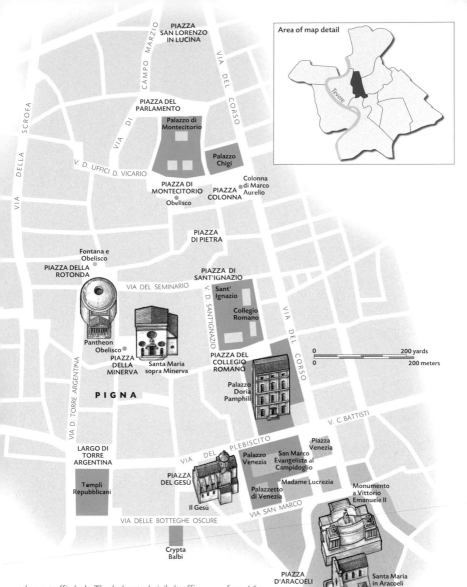

PIAZZA
SAN LORENZO
IN LUCINA

CAMPO MARZIO

VIA DEL CORSO

VIA DELLA SCROFA

VIA DI

PIAZZA DEL
PARLAMENTO

Palazzo di
Montecitorio

V. D. UFFICI D. VICARIO

Palazzo
Chigi

Colonna
di Marco
Aurelio

PIAZZA DI
MONTECITORIO

PIAZZA
COLONNA

Obelisco

PIAZZA
DI PIETRA

Fontana e
Obelisco

PIAZZA DELLA
ROTONDA

VIA DEL SEMINARIO

PIAZZA DI
SANT'IGNAZIO

Sant'
Ignazio

V. D. SANTIGNAZIO

Collegio
Romano

VIA DEL CORSO

Pantheon

Obelisco

PIAZZA
DELLA
MINERVA

Santa Maria
sopra Minerva

PIAZZA DEL
COLLEGIO
ROMANO

Palazzo
Doria
Pamphili

VIA D. TORRE ARGENTINA

PIGNA

0   200 yards
0   200 meters

V. C. BATTISTI

LARGO DI
TORRE
ARGENTINA

VIA   DEL   PLEBISCITO

Palazzo
Venezia

San Marco
Evangelista al
Campidoglio

Piazza
Venezia

Templi
Repubblicani

PIAZZA
DEL GESÙ

Il Gesù

Palazzetto
di Venezia

Madame Lucrezia

Monumento
a Vittorio
Emanuele II

VIA SAN MARCO

VIA DELLE BOTTEGHE OSCURE

Crypta
Balbi

PIAZZA
D'ARACOELI

Santa Maria
in Aracoeli

than a traffic hub. The helmeted *vigile* (traffic policeman) on his podium in the center of the intersection, is a fixture of the piazza and has appeared in countless films and advertisements.

From an architectural standpoint Palazzo Venezia marks the beginning of modern Rome, where medieval and Renaissance styles meld to form something entirely new. But it was the construction of the monument to Victor Emanuel II, at the end of the 19th century, that totally changed the look of the square. In order to create a clear view of the monument

from Via del Corso, the Palazzetto di Venezia, with its lovely courtyard and garden, was dismantled brick by brick and rebuilt around the corner in nearby Piazza San Marco. The Basilica of San Marco was founded in the fourth century to honor St. Mark, who some say wrote his gospel in a nearby oratory. Right outside is one of Rome's famous talking statues, the bosomy Madama Lucrezia. ■

Pantheon

Originally a pagan temple and later a Christian church, the Pantheon is a perfect example of classical architectural harmony. Gracefully combining a variety of shapes and forms, this circular building, or rotunda, features a massive dome—an architectural and engineering feat so important that it became a prototype in much of the world.

The Pantheon's large oculus lets in rain as well as light. There are drainage holes below, in the center of the pavement.

Wider than that of St. Peter's, the **cupola,** which was cast by pouring concrete over a temporary wooden frame, has a diameter of 142 feet (43 m). At the base, the dome measures almost 20 feet (6 m), but the thickness gradually diminishes with height, as do the widths of the five rows of coffers lining it. The architectonic function of these was to reduce the weight of the vault, but they also create an optical effect that draws attention toward the center.

The opening or "eye" in the ceiling is 30 feet (9 m) in diameter. Apart from any allusion to an eye looking at the cosmos, the *oculus*, as it is called in Latin, is the only source of light and air in the building, the walls of which are too thick (about 20 feet/6 m) to have made windows an option.

Built between A.D. 118 and 125 by the philosopher-emperor Hadrian to replace an earlier edifice, the Pantheon—it is important to remember—was also used as an astronomical instrument. The ancients gave great significance to the two equinoxes (March 21 and September 22), the dates when day and night are of equal length, and to the summer and winter solstices (June 21 and December 21 or 22), all of which had a particular significance for agriculture

INSIDER TIP:

If it's raining, head for the Pantheon. The sight of rain pouring through the oculus, the hole in the vast dome, is one of Rome's most remarkable.

—TIM JEPSON
National Geographic author

and for checking the accuracy of the calendar. It also had ceremonial possibilities. If every June 21 at noon the beam of light streaming through the oculus hit the floor right in front of the main door, it'd be a good time, wouldn't you think, for an appearance-conscious emperor in full regalia to make a sun-kissed entrance?

The Building's Exterior

The outside **portico**, once preceded by a short staircase, consists of 16 columns of red or gray granite, each 41 feet (12 m) tall and 15 feet (4 m) in circumference and only three of which (on the left side) are replacements. The inscription running below the pediment, *"M. Agrippa F.L.Cos. Tertium Fecit"* ("Marcus Agrippa, son of Lucius, in his third consulate, built this"), refers to the earlier structure erected in 27 B.C. by Agrippa to honor his friend and father-in-law, the Emperor Augustus. The bronze letters are new—19th-century fittings made for the original letter holes.

Other changes have been made to the Pantheon throughout the centuries. During his visit to Rome in 663, the Byzantine emperor, Constans II, plundered the gilded bronze sheeting that originally covered the dome; it was replaced with lead in the 8th century. The central bell tower added in the Middle Ages was replaced in the 17th century by twin turrets. Nicknamed "the donkey's ears," they were removed in 1883. The enormous **bronze doors** are ancient but may in fact have been taken from another structure.

Pantheon

 Map p. 127

✉ Piazza della Rotonda 12

☎ 06 6830 0230

🕐 Open daily

🚌 Bus: C3, 40, 46, 62, 63, 64, 70, 81, 87, 116, 119, 492, 628. Tram: 8

From Paganism to Christianity

As early as the sixth century, pagan structures in Rome were converted into Christian places of worship. However, the original buildings had all been constructed for secular, not religious, purposes. Take, for example, Santi Cosma and Damiano in the Roman Forum, and Santa Maria in Cosmedin near the Forum Boarium (see pp. 202–203).

Furthermore, many of the early Christian churches, such as San Giovanni in Laterano, Santa Croce, and indeed St. Peter's, were built on what were then the outskirts of the city. This made things easier for incoming pilgrims and also avoided offending Rome's pagan population. After all, the spread of Christianity did not take place overnight nor without considerable conflict and resistance.

In the seventh century, the Pantheon became the first pagan temple in Rome to be converted into a church. It was also the first temple-to-church conversion to take place at the very center of the city, a development of great consequence that demonstrated to everyone that Christianity had by then become the most important religion in Rome.

In the mid-1600s, Pope Urban VIII of the Barberini family ordered that the bronze covering of the portico beams be stripped away to make the cannon for Castel Sant'Angelo. For this act of vandalism came the famous Latin quip, *"quod non fecerunt barberi, fecerunt Barberini"* ("what the barbarians did not do, the Barberini did").

The Interior

The Pantheon is the best preserved ancient monument in Rome, largely thanks to its conversion to a Christian church after the Byzantine emperor Phocas gave the building to Pope Boniface IV in 608 or 609. And its interior is awe inspiring.

Unlike other pagan temples, the Pantheon's cavernous **central body** or *cella* was accessible to ordinary worshippers and not reserved for priests or notables alone. It is divided into three distinct segments. The lower part has six niches (not including the apse), which originally contained statues of the principal gods.

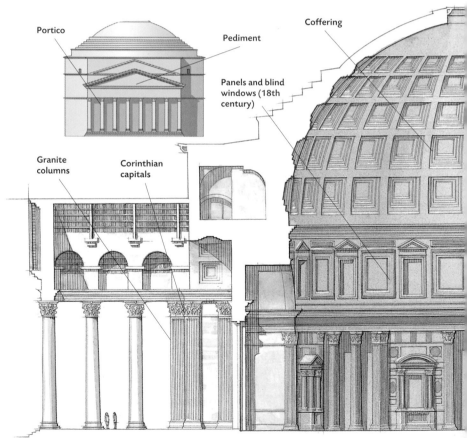

Portico
Pediment
Coffering
Panels and blind windows (18th century)
Granite columns
Corinthian capitals

Interior

In between are eight *aediculae* (shrines) flanked by marble columns. The floor, restored in 1872, repeats the colored, geometric patterns of antiquity. Except for a small area, the original marble decoration of the *attic,* the segment that runs around the base of the dome, no longer exists.

The current decor, begun in the 15th century but added to over the following 400 years, contains few major artworks. One exception is Lorenzetto's "Madon-na del Sasso" ("Madonna of the Stone"), which stands on the altar in the third aedicula to the left, above the **tomb of the painter, Raphael,** who died in 1520.

Two Italian kings and a queen are also buried here, as well as several other painters. This is not surprising since for centuries the Pantheon has been associated with the arts, and one of the most famous artists' groups in Rome, the Accademia dei Virtuosi, had its headquarters here.

The **fountain** outside, built in 1578, was designed by Giacomo della Porta. The Egyptian **obelisk** was placed on the fountain trough in 1711 by Pope Clement XI. ■

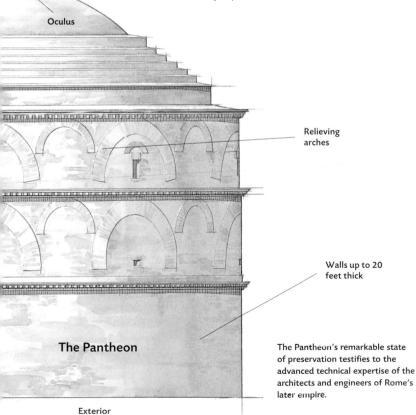

Oculus

Relieving arches

Walls up to 20 feet thick

The Pantheon

The Pantheon's remarkable state of preservation testifies to the advanced technical expertise of the architects and engineers of Rome's later empire.

Exterior

Coffee & Cafés

Coffee has been known to Italy since the 16th century, when a Venetian botanist brought some back from Egypt, and today it comes close to being a national obsession. To help you understand your many options, a primer might be in order.

A café does brisk business in the shadow of the Pantheon.

Unless you want a glass of milk, don't ask for a *"latte."* What you want is properly known here as a *caffèlatte,* a breakfast drink of warm milk with a small amount of coffee added. It is normally imbibed at home, especially by children, but can be drunk at the corner bar, where the custom is to take one's pleasure at the counter (although in most places at least some tables are generally available).

The most popular form of coffee outside the home is espresso. But wait! That would be too simple. Everyone crowding the counter seems to have his or her own special request.

Un caffè macchiato is an espresso with a few drops of warm milk (for cold milk you say *"un caffè macchiato freddo"*). Some prefer a somewhat weaker, more abundant *caffè lungo.* A really strong espresso is, instead, *un caffè ristretto.* And then there are those who don't like cups and want their coffee in a small glass *(un caffè al vetro).* A decaffeinated espresso is *un caffè Hag* or *un decaffeinato,* while the worker in overalls who's been toiling since 7 a.m. wants *un caffè corretto,* an espresso spiked with something alcoholic—grappa, brandy, or anisette.

Then, of course, there is the legion of cappuccino drinkers. Cappuccino, made with less

milk than a caffèlatte, is also generally a morning drink (and something an Italian would never even remotely consider drinking after a meal!). But here, too, there are variations. It can be ordered *senza schiuma* (without foam), *chiaro* (light), or *scuro* (dark). A *caffè americano* comes in a larger cup and is probably Nescafé, whereas a *caffè d'orzo* is made from barley.

Now that you know what to ask for, the next step is to get out and try a few cups.

The cafés in Rome are an integral part of everyday life.

EXPERIENCE: Finding Your Perfect Cup

The **Tazza d'Oro** on the corner of the Piazza della Rotonda sells excellent fresh-ground for home use in a mocha or Neapolitan coffeepot. Also in the piazza, a couple of blocks away, **Bar S. Eustacchio** uses a closely guarded procedure to make its particularly strong ristretto brew.

Ambience counts, too, and Rome boasts a selection of cafés where the city's denizens go to chat and people-watch, another national sport. Along with the cafés at Piazza della Rotonda, two others in this area offer ample indoor seating: **Giolitti** *(Via degli Uffici del Vicario 40)*, also known for its gelato, and **La Caffetteria** at Piazza di Pietra.

For decades, the best-known café in Rome was the **Caffè del Greco** on the fashionable Via dei Condotti, almost facing the Spanish Steps. This was the place where writers and artists gathered to discuss cultural trends and to gossip, and it is still a charming place (indoors only, however) for a rendezvous. But many prefer **Rosati** and **Canova** with their outdoor tables on opposite sides of the now car-free Piazza del Popolo.

Cafés now line Piazza Navona, but the Antico Caffè della Pace, located a block away on Via della Pace, has much more atmosphere. **Ciampini** on the repaved piazza in Lucina (off the Corso) is an in place. And if you happen to be on Trinità dei Monti, above the Spanish Steps, try Ciampini's outdoor café, immersed in greenery and overlooking the rooftops of Piazza di Spagna.

The weather-proofed sidewalk cafés that line the Via Veneto are pricey but make a nice change. If you're over on the Trastevere side of the river, **De Marzio** on Piazza Santa Maria di Trastevere, facing the facade of the basilica, isn't fancy but it's where most residents of Rome's "Greenwich Village" gather on weekend mornings. Other popular cafés in the area are **Ombre Rosse** at Piazza S. Egidio and **Friends** at Piazza Trilussa.

Santa Maria sopra Minerva

This lovely church, with its three aisles and vaulted ceilings, is said to be the one true Gothic church in Rome, although the facade is early Renaissance and the interior, complete with rose windows, has been changed all too often. The structure dates to the 13th century, when two monks began its construction as the religious center of the Dominican order.

The assumption of Mary into heaven was a major theme of the Renaissance.

This being Rome, however, the monks did not have to break new ground. An earlier church had already been erected on this site in the eighth century amid the remains of a pagan temple perhaps dedicated to the Roman goddess of war, Minerva. Note the wall plaques on the right side of the facade, which show the waterline from the frequent floods that inundated the area until the 19th-century Tiber embankments were built.

Because of the power and influence of the Dominicans—the order that would later spearhead the Inquisition and, together with the Jesuits, act as standard-bearers to the popes during the Counter-Reformation—Santa Maria sopra Minerva became a very prestigious church. Four popes are buried here, as are the Tuscan painter Fra Angelico, and St. Catherine of Siena, one of Italy's two patron saints (the other is St. Francis).

The Carafa Chapel

Many noble Roman families hired the most famous artists and architects to decorate their chapel inside the church. The Carafa family chapel at the end of the right transept boasts a splendid "Assumption" and an "Annunciation," as well as a cycle of glorious **frescoes** by

Filippino Lippi illustrating the life of the Dominican saint, Thomas Aquinas.

In the "Triumph of St. Thomas" on the right wall, the two small boys represent the future Medici popes, Clement VII and Leo X, who are buried in the church. On the left wall is the tomb of Pope Paul IV, who bears the blame for shutting Rome's Jews into their 16th-century ghetto.

To the left of the chapel, note the cosmatesque funeral monument (see p. 208), a mosaic "Virgin and Child Enthroned," flanked by two saints on a gold background. To the left of the main altar stands Michelangelo's **"Christ Bearing the Cross."**

In the fifth chapel on the right see the interesting detail in Antoniazzo Romano's "Annunciation," with the Madonna handing money bags (for dowries) to three girls. The seventh has the marvelous Renaissance tomb by

Andrea Bregno. The sarcophagus under the main altar holds the remains of St. Catherine, who convinced the popes to return from exile in Avignon.

Behind the altar are the wall tombs of Clement VII and Leo X, created by Antonio Sangallo the Younger. On the left, in a poorly lit passageway near the rear door, is **Fra Angelico's** strikingly simple floor **tomb.**

The Sacristy & More

Ask to see the *sacristia* (sacristy), where two papal conclaves were held in the 15th century, and the room where Catherine died, now a chapel. In the 1566 *chiostro* (cloister), the vaulted ceiling of the fourth arch on the right side of the portico bears the headless images of four Inquisitors, who were themselves tried and executed.

In the piazza outside is the delightful **stone elephant** designed by Bernini in 1667. Pope Alexander VII composed the inscription, which speaks of the elephant's wisdom and intelligence. ∎

Santa Maria sopra Minerva

- Map p. 127
- Piazza della Minerva 42
- 06 679 3926
- Open daily
- Bus: C3, 40, 46, 62, 63, 64, 70, 81, 87, 116, 119, 492, 628. Tram: 8

Galileo's Trial

It was in the monastery adjoining Santa Maria sopra Minerva that Galileo Galilei (1564–1642) was tried for heresy in 1633 and forced to repudiate his belief that the Earth moved around the sun. Legend has it that as he was getting off his knees, he whispered under his breath "E pur si muove—But it does move."

A Walk Through the Heart of Rome

As it has throughout the centuries, this area—really the heart of contemporary Rome—includes some of Rome's major political institutions. The walk will take you from Piazza di Montecitorio to Piazza San Marco, enabling you to bear witness to the city's intricate mix of old and even older.

Start at Piazza di Montecitorio, where one of the Egyptian obelisks (see p. 86) that Augustus brought back to Rome stands in front of the massive Palazzo dei Montecitorio, now the Chamber of Deputies, the lower house of Parliament. From this piazza, where protesters sometimes gather, walk right toward the Piazza Colonna, named as you will immediately appreciate for the **Colonna di Marco Aurelio** ❶ (Marcus Aurelius' triumphal column), erected in A.D. 193 to celebrate that emperor's victory over the Marcomanni, one of the barbarian tribes that were beginning to threaten Rome. The column stands in front of **Palazzo Chigi** (built in the 16th and 17th centuries), today the prime minister's office and the seat of the Italian government. The column may seem out of place, but, as with the Pantheon, it reminds us that this area was also very important in Roman times.

Leaving Piazza Colonna by Via dei Bergamaschi, you'll see 11 massive Corinthian columns in **Piazza di Pietra** ❷, now paved and closed to traffic. Embedded in the wall of the **Borsa,** or Rome Stock Exchange, these columns were once part of a temple built in A.D. 145 in honor of Hadrian by his successor, Antoninus Pius.

Continue in the same direction along Via del Burro, and you're in for another treat. **Piazza di Sant'Ignazio** ❸ is a rococo jewel, constructed by an 18th-century architect to resemble a theatrical stage. View it from the central door of **S. Ignazio** (see p. 142), a major Jesuit church. Walk along the side of the church (on Via di Sant'Ignazio), noting the overhead arch that connected the Jesuits to their Coun-

NOT TO BE MISSED:

Column of Marcus Aurelius • Piazza di Pietra • Sant'Ignazio • Il Gesù

ter-Reformation allies, the Dominicans, masters of the Minerva church (see pp. 134–135) around the corner. Via di Sant'Ignazio ends at **Piazza del Collegio Romano** ❹, where you'll find the entrance to **Palazzo Doria Pamphili** and Galleria Doria Pamphili (see pp. 139–140).

Turn right on Via di Pie'di Marmo, being sure to note the huge marble foot (from which this street gets its name) at the intersection with Via Santo Stefano del Cacco. Like the obelisk on the elephant in front of the Minerva church, it probably came from a nearby Temple of Isis and Serapis. Facing it at No. 21 is a marvelous chocolate shop.

The next cross street, just before you get to the Minerva church, is Via del Gesù. Turn left, making sure you peek into the courtyards, most of which have fountains (observe the beautiful water clock at No. 62). At the intersection with Corso Vittorio Emanuele II, you'll see the Jesuit mother church, **Il Gesù** ❺ (see pp. 140–141).

Turn right and walk a block to **Largo di Torre Argentina** ❻, more commonly known as Largo Argentina, to see the remains of four Republican-era Roman temples **(Templi Repubblicani).** On the other side of the Largo, cross Via delle Botteghe Oscure (Street of the Dark Shops) and walk back along it in the direction from which you just came. At No. 31 you'll spot the entrance to the **Crypta Balbi,** the section of the Museo Nazionale Romano (see p. 31) dedicated to medieval Rome. It's built over the ruins of an imperial-era theater.

Farther on, turn right on Via dei Polacchi and walk to lovely **Piazza Margana ➐**. Turn left here and take Via Margana to Via d'Aracoeli. On the right stand Santa Maria d'Aracoeli and the Campidoglio.

Turn left and return to the Botteghe Oscure, which becomes Via di San Marco.

Cross and walk right along Via di San Marco to **Piazza di San Marco ➑**, where you'll see the basilica (see p. 142) and the "talking statue," Madama Lucrezia (see p. 147).

🅰 Also see area map, p. 127
▶ Piazza di Montecitorio
↔ 1.5 miles (2.4 km)
🕐 2 hours
▶ Piazza San Marco

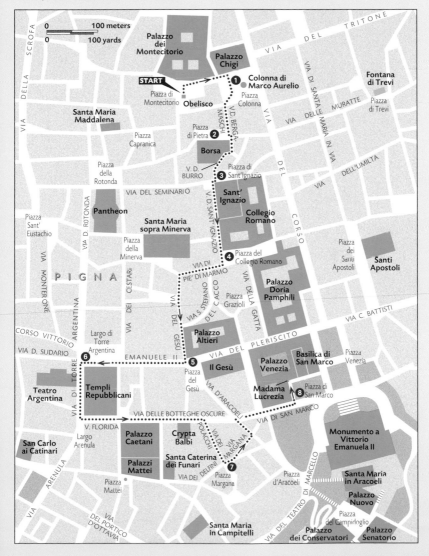

Piazza Venezia & Around

Begun in 1885 and inaugurated in 1911, the Vittoriano—the stark white marble monument to King Victor Emanuel II, the Savoy monarch associated with the Risorgimento and the first king of united Italy—dominates the piazza. Today it is home to Italy's Tomb of the Unknown Soldier and has acquired status as a patriotic symbol. Nearby are two important churches, Santa Maria d'Aracoeli and Il Gesù, and the impressive Palazzo Doria Pamphili.

The monument to Victor Emanuel II provides spectacular views of the city from the top terrace.

Piazza Venezia

🗺 Map p. 127

🚍 Bus: H, C3, 40, 46, 60, 62, 63, 64, 70, 81, 84, 85, 87, 95, 119, 170, 175, 628, 715, 716, 780

Vittoriano

✉ Piazza Venezia

☎ 06 699 1718

🕐 Open daily

Museo del Palazzo Venezia

✉ Via del Plebescito 118

☎ 06 32810

🕐 Closed Mon.

💲 $

The Vittoriano is also the site of the new Museo Centrale del Risorgimento as well as a venue, through an entrance on Via dei Fori Imperiali, for important exhibitions.

Built in the late 15th century by Venetian Cardinal Pietro Barbo (the future Pope Paul II), **Palazzo Venezia** was Rome's first important Renaissance palace, although by incorporating a pre-existing medieval tower and some battlements, it can be seen as a transition. The palace was built at a time of significant architectural change in Rome. Until the early 14th century, when the popes fled to Avignon in France, urban development was centered around the Lateran Palace, then the papal residence. On their return from

exile, the Lateran having fallen into disrepair, the popes moved to the Vatican, spurring growth in the area in between.

Over the centuries the palace has served as a papal residence, as the embassy of the Venetian Republic, and, from 1797 to 1916, as the residence of the Austrian ambassador to the Holy See. Under Fascism it was the headquarters of Benito Mussolini, whose major speeches were declaimed from its balcony. The building now houses the **Museo del Palazzo Venezia,** with a vast collection of artworks and objets d'art, which often hosts special exhibitions.

Santa Maria d'Aracoeli

Few other church in Rome better embodies the stratified

nature of Rome's architectural development, and this is not just because its 22 columns were recycled from some important Roman structures. Santa Maria d'Aracoeli (St. Mary of the Altar of Heaven) was built over the ruins of an ancient Roman temple to Juno.

The early Christian church marks the site where, in the first century B.C., Octavius, the future Emperor Augustus, is said to have experienced a vision foretelling the birth of Jesus. He built an altar here, and for this reason, in a break with tradition, he is depicted in the fresco on the arch of the apse—quite a place of honor for a ruler of Rome. Rebuilt in the 13th century by the Franciscans, the church has retained the rather austere Romanesque style of that era, intensified by the fact that the facade was never completed.

An Aura of Mystery: Inside, despite the chandeliers and considerable restoration, the church retains its aura of mystery. The cosmatesque pavement (see p. 208) is interspersed with floor tombs (Donatello created that of Archdeacon Crivelli). The ceiling decoration commemorates the

European naval victory at Lepanto in 1571.

Don't miss the **Bufalini chapel** (the first on the right) with Pinturicchio's magnificently colored rendition of scenes from the "Life of San Bernardino" (1485). Note how the Renaissance realism of this painting contrasts with the stylized Byzantine icon of the "Madonna" on the main altar. Other works are by Benozzo Gozzoli, Arnolfo di Cambio, Andrea Sansovino, and Pietro Cavallini.

Nearby is the chapel of the Santissimo Bambino (the Holy Infant). Romans were outraged when, in February 1994, thieves "abducted" its occupant, a gem-studded statue of an infant Jesus said to be carved out of olive wood from the garden of

The Climb Up

You'll surely notice the 132 wide steps that visitors need to climb to reach the entrance of Santa Maria d'Aracoeli. The painfully steep staircase—a reflection of the medieval view that salvation can only be obtained by sacrifice—was built in 1348, probably as a physical symbol of thanksgiving for the end of the Black Death.

Gethsemane and reputed to have miraculous healing powers. It was replaced by a copy.

Palazzo Doria Pamphili

This enormous block-long building, which today houses the Doria Pamphili Museum, dates

Santa Maria d'Aracoeli

- 🅼 Map p. 127
- ✉ Piazza del Campidoglio 4
- ☎ 06 679 8155
- 🕐 Closed 12:30–3 p.m. (summer) & 12:30– 2:30 p.m. (winter)
- 🚌 Bus: H, C3, 40, 46, 60, 62, 63, 64, 70, 81, 84, 85, 87, 95, 119, 170, 175, 628, 715, 716, 780

Palazzo Doria Pamphili

A Map p. 127

✉ Via del Corso 305

☎ 06 679 7323

⊕ Closed Thurs.

$ $$. Audio guide: $

🚌 Bus: 40, 46, 62, 63, 64, 70, 81, 85, 87, 95, 119, 175, 492, 628

www.doriapamphilj.it

Il Gesù

A Map p. 127

✉ Piazza del Gesù 1

☎ 06 697 001

⊕ Closed 12:45–4 p.m. St. Ignatius's rooms open 4–6 p.m. Mon.–Sat., & 10 a.m.–noon Sun.

🚌 Bus: 46, 62, 63, 64, 70, 81, 84, 87, 492, 628, 780

back to 1435, when it belonged to Cardinal Santorio, an obedient prelate who allowed himself to be "convinced" by Pope Julius II to cede the palazzo to the Duke of Urbino, who just happened to be the pontiff's nephew. The rococo facade on Via del Corso, considered notable, was added later.

The Pamphilis moved here in the 1700s, bringing with them the collection begun a century earlier by Donna (or Lady) Olimpia, when the family still lived at Piazza Navona. It is the largest and most important patrician collection still in private Roman hands, and the walls are really overcrowded. But as we are talking about works by the likes of Titian, Raphael, Velázquez, and Rubens, it's a minor annoyance. As there are no labels, use the free audio guide included in the entry price, or buy the museum catalog.

The Collection: The collection is spread through the first floor, the so-called *piano nobile* where the family lived, which runs around a vast courtyard that was once turned into a ballroom to honor a Hapsburg emperor!

The star attraction is probably the corner room (between corridors 1 and 2) in which the Velázquez portrait of Pope Innocent X (1644–1655) is displayed next to Bernini's bust of the same pontiff. Corridor 2 is a triumph of gold, crystal, and mirrors. Two Caravaggios (the "Maddalena" and the "Riposo Durante la Fuga in Egitto") are in Sala del 600, between corridors 2 and 3, and the third (a "San Giovanni Bat-

tista") is in corridor 4. There is fine statuary, Roman and otherwise, in the Sala Aldobrandini, where corridors 3 and 4 meet. And don't miss the wonderful bust of Lady Olimpia by Algardi in the corner. The private apartments, with their sumptuous decoration and artwork, are also open to the public.

INSIDER TIP:

The Doria Pamphili museum is a beautiful and often overlooked collection that the Pamphili family still owns. The current Doria Pamphili prince narrates the free audio guide.

—SARAH YEOMANS
Archaeologist & National Geographic contributor

Il Gesù

The mother church of the Jesuit order, this is a pre-baroque structure that, in ecclesiastical terms, fully embodies the Counter-Reformation spirit. Begun by St. Ignatius Loyola (1491–1556) to complement the new Jesuit headquarters at Collegio Romano, it was consecrated in 1584, although the decoration of the interior continued, to be completed in the 19th century.

The Opulent Interior: This church, like many, is built in the form of a Latin cross, meaning

The family still lives in the private apartments of the Doria Pamphili.

that there is a long central nave, making one of the four arms that radiate from the center under the dome longer than all the others. The decoration is extremely opulent. These things were done deliberately. To counter the influence of Protestantism (which stressed simplicity and personal responsibility), the Jesuits sought to emphasize the importance of the Church and the clergy.

The chapel on the right, by Pietro da Cortona, is dedicated to St. Francis Xavier; the relic case is said to contain the saint's arm. The chapel on the left belongs to St. Ignatius, whose remains are buried here. The silver statue of the saint is attributed to the sculptor Canova. It replaced a more valuable effigy, melted down by Pope Pius VI to pay a tribute to Napoleon. The ceiling fresco and the cupola, decorated with prophets, Evangelists, and Doctors of the Church, are from the end of the 17th century. The ornate bronze banister in front of the chapel is decorated with cherubs and with candelabra set on elaborate marble bases. Note the cherub at the top holding up a lapis lazuli globe.

Next door at Piazza del Gesù 45 are the **rooms where St. Ignatius lived.** There are paintings in a magnificent trompe l'oeil style by Padre Andrea Pozzo; some memorabilia are also displayed. ∎

Designed for Effect

Il Gesù's long nave made processions more dramatic, while darkness encouraged the faithful to focus on the priest, who stood on a raised main altar. The ample use of marble, gilded bronze, lapis lazuli, and silver in the decoration of the chapels, especially the two at the opposite ends of the main transept, was another way to stress the magnificence of God.

More Places to Visit

Piazza di Sant'Ignazio

Designed by architect Filippo Raguzzini, this piazza (1727–1728) resembles a theatrical stage set, especially when viewed from the central door of the church of **Sant'Ignazio** (tel 06 679 4560, closed 12:15–3:15 p.m.). Historically the official place of worship for the nearby Jesuit Collegio Romano, the church, completed in 1650, was built to celebrate St. Ignatius Loyola, the founder of the Jesuit order. Funds ran out before the cupola could be built, so ingenious artists painted a 56-foot-wide (17 m) circular trompe l'oeil canvas that simulates the interior of a dome. The best view is from the yellow marble disk set in the floor of the central nave.

Built in the form of a Latin cross, the church is heavily and ornately decorated with an abundance of stucco, gilt, and colored marbles. The most notable artwork is Padre Andrea Pozzo's ceiling fresco depicting "St. Ignatius' Entrance into Paradise" and, along the sides, his frescoes commemorating the order's missionary activities around the world. Note the four large female figures representing the continents on which the Jesuits were active. Guess which one is meant to personify the Americas.
🄼 Map p. 127   🚌 Bus: C3, 62, 63, 81, 85, 95, 116, 119, 175, 492, 628.

San Marco Evangelista al Campidoglio

One of Rome's 25 titular churches (nonparish churches founded in early Christian times), the basilica of San Marco was established by Pope St. Mark in A.D. 336 and dedicated to his namesake, St. Mark the Evangelist. It has been rebuilt and restored several times since. The apse mosaic, which dates from the ninth century, shows Jesus flanked by saints, his arm lifted in a blessing. Note that his fingers are positioned in the Greek style, with the index and middle fingers raised while the thumb is crossed over. This is said to mimic the first letters, in Greek, of "Jesus Christ," while the Western blessing style—the thumb plus the first two fingers—signifies the Trinity. Pope Gregory IV, on the far left, holds a model of the church.

A fine example of Renaissance church architecture, the facade, and its two-story portico, may be the work of Leon Battista Alberti. From the Palazzo Venezia (see p. 138) next door you can get a good look at the courtyard with its charming 18th-century fountain and its beautiful, if incomplete, two-story Renaissance loggia.
🄼 Map p. 127   ✉ Piazza San Marco 48
📞 06 679 5205   🕐 Closed noon–4 p.m.
🚌 Bus: H, C3, 40, 46, 60, 62, 63, 64, 70, 81, 84, 85, 87, 95, 119, 170, 175, 628, 716, 780. ■

Family & Papal Heraldic Crests

Bears, bulls, castles, bees, fleurs-de-lis, doves, and dragons are everywhere in Rome, gracing facades, fountains, occasionally a pavement, and often a ceiling (especially in churches). In case you've wondered about these ubiquitous symbols, they are the heraldic crests of Rome's noble families. These coats of arms may be carved in marble or wood, molded in bronze and in one case (in the Aracoeli Church) represented in stained glass. If the symbol is topped by a papal tiara (a large

beehive-shaped crown) and two criss-crossed keys, then there is a pope somewhere on the family tree. (A broad brimmed hat with tassels means a cardinal.) As the city's rulers over centuries, the pontiffs left more traces than most. Some, like Urban VIII Barberini (a baroque-era Donald Trump?), went on real building binges; in fact, the Barberini bees are probably more frequent than the Chigi star, the Farnese fleurs-de-lis, the Pamphili dove, or the Borghese dragon and eagle.

A buried Imperial stadium, Renaissance palaces, baroque
churches, medieval arches and passageways, and other intriguing
traces of the past

Campo Marzio

A cupid from the fountain
in Piazza Navona

Campo Marzio

Once separated from the Roman Forum by a land ridge, the Campo Marzio or Campus Martius (Field of Mars) was a broad expanse of land that stretched from the Quirinal Hill to the Tiber River. From about the fourth century B.C. on, the Romans used it first for military exercises and later for games and athletic competitions.

At first, Campo Marzio included most of what is today downtown Rome, with numerous porticoes built among the trees for the citizens' enjoyment and relaxation. Subsequently it shrank in size and came to be identified primarily with the area tucked into the curve of the Tiber that faces Castel Sant'Angelo and St. Peter's, enclosing more or less everything from Via del Corso to the river. Only in 1377, when the popes returned from Avignon and took up residence across the river in the Vatican, did this area become a focus for residential construction.

In fact, this is one of the oldest parts of modern Rome, and in vast areas much has remained more or less as it was before broad avenues like Corso Vittorio Emanuele II had even been imagined. Then, as now, there was a warren of narrow streets interrupted only by spacious squares such as Piazza Navona with its magnificent baroque fountains, Campo dei Fiori (a food and flower market), and Piazza Farnese, a study in Renaissance elegance.

You will find traces of the past everywhere in Campo Marzio. Beneath Piazza Navona lie the remains of Emperor Domitian's stadium, parts of which are visible several yards below modern ground level. To see them exit the square at its north end and turn left at the end of Via Agonale. Buildings here bear flood marks from the pre-embankment days, while medieval arches and passageways evoke images of tradesmen in leather jerkins and soldiers in suits of clanking armor.

It is also in this neighborhood that the Renaissance and baroque best meet. Renaissance palaces such as Palazzo Altemps and the Cancelleria alternate with baroque baronies and churches such as Palazzo Pamphili, Sant'Agnese in Agone, or Sant'Andrea della Valle.

Elegant high-rent streets such as Via Giulia, Via di Monserrato, and Via dei Coronari—with their churches, art galleries, and exquisite antiques shops—give way to humbler crossways. On Via dei Giubbonari and the streets that surround Teatro di Pompeo or, in the other direction, on Via del Governo Vecchio, you will find countless small *botteghe* (shops of craftsmen and artisans), the direct descendants of the guilds of an earlier era that more often than not gave their names to the streets of today. ∎

NOT TO BE MISSED:

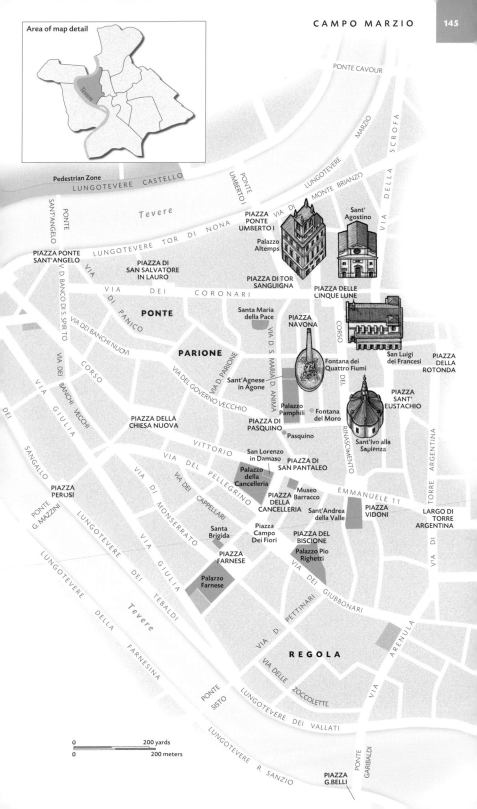

Area of map detail

Tevere

Pedestrian Zone

PONTE CAVOUR

LUNGOTEVERE CASTELLO

PONTE UMBERTO I

LUNGOTEVERE MONTE BRIANZO

VIA DELLA SCROFA

MARZIO

VIA DI MONTE BRIANZO

Tevere

SANT'ANGELO

PONTE

PIAZZA PONTE
SANT'ANGELO

LUNGOTEVERE TOR DI NONA

V. D. BANCO DI S. SPIRITO

VIA DEI BANCHI NUOVI

VIA DI PANICO

PIAZZA DI
SAN SALVATORE
IN LAURO

PIAZZA
PONTE
UMBERTO I

VIA DI

Palazzo
Altemps

Sant'
Agostino

VIA

PIAZZA DI TOR
SANGUIGNA

PIAZZA DELLE
CINQUE LUNE

VIA DEI CORONARI

PONTE

PARIONE

Santa Maria
della Pace

PIAZZA
NAVONA

CORSO DEL RINASCIMENTO

San Luigi
dei Francesi

PIAZZA
DELLA
ROTONDA

VIA D. S. MARIA D. ANIMA

Fontana dei
Quattro Fiumi

VIA DEL GOVERNO VECCHIO

VIA D. PARIONE

Sant'Agnese
in Agone

Palazzo
Pamphili

Fontana
del Moro

PIAZZA
SANT'
EUSTACHIO

CORSO

VIA DEI BANCHI VECCHI

VITTORIO

PIAZZA DI
PASQUINO

Pasquino

Sant'Ivo alla
Sapienza

VIA GIULIA

DEI

SANGALLO

PONTE
G. MAZZINI

PIAZZA
PEROSI

PIAZZA DELLA
CHIESA NUOVA

VIA DEL PELLEGRINO

San Lorenzo
in Damaso

Palazzo
della
Cancelleria

PIAZZA DI
SAN PANTALEO

VIA DI MONSERRATO

VIA DEI CAPPELLARI

VIA DEL PELLEGRINO

PIAZZA
DELLA
CANCELLERIA

Museo
Barracco

Sant'Andrea
della Valle

EMMANUELE II

PIAZZA
VIDONI

VIA DI TORRE ARGENTINA

LARGO DI
TORRE
ARGENTINA

Santa
Brigida

Piazza
Campo
Dei Fiori

PIAZZA DEL
BISCIONE

VIA ARENULA

LUNGOTEVERE DEI TEBALDI

VIA GIULIA

PIAZZA
FARNESE

Palazzo
Farnese

Palazzo Pio
Righetti

VIA DEI GIUBBONARI

Tevere

LUNGOTEVERE DELLA FARNESINA

VIA D. PETTINARI

REGOLA

PONTE
SISTO

VIA DELLE ZOCCOLETTE

LUNGOTEVERE DEI VALLATI

LUNGOTEVERE R. SANZIO

PONTE
GARIBALDI

PIAZZA
G.BELLI

0   200 yards
0   200 meters

Piazza Navona

One of the world's most beautiful squares, Piazza Navona gives the visitor an opportunity to grasp the complexity of 2,000 years of Roman history. A spectacular baroque composition, the piazza lies within the contours of an ancient Roman stadium. Today it plays host to those who flock here for a moment of relaxation—a chat, an *aperitivo*, a meal—against a backdrop of magnificent man-made beauty.

Giacomo della Porta's Fountain of the Moor

Piazza Navona

🗺 Map pp. 144–145

🚌 Bus: C3, 46, 62, 64, 70, 81, 87, 116, 280, 492, 628

In A.D. 86, the Emperor Domitian constructed a stadium, the Circus Agonalis, on this site. But urban development did not begin in earnest in this area until 1377, when the popes returned from Avignon and chose the Vatican as their new residence.

In 1477, Pope Sixtus IV moved the city's central market here from its historic location at the Capitol (Campidoglio). It remained here for 390 years and survives today in the traditional Christmas stalls set up by merchants every December to sell toys and decorations.

The modern Piazza Navona dates from the 1640s, when Pope Innocent X, a Pamphili, chose the square as the site of the new family residence. His plan included

INSIDER TIP:

The Piazza Navona is best experienced at dawn, before the crowds descend upon the place.

—SHEILA BUCKMASTER
National Geographic Traveler editor

elaborate fountains and a church. The Palazzo Pamphili, completed in 1650, and Sant'Agnese in Agone, completed more than a decade later, are the work of Francesco Borromini, Girolomo Rainaldi, and Rainaldi's son Carlo.

Palazzo Pamphili & Sant'Agnese in Agone

Now an embassy, Palazzo Pamphili boasts a series of **frescoes** by Pietro da Cortona that depict the story of Aeneas. **Sant'Agnese in Agone** was built over the spot where 13-year-old Agnes, a fourth-century Christian maiden who rejected the advances of a Roman official's son, was reportedly stripped naked in public. According to the story, the girl's hair grew so long and so fast that it quickly covered her body. Agnes was martyred all the same, beheaded in A.D. 304 during Emperor Diocletian's anti-Christian persecutions. The church's facade was designed by the temperamental Borromini, who worked on it until falling out with the family in 1657.

Fountains

The piazza's magnificent baroque fountains (see pp. 98–99) conceal yet another chapter in the legendary rivalry between Bernini and Borromini. Borromini lost his commission for the central Fountain of the Four Rivers (**Fontana dei Quattro Fiumi**) because of the savvier, more diplomatic Bernini's successful flattery of Donna Olimpia, the pope's sister-in-law. Although just a legend, the story goes that Bernini gave one of the fountain's statues a raised arm to ward off the imminent collapse of Sant'Agnese; Borromini's statue of the saint on the church, her hand on her heart, replies, "I will not fall." However, the fountain was completed in 1651, years before Borromini's facade.

The Fountain of the Moor (**Fontana del Moro**) is by Giacomo della Porta, but Bernini designed the central figure. ∎

Pasquino, the Talking Statue

In the 16th century, a Church official erected an ancient Roman statue near Piazza Navona in what is today known as the Piazza Pasquino. Hoping to incite the populace against the popes, dissidents and those opposed to the clerics began affixing radical messages to the torso of the statue, which was soon named Pasquino in honor of an outspoken neighborhood tailor. Later, several other "talking" statues popped up around Rome, including Marforio, the river god, now in the Capitoline Museum; the Facchino (the porter), on Via Lata off the Corso; Abbot Luigi, on Piazza Vidoni near Corso Vittorio Emanuele II; and buxom Madama Lucrezia, who today stands outside the Palazzetto di Venezia.

Palazzo Altemps

After a long period of decline and abandon, Palazzo Altemps—once the residence of 16th- and 17th-century noblemen and cardinals—has been superbly restored by the Italian government. Part of the Museo Nazionale Romano complex, it contains many priceless pieces of classical statuary, although the building's structure and decor compete for the visitor's attention.

The elegant central courtyard designed by Martino Longhi the Elder

Palazzo Altemps belonged to Cardinal Marco Sittico Altemps, who bought the building in 1568. In it he housed his magnificent collection of books and ancient sculptures. Today most of the original pieces are scattered among the world's major museums, although some of them have now been returned. The family sold the palace to the Holy See, which turned it into a seminary. In a dismal state, it was purchased by the Italian government in 1982 and transformed into a museum.

The Collection

The museum's inventory includes artworks from several major Roman art collections, in particular the Boncompagni Ludovisi collection that for years was accessible only to scholars. Now, world-famous pieces such as the magnificent **Ludovisi throne** depicting the birth of Aphrodite, the breathtaking **Grande Ludovisi Sarcophagus** with its violent battles between Roman and barbarian soldiers, the tragically moving "Gaul Committing Suicide," and the inspiring, noble "Ares" are all displayed here. The Painted Loggia on the first floor (one flight up) is now the setting for the Ludovisi **busts of the Caesars.**

In the 16th and 17th centuries, restoring sculpture meant

reconstructing the missing parts. The Altemps Museum is one of a very few that explains this. Panels near the statues use shading to indicate the parts that were added. There are also ample explanations in English.

Church of Sant'Aniceto

Inaugurated in 1617, this beautiful but tiny church may have been the only private church to house the remains of a saint. Anicetus was one of Rome's early popes and martyrs. The frescoes tell the story of his death by decapitation. In reality, however, the story of Anicetus was altered to resemble that of Roberto Altemps, who was sentenced to death by decapitation (for adultery) by Pope Sixtus V. Richly decorated in high baroque style, the church features striking examples of marble and mother-of-pearl inlay.

The Palazzo as Art

The palace's original **wall** and **ceiling decorations** have been restored so that the decor of this patrician palace embodies the gradual transition from Renaissance to baroque. The breathtaking **courtyard** features a nymphaeum: a curved wall-fountain decorated with mosaic, paste shells, and colored gravel of the type found in ancient Roman villas. Four of the statues in the courtyard come from the original Altemps collection.

And don't miss the Fireplace Room, with Cardinal Altemps's monumental fireplace and the room of the Painted Landscapes. The wall fresco in the Cupboard Room, once the 15th-century reception room, displays wedding gifts and greeting cards received by Girolamo Riario and Caterina Sforza, the palace's first occupants. ■

Palazzo Altemps

- Map pp. 144–145
- Piazza Sant'Apollinare 44
- 060608 or 06 3997 7700
- Closed Mon.
- $$. Audio guide: $ Tours in Italian on Sun. Tours in English on request: $$$$$
- Bus: C3, 30, 70, 81, 87, 116, 280, 492, 628

www.pierreci.it

EXPERIENCE: Attend a Concert in a Roman Church

There is something special about listening to music in a church. The lights are dim, a slight perfume of candles floats through the air, statuary and frescoed ceilings complete the hushed, solemn atmosphere as the strains of sacred choral music filter through the air. Whether in St. Ignazio Loyala or the Basilica of S. Eustachio, San Lorenzo in Lucina or Santa Maria Maggiore, this is a lovely way to spend an afternoon or evening in Rome.

The **Associazione Internazionale Amici della Musica Sacra** (www.amicimusicasacra.com, tel 06 6880 5816) offers a regular program of free concerts featuring choirs and choral groups from all parts of the world. All you have to do is turn up. Every Friday through much of the year (summer months excluded) young musicians hold chamber music concerts in the Borromini sacristy of **Sant'Agnese in Agone** church (see p. 147) in Piazza Navona (tickets €12 at the entrance or around the back at Santa Maria dell'Anima 30, or at www.classictic.com).

Other chamber music concerts organized by the Coro Polifonico Romano are held at the mannerist-frescoed **Oratorio del Gonfalone** (Via del Gonfalone 32a, tel/fax 06 687 5952, Mon.–Fri. 9:30 a.m.–5:00 p.m.). The **Festival Internazionale di Musica e Arte Sacra** (www.festivalmusicaeartesacra.net) takes place annually in the fall in some of the city's most famous and prestigious basilicas, including St. John's and even St. Peter's itself.

Four Campo Marzio Churches

With works by some of the Italy's most famous artists, four standout churches in Campo Marzio are a treasure to visit. San Luigi dei Francesi displays Caravaggio paintings, Sant'Agostino contains a magnificent Raphael fresco, Sant'Ivo alla Sapienza is an architectural play of fantasy and mystery, and Sant'Andrea della Valle features artwork by rivals Lanfranco and Domenichino.

Sant'Agostino was favored by Renaissance courtesans.

San Luigi dei Francesi

Although the statuary dates to the 18th century, the church itself, bearing a Renaissance facade attributed to Giacomo della Porta, was completed in 1589. It is dedicated to Louis IX, the French king later made a saint; the stone dragons that adorn the first story bear the fleur-de-lis.

Inside you will find an overwhelming profusion of marble decoration and monuments. The Contarelli Chapel, has three Caravaggio paintings, all scenes from the life of St. Matthew and masterpieces of chiaroscuro and realism. The dramatic content of "Vocation of St. Matthew," in which Jesus points at Matthew, its use of indirect lighting, and the incredulous expression on the saint's face are enough to rank Caravaggio among the world's greatest artists. Look for Domenichino's "Scenes from the Life of St. Cecilia" in the second chapel on the right.

Sant'Agostino

To reach Sant'Agostino, cross Piazza della Cinque Lune from San Luigi to a wide flight of stairs and an imposing Renaissance facade—possibly one of the earliest in Rome. Completed in 1483, although the main altar was refashioned in the 1600s, this church features Raphael's magnificent fresco of the "Prophet Isaiah." It decorates the third pilaster on the left, against which stands a lovely sculpture group, "St. Anne, the Virgin and Child" (1512), by Andrea Sansovino.

The first chapel on the left houses Caravaggio's remarkable "Madonna dei Pellegrini" (1605), highly controversial at the time because of its realistic depiction of its pilgrims as old and poor. To the right of the main portal stands Jacopo Sansovino's

"Madonna del Parto" (parto means "childbirth"), with unusual Junoesque proportions.

Sant'Ivo alla Sapienza

Named for the patron saint of lawyers, this church is located down Corso del Rinascimento and inside the Palazzo della Sapienza (sapienza means "knowledge" in Latin), today the National Archives. Until it moved, in 1935, this was the site of Rome's La Sapienza University, founded by Boniface VIII in 1303.

A number of popes commissioned a variety of artists to work on the structure, as you can see from the papal insignias in the courtyard—eagles and dragons for the Borghese family, bees for the Barberini. Designed by the temperamental Francesco Borromini, the 17th-century church mixes fantasy and mystery with Gothic overtones. Giacomo della Porta designed the courtyard and facade, of which the lower portion is concave. The convex curves of the cupola culminate in a spiral pinnacle. The all-white interior again alternates convex and concave forms.

Outside, around the corner to the right, look on the small **fountain** for the symbol of Sant'Eustacchio or Eustace: books, a cross, and the head of a deer. A Roman soldier who converted to Christianity after seeing a cross between the horns of a deer, Eustace was martyred and now gives his name to this neighborhood.

Sant'Andrea della Valle

Sant'Andrea della Valle stands farther down Corso del Rinascimento in Piazza Vidoni. Similar in style to Il Gesù (see p. 140), Sant'Andrea was designed by Giacomo della Porta, although the facade and the dome—the largest in Rome aside from St. Peter's—are fundamentally the work of Carlo Maderno.

INSIDER TIP:

Opera buffs should not miss a visit to Sant'Andrea della Valle, Piazza Farnese, or Castel Sant'Angelo, three locations used by Puccini in Tosca.

—DENNIS CIGLER
*Tour coordinator & guide,
In Italy's Companions*

According to one story, there were supposed to be two angels, not just one, on the top of the facade, but the sculptor, irritated by criticism, told his episcopal patron to "do it himself."

Inside, Lanfranco created the magnificent dome fresco, the "Glory of Paradise"; his archrival Domenichino painted the pendentives. Domenichino also painted scenes from the Life of St. Andrew in the upper portion of the apse, where two popes are buried. The lovely Strozzi chapel is in the Michelangelo style. The Barberini chapel, the first on the left, corresponds to the chapel Puccini chose as the setting for the first act of *Tosca*. Here Tosca accused her lover of betrayal when she noticed that the Mary Magdalen he was painting resembled another woman. ■

San Luigi dei Francesi

🅜 Map pp. 144–145

✉ Piazza San Luigi dei Francesi 5

☎ 06 688271

🕐 Closed 12:30–2:30 p.m. & Thurs. p.m.

🚌 Bus: C3, 30, 46, 62, 64, 70, 81, 87, 116, 280, 492, 628

Sant'Agostino

🅜 Map pp. 144–145

✉ Piazza di Sant'Agostino

☎ 06 6880 1962

🕐 Closed noon–4 p.m.

🚌 Bus: C3, 30, 70, 81, 87, 116, 280, 492, 628

Sant'Ivo alla Sapienza

🅜 Map pp. 144–145

✉ Corso Rinascimento 40

☎ 06 686 4987

🕐 Courtyard open daily. Interior open Sun. 9 a.m.–noon.

🚌 Bus: C3, 30, 46, 62, 64, 70, 81, 87, 116, 280, 492, 628

Sant'Andrea della Valle

🅜 Map pp. 144–145

✉ Piazza Vidoni 6

☎ 06 686 1339

🕐 Closed 12–4:30 p.m.

🚌 Bus: C3, 40, 46, 63, 64, 70, 81, 87, 116, 492, 628.

Medieval Mystery & Renaissance Riches Walk

In Roman times, the vast area of the Campo Marzio was given over to army encampments, stadiums, and pleasure porticoes. It's mostly all gone or buried now, but many of the medieval and Renaissance buildings that came later remain, bearing witness to the intrigues and riches of a not-so-distant past.

A view of Castel Sant'Angelo

NOT TO BE MISSED:

Domitian's Stadium • San Salvatore in Lauro • View from Ponte Sant'Angelo • Chiesa Nuova • Oratorio dei Filippini

This walk starts just north of Piazza Navona at **Piazza di Tor Sanguigna,** where a chunk of the first-century foundation of **Domitian's Stadium** still sits below the railing. The medieval tower behind you gave the piazza its name. **Via dei Coronari**—where vendors once sold *corone* (rosary beads) to Catholic pilgrims—begins on your left, near the lovely 17th-century wall *aedicola* (shrine) at No. 2. Today the street is filled with wonderful (and expensive) antiques stores.

On your left, down the Vicolo del Volpe, rises the colorful tiled spire of Santa Maria dell'Anima. On your right, the Vicolo di San Trifone is a really tight fit. Farther on you will find **Piazza di San Salvatore in Lauro ❶,** with the church of the same name. Here, be sure to see the church's beautiful double *chiostro* (cloister).

Return to Via dei Coronari and walk away from Piazza di Tor Sanguigna; turn right on Via di Panico. At No. 40 note the small marble relief on the wall, a stonecutter's shingle. At the end of the street, carefully cross the Lungotevere river road (Lungotevere Tor di Nona) to **Ponte Sant'Angelo ❷,** where you can enjoy a breathtaking view of Castel Sant'Angelo and St. Peter's dome. The bridge is magnificently decorated with monumental Bernini-designed statues, each holding a symbol (a crown of thorns, a whip, a nail) of the Crucifixion.

Cross back over the Lungotevere Tor di Nona, and this time take the Via del Banco di Santo Spirito. It is the middle street—note the columns of a medieval portico embedded in the corner building—of the three that fan out from what was formerly called Piazza del Ponte. Just after the church on your left, there is a dark, medieval passage on the other side of the street, the **Arco dei Banchi,** where an ancient inscription marks the height of the 1277 flood.

The road forks at the Banco di Santo Spirito at No. 3. Take the picturesque Via dei Banchi Nuovi on your left to **Piazza dell'Orologio ❸,** named for the large clock on the tower. On the left, take Vicolo degli Orsini, and at the end, sneak a peek at the lush, green inner courtyard of a baronial palace built by the Orsini.

Backtrack to the piazza and continue along the same street, now called Via del Governo Vecchio). Turn right on Via della Chiesa Nuova and right again at the end to find yourself in front of the late Renaissance church that Romans call the **Chiesa Nuova** ❹ (officially, Santa Maria della Vallicella). Stand near the statue for a better view of the church and the interesting Borromini facade of the **Oratorio dei Filippini** on the left. It has a curious porticoed courtyard and, upstairs on the top floor, a charming if somewhat musty library, the Biblioteca Vallicelliana, designed by Borromini in 1637. The church, which has a ceiling fresco by Pietro da Cortona, has three Rubens paintings over the main altar.

Leave by the side door and return to Via del Governo Vecchio, then proceed to **Piazza di**

Pasquino ❺, with its "talking" statue (see p. 147). The statue stands against the back wall of Palazzo Braschi, seat of the **Museo di Roma.**

Follow the street on the left, Via di Santa Maria dell'Anima, to **Tor Millina,** a medieval tower. Turn left and walk a block until you reach the beginning of Via della Pace and, facing you, Pietro da Cortona's spectacularly dramatic facade of the church of **Santa Maria della Pace.** The piazza here has some interesting cafés.

- Also see area map, pp. 144–145
- Piazza di Tor Sanguigna
- 1 mile (1.5 km)
- 1.5–2 hours
- Piazza Santa Maria della Pace

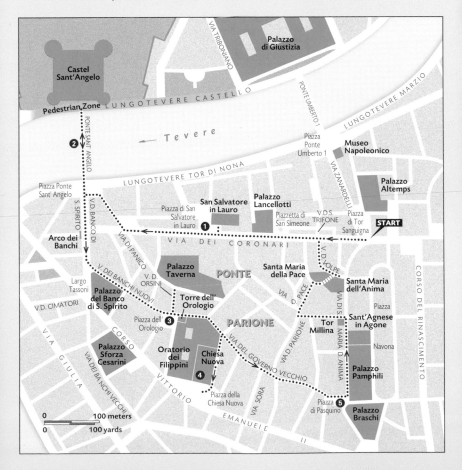

Piazza Campo dei Fiori

One of the liveliest spots in the city, Piazza Campo dei Fiori (its name means "field of flowers") has been an outdoor marketplace since 1869. On weekday and Saturday mornings you can buy fresh produce and fish. Come evening, young Italians and foreigners alike fill the square's inexpensive trattorias, while its bustling wine bars and pubs stay open late into the night.

A vibrant, open-air market moved here from Piazza Navona

Piazza Campo dei Fiori

🅰 Map pp. 144–145

🚍 Bus: C3, 46, 62, 64, 70, 81, 87, 116, 492, 628

Ditirambo

✉ Piazza della Cancelleria 74

☎ 06 687 1626

(See p. 251)

Campo dei Fiori is one of the few important squares not linked to a particular patrician family or an important edifice. The only building of note is the **Palazzo Pio Righetti,** built over the ruins of Pompey's Theater at its southeastern end. As is true of the rest of the Campo Marzio area, Campo dei Fiori became increasingly central after the Holy See's decision in the 14th century to set up residence in the Vatican. The square was, after all, directly on the Via Papalis (gone today) and the Via del Pellegrino, the pedestrian routes for pilgrims arriving from the city's south side.

After Pope Sixtus IV built his bridge over the Tiber (Ponte Sisto) for the 1475 Holy Year, this piazza became a transit point for anyone coming from Trastevere. Not surprisingly, until the 17th century, when most such activity moved to the Spanish Steps area, it was the center of a flourishing tourist trade. Indeed, the Albergo del Sole, just around the corner on Via del Biscione, is reputedly the oldest hotel in Rome. Number 13, on the corner of the Via dei Cappellari and Vicolo del Gallo, was an inn, La Vacca, run by Vanozza Cattanei, a grande dame who for a time was the mistress of Rodrigo Borgia (the future Pope Alexander VI), and mother of the lovely, but infamous Lucrezia.

INSIDER TIP:

For delicious and inventive food without sacrificing your budget, try Ditirambo in Piazza della Cancelleria, next to Campo dei Fiori.

—EMILIANO CATALDI
Tourism professional

The piazza's large, open space was once well suited to all sorts of games and processions—and executions. The scholar Giordano Bruno, whose statue stands in the square, was burned at the stake as a heretic by the Inquisition in 1600. ∎

EXPERIENCE: Outdoor Markets and Specialty Shops

In the past, before supermarkets and packaged food, a Roman housewife planned all of her family's meals around the seasonal products available in the nearest outdoor or *rionale* (neighborhood) food market. Although fewer in number today, those markets still exist (see below). If you are staying in an apartment while in Rome and have decided to cook—or if you want simply to walk in the footsteps of generations of Roman *casalinghe*—any morning (except Sundays) head straight to the Campo dei Fiori neighborhood (see opposite) and its famous market.

Campo dei Fiori is not the only area of old Rome where you can take an intriguing food-based walk. Alternatives include **Trastevere,** the ancient Jewish Ghetto area (see p. 206); **Testaccio,** under the shadow of the Aventine Hill; or **Piazza Vittorio Emmanuele II,** an immigrant area where the huge new indoor market offers foods from all continents.

The Freshest Produce

Some Romans still prefer to buy only produce that is in season, and you will soon see why. Make your way through the hodgepodge of vegetable and fruit stalls to get an idea of the richness and abundance of available fruit and vegetables.

If it is spring you will find peas and *fave* (Roman lima beans), which Romans like to eat with the tangy local *pecorino romano* cheese. In fall or spring you'll see the amazingly bright green *broccolo romano,* a cross between cauliflower and broccoli. You might even see an old woman bent over a tub filled with curly pale green stalks, the famous *puntarelle,* made by peeling a type of chicory known as Catalogna. It is served as a salad with olive oil and a garlicky anchovy sauce. Spring also brings piles of artichokes, the green-purple *romanesco* kind. In March, Sicily's blood-red oranges roll in, and in April or June you'll find tiny fragrant strawberries from nearby Lago di Nemi.

Meat & Fish

The **Macelleria Orelli** (butcher) at Piazza del Biscione 97 (next to Piazza Campo dei Fiori) specializes in local products like milk-fed lamb, *abbacchio,* or offal, which includes oxtail, tripe, liver, and heart. This area also boasts wonderful *norceria* (pork products stores) such as the **Antico Norcerina Viola** at number 43, where, along with the classic prosciutto, you'll find typical Roman products like *coppiette,* two dried strips of pork that are delicious as a snack with drinks; *coralline* salami, made from lean pork; and lard, traditionally eaten at Easter with *torta pasqualina* (a local savory tart). For fresh fish and shellfish of every type, walk across the street to **Attanasio** (*closed afternoons, Sundays and Mondays*).

From the Oven

And of course you mustn't forget breads. The locals head to **Il Forno,** which is located on the corner of Via dei Capellari and Campo dei Fiori. Here you will find, among others, typically Roman breads such as *rosette*—hollow, rose-shaped rolls—and *casareccio,* either Lariano or Genzano. Baked in wood-fired ovens, Genzano has a delicious thick brown crust and is ideal for classic *bruschetta.*

A few blocks away at Via dei Chiavari 34 is another forno, **Roscioli,** one of Rome's oldest. It offers excellent pizza and bread, as well as specialties such as basic Lariano bread to which raisins, nuts, or olives have been added. You can also get *ciambelle al vino,* cookies made to dip in wine; *castagnaccio,* a flat winter cake made with chestnut-flour, dried fruit, nuts, and a few sprigs of rosemary; and *pangiallo,* a hard, spicy Christmas cake. During Lent there are the fried, sugar-sprinkled *frappe* and *castagnole.*

Think you need help? English-speaking **Christine Georgeff** is a long-time resident of Rome and an expert who can guide you through a food walk tailored to your special interests. Contact her at *chgeorge@libero.it.*

Piazza Farnese

Palazzo Farnese is widely considered to be the most beautiful Renaissance building in Rome, if not in Italy, and the imposing structure cannot be separated from the lovely piazza in which it stands. Begun in 1514 by Alessandro Farnese (the future Pope Paul III), the palazzo's magnificent proportions are the work of some of the major architects of the time, including Antonio Sangallo; Michelangelo, who designed the cornice and the loggia on the facade; and Giacomo della Porta.

The Caracci Gallery is decorated with mythological love scenes like that of "Jupiter and Juno."

Piazza Farnese

🅰 Map pp. 144–145

🅿 Bus: C3, 23, 46, 62, 63, 64, 70, 81, 87, 116, 280, 492, 628

Today the Palazzo Farnese houses the French Embassy and is not open to the public. That is a shame since the interior— which was also decorated by some of the best artists of the era, including Annibale and Agostino Caracci, Domen- ichino, and Lanfranco—is inac- cessible. The fleurs-de-lis visible everywhere on the palace's exterior and on the fountains have nothing to do with France.

Rather, these are the Farnese lilies, the symbol of that noble Roman family.

The Palazzo

During the Renaissance a piazza was always considered an integral part of any aristocratic residence, and this one was adorned with granite basins from the Baths of Caracalla. It seems to be among the very few in the city not designed by

INSIDER TIP

For a great glass of wine, stop in Il Goccetto, which has no sign except a dusty "Vino e Olio" (wine and oil) above the door. It's at Via dei Banchi Vecchi 14, a few hundred yards northwest of Piazza Farnese.

—PAUL BENNETT
*National Geographic writer &
founder of Context Travel*

Giacomo della Porta. Della Porta is instead credited with the back facade of the palace, which faces the garden and the river. A project, attributed to Michelangelo, to link the palazzo to property on the Trastevere side of the river with an overhead bridge, was never completed. The only part of the project realized is the lovely arch that romantically spans the Via Giulia. The church of **Santa Brigida**, to the left of the palace, is the Swedish National Church. The convent next door is where St. Bridget died in 1373.

"Ecstasies"

The relatively small marble wall relief in the Casa di Santa Brigida showing St. Bridget's ecstatic face after a mystical communication with God was probably inspired by Bernini. But, truth be told, it cannot be compared to the Maestro's work. Bernini's marble rendering of the ecstasy of the "Blessed Ludovica Albertoni" in San Francesco a Ripa (see p. 198) is magnificent. As for the breathtaking and dramatically baroque "The Ecstasy of St. Theresa" in Santa Maria della Vittoria (see p. 92), it led one 19th-century traveler to quip, "If that's celestial ecstasy, I've experienced it, too." ∎

Casa di Santa Brigida
- 🅰 Map pp. 144–145
- ✉ Piazza Farnese 96
- ☎ 06 6889 2596
- 🕐 Closed 1–4 p.m., Mon. a.m., Thurs. & Fri. 11:30–4 p.m.; ring bell for access

Street Names

In medieval and Renaissance times, artisans typically set up shop in clusters, a practice often imposed by law as well as by convenience. Many of the streets in this central area of old Rome took, and kept, their names from the tradesmen who once worked there. Thus we have Via dei Cappellari, the street of the hatmakers, which starts at the northwest corner of Campo dei Fiori; Via dei Baullari, the street of the trunkmakers, which leads toward Piazza Navona; and Via dei Giubbonari, the street of jacket- or jerkinmakers, which runs toward Via Arenula and the Ghetto. Other examples are Via dei Chiavari, the street of the locksmiths; Via dei Sediari, the street of the chairmakers; and Via dei Balestrari, the street of the crossbowmakers. On Via dei Coronari, artisans specialized in the making of rosaries; the Cestari and the Canestrari made baskets; the Funari made ropes; the Staderari weighed things; and, on Vicolo del Bollo, jewelers brought gold or silver to be hallmarked. Piazza del Fico is named after its centuries-old fig tree, Via del Governo Vecchio after the large building that was once the seat of government, while Via dei Soldati, near Piazza Navona, was on a military patrol route. A small Italian-English dictionary will help you get a better idea of the historical context.

Among Popes & Princes Walk

This walk will let you feast your eyes on a wealth of Renaissance and baroque detail. Unlike other areas of Rome, the Campo Marzio is remarkably homogeneous. This is because most construction here took place only after the popes returned from exile in Avignon in 1377 and decided to set up house in the Vatican, setting off a new period of urban development in the area.

An ivy-draped arch over the Via Giulia

NOT TO BE MISSED:

San Girolamo della Carita
• Via Giulia • Galleria Spada
• Sant'Andrea della Valle

Facing the Palazzo Farnese, take Via di Monserrato on the right. Though tiny, the first square you come to, Piazza Santa Caterina della Rota, has three churches. The cream-colored **San Girolamo della Carita** ❶ on your left (1650–1660) is a must. The Spada Chapel, to the left of the entrance, has opulent polychromatic marble decor created by Francesco Borromini. Note the drapery between the two kneeling angels; it looks like cloth but is really marble.

Continue along Via di Monserrato until you reach Piazza dei Ricci with its *palazzo istoriato* (painted building)—the L-shaped, 16th-century **Palazzo Ricci** ❷. At the intersection of Monserrato and Via del Pellegrino, where **Via dei Banchi Vecchi** ❸ begins, don't miss the marble plaque, inscribed in Latin, on No. 145.

Dating from the reign of Emperor Claudius (A.D. 41–54), it marks the perimeter of an ancient Roman neighborhood. Via dei Banchi Vecchi has charming little shops selling antiques and bric-a-brac. Take a peek into the old pharmacy at No. 24 (red lanterns hang outside above the door), then cross the street to look at its facade. You'll see why the building is called the **Palazzo dei Pupazzi** (puppets). At No. 118 you'll see the imposing *portone* to the **Palazzo Sforza Cesarini**, originally built by the infamous 15th-century Borgia pope, Alessandro VI.

Continuing on, you will come to Via dei Cimatori, which leads to the most beautiful street in Rome—the Via Giulia—built by Pope Julius II in the early 16th century to provide a better link to the Vatican. To the right is the church of the Florentine residents of Rome, **San Giovanni dei Fiorentini.**

Turn left on **Via Giulia** ❹. At No. 85, note the inscription "*Raf Sanzio*" (for Raphael, the painter) above the second-floor balcony. In Renaissance times many famous architects lived next door to their patrician clients. The travertine "sofas" on the building at No. 62 were part of the grandiose courthouse (Palazzo dei Tribunali) begun by Bramante for Julius II but never completed. Just past the ivy-clad overhead arch is the rear facade of **Palazzo Farnese**. After the arch is the striking Mascherone fountain, which incorporates a giant marble mask of ancient Roman origin.

Turn left on Vicolo del Polverone. Walk up to the Piazza Capo di Ferro to No. 13, the **Galleria Spada** ❺ *(tel 06 6832 409, closed Mon., www.ticketeria.it/spada-eng.asp),* which contains paintings by Rubens, Titian, Guido Reni, Andrea del Sarto, and others. The palazzo is equally interesting. Note the magnificent stucco decorations—including statues of Caesar, Augustus, and Trajan—on its facade. From the central courtyard you can look at Borromini's famous trompe l'oeil perspective; the optical illusion created makes a tiny statue at the end of a short, 30-foot (9 m) corridor appear to be a colossus at the end of a long, imposing hallway.

From Piazza Capo di Ferro, walk down Via dei Balestrari, skirt the end of Piazza Campo dei Fiori, and bear right to the Piazza del Biscione. Venture through the iron gate at the far end and down the covered passageway (Passetto del Biscione) to **Via di Grotta Pinta** ❻. The buildings here were are constructed over the stands of Pompey's Theater (Teatro di Pompeo), the probable site of Julius Caesar's assassination. Heading left, cross the Largo del Pallaro and follow Via dei Chiavari to Corso Vittorio Emanuele II. The large church on your right is **Sant'Andrea della Valle** (see p. 151).

🗺 Also see area map, pp. 144–145
▶ Piazza Farnese
↔ 1.5 miles (2.5 km)
🕐 2.5–3 hours
▶ Sant'Andrea della Valle

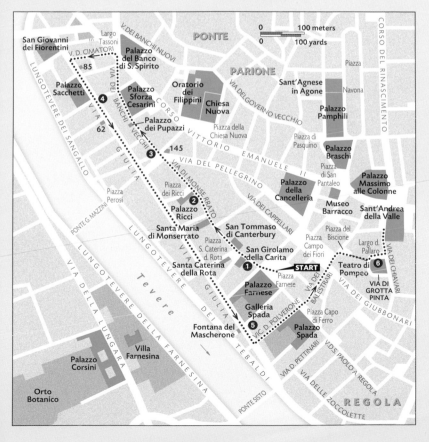

More Places to Visit

Museo Barracco

This little-known but delightful museum is commonly called La Piccola Farnesina. The building has no connection with the Palazzo Farnese, but its builders, a French noble family named Le Roys, were allowed to use the royal fleur-de-lis in their coat of arms. Built in 1523, probably by Antonio Sangallo the Younger, it has been altered several times. Currently the property of the Rome city government, it now houses the Barracco collection of ancient artwork, primarily sculptures. The collection, donated to the city in 1902, includes Egyptian, Greek, Assyrian, Etruscan, and Roman pieces. The late Roman ruins beneath the museum are often accessible to the public.
en.museobarracco.it 🗺 Map pp. 144–145
✉ Corso Vittorio Emanuele II 166/A
☎ 060608 🕐 Closed Mon. 💲 $. Audio guide: $ 🚌 Bus: C3, 40, 46, 63, 64, 70, 81, 87, 116, 492, 628

Palazzo Della Cancelleria

Completed in 1517, this palazzo ranks as one of the finest Renaissance buildings in the city, with a history intimately linked to the Roman nobility. It was paid for with the 60,000 scudi that Raffaele Riario, a nephew of Pope Sixtus IV, received from Franceschetto Cibo, the nephew of Pope Innocent VIII, as payment for a gambling debt. The stone roses on the facade and in the courtyard were the heraldic symbol of the Riario family. Today, it is owned by the Vatican, which at one time used it as a chancellery, and it enjoys extraterritorial status. Bramante did some work on the palazzo, and you should not miss its marvelous *cortile* (courtyard) with its impressive two-story double loggia.

Concerts are sometimes held upstairs in the **Sala dei 100 Giorni** *(tel 06 6989 3405)*, the Hundred Days Room, which features frescoes by Giorgio Vasari depicting scenes from the life of Pope Paul III, a Farnese. Vasari's claimed to have painted the room in 100 days, to which Michelangelo reportedly responded, *"Si vede bene"* ("You can tell"). Incorporated into the palazzo on the right is the church of **San Lorenzo in Damaso**. Take note of the columns in the courtyard, some of which were taken from a preexisting fourth-century church.
San Lorenzo in Damaso: 🗺 Map pp. 144–145
✉ Piazza della Cancelleria 1 ☎ 06 6889 1661
🕐 Closed 12–4:30 p.m. 🚌 Bus: C3, 40, 46, 63, 64, 70, 81, 87, 116, 492, 628

Caravaggio

Born Michelangelo Merisi in September 1573, Caravaggio was later known only by the name of the tiny northern town of his birth. He trained in Milan, far from the centers of classical Renaissance art, where he developed a style of painting that mixed realism and dramatic lighting.

Caravaggio arrived in Rome at the age of 17 and took the art world by storm. He was one of the first painters to contrast light and dark to maximum effect, a technique known as chiaroscuro. His wealth of detail and his ability to depict human-

ity with all of its defects and frailty were also exceptional. However, not everyone loved his work. The priests of San Luigi, rejected his first version of "St. Matthew and the Angel," labeling its extreme realism "disrespectful."

Caravaggio's life in Rome was marked by drunkenness, scrapes with the law, murder (albeit unintentional), poverty, illness, and, finally, death at 37. Today his works can be found in Sant'Agostino and Santa Maria del Popolo, as well as in most of Rome's leading museums.

The world's smallest independent state, the historic seat of Roman Catholicism, and the repository of several major artistic treasures

Vaticano

Detail from Michelangelo's ceiling fresco of the "Creation" in the Sistine Chapel

Vaticano

St. Peter's—the church built over the tomb of the Apostle Peter—is the center of Roman Catholicism and the largest basilica of Christianity. It is also the external face of the Vatican, the world's smallest independent city-state. Despite its minuscule geographical dimensions, however, the Vatican wields immense power and influence.

Built to keep out marauding Saracens, the walls of the Vatican enclose a miniature urban tapestry. The Vatican has its own post office and stamps, judicial system, pharmacy, gas station, railway station, commissary, television station, and special police force, the Swiss Guards corps, that dates back to 1505. It publishes a daily newspaper, the influential *Osservatore Romano*, and sends out daily radio broadcasts in more than a dozen languages. The Church once ruled much of Italy, but between 1860 and 1870, Piedmontese troops conquered the Papal States. As a result, the pope did not leave the Vatican until peace was made with Italy in 1929 through the signing of the Concordat.

The popes have lived in the Vatican since the end of the 14th century, when they returned from exile in Avignon and found the Lateran Palace (see p. 79) in ruins. Settlement of the Vatican plain (Ager Vaticanus) occurred slowly, but the papal move to the Vatican accelerated development. The 15th and 16th centuries saw a rash of construction on what was called the Mons Vaticans. The result, a labyrinthine complex of interconnected palaces, grew up around St. Peter's in a largely disordered fashion.

In the mid-1400s, Nicholas V (1447–1455) enlarged and beautified earlier structures, and his successors followed suit. Sixtus IV built the

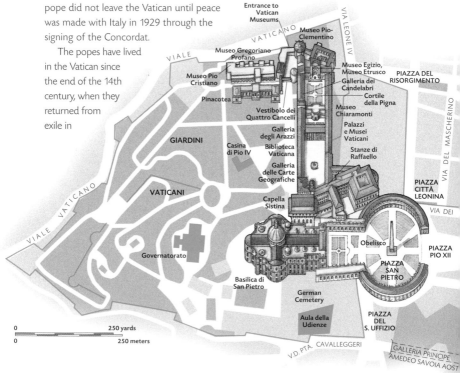

Entrance to Vatican Museums

VIA LEONE IV

VATICANO

VIALE

Museo Pio-Clementino

Museo Gregoriano Profano

Museo Pio Cristiano

Museo Egizio, Museo Etrusco

PIAZZA DEL RISORGIMENTO

Galleria dei Candelabri

Pinacotea

Cortile della Pigna

Vestibolo dei Quattro Cancelli

Museo Chiaramonti

Galleria degli Arazzi

Palazzi e Musei Vaticani

GIARDINI

Casina di Pio IV

Biblioteca Vaticana

Stanze di Raffaello

Galleria delle Carte Geografiche

VIA DEL MASCHERINO

VATICANI

Capella Sistina

PIAZZA CITTÀ LEONINA

VIA DEI

VIALE VATICANO

Obelisco

PIAZZA PIO XII

VIALE

Governatorato

PIAZZA SAN PIETRO

Basilica di San Pietro

German Cemetery

Aula della Udienze

PIAZZA DEL S. UFFIZIO

0   250 yards
0   250 meters

V.D. PTA. CAVALLEGGERI

GALLERIA PRINCIPE AMEDEO SAVOIA AOST

Near St. Peter's

Outside, the Borgo neighborhood is flanked by the remains of the ninth-century Leonine Wall, a portion of which connects the Vatican to Castel Sant'Angelo. Built as a mausoleum for a Roman emperor, the castle later operated as a fortress and a papal refuge. In the 1930s, Mussolini gave Pope Pius XI (1922–1939) permission to connect the Vatican and the castle with the broad Via della Conciliazione (reconciliation). This made St. Peter's more visible but destroyed a historic neighborhood in the process.

Much of the Vatican today is occupied by the Musei Vaticani or Vatican Museums, which, along with the Sistine Chapel and the Rooms of Raphael, include the Museo Pio-Clementino, the Pinacoteca, and the Gregorian Profane, the Egyptian, and the Etruscan museums. The entrance is well around the back of Vatican City—beyond Piazza del Risorgimento—on winding Viale Vaticano. To the right of St. Peter's, instead, is the Apostolic Palace with Bernini's Portone di Bronzo, the Papal Apartments (the Pope appears in a window every Sunday when he is in residence to bless the faithful), and the offices of the Secretariat of State (the foreign ministry). It is from here that the pontiff rules his largely (but not entirely) spiritual empire. ■

chapel that bears his name (the Cappella Sistina), on top of which Alexander VI (1492–1503) built a tower (Torre del Borgia), and Julius II (1503–1513) arranged for Bramante, Raphael's mentor, to construct the new St. Peter's.

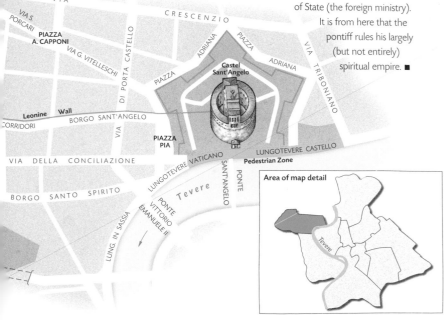

Basilica di San Pietro

Nobody knows exactly in what year Peter came to Rome, other than that it was after A.D. 50. And no one knows the exact year of his martyrdom, only that he was crucified in an Imperial Circus near the Vatican during Nero's persecutions and therefore sometime between A.D. 64 and 67. What we do know is that from early on his gravesite assumed a particular importance for the members of the then recently born Christian sect.

Just another day in St. Peter's Square

Basilica di San Pietro

- 🅰 Map pp. 162–163
- ✉ Piazza di San Pietro
- ☎ 06 6988 1662
- 🕐 Open daily
- 🚌 Bus: 23, 34, 40, 46, 49, 62, 64, 81, 115, 116, 590, 881, 982, 990

The Basilica's History

Eager to help—and perhaps to be helped—by the growing Christian religion, Emperor Constantine laid the foundations for the first St. Peter's in the early fourth century. Consecrated by Pope Sylvester I in A.D. 326, the new church had a spacious atrium and elaborate decorations. When the popes returned from Avignon, they found that

the old building had deteriorated and risked collapse. Exactly 1,300 years later to the day (November 18, 1626), a new St. Peter's opened its doors, but its birth was slow and painful.

Shortly after his reign began, Julius II (1503–1513) commissioned Bramante to build a new church on top of Peter's tomb, and in 1506 the foundation stone was laid. However 120 years passed before this massive new structure was completed.

Construction of a Masterpiece

So just who did build St. Peter's? The answer is, just about everyone. And the fact that so many cooks did not spoil the broth is in itself a minor miracle. Nevertheless, the city's architects did argue over the basic plan.

Some, like Baldassare Peruzzi, wanted St. Peter's to be built in the shape of a Greek cross, with four arms of equal length. Bramante, for example, thought it should resemble Santa Sophia in Constantinople. Michelangelo, who joined the fray in 1546 but only had time to conceive the giant dome that dominates much of the Roman skyline, was also in favor of the Greek cross plan. Others, including Raphael and Antonio Sangallo the Younger, preferred the shape of a Latin cross, which has a long vertical arm and a shorter crossbar toward one end, like a crucifix. In the end, Pope Paul V (1605–1621) finally decided in favor of the Latin cross, awarding the commission to architect Carlo Maderno in 1607.

At that time, the Catholic Church was fully caught up in the

INSIDER TIP:

The cupola atop St. Peter's basilica affords a wonderful view of the city, not to mention an eerie, if a bit claustrophobic, climb through the inside of the dome [see p. 170].

—RUTH ELLEN GRUBER
National Geographic author

Counter-Reformation, and Paul wanted the church to be at least as big as its predecessor. He also wanted it to have an even longer nave (615 feet/187 m), which would heighten the importance of ritual and make processions and other rites more dramatic.

The pope's plans for the new church meant that the dome would not be immediately visible to the entering faithful as originally planned. When completed, the dome designed by 71-year-old Michelangelo was also higher and more elaborately decorated than anyone had intended. Nevertheless, his mark on the church's structure, including the massive

pilasters and the magnificent windows, is indelible.

St. Peter's Square

In contrast to the basilica, there is no doubt about who created **Piazza di San Pietro** (St. Peter's Square). With its elliptical shape and its two semicircular colonnades, Gian Lorenzo Bernini's design, commissioned by Pope Alexander VII Chigi (1655–1667), has been universally acclaimed as an architectural masterpiece.

The square features 284 gigantic Doric columns in the colonnade, 88 other pilasters, and 140 statues. Statues of Jesus, John the Baptist, and 11 apostles decorate the church facade. Three sets of steps, flanked by statues of St. Peter and St. Paul, lead to the entrance. In the middle of the piazza are two fountains, one by Maderno and a copy created in 1677 by Bernini, and an Egyptian obelisk (see p. 86), placed there before the creation of the colonnade. Halfway between the obelisk and each fountain is a plain stone disk reading "Centro del Colonnato." Stand on one and see the four rows of columns in the corresponding hemicycle miraculously line into one.

The Facade & Portico

Carlo Maderno also created the basilica's travertine facade— white and ocher, with red and green accents on the Loggia della Benedizione. Newly renovated, this internationally known landmark did not please everyone. French painter Henri Matisse once said that the wide (360 foot/110 m), two-story facade looked more like a train station than a church.

There are five entrances into the portico (and another five doors into the church). Inside—where you can see Maderno's stuccoed ceiling, now gloriously restored—note the two equestrian statues: "Constantine" by Bernini on the extreme right and "Charlemagne" (1725) on the extreme left. Together they represented the temporal power of the Church.

Directly over the central doorway, but very difficult to see, is what is left of the famous "Navicella" mosaic ("Jesus Walking on Water") by Giotto, which once graced the atrium of the old St. Peter's built by Constantine. The "Navicella" is best seen if you stand with your back to the church's central bronze doors. Also from Constantine's time, the doors were decorated in the 15th century by Florentine sculptor, Filarete (Antonio Averulino). Opened only during Holy Years, the **Holy Door**, or Porta Santa, is the one on the far right. The pope uses the central loggia when he delivers his *Urbi et Orbi* ("To the city and to the world") blessing on Christmas and Easter. It is also used for the "*habemus Papem*" announcement after a papal election.

Inside the Basilica

Bernini must get much of the credit for the overwhelming baroque interior of St. Peter's. Enter through Filarete's doors,

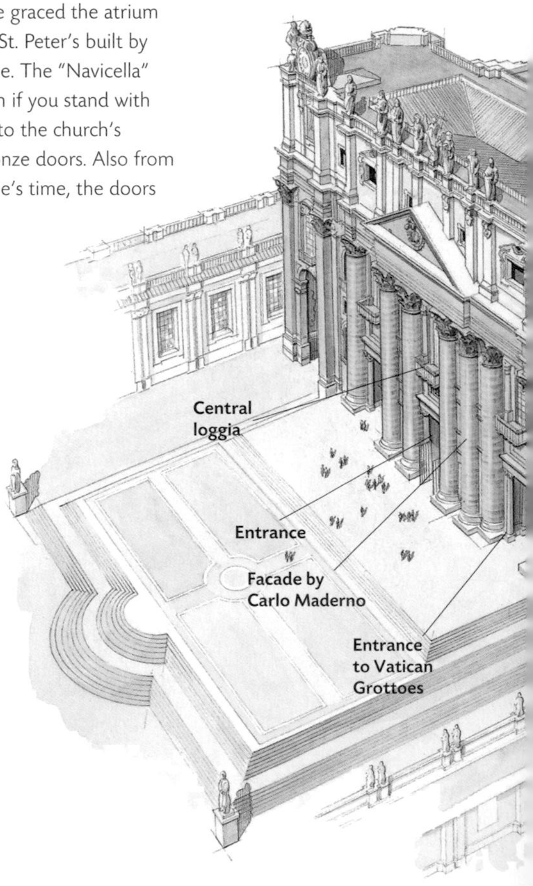

Central loggia

Entrance

Facade by Carlo Maderno

Entrance to Vatican Grottoes

and stand briefly on the large porphyry circle just inside, the spot where Charlemagne and others after him knelt when crowned emperor. Walk straight up the nave to the transept. The bronze strips on the floor mark the lengths of other famous, but shorter, cathedrals.

Just as Bernini intended, your eyes go immediately to the

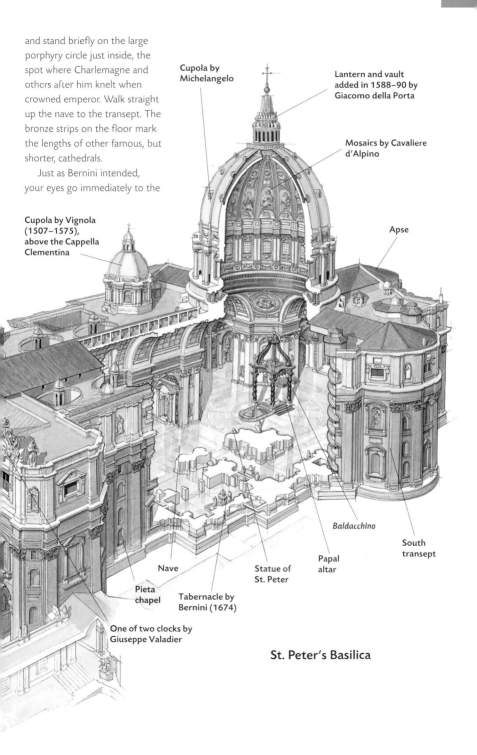

Cupola by Michelangelo

Lantern and vault added in 1588–90 by Giacomo della Porta

Mosaics by Cavaliere d'Alpino

Cupola by Vignola (1507–1575), above the Cappella Clementina

Apse

Baldacchino

South transept

Nave

Statue of St. Peter

Papal altar

Pieta chapel

Tabernacle by Bernini (1674)

One of two clocks by Giuseppe Valadier

St. Peter's Basilica

enormous bronze canopy (baldacchino) over the papal altar, made with bronze stripped from the portico of the Pantheon. Don't miss the "Woman-in-childbirth" sequence on the column bases; marble reliefs depict her changing expressions and end with a smiling *bambino* (baby). The sunken *confessio* in front of the canopy, designed by Maderno, is surrounded by a balustrade with 95 perennially lit lamps. It marks St. Peter's tomb several levels below.

The *gloria* or sunburst in the apse is part of a magnificent baroque monument, the **"Cattedra Petri,"** into which Bernini incorporated an early ninth-century papal throne once thought to have been Peter's. An alabaster window with a dove, the symbol of the Holy Spirit, at its center is flanked by the tombs of Pope Paul III (left) and Pope Urban VIII (right).

The Dome

Although completed well after his death in 1564, the basilica's cupola is Michelangelo's architectural masterpiece. Warmly illuminated by the light from 16 windows and, in the upper portion, divided into 16 wedges by ribs that run up to the lantern at the top where God the Father is depicted, the dome is supported by four enormous pilasters. Note the mosaic decoration in the four pendentives, the triangular spaces where the pilasters reach the dome. Each represents one of the four Evangelists. Note the enormous proportions; St. Mark's pen is

INSIDER TIP:

Bring a small pair of binoculars to Rome—not for birding, but for the close-up details of the ceiling paintings and mosaics in the vast churches and basilicas.

—TIM JEPSON
National Geographic author

more than 5 feet long (1.5 m). The Latin inscription around the base of the dome comes from the gospel of St. Matthew (16:18) and affirms the importance of Peter and his successors: "You are Peter and on this rock I will build my church. I will entrust to you the keys to the kingdom of Heaven."

Pope Urban VIII requested that Bernini decorate the dome's four enormous **supporting piers** with large *aedicolae* (niches) holding oversize statues, each more than 16 feet (4.8 m) tall: St. Longinus (created by Bernini), St. Andrew, St. Veronica, and St. Helen Sometimes precious relics are exhibited on the balconies above the statues: the lance of St. Longinus (the Roman soldier who prodded the crucified Jesus with his spear), portions of the cross brought back from the Holy Land by St. Helen, and St. Veronica's veil, said to bear the image of Jesus' face. Against the Longinus pier stands Arnolfo di Cambio's wonderful bronze **statue of St. Peter.** Once thought to be much older, it dates from the late 1200s.

EXPERIENCE: Papal Audience

If you have always wanted to receive a papal blessing, you will find it fairly easy to arrange one during your stay in Rome. You won't be alone, of course; thousands turn out week after week. In fact, during much of the year, the Wednesday General Audiences are held in the Pope Paul VI hall, which can hold more than 10,000 people. But never mind. Once seated in the modern auditorium, you will be so caught up in the proceedings that you will feel as if it has all been arranged for your benefit.

People have been visiting Rome for nearly three millennia. After the onset of the Christian era, or rather since Rome became the center of the Christian faith, a huge number of those people have been pilgrims. While legions of ancient pilgrims may feel distant to us, they nevertheless had something in common with today's visitors, whether Roman Catholic or not. They wanted to visit the seat of Christianity and, if possible, see the Pope and obtain a papal blessing.

Two musts for the devout: St. Peter's (above) and a papal audience

The Audience

Once you have applied for and received your free tickets (see below), you will file into the spacious hall and take your seat among lay people, clerics, and nuns, from all over Italy and almost every country in the world. In summer, the general audiences are held in St. Peter's Square or at the pope's summer residence in Castel Gandolfo in the Alban Hills.

The ceremony begins with the papal address, during which you may hope to hear at least parts in a language you understand. Afterward, representatives of groups from selected countries may be asked to stand and even perform, possibly a song, a little dance, a piece of music, or a reading. The pontiff will then thank them in their own language. And the two-hour meeting—a cross between a revival meeting and a pop concert—will end with a solemn blessing that will likely make you, and everyone else in the room, feel simply splendid.

Getting Tickets

Tickets are available at the Prefettura della Casa Ponteficia on the north side of St. Peter's Square (tel 06 6988 4857) on Monday and Tuesday mornings from 9 a.m. to 1 p.m. A better option is to pre-order them by mail from **Prefettura della Casa** (Pon- teficia 00120, Città del Vatican, fax 06 6988 5863) or online (www.vatican.va). Another way to reserve tickets (but only for the Wednesday general audiences) is through the website of the **Santa Susanna church** in Rome. Visit their website as www .santasusanna.org and click on "Pope & Vatican." Your parish priest may also be able to help secure tickets.

Another Option

No tickets are necessary to see the pope, albeit from a great distance, at the Sunday midday Angelus in St. Peter's Square, when he appears in the library window to deliver his weekly homily and blessing.

The Pietà

You wouldn't want to travel all the way to St. Peter's in Rome and not see Michelangelo's "Pietà." The famous statue can be found in the first chapel of the right aisle. This is Michelangelo's only signed sculpture—see his signature on the sash across the Virgin's breast. The work has been protected by a transparent bullet-proof panel ever since a deranged man attacked and damaged it with a hammer in 1972.

Tombs & Monuments

At present, 147 popes are buried in St. Peter's. You can visit the **tomb of Alexander VII,** a Chigi, in a corridor off the left transept. Rich in colored marbles and statuary, this magnificent late work (1678) of Bernini's shows the pope kneeling in prayer and surrounded by statues representing the virtues. Look closely and you will notice that from beneath the folds of patterned marble, Winged Death—with hourglass in hand—rears his ugly head.

The **tomb of Innocent VIII** stands against a pilaster in the left aisle. It was created by Antonio del Pollaiuolo and is the only papal tomb taken directly from the old St. Peter's, other than those in the Grottoes.

Only three monuments in the church are dedicated to women. Queen Christina of Sweden abdicated her throne in 1654 to convert to Catholicism. Countess Matilda of Tuscany sided with the papacy in the 11th-century conflict with the Holy Roman Emperor. And Maria Clementina Sobieski (1702–1735) was mother to the last two Stuart pretenders to the English throne, Bonnie Prince Charlie and Henry Stuart.

With only two exceptions (the ceiling fresco over the "Pietà" and the Pietro da Cortona oil in the Cappella del Santi Sacramento) all the "paintings" you see here are actual mosaic copies of famous paintings in other churches or in the Vatican Museums.

Other Attractions

Consider spending some time in the **Treasury Museum** (located off the left transept), where, for a small fee, you can see magnificent church vestments and crucifixes, a Bernini angel, another Pollaiuolo tomb, and the **Grottoes.** Many popes are buried here, including John Paul II, who died in 2005.

A visit to the museum will also allow you a glimpse of St. Peter's shrine. Do not miss the **dome** or cupola. Take the elevator (there is a charge) from the far end of the portico to get to the first level. A short climb from there will get you inside the dome, where you can really appreciate the church's immense proportions. Another narrow, seemingly endless circular staircase will take you to the balcony atop the cupola from which the view is superb. But be sure you're physically fit and not claustrophobic. This closed-in staircase is one-way, so you can't change your mind halfway up. ■

Musei Vaticani

It is hard to think of any greater museums than those of the Vatican. Other galleries may match the broad span and myriad origins of its artifacts, but none can also offer works of art that include entire rooms painted by Raphael and the ceiling frescoes of the Sistine Chapel.

The Sistine Chapel is the place where the College of Cardinals meets to elect the pope.

Visiting the Museums

The Vatican Museums are immense, and you cannot see everything in one visit. Select the sections that interest you the most and head straight there; do not try to absorb or read everything along the way. And remember, there is a lot of walking: about 0.3 mile (0.5 km) from the museum entrance to the Sistine Chapel alone! If you can, try scheduling your visit later in the morning, around 11:30, to avoid the long lines that form when the museum opens. Admittance stops at 4:00 in the afternoon..

Getting Your Bearings

Once through the brand new entrance on the Viale Vaticano, climb the few steps and take the escalators to the top. The **Pinacoteca** (painting gallery; see p. 176) is to the right. Most first-time visitors, however, will want to head straight for the Rooms of Raphael and the Sistine Chapel. To do this, proceed left to the **Vestibolo dei Quattro Cancelli** (Vestibule of the Four Gates).

Musei Vaticani

- Map pp. 162–163
- Viale Vaticano
- 06 6988 3041
- Open 8:30 a.m.–6 p.m. (last entrance 4 p.m.). Closed Sun. 2 p.m. (last entrance 12:30 p.m.)
- $$$. Free last Sun. of month. Audio guide: $$. Tours ($$$) every day except Sun. Call 06 6988 4947 for reservations
- Bus: 32, 49, 81, 98, 492, 990

Note the enormous bronze Roman *pigna,* or pinecone, in the courtyard **Cortile della Pigna,** through the door facing the other side of the *vestibolo.* Now turn left and walk up the stairs to the first landing and the **Greek Cross Room,** part of the Pio Clementine Museum (see p. 175). Don't miss the stupendous fourth-century porphyry sarcophagi; St. Helena, Constantine's mother, was buried in the one on the right, decorated with battle scenes.

Take the stairs to the second floor and walk down a long corridor divided into three sections: the **Galleria dei Candelabri** (candelabras); the **Galleria degli Arazzi** (tapestries); and the **Galleria delle Carte Geografiche,** which features interesting map frescoes depicting Italy's and the Church's possessions in the 1580s. The windows on the right look out on a Renaissance villa, the **Casina di Pio IV,** and the **Vatican Gardens.** The Sala dell'Immacolata, at the end of the corridor, leads to the Stanze di Rafaello.

Stanze di Raffaello

The Stanze di Raffaello or Raphael's Rooms, of which there are four, were commissioned by Julius II in 1508, supposedly because the existing papal apartment reminded him too much of his hated predecessor, Alexander VI (a Borgia). The order of the visit described here is subject to change.

Used by Julius as a library, the **Stanza della Segnatura** is considered one of Raphael's greatest works. It contains two of his best known works, painted between 1508 and 1511. In the **"Disputation of the Sacrament"**—meant to glorify faith—Jesus, the Virgin, and St. John the Baptist are flanked by figures from the Old and New Testaments; those from the New Testament have halos. Below is an altar with the Host and, farther down, Doctors of the Church, saints, and scholars. Dante appears on the right in the lower section.

INSIDER TIP:

The Vatican Museums and Sistine Chapel have extended their opening times; last entrance is now at 4:00 p.m. It's much less busy after lunch, when most of the big tour groups have left.

—ANTONIO BARBIERI
National Geographic contributor & co-founder, Concierge in Rome

A tribute to philosophy, the **"School of Athens"** depicts Plato and Aristotle in animated conversation inside a large classical building. Raphael, who clearly enjoyed painting his contemporaries into historical tableaus, painted himself second to last in the group of hatted gentlemen on the right. Just in front is Bramante, in the guise of Euclid, who is bending over, compass in hand, to explain a problem to his students. (Bramante also appears in the "Disputation of the Sacrament," leaning over the bannister, on the far left.) The pensive figure seated in the forefront, his head leaning on his left hand, is Michelangelo as Heraclitus, the pessimist.

Originally a bedroom, the **Stanza di Eliodoro** (Heliodorus), which was decorated between 1512 and 1514, is noted for its stunning use of color and the dramatic lighting in **"The Liberation of St. Peter."** The room also contains the **"Expulsion of Heliodorus"** (from the temple in Jerusalem), and **"Pope Leo Meets Attila the Hun,"** recounting how St. Leo the Great (Pope Leo I, 440–461) turned Attila and his Huns away during a fifth-century attack on Rome. After Julius II died, Raphael repainted the face of St. Leo with the features of the new pope, Leo X (1513–1521). However, Leo X already appeared in the painting as a cardinal, so now he appears twice in the same scene.

Raphael's students painted the **Stanza dell'Incendio** (fire), formerly a dining room, between 1514 and 1517. Based on Raphael's designs, it depicts events from the lives of Leo III and Leo IV, the pope who built the Vatican walls in the ninth century. The most famous painting shows how, in 847, Leo IV quenched a fire in the surrounding Borgo neighborhood by making the sign of the cross. Nearby is the small **Cappella di Niccolo V** (Chapel of Pope Nicholas V), frescoed by the Florentine artist Fra Angelico.

Before reaching the Sistine Chapel, you might want to visit

The Sistine Hall, part of the extensive Vatican Library

the **Borgia Apartment,** decorated with lovely frescoes by Pinturicchio and his disciples.

The **Sala di Costantino** was finished in 1524, after Raphael's death, and he probably only did some preliminary sketches. The underlying theme of this room, attributed largely to Giulio Romano, Francesco Penni, and Raffaellino del Colle, and told through scenes from the life of Constantine, is the triumph of Christianity over paganism.

Cappella Sistina

Built by Giovanni di Dolce during the reign of Sixtus IV (1471–1484), the Sistine Chapel has seen a lot of history. This rectangular hall was the private chapel of the pontiffs, and for centuries it has been the room where the conclaves, or papal elections, are held.

The floor is decorated in an exquisite "*opus alexandrinum*" pattern reminiscent of the

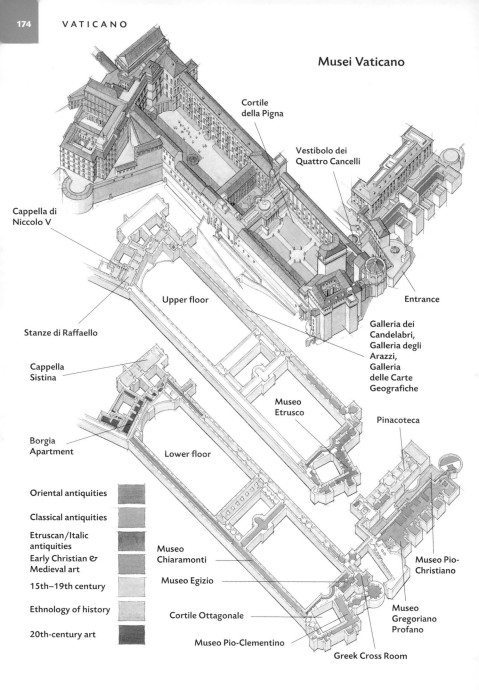

Musei Vaticano

Cortile
della Pigna

Vestibolo dei
Quattro Cancelli

Cappella di
Niccolo V

Upper floor

Entrance

Stanze di Raffaello

Galleria dei
Candelabri,
Galleria degli
Arazzi,
Galleria
delle Carte
Geografiche

Cappella
Sistina

Museo
Etrusco

Pinacoteca

Borgia
Apartment

Lower floor

Oriental antiquities

Classical antiquities

Etruscan/Italic
antiquities

Early Christian &
Medieval art

Museo
Chiaramonti

Museo Pio-
Christiano

15th–19th century

Museo Egizio

Ethnology of history

Cortile Ottagonale

Museo
Gregoriano
Profano

20th-century art

Museo Pio-Clementino

Greek Cross Room

cosmatesque pavements (see
p. 208) from the 13th and 14th
centuries. An elegant sculpted
screen—by Mino da Fiesole,
Andrea Bregno, and Giovanni

Dalmata—divides the chapel into
two sections. But the room is
best known for the recently restored wall and ceiling frescoes,
considered by many to be the

supreme example of Renaissance, if not universal, art.

The decoration of the Sistine Chapel can be divided into three periods, each coinciding with an important stage in the development of Renaissance art. The frescoes on the long walls were painted between 1481 and 1483; the ceiling was painted by Michelangelo between 1508 and 1512; and his "Last Judgment" was executed some 20 years later, between 1534 and 1541.

The Long Walls: The long walls were decorated by some of the most important 15th-century Renaissance painters (Pinturicchio, Botticelli, Perugino, Ghirlandaio, Rosselli, Signorelli), all of Tuscan or Umbrian origin. During this period, under the impetus of a reinvigorated and dynamic papacy, the cultural epicenter of the Renaissance was shifting from Florence and its environs to Rome.

On the left, starting from the "Last Judgment," are **scenes from the Old Testament** including the "Burning Bush" and "Moses Slaying Egyptians" (Botticelli), the "Punishment of Korah, Dathan, and Abiram" (Botticelli), and the "Last Days of Moses" by Signorelli. The scenes on the right, from the New Testament, include the "Baptism of Jesus" (Pinturicchio or Perugino), the "Temptation of Christ" (Botticelli), the "Calling of Peter and Andrew" (Domenico Ghirlandaio), and "Jesus Giving the Keys to Peter" (Perugino). On the end wall, opposite the "Last Judgment,"

are the "Resurrection" by Ghirlandaio and Salviati's "St. Michael," both later repainted.

The Ceiling: Michelangelo's decoration of the ceiling (originally blue with stars) coincided with the mood of cultural and political self-confidence that characterized the early Renais-

Giuseppe Momo's monumental spiral staircase

sance. Not particularly keen on accepting this commission, Michelangelo, who considered himself a sculptor, not a painter, wanted to keep working on the marble tomb of Julius II. When he did accept (possibly to foil his implacable rival, Bramante), he turned a simpler project (the "Twelve Apostles") into the more ambitious "Creation." As most everyone now knows, he spent four years lying on his back on scaffolding to do it.

Michelangelo's choice of subject matter was not accidental. The cosmology of the time divided world history into various epochs: the period before the

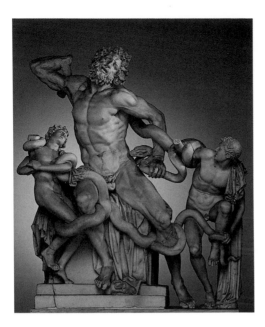

The exquisite Laocoön was found in 1506.

Law, the period of Law as given to Moses, and finally the period of Grace, which began with the coming of Jesus. The older decoration on the side walls corresponded to the eras of Law and Grace, so Michelangelo decided to dedicate the ceiling to the pre-Law era, that is, to the Creation, the Garden of Eden, and original sin. The decoration is sublime. Ideally, you will have brought your binoculars or at least a decent-size mirror to view the ceiling comfortably. Remember, start your gazing from the altar end of the room.

There are nine central scenes on the ceiling. Alternating in larger and smaller rectangles are "The Separation of Light and Darkness"; "The Creation of the Sun, the Moon, and Planets"; "The Separation of Land from the Sea" and "The Creation of Plants and Animals"; "The Creation of Adam"; "The Creation of Eve from Adam's Rib"; "The Expulsion from the Garden of Paradise"; "The Sacrifice of Noah"; "The Flood"; and "Noah Drunk."

Portraits of prophets form a border around them (going clockwise Jonah, Jeremiah, Ezekiel, Joel, Zecheriah, Isaiah, Daniel). Alternating with these are sibyls, the oracles of the ancient world (clockwise the Persian, Erythrean, Delphic, Cumaean, and Libyan sibyls). The triangular lunettes between the sibyls and prophets contain images of the forerunners and ancestors of Jesus Christ, while the four larger corner lunettes represent Old Testament scenes. Between the prophets and sibyls and above the triangular lunettes, are figures known as the "Ignudi," athletic male nudes, painted in various poses between low, trompe l'oeil pedestals.

"The Last Judgment": By the time Michelangelo got around to painting "The Last Judgment," commissioned by Pope Paul III (1534–1549), the mood in Rome had changed drastically to one of pessimism. The 1527 Sack of Rome had created insecurity, and the burgeoning Protestant movement was stimulating renewed religious uncertainty and fervor. In the "Last Judgment" (which received far less favorable reviews than the "Creation," with many critics crying obscenity), you can read the drama, terror, and pathos of the era.

In the center of the composition is an athletic, beardless,

and severe Christ in Judgment, flanked by Mary and a collection of saints. Below, on the left, are the blessed on their way to Heaven; note the two figures suspended by a rosary, a clear anti-Lutheran statement.

In contrast, on the right the damned are being pushed down to Hell while Charon, in his boat, watches. Michelangelo gave Minos, the judge of the damned, the face of one of his sharpest critics, Biagio da Cesena, a member of the papal court. He is the figure in the lower right-hand corner with the donkey's ears entwined in a serpent's coils. Below and right of the Redeemer, St. Bartholomew holds his flayed skin, recalling the method of his martyrdom, but he has no beard. Why? Because his is the face of the beardless Michelangelo.

Museo Pio-Clementino

Access to the Pio-Clementine Museum is through the ground-floor Cortile della Pigna and up the stairs to the Palazzo del Belvedere, built during the reign of Innocent VIII. This museum has a variety of sections, but the most impressive may well be its vast display of classical statuary in the Cortile Ottagonale. You could say that the foundations of the entire Vatican museum complex were laid right here when, in 1503, Pope Julius II placed a statue of Apollo, ever since called the **Belvedere Apollo,** in the Belvedere's courtyard. Clement XIV significantly enlarged the collection in 1770, and the museum was opened shortly thereafter.

The list of sculptures is endless, but there are several pieces that are not to be missed, especially the **"Laocoön"** (see sidebar p. 178). The Cabinet of Apoxyomenos, just beyond the round vestibule, houses a statue known as the **"Apoxyomenos Athlete,"** a first-century Roman marble copy of a bronze statue by Lysippus from about 320 B.C. Found in Trastevere

(see sidebar p. 178)

Skip the Lines

One way to skip waiting in line at the Vatican is to sign up for a tour *(www .vaticano.va)*. Another is to buy tickets from an online agency that organizes a tour—though, once inside, they often leave you to visit the museums on your own (sometimes with an audio guide). You may still encounter a wait, but it generally won't be more than 30 minutes.

Naturally, these services costs more than the Vatican's normal entrance fee, but you may well decide it is worth it. (If not, try going to the Vatican just after lunch, when the regular line is likely to be much shorter.)

You can also avoid the line at the Colosseum by signing up for a guided tour. Or you can prearrange your visit online at www.pierreci.it, or by telephone at 060608 (see sidebar p. 10) or 06 3996 7700 (€1.50 surcharge). You get immediate access with the Roma Pass (see sidebar p. 9) or by simply going first to the Palatine Hill or the Roman Forum, where the ticket you buy also is good for the Colosseum.

Online sites which offer Skip-the-line tickets for the Vatican and/or the Colosseum include www.Rome-museum.com; www.viator.com; www.traveltoe.com; www .prestotours.com; and www.aboutroma.com.

in 1849, it shows an athlete in the process of scraping oil from his body. The street where is was found is now called the Vicolo dell' Atleta. The remaining rooms include the Animal Room, the Gallery of Statues, the Gallery of Busts, the Mask Room, and the Hall of the Muses. Near the exit is a domed room with a reconstructed *biga*, or two-horse chariot.

The "Laocoön"

In the Octagonal Court you'll find the "Laocoön," possibly the most sublime classical marble group to have survived. Excavated in 1506 on the Esquiline Hill and possibly from the Domus Aurea, it is attributed to three first-century sculptors from Rhodes working from an older bronze original. It tells the story (related by Virgil in the *Aeneid*) of the Trojan priest, Laocoön, and his two sons whose warnings about the wooden horse angered Athena, who sent two huge serpents to kill them. Their facial expressions convey human suffering in an unparalleled fashion.

The Pinacoteca & the Other Museums

As you can imagine, over the centuries the popes have also built quite a collection of paintings. You can see them in the **Pinacoteca.** (Turn right at the top of the escalator instead of left.) Although not enormous, the collection is impressive and includes Raphael's "Transfiguration," his "Madonna di Foligno," and his "Coronation of the Virgin," all in the same room. There are also paintings by Giotto, Fra Angelico, Simone Martini, Perugino, Bellini, and Titian, to name only a few.

For more specialized interests, there are the **Museo Egizio** (Egyptian Museum), the **Museo Etrusco** (Etruscan Museum), and the **Museo Gregoriano Profano** (Gregorian Profane Museum), which displays several Greek and Roman collections, arranged either by era or thematically. It is in this museum that you can see the famous mosaics of athletes found in the Baths of Caracalla (see pp. 212–213).

The Braccio Nuovo of the **Chiaramonti Museo,** a smaller adjunct to the Pio-Clementino that was organized by the sculptor Canova in the early 19th century, also displays Roman floor mosaics. There you will also find the famous statue of Augustus from the villa of his wife, Livia, at Prima Porta. The **Museo Pio-Christiano** (Pio-Christian Museum) displays early Christian antiquities.

It is also possible to visit the 16th-century **Giardini Vaticani** (Vatican Gardens). On guided tours that last about two hours, you get to see the medieval German cemetery attached to the Teutonic College, several major fountains, and the main buildings (mostly from outside) including the new (1971) Aula delle Udienze (Audience Hall), the Governatorato (Governor's Palace), and Casina di Pio IV, today seat of the Pontifical Science Academy. ■

Castel Sant'Angelo

Built as a mausoleum by Emperor Hadrian (but completed after his death), Castel Sant'Angelo has also been a fortress, a prison, a papal refuge, a barracks, and a pleasure palace. This circular structure was once topped with trees and, possibly, a large statue of the emperor.

The ancient Pons Adrianus in front of Castel Sant'Angelo was built in the second century A.D.

At the end of the sixth century, with Rome decimated by plague, Pope Gregory the Great led a massive procession to St. Peter's to ask for divine intercession. Along the way, he saw the Archangel Michael standing above the mausoleum and sheathing his sword as if to mark the end of the scourge. Subsequently, a statue of the Archangel was placed atop the tomb, which was renamed Castel Sant'Angelo. Erected in 1753, the bronze statue you see today replaced an earlier stone one created by Raffaele da Montelupo.

Throughout the Middle Ages, the papacy and Rome's noble families frequently vied for control of the castle, and thus the city itself. During the Sack of Rome in 1527, Clement VII took refuge here, probably using the secret corridor *(il passetto)* that was built into the Leonine wall in 1277; you can see it on a guided tour of the castle.

Because bits and pieces have been added on over the centuries, you'll need imagination and a discerning eye to separate the original Roman portions from the additions of later eras. The vestibule downstairs was the original entrance. A statue of Hadrian probably stood in the niche at the far end. Like the rooms directly above it, the vestibule is in the central Roman

Castel Sant'Angelo

- Map pp. 162–163
- Lungotevere Castello 50
- 06 681 9111 or 06 3996 7600
- Closed Mon.
- $. Audio guide: $. Tours in English on request: $$$$$
- Bus: 23, 34, 40, 49, 87, 280, 492, 926, 982, 990

www.pierreci.it

core of the building. Walk up the long ramp, which still has portions of the original mosaic floor. Go left and continue until you reach the **Cordonata di Alexander VI,** a gradual staircase that cuts diagonally across the structure and eventually ends at the **Cortile dell'Angelo.** Along

The Prison

For centuries parts of Castel Sant'Angelo were used as a prison. Benvenuto Cellini, a 16th-century Florentine goldsmith, tells in his autobiography of being imprisoned there, and Puccini made it the scene for Tosca's suicide. In the 1930s, it was restored and turned into a museum.

the way you will walk over a drawbridge, which, until 1822, could be pulled up to protect the upper stories of the castle from intruders. The bridge spans the funeral chamber, where Hadrian's remains were originally kept. Named after the cannonballs stored there, the Cortile delle Palle is also known as the Cortile dell'Angelo because it housed da Montelupo's gigantic angel statue after its replacement.

The rooms on the left are named for the various popes who inhabited them or for the subject matter of their decoration. The **Sala di Apollo** has lovely "grotesque" decoration on the walls. When you come to the **Sala di Giustizia,** once a courtroom, you will be back in the Roman part of the structure. Be sure to note the fresco of the Angel of Justice, over one of the doors, by Perin del Vaga.

A corridor from the Apollo Room leads to a courtyard, called either the **Cortile del Teatro,** because theatrical performances were given there during the Renaissance, or the Cortile del Pozzo dell'Olio, because of the wellhead. Just past the entrance, a short flight of stairs through the door on the right takes you to **Pope Clement VII's bathroom,** with frescoes by Giulio Romano. The courtyard's other rooms were used as **prison cells;** the ones on this floor were for VIPs; the ones downstairs, for ordinary prisoners.

Farther upstairs, the **Loggia of Julius II** overlooks the Ponte Sant'Angelo. Its walls were lengthened in the 19th century when the walls along the Tiber were built.

Up a short flight of stairs from the loggia are the **Papal Apartments** frescoed by Perin del Vaga for Paul III (1534–1549). Note another angel frescoed on the far wall and the amusing portrait of a gentleman peering out of a trompe l'oeil door. A curving corridor, decorated with more grotesques, leads to what was once the library; only the upper portion of the walls was frescoed because bookcases covered the lower part.

Through a door in the center of the wall is the **Camera del Tesoro** or dell'Archivio Segreto. Until 1870 the Vatican kept its secret archives here. A narrow winding staircase carved into the thick walls leads up to the terrace, where you will find a spectacular view of St. Peter's and the city. ■

A warren of narrow streets and small squares traditionally inhabited by transplanted foreigners and nonconformists

Trastevere to Gianicolo

Detail of the ceiling of the master bedroom in Villa Farnesina

Trastevere to Gianicolo

To the Italians, Trastevere is a *popolare* neighborhood, one of the few still inhabited by "real" Romans. Until recently it was a working-class area, where typical *Trasteverini* were lower-income, extroverted, sharp-tongued—and possibly a bit arrogant, since they consider themselves to be the true descendants of the ancient Romans.

No one really knows why, but the Trasteverini tend to have loud, rather hoarse voices and to speak with a very heavy Roman accent. They drink lots of coffee, breakfast on *maritozzi* (a plain, sweet roll filled with fresh whipped cream), and favor heavy dishes such as *spaghetti cacio e pepe* (spaghetti with grated *caciotta* cheese and pepper) and *coda alla vaccinara* (oxtail in tomato sauce). Over the past several decades their numbers have dwindled. Some have left the area either by choice, preferring the newer, more modern apartments built in the postwar period. Others have been forced out by gentrification and spiraling rents. But enough Trasteverini remain to allow the neighborhood to keep much of its traditional color and character.

At the same time, Trastevere—which means trans-Tiber (across the Tiber)—also has a long history as a favorite residential area for foreigners and nonconformists. This was true even in ancient Roman times, when many outsiders settled here, including tens of thousands of Jews. According to local parish officials, there may once have been as many as ten synagogues in the neighborhood. The first Christians, for the most part converted Jews, settled here as well. And the area's international flavor was certainly heightened following World War II, when many foreigners settled here because of its traditions and because it was considerably cheaper than other central neighborhoods.

Artisans abound, as do small shops, bars, and eateries. In fact, the trattorias of Trastevere have always drawn outsiders, especially on weekends and during July's Festa de'Noiantri (Our Own Festival). These days, in the evenings the restaurants have been supplemented by scores of small *locali* (clubs), sometimes only a few tables or a bar counter, which appeal to young people. Many intellectuals—filmmakers, artists, and students—also live here. This, along with an abundance of street peddlers, art galleries, and boutiques, explains why Trastevere is often compared to Soho in London or New York's SoHo or Greenwich Village.

NOT TO BE MISSED:

GALLERIA PRINCIPE
AMEDEO SAVOIA AOSTA

PONT
PR. AMEDE
SAVO
AOS

VIA LUNGOTEVE DELL

VIALE DELLE

Sant'
Onofrio

Tasso's
Oak

Passeggiata

Faro

Monumento ad
Anita Garibaldi

MONTE

MURA del

Villa
Lante

Monument
a Giuseppe
Garibaldi

PIAZZALE
G. GARIBAL

AURELIE

Porta S
Pancra

Trastevere stretches upriver from Viale Trastevere to the Vatican and nestles on the lower slopes of Monte Gianicolo (Janiculum Hill). It also extends downriver beyond the Viale, running by Tiber Island and including lovely Piazza in Piscinula, the church of Santa Cecilia, and, at its outer limit, Porta Portese. The heart of the neighborhood, however, is Piazza Santa Maria in Trastevere, which faces the magnificent basilica of the same name and which, with its cafés and restaurants, newsstand, and pharmacy, is akin to a village square for the area's residents.

Many people still shop in the outdoor market at nearby Piazza San Cosimato or buy bread on Sunday mornings at the *forno* in Via del Moro. Pass through Porta Settimiana on Via della Lungara, for centuries the only road linking Trastevere to the Vatican, and you will come to the Botanical Gardens, once part of the beautiful, post-baroque Palazzo Corsini, and to Villa Farnesina, where archaeologists found the ruins of a splendid villa. Above looms the Janiculum Hill, where San Pietro in Montorio and Sant'Onofrio compete for attention with the breathtaking Roman panorama. ■

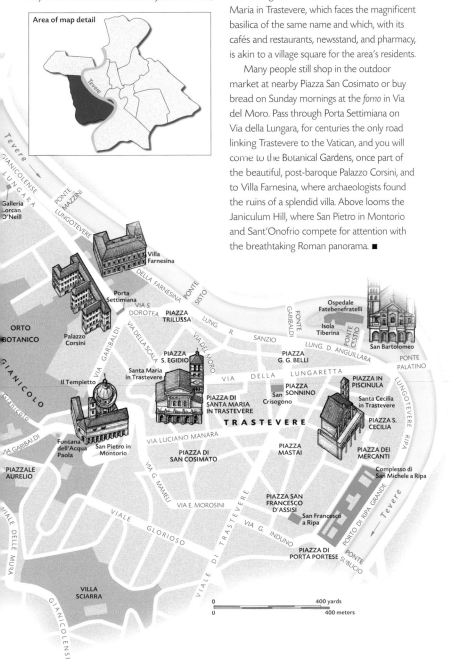

Area of map detail

Santa Maria in Trastevere

According to St. Jerome, oil gushed from the ground in a veterans' hospital in Trastevere at the time of Jesus' birth, a clear sign of "the grace of Christ that would come to humanity." In the third century, a church was founded (probably by St. Calixtus) where the miracle supposedly took place. An inscription on the church floor, to the right of the altar, marks the spot.

In Christian iconography, the 12 Apostles were often shown as sheep in mosaics.

Widely believed to be one of the first churches in Rome, Santa Maria in Trastevere was certainly the first to be dedicated to Mary. As we see it today, with its charming *campanile* (bell tower), the basilica—completed in the 1140s—is primarily medieval in style. Somehow the 12th-century aura has lingered, despite later additions such as Domenichino's gilded, coffered ceiling (1617) and Carlo Fontana's portico (1702) with its statues of four saints, including St. Calixtus.

The church is notable for its use of classical Roman architectural forms. The 22 columns in the nave, of various dimensions, types

of stone, textures, and colors, were looted from ancient ruins. The straight trabeation (or architrave) over the columns evokes classical Roman construction, a temporary rejection of the arches preferred by earlier and later architects.

Mosaics & More

What truly sets Santa Maria apart are its glowingly beautiful mosaics, which mark a return to a tradition that had been largely discontinued. For this we can probably thank Abbot Desiderius of Monte Cassino, who, toward the end of the 11th century, brought mosaic workers from Constantinople and used them to train local artisans. In this regard, note the cosmatesque pavement (see p. 208) that, though restored in the 19th century, dates to the 1100s.

The mosaics on the facade date from the 12th or 13th century and show a Madonna enthroned, flanked on either side by five women. They probably represent the Wise and Foolish Virgins from the Gospel, although some historians believe that the scene depicts a procession of eight virgins and two widows. The widows, they insist, are the women whose lamps have gone out. The two tiny figures at the Madonna's feet represent the donors who financed the piece.

The mosaics inside the church are even more exceptional. Those in the half-dome of the apse date from the 12th century and show Mary, enthroned, next to Jesus, who has his arm around his mother's shoulder. They are flanked by a collection of saints including, on the left and holding a model of the church, Pope Innocent II, the donor. The prophets Isaiah and Jeremiah are on the two sides of the apse. On the next row down is Pietro Cavallini's 13th-century mosaic of the "Life of the Virgin Mary" in six masterful scenes. Cavallini also created the mosaic showing the "Madonna and Child between St. Peter and St. Paul" on the apse's central lower segment.

The altar canopy has four porphyry columns. The sumptuous **Altemps Chapel** on the right (designed by Martino Longhi the Elder in the 1580s) has an ornate ceiling and numerous frescoes, including one that depicts the Council of Trent (1545–1563; see sidebar, p. 24), a major event in Roman Catholicism's response to the Protestant challenge. Also interesting are the marble fragments embedded in the walls of the facade, bearing catacomb inscriptions from the third and fourth centuries. Between the gate and the facade are four magnificent medieval floor tombs. ■

Santa Maria in Trastevere

🅰 Map pp. 182–183

✉ Piazza Santa Maria in Trastevere

☎ 06 581 4802 or 06 581 9443

🕐 Open daily

🚌 Bus: 23, 115, 125, 175, 280. Tram: 3, 8

EXPERIENCE: Cooking Classes

You know you are in love with Roman food when your mouth waters every time you think of those artichokes—*alla romana* or *alla giudea* (Jewish style), the fried zucchini flowers, that luscious *saltimbocca,* the scrumptious *pollo con pepperoni,* the tripe or oxtail in tomato sauce, the sauteed chicory, the fried mozzarella, and all those wonderful pasta dishes.

Sure, you can eat all these dishes, and scores more, in most Roman restaurants, but why not learn to cook them for yourself? If you do, you'll have more than just some photos and a few souvenirs to show your friends when you get home. Surprisingly, this is something you can do fairly easily, as long as you are willing to make arrangements in advance. Here are some suggested companies that offer cooking classes in Rome to make your search easier:

Torre di Babele www.torredibabele.com
Maureen Fant www.contextrome.com
IT-SCHOOLS www.it-schools.com
Cook Like Romans Cook
    www.liveromelikearoman.com
Diane Seed's Roman Kitchen
    www.italiangourmet.com

A Taste of Trastevere Walk

This two-part walk around Trastevere will give you a feeling for a neighborhood that boasts a vast spectrum of sights and sounds. Local artisans, young professionals, American college students, and transplanted foreigners congregate here to enjoy what many people say is one of the last remaining enclaves of "the real Rome."

Start at Piazza Santa Maria in Trastevere (see p. 184), where you can enjoy a coffee at the Café de Marzio while taking one more look at the Basilica of Santa Maria's glorious facade. Wear your bags or cameras across your chest. Or, better yet, don't carry a bag at all; a Roman purse-snatcher can spot a tourist a mile off. Exit the piazza by the newsstand and take Via della Lungaretta to Viale di Trastevere. On your right, **San Crisogono** ❶ (see p. 198) has an exceptional cosmatesque pavement (see p. 208).

INSIDER TIP:

Romans are fond of strolling through the Orto Botanico, a refreshing sanctuary boasting a variety of cacti and flora...as well as several inviting patches of grass, perfect for napping.

—NATASHA SCRIPTURE
National Geographic contributor

Carefully cross the busy avenue, and continue along Via della Lungaretta, which takes you through a deliciously old neighborhood, to charming Piazza in Piscinula, where the Mattei family once had a palace. Before entering the piazza, turn right at the hilly Arco dei Tolomei, which brings you under a fascinating medieval archway. Turn left at Via dei Salumi and then right on Via dei Vascellari, which soon becomes Via di Santa Cecilia and takes you to the piazza and church of **Santa Cecilia in Trastevere** ❷ (see pp. 194–95).

After visiting the church, check out lovely **Piazza dei Mercanti,** which is located between

NOT TO BE MISSED:

San Crisogono • Santa Cecilia in Trastevere • San Francesco a Ripa • Villa Farnesina

Piazza Santa Cecilia and the river, but avoid the restaurants; they are way too touristy. Continue along Via di Santa Cecilia toward Via Madonna dell'Orto. Note the long **Complesso di San Michele a Ripa** building on your left. A poorhouse in the 17th century, today it is used for governmental offices (see p. 198). **Santa Maria dell'Orto** ❸, the facade at the end of the Via Madonna dell'Orto curiously decorated with obelisks, was once the headquarters for many guilds of the more humble occupations, such as fruit vendors and chicken keepers. If it's between 2:00 p.m. and 4:00 p.m. on a Tuesday or Thursday afternoon, make a brief detour right on Via Anicia and ring the bell at No. 12. The custodian will let you into the magnificent, hidden 15th-century cloister of **San Giovanni dei Genovesi** ❹.

After leaving the cloister, retrace your steps and continue along Via Anicia until you come to Piazza San Francesco d'Assisi and the church of **San Francesco a Ripa** ❺ (see p. 198), where one of Bernini's three "Ecstasies" is displayed. Via San Francesco a Ripa, which faces the church, will take you back to Viale di Trastevere. Cross over and, at the intersection with Via Luciano Manara, look left up the street at the lovely, moss-covered fountain set against the lower slope of the Janiculum Hill. Continuing along Via San Francesco a Ripa will bring you to Piazza di San Callisto and then to **Santa Maria,** where you began.

The second, and shorter, part of this walk starts from the Via della Paglia (the street opposite the newsstand) and takes you to **Piazza Sant'Egidio** ❻ on the right, where there is a folk art museum (Museo di Roma in Trastevere) and the church's socially activist Comunità di Sant'Egidio. Here you have a choice. If you leave the Piazza by Via della Scala (the street on the left) you will come to Piazza della Scala, where the Carmelite church of **Santa Maria della Scala** contains paintings by some of Caravaggio's pupils. The pharmacy outside is also very old. At the end of Via della Scala is the old stone **Porta Settimiana** gateway and Via della Lungara, which takes you to the **Orto Botanico** (Botanical Garden), **Palazzo Corsini**, and **Villa Farnesina** ❼ (see pp. 188–189).

If you take Vicolo del Cinque, the right-hand exit out of Piazza Sant'Egidio, you'll reach **Piazza Trilussa** and the wonderful fountain facing the Ponte Sisto pedestrian bridge spanning the Tevere, or Tiber River. Follow Via Santa Dorotea on the other side of the fountain to Porta Settimiana. The house to the right of the arch, **Casa della Fornarina** (today a restaurant), is said to have been the home of La Fornarina, Raphael's mistress.

Ⓜ	Also see area map, pp. 182–183
►	Santa Maria in Trastevere
↔	1.5 miles (2.5 km)
⊕	2 hours
►	Villa Farnesina

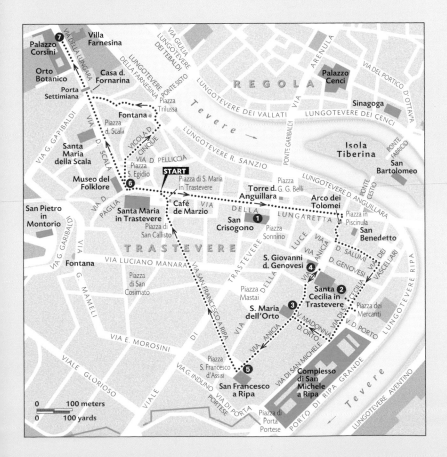

Villa Farnesina

Considered a gem of Renaissance architecture, Villa Farnesina—about a block from Porta Settimiana—was built in the early 1500s as a country villa for Sienese banker and businessman Agostino Chigi and later sold to the Farnese family. Chigi spared no expense in furnishing his new residence, decorating it with scenes from Greek and Roman mythology.

Il Sodoma's painting of the wedding of Alexander and Roxanne

The Galatea Room

The first room on the ground floor, the Galatea Room, was once an open loggia. Today it is known primarily for Raphael's **"Triumph of Galatea."** This wonderful fresco, dated around 1513, shows the sea nymph, wearing a red cloak, riding the ocean waves. Two straining dolphins, one of which is breakfasting on a small squid, pull her seashell carriage, which is surrounded by cupids. A triton appears to be molesting Galatea's handmaiden.

Created by Peruzzi, the sumptuous **ceiling** depicts the planets and constellations at the time of Chigi's birth. Some of the lunettes (by Sebastiano del Piombo) contain scenes from Ovid's *Metamorphoses*.

Next is the magnificent **Loggia of Cupid and Psyche,** which Raphael designed to look like a summertime pergola with fruit and flowers, although most of the artwork was done by his pupils. Craning at the ceiling may give you a stiff neck, but the two large **ceiling frescoes—**

INSIDER TIP:

To complement Rome's rich artistic legacy and to get a feel for how Romans kick off the evening, check out exhibition openings at contemporary galleries, such as the recently opened Lorcan O'Neill in the bohemian neighborhood of Trastevere.

—FILIPPO COSMELLI
Founder & Director,
IF Lifestyle Management

the "Wedding of Cupid and Psyche" and the "Council of the Gods"—are breathtaking. Of the "Three Graces" in the fresco in the corner right of the door, the one with her back to you was probably Chigi's mistress and may have been painted by Raphael himself. The lunettes recount the various stages of Psyche's troubled relationship with the jealous Venus.

Upstairs

The upper floor is equally exciting. In the **Sala delle Prospettive,** the living room, Peruzzi repeated his indoor-outdoor theme, relying heavily on trompe l'oeil landscapes and urban scenes with real landmarks such as Porta Settimiana, an aqueduct, and the campanile of Santa Maria in Trastevere. Note the unfortunate graffiti, left by marauding soldiers during the Sack of Rome in 1527.

Next door you will find the villa's rather small **master bedroom.** Despite its size, however, the room is a magnificent riot of color, painted mostly by Giovan Antonio Bazzi, generally referred to as Il Sodoma (the Sodomite) because of his homosexuality. The central wall, the "Wedding of Roxanne and Alexander" (the Great), is considered Bazzi's masterpiece. The right-hand wall, "Alexander's Meeting with the Family of Darius of Persia," is less accomplished; the artist reportedly felt he was being underpaid. Whereas the central portion of the left-hand wall, the "Taming of Bucephalus" (Alexander's horse), was clearly painted by someone else. When Chigi's enormous gem-encrusted bed was moved out of the house after his death, it left an empty space that had to be filled.

Chigi's Theatrics

Chigi was a very wealthy bon vivant with a keen sense of one-upmanship. A lavish reception organized in 1518 in honor of Pope Leo X was staged in the stables, which were appropriately decorated for the occasion. The idea was to embarrass the Riario family across the street by demonstrating that the Chigi stables were as elegant as the Riario's dining rooms. Later the same year another reception was held at a loggia on the riverbank. Guests were surely impressed (or perhaps horrified?) when, at the end of each course, the servants tossed the silver dishes into the Tiber. But not to worry—Chigi had strung nets below to retrieve them. ∎

Villa Farnesina

🅰 Map pp. 182–183

✉ Via della Lungara 230

☎ 06 680271

🕐 Open Mon.–Sat. 9 a.m.–1 p.m. Closed Sun.

💲 $

🚌 23, 116, 125, 280

Galleria Lorcan O'Neill

🅰 Map pp. 182–183

✉ 1e Via Orti D'Albert

☎ 06 6889 2980

🕐 Open Mon.–Fri. noon–8 p.m. , Sat. 2–8 p.m., Closed Sun.

www.lorcanoneill .com

Palazzo Corsini

Across the street from Villa Farnesina is the Palazzo Corsini, an 18th-century reconstruction and amplification of the Renaissance palace owned by the Riario family in the 15th century. In the 17th century it became the home of Queen Christina of Sweden, a convert to Catholicism who had abdicated and moved to Rome in 1655. The Corsini, who were Florentines, moved to Rome after Lorenzo Corsini was elected to the papacy as Clement XII in 1730.

Palazzo Corsini
- Map pp. 182–183
- Via della Lungara 10
- 06 6880 2323
- Closed Mon.
- $
- Bus: 23, 116, 125, 280

www.ticketeria.it/ corsini-eng.asp

The 18th-century architect Ferdinando Fuga directed the restructuring, creating a new light-filled central body with an impressive and stately ceremonial double staircase leading up to the gallery and a monumental three-arched entryway. He also added another wing that was used to house the priceless Corsini library.

In 1883 the building and its art collection were bought by the Italian government, and today the building also houses the Accademia dei Lincei (1603), an academy of scholars founded to promote learning, and said to be the oldest of its kind.

The **Galleria Corsini,** a suite of eight rooms that give off the atrium (one floor up), contains part of the collection of the Galleria Nazionale d'Arte Antica (see pp. 100–101). The paintings, from the 14th to the 18th century, are somewhat haphazardly displayed but include one Caravaggio ("San Giovannino, The Young John the Baptist"), a lovely "Madonna and Child" by Beato Angelico, and a bust of Pope Alexander VII, a Chigi, by Bernini. There are also works by Rubens, Van Dyck, Murillo, and Poussin, as well as sculptures, bronzes, and furniture from the 1700s.

Queen Christina of Sweden is one of only three women accorded monuments in St. Peter's Basilica (see p. 170). Despite several remodelings, the room in which she died on April 19, 1689, has remained as it was. Lavishly decorated, it has two yellow faux-marble columns as well as elaborate ceilings.

From the back rooms there is a lovely view of the Botanical Garden (formerly the gardens of the Palazzo) and of the lower slopes of the Janiculum Hill. ∎

The Seven Hills of Rome

Many people think that the Janiculum was one of the original seven hills of Rome. But they are wrong. The seven hills of Rome are all on the other side of the Tiber. The Palatine, close to the river, was the site of the earliest settlements and later of the emperors' opulent residences. On the Capitoline were Rome's most important temples, and in between the two hills was the magnificent Roman Forum. The remaining hills, which do not actually seem terribly high, are the Caelian, the Esquiline, the Aventine, the Viminal, and the Quirinal, now the Italian president's residence (see pp. 92, 98).

San Pietro in Montorio & Bramante's Tempietto

This magnificently placed Franciscan church is generally the first stop for visitors to the Janiculum Hill. The view of the city from the entrance steps is superb, and the church itself, with its fine travertine facade, is lovely. Dating from 1481, San Pietro in Montorio once enjoyed special significance in the erroneous belief that the cloister next door was the site of St. Peter's crucifixion.

From Trastevere a series of steps starting in Via Masi leads up to this landmark church.

Inside, there is a beautiful "Flagellation" by Sebastiano del Piombo, and works by Peruzzi, Pomarancio, and Vasari. Bernini designed the second chapel on the left. Somewhere underneath is the grave of the young noblewoman Beatrice Cenci, whose 1599 execution at the age of 22 for patricide excited the popular imagination. She was the subject of poems, plays, and paintings, such as Guido Reni's portrait in the Barberini Museum.

In the courtyard of the adjacent monastery is the small, circular **Il Tempietto** ("Little Temple") designed by Bramante and paid for by King Ferdinand and Queen Isabella of Spain to mark the birth of their son. The structure—a colonnade with Doric capitals topped by a balustrade and a cupola—is thought to embody the Renaissance ideal of classical harmony and proportion. Farther up the hill in a commanding position is the **Fontana dell'Acqua Paola** (otherwise known as the Fontanone or Big Fountain). Like the Trevi Fountain, this is the *mostra terminale* of an aqueduct, the point where water first arrives from an extra-urban source. Built of material plundered from the Roman Forum, it is composed of three large central niches flanked by two smaller ones. Water gushes from all five into the pool below (see pp. 96–97). ■

San Pietro in Montorio & Bramante's Tempietto

 Map pp. 182–183

✉ Piazza di San Pietro in Montorio 2

☎ Church: 06 581 3940. Tempietto: 06 581 7377

🕐 Church: closed noon–3:30 p.m. Tempietto: closed 12:30–2 p.m. (winter), 12:30–4 p.m. (summer) & Mon.

🚌 Bus: 115, 870

Gianicolo

The Gianicolo, or Janiculum Hill, which runs from Trastevere to the Vatican more or less parallel to the Tiber, has little significance for ancient Roman history but was intimately associated with the Italian *Risorgimento* unification movement of the 19th century. The Porta San Pancrazio, at the top of the hill, and the surrounding area saw major battles between the French and the Romans and Italians. In the 1890s the entire area was turned into a public park.

Romans love to drive to the Janiculum Hill to enjoy the spectacular panoramic view of the city.

Gianicolo
- Map pp. 182–183
- Bus: 115, 870

Look for the main entrance to the Gianicolo Promenade or **Passeggiata del Gianicolo** on the right just, past the Fontana dell'Acqua Paola or Fontanone. The promenade has a lovely tree-lined avenue, an equestrian statue of Garibaldi, and busts of Italy's most important patriots. A favorite place for the *passeggiata domenicale* (Sunday walk), it also offers pony rides, puppet shows, and, in the evenings, ample space for couples to park.

The incomparable view of Rome, however, is the major attraction. This vantage point offers an unobstructed vista of all of the city's major landmarks and magnificent domes. On a clear day, you can see all the way to the Alban Hills. The view is also superb from the faro (lighthouse) beyond **Villa Lante**, which Italians in Argentina donated to the city in 1911.

Little is left of **Tasso's Oak**, the tree under which the 16th-century poet liked to sit. Tasso died in 1595 in the convent of nearby **Sant'Onofrio**, a small, single-nave church. It boasts a lovely two-part "Annunciation" by Antoniazzo Romano and a 15th-century cloister with frescoes from the life of Sant'Onofrio. ■

EXPERIENCE: Appreciating the *Aperitivo*

It's late afternoon but too early for dinner. You have finished your shopping and touring and want to enjoy the afternoon sun or the sunset. What should you do? Everywhere you look, Romans are sitting at outdoor cafés with colored drinks and nibbles in front of them and enjoying chit-chat, people-watching, and the view of some gorgeous ancient Roman monument or, if seated on a terrace or hill, the city below. You should join them.

The *aperitivo*—which has existed in Italy in some form or other for millennia—is an aromatic or alcoholic drink designed to encourage social contact and stimulate the appetite. Its first appearance in modern Italy may have been in Turin in 1796, when Anronio Benedetto Carpano invented his vermouth drink, later renamed "Punt e Mes" by Italian King Victor Emanuel II. Others say the tradition began in Milan, where the Ramazzotti brothers invented their "amaro," mixing 33 herbs and roots in an alcohol base. Also in Milan, the Martini family came up with their vermouth drinks, first Martini bianco and then Martini dry, and in 1862, Gaspare Campari created Campari Bitter.

The Roman Take

Whatever its origins, the aperitivo tradition is now in full swing in Rome, too. At **Ombre Rosse** *(Piazza S. Egidio)* in Trastevere, where you can enjoy free buffet from 7 p.m. to 9 p.m, the aperitivo of choice these days is a "spritz" made with white wine, the orange-colored non alcoholic Aperol, and soda. Elsewhere people choose the more traditional drinks, like a Negroni (vermouth, gin, and Campari over ice)

or a non-alcoholic Crodino. Drinks newer to Italy, like the Brazilian Caipirinha or the Cuban Mojito, also abound, as do classics like the Bellini (champagne and peach juice) or a simple glass of sparkling Prosecco. But really, what's most important is your mood, that feeling of joie de vivre and expectation—whether for dinner or something else.

INSIDER TIP:

Start a meal with an aperitivo: It doesn't need to be Campari and soda—the non-alcoholic Crodino is also very popular.

—TIM JEPSON
National Geographic author

Stellar Views

To heighten the aperitivo experience even further you should combine your pre-dinner drink with nothing less than an astounding view. One way to do this is to head either for the cafès at **Piazza della Rotonda,** where the magnificent second-century Pantheon stares you in the face, or those at **Piazza Navona,** where your eyes

can feast on Bernini's magnificent fountains. Or you can aim for **Rosati** in Piazza Del Popolo, where you can look up toward the Pincio and think about Daisy Miller riding in her carriage there.

Another possibility Is to choose the "high road" instead. Several of Rome's hotels have terraces from which you can get a magnificent view while sipping your Campari and orange juice: the **Raphael** (see p. 250) near Piazza Navona overlooks the rooftops of medieval Rome, the **Minerve** (see p. 249) has a splendid view of the back of the Pantheon, the **Forum** (see p. 244) looks out over the Forum, and the **Eden** (see p. 246) overlooks Villa Medici and Trinità dei Monti. Two other deluxe hotels—the **Hassler** (see p. 247) and the **De Russie** (see p. 247)—don't have views but offer wonderful gardens for a pre-dinner drink.

If you have spent the morning or afternoon at the **Capitoline Museums,** another "high" is to sip something from the Museum's terrace bar as you scan the city's rooftops. And then, of course, there is the **Janiculum Park** above Trastevere, from which, as you sip, you can see all of Rome unfold before your eyes.

Santa Cecilia in Trastevere

An oasis of peace and quiet in a noisy neighborhood, this church was built to honor St. Cecilia, a very important early Christian saint, martyred by the Romans, together with her husband, Valerianus. It is said that on her wedding night, the well-born Cecilia converted her husband and the two then lived together platonically. The remains of their house, containing some sarcophagi, mosaic floors, and remnants of other classical structures, are under the church and can be visited during church hours.

Sculptor Stefano Maderno carved this statue of the dead St. Cecilia after viewing her body.

Some say that Cecilia, the patron saint of music, invented the organ. Others claim that she sang hymns for three days while confined to the *calidarium* (steam bath) of her house in a first, botched attempt by third-century Roman authorities to murder her. She was eventually stabbed in the neck, although decapitation proved, miraculously, impossible.

Pope Paschal I (817–824), who moved Cecilia's body here after seeing the location of her grave in a vision, first built a basilica on this site. Today's church is a hodgepodge of styles and colors. Ferdinando Fuga's monumental doorway opening onto a garden with a fountain is early 18th century, as is the facade. The bell tower, however, and the portico, with its lovely mosaic decoration, are 12th century.

Inside, the church has a bland, 18th-century look, probably because of the rash decision to encase the Roman columns in concrete pilasters, but there are some marvelous remnants of the more distant past. The ninth-century **mosaic in the apse** showing Jesus flanked by St. Paul, St. Agatha, and St. Valerian on the right side and by St. Peter and St. Cecilia on the left is a more Byzantine version of the one visible in Santi Cosma e Damiano (see p. 46). The figure farthest on the left, holding a model of the church, is Paschal, who cleverly had himself placed on equal footing with the saints and introduced to Christ by an affectionate St. Cecilia. The cosmatesque pavement (see p. 208) is, of course, medieval. The beautiful Gothic **altar canopy** by Arnolfo di Cambio dates from the late 13th century and is considered his masterpiece. Below is the heart-wrenching statue of Cecilia sculpted by Stefano Maderno, who viewed the supposedly intact body when the tomb was temporarily opened in 1599. In the chapel at the end of the right aisle, a damaged 12th-century fresco depicts the discovery of the saint's body.

Unfortunately, Church authorities have closed off the corridor where the calidarium was located and which also has a Guido Reni painting. And you can only look into the Ponziani Chapel. But don't despair. Every morning, for a small fee, the Benedictine nuns of the adjacent convent allow you to see the enthrallingly warm colors of **Pietro Cavallini's fresco of the "Last Judgment."**

Rediscovered in 1900, but dating from 1293, the fresco is the only major Cavallini to survive. Christ is shown enthroned and surrounded by Apostles, saints, and angels whose multicolored wings run from cream to rose. The nuns of Santa Cecilia have an extra behind-the-scenes job. Every year they are entrusted with two lambs blessed by the pope. They keep them until Easter, when they shear the wool—used to make the *pallia* (stoles) given to new patriarchs and archbishops. ■

Santa Cecilia in Trastevere

- 🅰 Map pp. 182–183
- ✉ Piazza Santa Cecilia 22
- ☎ 06 589 9289
- 🕐 Basilica: closed 12:30–4 p.m. Cavallini fresco: open Mon.–Sat. 10:15 a.m.–12:15 p.m. & Sun. 10:15 a.m.–11:15 p.m.
- 🚍 Bus: H, 23, 75, 115, 125, 280, 780. Tram: 8

Street Markets

A well-established tradition in Italy, street markets for used clothing, antiques, gifts, and bric-a-brac can be found throughout Rome. The Romans call them *mercatini* to distinguish them from the city's neighborhood food markets or *mercati rionali*. For years, the giant flea market held Sunday mornings at **Porta Portese** on the far side of Trastevere *(5 a.m.–2 p.m)* was the sole option for bargain-hunters and browsers in Rome. But nowadays, if you want to spend your Sunday looking for a treasure, you have several options.

Every Sunday from 10 a.m. to 7 p.m. at the **Borghetto Flamino** *(Piazza della Marina 32, Metro A, Flaminio stop, and then walk)*, you can browse the 240 stands for

everything from linens to old records. Or try the market at **Via Conca d'Oro**, where you can also taste specialties from the Italian south. Another is the **Isola del Tesoro** antiques fair in the outlying Tiburtina quarter *(Metro B, Pietralata stop)*, where 80 stands offer everything from books to antique watches.

Other Sunday markets (see Travelwise, p. 259) operate only once a month from September to June, although some, like the open-air market in **Via Sannio** near San Giovanni, are open all the time. And if antique prints are your thing, the **Mercato delle Stampe** in Largo della Fontanella Borghese (near the Spanish Steps) offers vintage prints, books, and magazines.

Isola Tiberina & San Bartolomeo

A tiny gemstone of travertine and plane trees located in the midst of the river, Isola Tiberina (Tiber Island) has long been associated with both medicine and religion. Connected to both shores of the Tevere (Tiber), it is the site of a major hospital, Fatebenefratelli (Do good, brothers) and a small synagogue.

Ponte Quattro Capi connects the island to the east side of the Tiber and the Ghetto.

San Bartolomeo
- Map pp. 182–183
- Isola Tiberina 22
- 06 687 7973
- Closed Mon.– Sat. 1:30–2:30 p.m. & Sun. after 1 p.m.
- Bus: H, 23, 63, 125, 280, 780. Tram: 8

Isola Tiberina

Legend has it that in the third century B.C. a delegation of Romans returned from a visit to the sibyl in Epidaurus (Greece) with instructions to build a temple to Aesculapius, the god of healing, if they wanted an outbreak of the plague to be quelled. As they sailed up the Tiber in 219 B.C., they saw a snake like the one wound around Aesculapius's staff (traditionally the doctor's symbol). It supposedly slithered off the ship and swam to the island, indicating its choice of a temple site.

Over the centuries, the island became so closely associated with this ancient story that travertine blocks were used to give the island itself the appearance of a prow and a stern, and vestiges of this construction in the form of a trireme's keel—including a relief depiction of the sacred snake—can still be

Il Tevere

Although it runs right through the city, these days Il Tevere, or Tiber, does not play much of a role in the lives of everyday Romans. It's there, it's picturesque, and it is spanned by a variety of bridges, including charming Ponte Sisto, from which there is a glorious view that includes St. Peter's Basilica. But ever since the end of the 19th century, when high embankments were built to put an end to frequent flooding, the *Biondo Tevere* ("blonde Tiber," named for its yellowish, muddy bottom) has taken a backseat to the Thames, the Seine, and the other major urban rivers of the world.

This was not always the case, however. Romulus and Remus, supposedly the founders of Rome, were said to have been discovered on the banks of the Tiber by the she-wolf who adopted them. In ancient times, the Tiber was a major point of access for ships sailing the Tyrrhenian Sea off the western Italian coast. And the Ripa Grande, the large commercial river port in Trastevere, and the smaller Porto di Ripetta (which until the 19th century boasted a monumental, tiered riverside staircase believed to have been the inspiration for the Spanish Steps), were both of vital ecomonic importance to the city.

---

seen on the side of the island that faces the synagogue.

Centuries later, the young Holy Roman Emperor Otto III chose the ruins of Aesculapius's temple as the site for a new church dedicated to his friend Adalbert, the first bishop of Prague, who had been martyred a year earlier in A.D. 997. Otto is said to have personally directed the building, using Roman columns and other ancient remnants for the nave and the portico. Somehow, however, poor Adalbert got lost in the shuffle.

Shortly after beginning construction, Otto perished in a skirmish with the rebellious local population. He had returned from a trip to Benevento in the Italian south with the remains of the Apostle Bartholomew and deposited them—temporarily, he thought—in his church. But when he died, St. Adalbert was quickly forgotten and the church was subsequently rededicated to St. Bartholomew instead.

San Bartolomeo

Rebuilt in 1113 and again in 1624, San Bartolomeo has a 12th-century campanile and baroque facade. Inside, a marble wellhead located on the steps leading up to the tribune bears four carved figures: Jesus, St. Bartholomew (holding the knife with which he was martyred), St. Adalbert with his bishop's staff), and Otto III with his crown and scepter. ∎

INSIDER TIP:

In 2003, the Tiber opened its waterways for tours of the Eternal City. Gain a different perspective of Rome by taking a boat tour—for information, go to *www.rexervation.com/crociere.asp*.

—MAURO PELELLA
National Geographic researcher

More Places to Visit

Complesso di San Michele a Ripa

Today the massive 1,099-foot-long (335 m) San Michele complex houses government offices and a branch of the Central Restoration Institute. Located on the bank of the Tiber once occupied by the ancient river port Ripa Grande, San Michele was founded in the late 17th century as a refuge for orphans, delinquents, and vagabonds. It was also a home for old folks and spinsters. Its upper end faces the Porta Portese gate, one of the entrances to the Sunday flea market. ▲ Map pp. 182–183 ✉ Via de San Michele 25 ☎ 06 5843 4437 🕐 Varies by exhibit 💲 Varies by exhibit 🚌 Bus: 23, 75, 115, 125, 280. Tram: 3, 8

San Crisogono

Situated on busy Viale di Trastevere, this large church is sadly often passed over by tourists. Built in the style of a classical Roman basilica, its cosmatesque pavement (see p. 208) may be one of the most beautiful in Rome. The baroque facade and interior decoration give little clue to its medieval beginnings; only the Romanesque campanile (one of the few in Rome with a triangular top) and the right flank are a giveaway to the church's 12th-century origins.

The two porphyry columns supporting the triumphal arch are the largest in Rome. The gilded and blue coffered ceiling is a masterpiece of the genre, but the 17th-century painting on the ceiling (the "Triumph of St. Crisogono" by Guercino) is a copy. The original is in Stafford House in London. The medieval altar has a cosmatesque finish, and the framed late 13th-century mosaic in the apse ("The Virgin Between Two Saints") has been attributed to Pietro Cavallini. The **underground ruins** of the original fifth-century paleo-Christian church are open to the public, although large groups should reserve. During the July Festival of Noiantri the church becomes a Marian sanctuary.

"The Virgin of Mount Carmel," an icon, is carried in procession through the streets and put on view in the church for eight days. ▲ Map pp. 182–183 ✉ Piazza Sonnino 44 (Viale Trastevere) ☎ 06 581 8225 🕐 Upper church: closed 11:30 a.m.–4:15 p.m. Mon.–Sat., 1:15–4:15 p.m. Sun. Underground church: closed 11 a.m.–4:30 p.m. Mon.–Sat., 1–4:30 p.m. Sun. 💲 Underground church: $ 🚌 Bus: H, 23, 125, 280, 780. Tram: 8

San Francesco a Ripa

St. Francis took a vow of poverty, but at St. Francis on the Riverbank (named for the ancient riverport that once existed near here) someone may not have been paying attention. When the 13th-century church (erected on the site of a hospice where the saint had once stayed) was rebuilt in the 17th century, it was done in no-holds-barred baroque—the decor is deliciously dramatic with opulent paintings, gold leaf, and stucco everywhere. The **Pallavicini Chapel** at the end of the right aisle nearest the altar is a triumph of multicolored marble; wall tombs sport garishly wicked winged skeletons. The **Altieri Chapel** across the aisle holds one of Bernini's majestic "Ecstasies," the magnificently dramatic statue of the "Blessed Ludovica Albertoni" (1674). Pay no attention to the stucco putto heads gazing down on the blessed Ludovica as she reclines in mystical ecstasy; they were added later. Bernini preferred natural and concealed lighting, but if the light from the side window is not enough for you, ask the sacristan to turn on the electric light for a moment. He'll also take you to visit St. Francis's cell with its stone pillow. ▲ Map pp. 182–183 ✉ Piazza di San Francesco a Ripa 88 ☎ 06 581 9020 🕐 Church: closed noon–4 p.m., & Sun. 1–4 p.m. St. Francis's cell: closed noon–4 p.m., Thurs., & Sun. a.m. 🚌 Bus: H, 23, 115, 125, 280, 780. Tram: 3, 8. ■

The remains of ancient temples and monuments, Piazza Venezia,
the 16th-century Jewish Ghetto, and the quieter Aventine Hill

Forum Boarium to Aventino

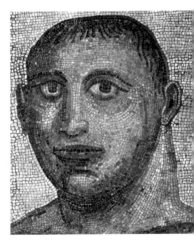

Floor mosaic at Terme di Caracalla
depicting a gladiator

Forum Boarium to Aventino

Some 2,000 years ago, the area between the Campidoglio and the Tiber was the location for the Forum Boarium and the Forum Holitorium, two bustling outdoor markets for, respectively, cattle and vegetables. The Velabrium, as it was called, straddled a road that led straight to the city center, the Roman Forum.

The adjacent area also abounds in vestiges of Roman rule. The remains of the Teatro di Marcellus, designed by Julius Caesar's architects but completed by Augustus, were incorporated into an elegant 16th-century palazzo. Three columns from the temple of Apollo Sosianus are dramatically outlined against a medieval urban background, and the remnants of the Portico d'Ottavia, which Octavius dedicated to his sister, lie within the area known as the Ghetto, to which the Jews of Rome were confined for centuries.

A large modern thoroughfare, opened in 1933 and now called Via Luigi Petroselli, takes car and bus traffic north past the central Registry Office (the Anagrafe) north to Piazza Venezia. But some remarkable remnants of those earlier times remain; all you need to enjoy them is a vivid imagination. Picture the cattle traders as they crowded under the Arch of Janus to avoid the winter rain or the scorching summer sun. Imagine how they decided to build a second arch (the Arch of the Moneylenders) to honor Emperor Septimius Severus. Surely you can appreciate why an anonymous wealthy cattleowner would be willing to spend

NOT TO BE MISSED:

many *sesterces* to build a circular temple in honor of Hercules Victor, the god of merchants and traders. A second rectangular temple was built to provide offerings to Portunus, the god of ports. The church of San Nicola in Carcere incorporates the ruins of three other temples (note the columns embedded in its walls). Several of the other churches in the

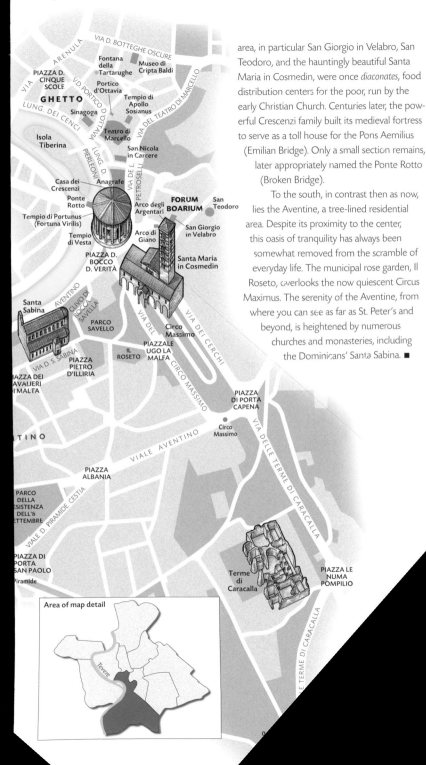

area, in particular San Giorgio in Velabro, San Teodoro, and the hauntingly beautiful Santa Maria in Cosmedin, were once *diaconates*, food distribution centers for the poor, run by the early Christian Church. Centuries later, the powerful Crescenzi family built its medieval fortress to serve as a toll house for the Pons Aemilius (Emilian Bridge). Only a small section remains, later appropriately named the Ponte Rotto (Broken Bridge).

To the south, in contrast then as now, lies the Aventine, a tree-lined residential area. Despite its proximity to the center, this oasis of tranquility has always been somewhat removed from the scramble of everyday life. The municipal rose garden, Il Roseto, overlooks the now quiescent Circus Maximus. The serenity of the Aventine, from where you can see as far as St. Peter's and beyond, is heightened by numerous churches and monasteries, including the Dominicans' Santa Sabina. ■

Area of map detail

Forum Boarium's Temples, Arches, & *Diaconates*

The massive fourth-century Arco di Giano, or Arch of Janus, hasn't much in common with the triumphal arches built by emperors such as Titus and Septimius Severus, but that's because its purpose was primarily practical. Despite its decorations (the niches on the facades held statues, and various deities are depicted above the archways), this was primarily a covered crossway, erected to protect the cattle traders of the Forum Boarium from inclement weather.

The Arch of Janus stands over the Cloaca Massima, the Roman Forum's main sewage drain.

n Boarium
pp.
01
3, 81,

Arco degli Argentari

The same is true of the tiny Arco degli Argentari (Arch of the Moneychangers), attached to the church of San Giorgio al Velabro. Erected in A.D. 204 by the cattle merchants and their financial kers, and dedicated to the ns, the arch was basically ay to the cattle market. varfish, remember

that centuries of silt and debris accumulation have raised the ground level, thus hiding a good part of the bottom section, which was made of plain travertine to avoid the wear and tear caused by passing bovines. The upper portion, made of white marble, is decorated with reliefs showing members of the imperial family performing religious rituals. Septimius Severus and his wife are on the right and Caracalla, who erased his brother Geta's image after murdering him, is on the left.

Facing the arch, at Via del Velabro 3, is an iron gate and a lovely arched passageway, unfortunately now inaccessible, which leads to an entrance to the **Cloaca Massima,** the enormous sixth-century B.C. drainage system that ran from the Roman Forum to the Tiber.

San Giorgio in Velabro

This former *diaconate* or food distribution center is dedicated to St. George (of dragon-slaying fame), who, contrary to popular belief, was not British but rather an early Christian martyr from Palestine. Here you will find a 13th-century **Madonna and Saints fresco** attributed to Pietro Cavallini and a lovely 12th-century **portico and bell tower.** The saint's relics (including, they say, his head) were brought to this church in the middle of the eighth century, when Pope Zaccaria reportedly found them languishing in the Lateran Palace.

Tempio di Portunus

Across Via Petroselli, a stone's throw from the river, stands this first-century B.C. temple dedicated to Portunus, the god of harbors. Rectangular, with a colonnaded porch and remnants of the stucco used to create a marblelike effect, it is an excellent example of temple architecture and is remarkably intact. Beginning in the ninth century, this building, like many others,

was converted into a church.

The medieval **house of the Crescenzi family** across the narrow Via del Ponte Rotto has Roman columns embedded in its walls and a classical architrave made from ancient fragments.

INSIDER TIP:

You will find useful information about what's going on in Rome at *www.roma turismo.com.* Once in the city, pick up a copy of *Roma C'è,* a local weekly that keeps you updated on events around town.

—ANTONIO BARBIERI
*National Geographic contributor &
co-founder, Concierge in Rome*

Tempio di Ercole

Just behind is the lovely round shrine that for centuries was mistakenly called the Tempio di Vesta because of its resemblance to the temple of that name in the Roman Forum. Instead, experts now say it was almost certainly dedicated to Hercules Victor, who slew the giant Cacus for stealing his cattle. Indeed, the god's image is on the upper left of the Arco degli Argentari. This temple, too, was converted into a church, but its original pieces, in white marble, are easy to spot. Many of the 20 Corinthian columns are also original. ■

Romans, Jews, & Christians Walk

This part of Rome encompasses the Jewish Ghetto and the few remains of an area that the ancient Romans dedicated to knowledge and entertainment as well as to commerce. Today it is home to many artisans and merchants, Jewish and not. It is also a desirable address for up-and-coming professionals.

Begin in front of the Tempio di Portunus and proceed up to the Lungotevere. Traffic permitting, cross the street for a magnificent view of **Isola Tiberina** (Tiber Island). To the right, the restored Torre dei Caetani, or Pierleoni tower (recently renovated), stands like a sentinel over the oldest bridge in the city, the Ponte Fabricio or Ponte Quattrocapi, constructed in 62 B.C. At the stoplight by the bridge, cross back (in greater safety) and you will find yourself at the beginning of the **Via del Portico d'Ottavia ❶**, the main street of the Ghetto (see p. 206). The square-dome building on your left is Rome's main synagogue, built a century ago in an odd, but not

NOT TO BE MISSED:

View of Tiber Island • Casa di Lorenzo Manilio • Fontana delle Tartarughe

INSIDER TIP:

Even the pope is said to be a fan of the cinnamon and almond biscotti, sweet "Jewish pizza," and other goodies at Boccionne, the kosher pastry shop in the old Jewish Ghetto.

—RUTH ELLEN GRUBER
National Geographic author

unpleasing, mock Assyro-Babylonian style. The temple and museum *(tel 06 6840 0661, ~ww.museoebraico.roma.it, closed Fri. p.m. & Sat., hourly tours in English)* are worth a visit.

~he small church on your right is **San Gre- ~ella della Divina Pietà**, one of the churches ~vs were forced to attend Christian ~ey could avoid this only by paying a

bribe or, as many did, using earplugs. Over the door there are Latin and Hebrew inscriptions.

Walk down the Via del Portico d'Ottavia to the large marble pediment supported by columns, all that's left of the **Portico d'Ottavia ❷**, the huge colonnade built by Augustus in 23 B.C. for his sister, Octavia. In the Middle Ages, the church of **Sant'Angelo in Pescheria** (*pescheria* means "fish market") was built into its ruins. The marble plaque on the far right pilaster says that any fish head (considered quite a delicacy) longer than the plaque itself was to be handed over to city officials.

Where the street turns 90 degrees, go left; note that the buildings on the left are newer than those on the right. Because of poor sanitary conditions in the overcrowded Ghetto, a century ago everything from here to the river was razed and rebuilt. At Nos. 1 and 2 is the **Casa di Lorenzo Manilio ❸**, built in 1497. Classical inscriptions and beautiful Roman reliefs are embedded in the walls. Boccione, the pastry shop on the corner (at No. 1), makes delicious Jewish cakes and pastries.

Backtrack to the Via della Reginella, which leads to Piazza Mattei with its delightful **Fontana delle Tartarughe ❹** (Tortoise Fountain, see p. 99), designed by Giacomo della Porta in the 1580s. Take Via dei Funari (the Street of the

Ropemakers) and peep into the courtyard of Palazzo Caetani at No. 31 to observe the fragments of classical sculpture covering the walls. **Santa Maria in Campitelli 5** (1662–1667), in nearby Piazza di Campitelli, is architect Carlo Rainaldi's masterpiece.

Exit the square from its farther end. On your right you'll see the remains of the **Teatro di Marcello** and the three surviving columns of the **Tempio di Apollo Sosianus.** The theater was erected between 13 and 11 B.C. and dedicated to Marcellus, Augustus' nephew. A short distance on is **San Nicola in Carcere 6**, the medieval church built into the remains of the Forum Holitorium's three temples. Proceed along Via Petroselli to **Santa Maria in Cosmedin 7** (see pp. 207–208).

🅰	Also see area map, pp. 198–199
▶	Temple of Portunus
⬌	1 mile (1.5 km)
🕐	1.5 hours
▶	Santa Maria in Cosmedin

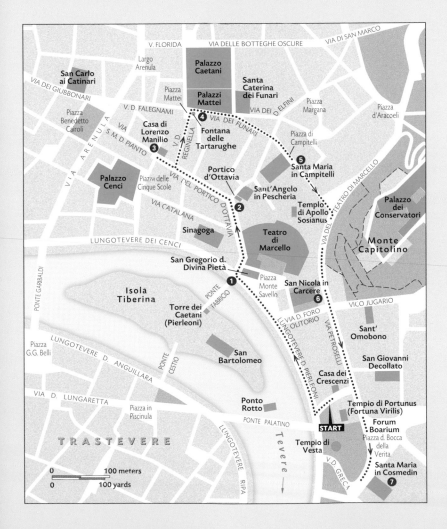

The Ghetto

The papal bull issued by Pope Paul IV on July 12, 1555, confined the Jews of Rome to a walled-off area of less than 3 acres (1.3 ha), where they were forced to live for more than 300 years. He was motivated in part by simple anti-Semitism. But the Counter-Reformation zeal inspired by the Protestant schism probably also played a key role in the creation of the Ghetto, which was not formally abolished until 1883.

The Ghetto

🔲 Map pp. 200–201

🚌 Bus: C3, H, 23, 40, 46, 62, 63, 64, 70, 87, 95, 119, 170, 280, 493, 715, 716, 780. Tram: 8

Jews have lived in Rome since the second century B.C., settling first in areas favored by foreigners, such as the Aventine and Trastevere. By the 16th century, however, many Roman Jews, especially merchants, had moved to this thriving commercial riverport neighborhood. Tiber Island was often referred to as the Pons Judaeorum, and the **Piazza delle Cinque Scole** (off today's Via Arenula), with its five temples, was called Piazza Giudea by everyone, Jews included. Today the area is dominated by an imposing synagogue. Pope John Paul II made history with his unprecedented visit here in 1986.

The papal edict made it illegal for Jews to live anywhere else in the city, barred them from certain

INSIDER TIP:

Rome's quietest and prettiest late-night stroll is through the old Ghetto district east of Via Arenula.

—TIM JEPSON
National Geographic author

professions, and forced them to attend church services. Although enforcement was patchy, severe overcrowding was inevitable. In the 1600s, some 6,000 people crammed into this tiny area when the gates closed at sunset.

Rome's Jews are neither Ashkenazi nor Sephardic and pride themselves on being part of a community that preexists the destruction of the Jerusalem temple in A.D. 70, a distinction that entitles them to certain privileges such as eating lamb at Passover.

Jewish people have been in Rome so long that Jewish and Roman cuisines, pork dishes excluded, are now almost indistinguishable. Some favorites of Jewish origin are *carciofi alla Giudea* (fried, whole artichokes), *filetti di baccalà fritti* (fried codfish fillets), and marinated zucchini. The Jewish bakery on **Via del Portico d'Ottavia** is known for its delicious ricotta cheesecakes (chocolate or berries). ∎

A Unique Jewish Community

The Babylonian exile of the sixth century B.C. dispersed Jews throughout the known world. Rome's Jewish community first developed a few hundred years after the diaspora, making their descendants part of the oldest continuous Jewish community in the world today.

Santa Maria in Cosmedin

Set in the heart of an area rich in ancient monuments and memories, Santa Maria in Cosmedin is unfortunately known primarily for the Bocca della Verità (Mouth of Truth). This stone disk adorned with the carved image of a sea god tempts hordes of tourists to see whether, as medieval legend had it, the mouth will bite off a liar's hand. Don't waste your time. The church has enough real treasures to further illustrate this city's perennial transformations.

A Diverse History

The two columns flanking the door inside, the three others embedded in the left wall, and the freestanding, shorter column in the sacristy are remnants of an earlier structure. In the fourth century, this building was the seat of the *statio annonae*, the city office for food distribution and market inspection. By the sixth century it had become a *diaconate*, a center set up by the Church to provide food and other services to the poor.

An oratory was also added in the sixth century, but it was only in the eighth century that Pope Hadrian (772–795) turned the structure into a bona fide church, donating it to Greek Christian refugees from the religious turmoil in Byzantium. Thus it became Santa Maria in Cosmedin, or, as it was sometimes called, Santa Maria de Schola Graeca.

Whichever name you prefer, both testify to the Eastern origin of the new church's parishioners. Cosmedin is no doubt derived from Constantinople's famous Kosmidion Monastery and neighborhood whereas Schola Graeca (which means "Greek School") speaks for itself.

Damaged during the Norman invasion in the late 11th

The Romanesque bell tower of Santa Maria in Cosmedin

century, the church was restored in the early twelfth century. The redbrick columned porch, the portico, and the lovely seven-story Romanesque bell tower also date from this period.

Church Porch & the Bocca della Verità

The Bocca della Verità was placed on the left-hand wall 370 years ago, but the porch shelters far more interesting treasures. The marble decoration around

Santa Maria in Cosmedin

 Map pp. 200–201

✉ Piazza Bocca della Verità 18

☎ 06 678 1419

🚌 Bus: C3, 23, 81, 95, 170, 280, 715, 716, 780

INSIDER TIP:

Many churches in Rome sit on top of ancient ruins or incorporated much older buildings into their construction. Keep an eye out for these anachronisms.

—SARAH YEOMANS
Archaeologist and National Geographic contributor

the portal dates from the 11th century. The tomb to its right is that of Alfano, the papal chamberlain who supervised the 12th-century restoration. The inscriptions on the wall record ninth-century donations.

Inside the Church

In the hush of the church's penumbra it is easy to feel yourself transported back in time and possibly moved to spiritual contemplation. This church abounds in Eastern or Byzantine influences, primarily the *schola cantorum,* the walled-off area reserved for worshippers; *matronei,* the balconies reserved for women; and the *iconostasis,* the marble divider delimiting the priests' domain.

The magnificently patterned floor is pre-cosmatesque, whereas the decorated Gothic canopy over the main altar is dated 1294 and is signed by Deodato, a son of one of the Cosmas (see below). There is cosmatesque decoration on the paschal candlestick—note the stylized lion at its base—just behind the right pulpit. And don't miss the framed eighth-century mosaic in the sacristy with its fine gold background, which comes from the original St. Peter's. It may be a scene from the Adoration of the Three Kings. ∎

The Cosmati Marble Workers

Many of Rome's greatest 12th- and 13th-century stonecutters bore the surname Cosma, perhaps because the name was common or perhaps for some other reason. We do know that these "Cosmati" reinvented mosaic art.

The cosmati technique or cosmatesque are the terms now used to describe their type of inlay decoration, which relied on the use of tiny pieces of colored marble—red, green, black, white—to create intricate patterns, at times resembling Islamic geometric motifs. Often, in a break from ancient Roman techniques, the Cosmati combined them with larger stone rounds and strips to make multicolored pavements such as those in Santa Maria in Cosmedin, San Crisogono, and Santa Maria in Trastevere.

Cosmati work was also applied to church accessories such as paschal candlesticks (notable in San Lorenzo), tombs, episcopal chairs and pulpits, and the small columns often used in church cloisters. The most impressive columns in Rome can be found in the cloisters of San Giovanni in Laterano and San Paulo fuori le Mura, both of which are signed by Pietro Vassalletto and his son, masters of this kind of workmanship.

The production of cosmati work was interrupted in the 14th century, when the popes fled temporarily to Avignon, and it never again reached its former levels.

Circo Massimo

If you look down at the Circo Massimo (Circus Maximus) from the imperial residences on the Palatine Hill, you can almost hear the crowds cheering on the city's most popular charioteers as their two-wheeled chariots rounded the course for the seventh and last time.

More people in ancient Rome watched chariot racing than any other sport.

Charioteers once raced here, their colors—white, red, green, or blue—signifying membership in one of the *factiones* or parties that paid for the outfitting of the equestrian teams. Today, however, there is little to see. Archaeologists say that the starting gates and the *spina,* or raised spine that ran down the middle of the race course, still exist. But they have yet to be excavated, and you will have to use your imagination to picture what may have been one of the largest stadiums that humankind has known. A long rectangle about the size of a football field, it had a triple tier of stone and wood bleachers believed to have held more than 250,000 people.

Tucked into the valley between the Palatine and the Aventine, the Circus Maximus dates back to the fourth century B.C. and is the oldest of the known Roman circuses. During the frequent *ludi* (games), the circus was primarily for horseracing and chariot races, although gladiatorial exhibitions were sometimes held there, as were public executions. It was last used as a Roman circus in A.D. 549, during the reign of the Ostrogoth (barbarian) king, Totila, who had temporarily won control of Rome from the city's Byzantine rulers. It then gradually fell into disuse (at one point cabbages were grown here).

The small medieval tower at the eastern end has nothing to do with the original circus. It belonged to the Frangipane family, which during the Middle Ages controlled much of this area. ∎

Circo Massimo

🅰 Map pp. 200–201

🚌 Bus: C3, 60, 75, 81, 118, 175, 628, 673, 715. Tram: 3. Metro: Linea B (Circo Massimo)

Aventino

The most picturesque way to get up to the Aventino (or Aventine Hill) and to Santa Sabina is to walk up the lovely cobblestone street called Clivo di Rocca Savella, which starts about 110 yards (100 m) from Santa Maria in Cosmedin (along Via Santa Maria in Cosmedin, the continuation of Via Petroselli).

Visitors enjoy the remarkable view from the top of the Aventine Hill.

Aventino
🗺 Map pp.
200–201

Parco degli Aranci

A gate in a medieval wall that was once part of the powerful Savelli family's fortress leads to the Parco Savello, also called the Parco degli Aranci because of the orange trees brought from Spain in the 13th century by St. Dominic, founder of the Dominican order. An oasis of peace and quiet, this lovely spot affords an unbelievable panoramic view of the city.

The imposing rear view of the Dominican basilica of **Santa Sabina** makes it easy for you to grasp the essentials of fifth-century church architecture in

Rome. The apse is clearly outlined, and you can see how the center part of the church, over the nave, is higher than the sides, permitting greater illumination through the clerestory windows.

By the time this church was built, Christianity had become a mainstream religion and, as you can see from the 24 fluted Corinthian columns, the remaining mosaic decorations above the entrance door, and the beautiful Roman marble inlay ornamentation above and between the arches, it was built to be seen.

The mosaic over the entrance is particularly interesting. Two female figures, resembling classical Roman matrons, represent the major components of early Christianity, the pagans or gentiles (Ecclesia Ex Gentibus), and the Jews (Ecclesia Ex circumscisione). The gold lettering on a deep blue background is striking. And don't miss the cypress door on the far left of the portico. Its 18 fifth-century paleo-Christian panels depict scenes from the Old and New Testaments, including one of the earliest surviving representations of Jesus' crucifixion.

Leave the park through the main entrance. Note the superb *mascherone* (mask) on the wall to your right, used in the fountain by Giacomo della Porta.

Piazza dei Cavalieri di Malta

Farther along Via di Santa Sabina you'll come to Piazza dei Cavalieri di Malta, a quaint space designed by 18th-century graphic artist,

INSIDER TIP:

Climb the Aventine Hill and find the *buco della serratura*, a keyhole through which you'll see Rome's most unique and memorable view of the dome of St. Peter's.

—CJ FAHEY
National Geographic International Channel

Giovanni Battista Piranesi. The monumental entrance leads to the residence of the Grand Master of the Knights of Malta, **Villa del'Ordine dei Cavalieri di Malta.** Piranesi (who is buried there) also designed the church, **Santa Maria del Priorato.** Peep through the keyhole to see the justifiably famous picture-postcard view of the dome of St. Peter's. ∎

Santa Sabina
- 🅰 Map pp. 200–201
- ✉ Piazza Pietro d'Illiria 1
- ☎ 06 57 941
- 🕐 Closed 12:30– 3:30 p.m.
- 🚌 Bus: C3, 23, 81, 95, 170, 175, 280, 628, 715, 716

EXPERIENCE: Body Beautiful

After looking at all the sleek, well-groomed people around you, you might well notice that the body beautiful is *molto importante* here. Many Romans— women as well as men—take advantage of an array of available beauty treatments.

Want a lympho-drainage massage, a shiatsu treatment, or a soothing ayurvedic facial done with Dead Sea mud? Feel like having your body coated with clay and then massaged with essential oils? Want to soak in rose petals while you sip luscious fruit drinks? Or do you yearn to pretend you are an ancient Roman at the imperial baths, passing from the caldarium to the tepidarium to the

frigidarium. Rome is filled with *istituti di bellezza*, so these treatments are not hard to find. Here are some suggestions for those located in central Rome: **Acanto Day Spa** (*Piazza Rondanini 30, tel 06 6813 6602, acantospa.it*), **AcquaMadre Hammam** (*Via di S.Ambrogio 17, tel 06 686 4272, www.acquamadre.it*), **Wonderfool** (*for men only; Via dei Banchi Nuovi 39, tel 06 6889 2315, www.wonderfool.it/home*), and the less expensive **Becos Club** (*800-603000*). There are 14 Becos locations in Rome; the most convenient branch is at the Roman Sport Center gym at Villa Borghese (*Via del Galoppatoio 33, tel 06 323 4450*). You can use the gym for a €25 daily fee.

Terme di Caracalla

Begun in A.D. 206 and inaugurated in 217 by Caracalla, the mammoth Baths of Caracalla went beyond simple hygiene and pleasure to satisfy the needs of the leisured class. Romans came here not just for a swim and a sauna but, as in any elitist club, to while away a lazy afternoon, to catch up on some reading, or even to make a business deal or two.

...ths of Caracalla, an average of 9,000 workers were employed daily for five years.

The Baths of Caracalla have been "out-of-order" since the sixth century, when the invading Goths destroyed the aqueducts and cut off their water supply. The majestic ruins, which loom in the shadow of the second crest of the Aventine Hill, will give you only a partial idea of the baths' extravagant scale.

Along with the bathing rooms, there were libraries (Greek and Latin), art galleries, meeting halls, and a stadium. The buildings were surrounded by a shaded esplanade with fountains, playing fields, and a covered portico.

The materials used to decorate the baths were lavish, as can be seen from the mosaics now displayed in the Vatican Museums, such as the "athletes in training." Monumental sculptures included the granite basins since incorporated into the fountains of the Piazza Farnese, and the so-called Farnese Bull and Farnese Hercules, both in the Naples archaeological museum.

Plundered over the centuries, the baths' retain little of their

EXPERIENCE: Learn Your Local Snack Options

In the 1970s, eating on the street, except for gelato, was done only by Americans and was strongly frowned upon. But that's no longer the case, and today Romans, too, carry snack food around with them or eat standing up at a counter. When you don't want a full meal, or if you are feeling hungry between meals, you will find a wealth of snack options. Here's a primer:

In late morning, you might stop by the local *forno* (bakery) and ask for a slice of *pizza rossa* (pizza with some tomato conserve on it) or, better yet, *pizza bianca*, a slightly thicker, plain warm pizza that is delicious with prosciutto but even better, in the summer, with fresh figs. Local legend has it that Roman bakers invented *pizza bianca* when they rolled out some

extra dough to make sure their ovens were at the right temperature. Or it may just be another variety of Mediterranean flat bread, similar to pita.

But that's just the start of your snack discoveries. Other Roman nibbles started out in life as a way of using leftover risotto. These include *supplì al telefono*, egg-shaped rice croquettes with mozzarella and ragu, and *arancini di riso* (little oranges), fried rice balls with meat sauce and peas inside, originally a Sicilian recipe.

And then there are the various sandwiches you can buy at most cafès: *tramezzini*, which are white bread sandwich halves, panini, sandwiches on a roll, and *piadine*, sandwiches on flat bread that need to be toasted.

original grandeur. As elsewhere, you must use your imagination.

The main bathing rooms—which could reportedly seat 1,600 people at one time—formed an axis of the central quadrilateral. Secondary rooms were arranged around the *apodyterium* (dressing room), the *palaestrae* (open-air exercise rooms), the *calidarium* (hot room), *tepidarium* (warm room), and the *frigidarium* (cold room). Other structures, like the libraries, were outside the perimeter.

Your visit begins in one of the two workout rooms (palaestrae). This, like its twin on the far side of the complex, contains segments of black and-white, and patches of multicolor, mosaic flooring. One door out of the workout room leads to a dressing room with a black-and-white pavement, a vestibule, and then, a few steps down, a *natatio* (swimming pool). Another brings you to an atrium

and then into the frigidarium. If you walk straight through here and the transition room on the other side, you'll come to the other palaestra with its many mosaic panels. Next to nothing remains of the enormous and circular calidarium, with its seven plunge baths, except two brick pilasters. The dome was said to have been as big as the Pantheon's. ∎

INSIDER TIP:

What better place to enjoy a Puccini aria than at the imposing ruins of Terme di Caracalla? Various Italian operas are performed at this ancient bathhouse in the summer.

—SOPHIE GORDON
Travel journalist

Terme di Caracalla

- Map pp. 200–201
- Via delle Terme di Caracalla 52 (at the intersection with Via Antonina)
- 06 3996 7700
- $$. Audio guide: $
- Open daily, but closed Mon. after 2 p.m.
- Bus: 60, 75, 118, 628, 673. Tram: 3. Metro: Linea B (Circo Massimo)

www.pierreci.it

More Places to Visit

Museo Della Civiltà Romana

This little-known treasure-trove is in the modern EUR (Esposizione Universale di Roma) quarter. It showcases replicas of artifacts, implements, and architectural reconstructions (arches, aqueducts, bridges, baths, etc.) of Roman civilization. Don't miss the set of plaster casts of Trajan's entire column in the basement and a room-size plaster model of the capital as it appeared in Constantine's day (early fourth century). en.museociviltaromana.it ▲ Map pp. 200–201 ✉ Piazza G. Agnelli, 10 ☎ 060608, 🕐 Closed 2 p.m. & Mon. 💲 $$. Tours in English on request: $$$$$ 🚇 Metro: Linea B.

Museo Montemartini

This former power station on the Via Ostiense has transformed into a small branch of the Capitoline Museums, a provocative setting for the classical beauty of 400-odd Capitoline marbles. Pediment sculptures, friezes from temples and Pompey's Theater, statuary from the *horti* (extensive monumental gardens of ancient aristocratic residences), mosaics, and Republican-era busts are dramatically displayed amid the equipment once in use in the likes of the Machine, Furnace, and Column Rooms. en.centralemontemartini.org ▲ Map pp. 200–201 ✉ Via Ostiense 106 ☎ 060608 or 06 8205 9127 🕐 Closed Mon. 💲 $. Tours in English on request: $$$$$ 🚌 Bus: 23

Protestant Cemetery

Officially named the Non-Catholic Cemetery, this burial place was founded in 1738 to provide a final resting place for those foreigners who not only visited Rome but died here as well. These include the famous—such as Keats and Shelley—and the ordinary, such as 16-year-old Rose Bathurst, who, in 1824, fell off her horse and drowned in the Tiber, and Devereau Plantagenet Cockburn, who

died in 1850 at the age of 21 after vainly traveling through Europe in search of a suitable climate. Banked up against a piece of the Aurelian Wall, their final resting place—now almost filled to capacity—is verdantly tranquil, a place of blossom and birdsong and a refuge for some of the city's most beautiful felines.

Pull the bellcord and tell the gatekeeper which tomb you wish to visit. Genuine mourners pay nothing; tourists are asked to make a small donation (€2 suggested). If you're short of time, remember you can see

INSIDER TIP:

The Protestant Cemetery is an oasis of peace and beauty and the resting place of many famous non-Italians, including Keats and Shelley.

—PATRICIA GLEE SMITH
Travel writer & illustrator

Keats's grave from outside, through a small window in the cemetery wall at the start of Via Caio Cestio, a street named, interestingly enough, after the first well-known non-Catholic to be buried in the area: Caius Cestius, a senior Roman magistrate who died in 12 B.C. but not before building himself a pyramid (on the next corner) for a tomb **(Piramide di Caio Cestio).** In the third century A.D., like other preexisting monuments, the tomb was incorporated into the walls built to protect the city from the growing threat of barbarian attack, which probably accounts for its survival over the centuries. www.protestantcemetery.it ▲ Map pp. 200–201 ✉ Via Caio Cestio 6 ☎ 06 574 1900, 🕐 Closed Sun. p.m. 🚌 Bus: 3, 23, 30, 60, 75, 95, 175, 280. Tram: 3. Metro: Linea B (Piramide) ∎

Early Christian catacombs, a contemporary world-class music venue, and the lovely Appian Way

Fuori le Mura (Outside the Walls)

Classical motif detail from Santa Costanza mosaic

Fuori le Mura

Rome, like most ancient settlements, was a walled city. Today the walls that once surrounded almost all of inhabited Rome no longer have the same function or import as in the past. Nevertheless, the words *fuori le mura*, or outside the walls, continue to have particular significance even for modern Romans.

In the sixth century B.C., an early king named Servius Tullius built fortifications to protect the nascent city, the so-called Servian Walls, of which only a few small sections remain. In the third century A.D., Emperor Aurelian began construction on a 12-mile (19 km) wall around the city. Maxentius continued the wall, which eventually doubled in height under subsequent emperors. When it was finished, the Aurelian Wall, as it is called, enclosed all seven hills, the Campus Martius, and Trastevere.

The mammoth ring of brick wall had an obvious function and a corresponding significance. Aurelian, who had already re-pelled the Alemanni, built the wall to protect the city in the event of another barbarian onslaught. All remained quiet until A.D. 410, when the Goths sacked the city, a prelude to the conquest of Spain. Romans hunkered down inside the city, leaving vulnerable everything fuori le mura—the catacombs, monasteries, vineyards, and farmland. The growing feeling that the walls were necessary marked the decline of an empire that once seemed invincible.

As built by Aurelian, the wall was inter-spersed by a series of 18 *porte* (gates), many of which are still in use today. The porte often became the gateways or portals for the roads used by the consuls, the leaders who took the place of the kings in the Republican era. Together with the aqueducts, these roads made the Romans famous throughout the world.

The first consular road, leading out from the massive Porta San Sebastiano, was the Via Appia, or Appian Way, inaugurated in 312 B.C. and named for the city's ruler, Appius Claudius Caecus, who also built the first aqueduct (the

Appia). During this period, Rome was becom-ing a force to be reckoned with. The Roman Republic, founded in 509 B.C., had quickly conquered the rest of Italy and soon after had begun its expansion into much of the known world. Military campaigns meant troop move-ments, which made good roads a necessity. In its first stage, the Via Appia—dubbed Regina Viarum, the Queen of Roads, by the historian Statius—ran only to Capua in the Italian south. Later the road's importance was assured when it was extended to Brindisi and Taranto in Apu-lia, in the heel of the Italian "boot," effectively becoming a pathway to the Middle East.

The Via Appia, once the site of grandiose funeral processions, such as that of the Emperor Augustus in A.D. 14, and of triumphal marches into the city by returning army legions, soon

---

NOT TO BE MISSED:

became a cemetery for the rich and powerful. The Romans, who considered it unsanitary to bury the dead within the city, lined the first section of the road with commemorative tombs, a small number of which have survived intact. Crowded with statues, friezes, and Latin inscriptions, the Via Appia was no doubt a sight to behold. Beginning in the first century A.D., when Christianity took root and began to spread throughout the empire, and lasting until about the fifth century, catacombs were carved out of the soft tufa rock to build deep, underground cemeteries for the multiple burials of the Christian dead. The damp, underground galleries, which sometimes ran for many miles, contain interesting Greek and Latin inscriptions, faded frescoes, imperial seals, and sarcophagi. ■

Rome

G.R.A.

A24

G.R.A.

Tevere

A1 dir.

Area of map detail

0   2 kilometers
0   1 mile

CORSO D FRANCI

VILLA GLORI
FLAMINIO
PARIOLI
VILLA ADA
TRIESTE

Museo MAXXI
(Opening late 2009)
Parco della Musica

VIA FLAMINIA

VIA SALARIA

NOMENTANA

PINCIANO

VIA

Sant'Agnese
fuori le Mura

Tevere

VILLA BORGHESE
SALARIO

VIA

VILLA TORLONIA

NOMENTANO

PRATI

Mura Aureliane

TIBURTINA

CITTÀ DEL VATICANO

San Lorenzo
fuori le Mura

CIMITERO DI CAMPO VERANO

A24

VIA GREGORIO VII

ROMA

TIBURTINO

AURELIO

VIA

PRENESTINA

PRENESTINO-LABICANO

VILLA DORIA PAMPHILI

TRASTEVERE

VIA

CASILINA

Terme di Caracalla

PARCO D. SCIPIONI

VIA APPIA

TUSCOLANO

Mura Aureliane

Casa del Cardinale Bessarione

Arco di Druso

Porta San Sebastiano

VIA OSTIENSE

GIANICOLENSE

VIALE MARCONI

Domine Quo Vadis

VIA APPIA ANTICA

VIA APPIA NUOVA

VIA PORTUENSE

VIA MAGLIANA

GARBATELLA

Catacombe di San Callisto

Mausoleo di Romolo

Circo di Massenzio

San Paolo
fuori le Mura

VIA CRISTOFORO COLOMBO

Catacombe di San Sebastiano

Mausoleo di Cecilia Metella

PORTUENSE

OSTIENSE

Tevere

VIA D.

EUR

Casal Rotondo

Museo della Civiltà Romana

Via Appia Antica

Believe it or not, those large, irregular flagstones that still pave some sections of the Via Appia Antica—often rutted by the wheels of carts and chariots that passed here so very long ago—are original, hewn by hand from the basaltic lava cliffs. In many ways, given the impact of nature, the scene here has not changed all that much over the centuries.

Via Appia Antica
 Map p. 217
Bus: 118, 218, 660, & Archeobus

Appia Antica Park
✉ Via Appia Antica 42
☎ 06 512 6314
🕐 Sun., closed to motor vehicles
💲 English tours on foot or bike: $$$ (min. 12, booking required, fax 06 513 5316

Museo delle Mura–Porta San Sebastiano
✉ Via di Porta San Sebastiano 18
☎ 060608 or 06 7047 5284
🕐 Open Tues.–Sun. 9 a.m.–2 p.m.
💲 $. Tours in English on request: $$$$
Bus: 118, 218, & Archeobus

www.museo dellemuraroma.it

Imperial roads are the most graphic evidence of Roman expansion.

The Via Appia Antica formally begins at **Porta San Sebastiano,** the gate in the Aurelian Wall once called Porta Appia. Here, at the end of lovely Via de Porta San Sebastiano, is a small, interesting **museum** that allows access to the tower—with a great view—and a walk along the inside parapets.

You will have already passed, at the beginning of the road, the Renaissance **Casa del Cardinal Bessarione** (on the right at No. 9) followed, farther up on the left, by the verdant **Parco degli Scipioni,** where the remains of the Tomb of the Scipios can be found. Out the other side of the park, across Via di Porta Latina, is the picturesque church of **San Giovanni a Porta Latina.**

Along the Road

Having passed through the Porta, you are now on the Via Appia. About 100 feet (30 m) along stands the road's only extant original Roman milestone.

About half a mile (1 km) farther, on the left, is the **Domine Quo Vadis,** where Jesus is said to have appeared to Peter as he was fleeing Nero's persecutions and convinced him to return to Rome and certain martyrdom. This church faces a clearly marked entrance to the Catacombe di San Callisto—another entrance lies about half a mile (1 km) down the road.

Catacombe di San Callisto: The Catacombs of San Callisto are the best known of the

Roman catacombs and the first official underground burial site for early Christians, including numerous second- and third-century martyrs. Excavations have revealed five different levels of *loculi*, niches where the bodies, wrapped in sheets, were placed in tiers. The openings to the loculi were closed with slabs of marble, but these have long since disappeared, as have any artifacts of value.

A major attraction of the 40-minute guided tour (available in different languages) is the **papal crypt,** which holds the remains of several martyred early popes. Nearby, with its Byzantine frescoes, is the **Cubiculum of St. Cecilia.** You won't find her body here, however; Pope Paschal I moved it to Santa Cecilia in Trastevere (see pp. 192–93).

Other cubicles have frescoes and Christian symbols carved on the walls. In the **crypt of St. Eusebius** you will see a sarcophagus that contains two mummified bodies.

Catacombe di San Sebastiano: Only a little farther, along in the Church of San Sebastiano, are the catacombs of the same name. The church dates back to the early fourth century, when it was called the Basilica Apostolorum because the bodies of Peter and Paul were hidden here during one of the more violent periods of anti-Christian persecution.

Inside the catacombs of San Sebastiano, archaeologists have excavated four levels. The tour of this catacomb, which has second-century **pagan tombs** along with Christian chapels, will take you down a staircase studded with pieces of sarcophagi with imperial seals. Underneath the church, you'll see an area

Catacombe di San Callisto

- Map p. 215
- Via Appia Antica 126
- 06 513 01580
- Closed 12–2 p.m., all day Wed., & month Feb.
- $
- Bus: 118, 218 & Archeobus

www.catacombe
.roma.it/en/info2
.html

Catacombe di San Sebastiano

- Map p. 215
- Via Appia Antica 136
- 06 785 0350
- Closed 12–2 p.m. & all day Sun. & from Nov. 15–Dec. 15
- $$
- Bus: 118, 660, & Archeobus

www.catacombe.org

EXPERIENCE: Going to a Soccer Game

Italy is a soccer-crazy country, and Rome is no exception. The city's inhabitants have two excellent teams to boast and argue about: AS Roma and SS Lazio. Wrap yourself in a red-and-yellow Roma scarf or a blue-and-white Lazio T-shirt any weekend from September to June and join the happy throngs heading to **Olympic Stadium** (Viale dello Stadio Olimpico, tel 06 323 7333), which the two teams share.

Inside the massive structure near Monte Mario, originally built for the 1960 Olympics, up to 81,000 fans make their way into the tribunes, or, if they've paid less, to the bleachers: la curva nord (north) if they are Lazio fans, la curva sud (south)

for Roma fans. And then it's kickoff, followed by lightning-rapid play after play, many accompanied by the singsong chants of the tifosi (fans). Other fans wave banners or cheer on their favorite players.

You can buy tickets for upcoming matches online (www.lis-ticket.it/calcio) or at one of the city's many ricevitorie. Just look for a tobacconist's shop that says T and Lotto. Be aware that you cannot buy tickets at the stadium.

A word of caution: Romanisti and Laziali have a noted distaste for one another. If the scheduled match is a "derby" (a Roma vs. Lazio game), when tempers may really flare, it might be best to stay away.

**Circo di
Massenzio e
Mausoleo di
Romulo**

▲ Map p. 217

✉ Via Appia Antica
153

☎ 06 780 1324

🕐 Open Tues.–Sun.
9 a.m.–2 p.m.;
closed Mon.

$ $

🚌 Bus: 118, 660, &
Archeobus

**Mausoleo di
Cecilia Metella**

▲ Map p. 217

✉ Via Appia Antica
161

☎ 06 3996 7700

🕐 Closed Mon.

$ $

🚌 Bus: 118, 660, &
Archeobus

with three decorated pagan tombs with some very attractive frescoes and a floor mosaic.

It is believed that both Christian and pagan funerals were held in the elaborate central chapel, the vault of which has acanthus and lotus-leaf stucco decorations. The **Chapel of Symbols** has early Christian symbols carved in it. Up another staircase is a **dining room** for funeral banquets. The graffiti date back to the second century.

Farther Along the Via Appia

If you've enjoyed yourselves so far, now you are really in for a treat. For those with a good legs, or a bicycle, the next several kilometers of the Appian Way become increasingly beautiful and evocative.

First, on the left, are the fascinating remains of the fortified **villa** built by Maxentius (A.D. 306–312), whose siege mentality led him to avoid the Palatine Hill. The site includes the **Mau-**soleo de Romulo (Mausoleum of Romulus), his young son, and the **Circo di Massenzio,** a Roman circus that is smaller but better preserved than the Circus Maximus. The stone remnants on the ground between the two towers at the western end show you where the 12 *carceres,* or starting gates, were located. You can also clearly see the *spina* which ran down the middle of the track and around which the chariots would have raced.

Next comes the massive, circular tower-tomb of **Cecilia Metella.** In the 13th century, the powerful Caetani family transformed it into a sort of medieval fortress. It's round shape clearly indicates that originally this was the tomb. The marble frieze has reliefs of flowers, ox-skulls, and weapons.

Traveling on, you will find yourself increasingly in the open countryside, where umbrella pines alternate with funerary remains. Off to the left, you can see the ruins of the impressive **Acqua Marcia** aqueduct. ∎

EXPERIENCE: Rome for Kids

Many youngsters will enjoy the **Museo della Civiltà Romana** (en.museociviltaromana.it; see p. 216), which has a giant plaster cast of ancient Rome as well as ancient weapons, boat models, and artifacts.

Children twelve and under will want to visit **Explora**, the Children's Museum of Rome (Via Flaminia 82, www.mdbr.it), a few blocks from Piazza del Popolo. This interactive site is organized as a "city on a child's scale where everything can be observed, touched and experimented with." The miniature city includes a bank, a post office, grocery store, television studio, and more. Every attraction is interactive and has both Italian and English instructions.

Technotown (www.technotown.it), in the Villa Torlonia on Via Nomentana, is similarly organized but geared for teenagers. The museum, which specializes in space-age technology, boasts interactive installations including a virtual TV set, 3-D theater, graphic representations of musical scores, sculpture robots, and materials of the future. Although everything is written in Italian, the personnel speaks English.

Three Churches Outside the Walls

The Aurelian wall encircled central Rome, but some important churches remained outside the fortifications: San Paolo, San Lorenzo, and Sant'Agnese, all of which have "fuori le mura" attached to their names to distinguish them from similarly named churches downtown.

San Paolo fuori le Mura

San Paolo Fuori le Mura (St. Paul Outside the Walls) seems isolated today, but until the eighth century, the church was linked to the city by a long, covered portico that led to Porta San Paolo, the city's southernmost gate. It was built over the spot where St. Paul was buried after having been beheaded at the nearby Abbey of the Three Fountains.

A small basilica built here by Constantine was enlarged by subsequent emperors. By the ninth century, it was the largest church in Rome and reputedly the most beautiful. Unfortunately, it was almost totally destroyed in an 1823 fire. However grandiose its 19th-century replacement may be, it lacks warmth—but it will provide a good idea of what a classical Roman basilica looked like.

San Paolo's large central nave is flanked by two aisles that are separated by 80 enormous columns. The **bronze doors,** which survived the fire, were made in Constantinople in 1070. Other pre-fire survivors include the fifth-century mosaics in the **Triumphal Arch,** a 13th-century mosaic in the apse, and more mosaic decoration on the inner side of the arch. Arnolfo di Cambio created the Gothic canopy over Paul's tomb in 1285. Don't miss the 18-foot (5.5 m)

Many consider San Paolo's cloister Rome's most beautiful.

13th-century cosmatesque **paschal candlestick,** decorated with scenes from the Passion of Christ. The Cosmati who fashioned it also worked on the church's small **cloister,** which has lovely fluted and spiraling colonnettes.

San Lorenzo fuori le Mura

On the other side of Rome is another of the seven pilgrim

San Paolo fuori le Mura

- Map p. 217
- Via Ostiense 186
- 06 541 0341
- Open daily
- Bus: C6, 23, 128, 761, 766. Metro: Linea B (Basilica San Paolo)

San Lorenzo fuori le Mura

- Map p. 217
- Piazzale del Verano 3
- 06 491 511
- Closed 12:30–4 p.m.
- Bus: C2, C3, 71, 93, 492. Tram: 3, 19

Sant'Agnese fuori le Mura

- Map p. 217
- Via Nomentana 349
- 06 8620 5456
- Church: closed noon–4 p.m. Catacombs: closed noon–4 p.m. & Nov.
- $. Guided visit: $$
- Bus: 60, 84, 90

churches, San Lorenzo fuori le Mura (St. Lawrence Outside the Walls), the only church in Rome to have suffered serious bombing damage during World War II. Unusually, it was formed from the fusion of two early churches, the Minor and Major Basilicas.

In A.D. 330, Emperor Constantine built a church to honor the martyr St. Lawrence (see sidebar). In the sixth century, Pope Pelagius rebuilt the Minor Basilica next door to a fifth-century place of worship honoring the Virgin Mary. In 1216, Honorius III knocked down their apses and joined the buildings together. The **chancel** and the ten superb Corinthian columns surrounding it are from Pelagius' church.

The **nave** and **aisles,** slightly lower in level, belonged to the second church. Its splendid 12th-century cosmatesque (see p. 208)

St. Lawrence

St. Lawrence, one of many early Christian martyrs, died a particularly grue-some death: He was roasted alive in A.D. 258 on a smoldering grid. Like many early Christians, he was buried in a cata-comb outside the city on the ancient Via Tiburtina. His grave site quickly became a popular destina-tion for pilgrims.

pavement was reconstructed after the war. In the portico, lovely frescoes dramatize the lives of the two saints. The remains of both, together with those of St. Justin,

are in the crypt. From the sacristy, in the right aisle, you exit into a charming 12th-century cloister.

Sant'Agnese fuori le Mura

About two miles (3 km) north of San Lorenzo lies the church of Sant'Agnese, who was martyred in A.D. 304 at only 13. Her cult became so popular that by the end of the century a basilica had been built over her tomb. The church was founded by Emperor Constantine's daughter Costantina (or Costantia), or perhaps by a granddaughter of the same name; Costantina/Costantia later built her own mausoleum, Santa Costanza.

Sant'Agnese fuori le Mura was built over Agnes' catacomb by Pope Honorius I (A.D. 625–638). Enter the complex on ground level from Via Nomentana and then descend a broad staircase to reach the front entrance. Note the early Christian tombstones and inscriptions embedded in the walls.

The seventh-century **apse mosaic** has a gold background against which Sant'Agnese (with the sword of martyrdom at her feet) stands between two popes. The figures are totally Byzantine, with no trace of substance or mass beneath their garments.

In contrast, the mosaic decoration in the ambulatory, or arcade, of **Santa Costanza** is an eloquent example of classical mosaic art. Note the absence of any explicit Christian symbolism or iconography, which had probably not yet developed. The ceiling is covered with a variety of distinctly pagan motifs—geometric, classical leafy scrolls, trees, and animals. ∎

MAXXI & Parco della Musica

Two inviting cultural sites beckon visitors beyond the city wall. MAXXI, opening in late 2009, promises to be a premier museum of contemporary art and architecture, while the Parco della Musica, inaugurated in 2002, is one of the largest multifunctional music and events venues in the world.

MAXXI

MAXXI stands for **Museum of the Arts of the 21st Century** (*Museo nazionale delle arti del XXI secolo*). But in Italian the name is particularly evocative since, in contemporary jargon, "maxi" means extremely large or important, be it a film screen or a building. And this museum, scheduled to open in the second half of 2009, is the latest addition to Rome's "maxi" campaign. Conducted by Rome's municipal government, the campaign means to brush off some of the dust accumulated on the Eternal City's image in the world of contemporary art and architecture.

The new museum also aspires to put Rome on the map for contemporary art and aims to be included on the short-list of world-class museums such as the Tate Modern in London, MoMA in New York, the Reina Sofia in Madrid, and Beaubourg in Paris.

The 310,000-square-foot (29,000 sq m) museum complex will be housed in a former military barracks in the Prati neighborhood, within walking distance of Renzo Piano's Parco della Musica. Of the 15 semi-finalists in the 1999 international competition, the project presented by London-based superstar architect Zaha Hadid (with Patrik Schumacher) to create an urban campus dedicated

Parco della Musica's 2,700-seat Santa Cecilia Hall

to art and culture was judged to be the best. When completed, the 107,000-square-foot (10,000 sq m) display area will be divided into two main sections: MAXXI Art and MAXXI architecture.

The Museum's art collection (61,000 square feet/5,700 sq m of display space) already counts more than 300 works by artists like Boetti, Clemente, Kapoor, Kentridge, Merz, Penone, Pintaldi, Richter, and Warhol. The architecture section (32,000 square feet/3,350 sq m) will include the archives of world-class architects such as Carlo Scarpa, Aldo Rossi, and Pierluigi Nervi, as well as projects by contemporary architects like Toyo Ito, Italo Rota, and Giancarlo De Carlo.

In addition to display space, the MAXXI complex will include

MAXXI
Map p. 217
Via Guido Reni, 2 F
06 321 0181
www.darc.beniculturali.it/MAXXI

Parco della Musica

 Map p. 217

✉ Viale Pietro de Coubertin

☎ 06 8024 1281 (Infoline), 199 109 783 (box office)

🚇 From Termini Station: 910, 217, Linea M (every 15 minutes from 5 p.m to end of last event); From Piazza Mancini: 53, 231 (Sat. & Sun.), Tram 2; From Piazzale Canestre: 231 (Sat. & Sun.); From Piazza San Silvestro: 53; From Viale XVII Olimpiade: 217; From Piazza Flamino: Tram 2; Via Metro: Linea A to Piazza Falmino & then Tram 2

www.auditorium.com

an auditorium, library, bookshop, cafeteria, and areas indoor and out for temporary exhibits.

Parco della Musica

Not all of the Fuori le Mura sites have been around for millennia. The Parco della Musica, inaugurated in 2002, is the biggest multifunction complex in Europe and one of the ten largest in the world. It already boasts one of the highest rates of attendance among similar structures, probably thanks to the wide variety of special events it hosts in addition to its regularly scheduled chamber music, symphonic, jazz, and rock concerts.

Designed by internationally acclaimed architect Renzo Piano, the main attractions are the three mushroom-shaped halls for indoor concerts. They are clustered around an **open-air amphitheater** *(cavea)* that, in summer, constitutes a fourth venue. There are also conference rooms, spaces for temporary exhibits, a bookshop, library, bars, and even the remains of a Roman imperial villa.

Opened in early 2008, the **Museo degli Strumenti Musicali** (Museum of Musical Instruments) houses one of Italy's main collections of musical instruments *(open 11 a.m.–6 p.m., closed Wed.)*. But it is best known as the home of Rome's increasingly polished symphonic orchestra and choral group, the Accademia Nazionale di Santa Cecilia.

Named after the patron saint of music, the group is the oldest in Italy that dedicates itself exclusively to a symphonic repertory. Its current permanent conductor, Antonio Pappano, follows in the steps of illustrious peers such as Mahler, Debussy, Strauss, Stravinsky, Toscanini, and Karajan, who have all conducted, in its previous concert halls, the orchestra of the Academy. The traditional concert season lasts from October to early June. Check online *(www.santa cecilia.it)* for a schedule.

And if you happen to be in Rome in winter, you might want to attempt a few double toe-loops in the artificial ice-skating rink set up annually in the museum's cavea. ■

EXPERIENCE: Parco della Musica

The tables at the RED bar are filling up. Next door, a crowd presses to get into the art gallery, where an exhibition has just opened. Farther on, people jam the aisles of the Notebook bookstore. No, you're not in one of Rome's bustling downtown streets—you're under the arcade of Rome's massive Parco della Musica, inaugurated in 2002 and today home to the Symphonic Orchestra of the **Accademia di Santa Cecilia** *(www.santacecilia.it)* and host of many musical and art events.

Like jazz? Several times a month you can hear famous performers here. Love movies? Every fall this is the site of the new **Rome International Film Festival** *(www.riff.tv)*. Adore classical, symphonic, or chamber music? Well, then, this is the place for you. Buy a ticket at the *botteghino* (box office) and follow the well-dressed crowd into the cavernous, cherry wood-panelled expanse of the massive Santa Cecilia Hall. Don't be late; there is no admittance after the concert starts.

Bewitching scenery, seaside resorts, lakes, charming hill towns, and important historical monuments

Excursions

Detail of the Fontana della Natura in the Villa d'Este in Tivoli

Excursions

At its height, the influence of the Roman Empire extended as far north as Britain, as far south as North Africa, and over all of Asia Minor and much of the Middle East. But the first focus of Roman expansion was, as is natural, close to home.

According to legend, Ancus Marcius, the fourth king of Rome, founded Ostia, the seaport at the mouth of the Tiber River. However, this is almost certainly just a legend; the earliest remains found at Ostia date from the fourth century B.C., and the colony, in the form of a *castrum* (fortified city), was probably founded at that time.

Legend or not, it was clear from the start that an outlet to the Mediterranean was essential for growth and expansion, and indeed Ostia was to have immense strategic and commercial importance for Rome. It was, for example, the terminus for the massive grain imports from North Africa that allowed Rome to implement its policy of *panem et circensis* (bread and circuses), which proved successful in assuring the affections of the populace. Ostia Antica was the headquarters for the Annona, which was responsible for supplying Rome with grain and distributing it (generally at no cost) to the people. The Annona's presence in Ostia gave impetus to the proliferation

INSIDER TIP:

Rome is a big, bustling city—if you need to slow it down for a day, take a local train to one of the small, charming towns just outside the city. You'll be surprised at how dramatically the landscape changes from urban to pastoral in only 12 miles (20 km).

—SARAH YEOMANS
*Archaeologist & National
Geographic contributor*

NOT TO BE MISSED:

---

of guilds and corporations involved in other kinds of trade. The mosaic remains of their storefronts in the Piazzale delle Corporazioni testify to their importance. So does the advanced level of decorative embellishment in the city in general, the proliferation of baths and temples, and of the *insulae* (multistory apartment houses) that will give you a good idea of what life was like in Rome as well.

Early expansion also looked eastward, and it wasn't long before the Romans set their sights on Tibur (modern-day Tivoli) in the Sabine Hills. Originally inhabited by tribes such as the Sabines and the Volsci, Tibur was conquered first by Tiburnus or Tiburtus, the son or grandson of a Greek hero named Amphiaraos, and quickly became the object

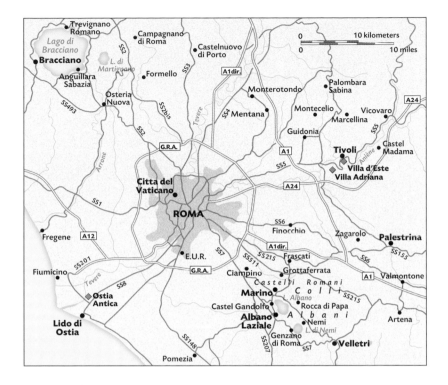

of Roman attentions because of its strategic location on the banks of the Aniene river. Not surprisingly, when conflict between the two finally broke out, Rome emerged as the victor and Tibur's fate was sealed.

By the first century B.C. Tibur's relatively cool climate and lush vegetation had made it a highly touted holiday resort for well-born, well-off Romans. It was here, in fact, that Augustus came to consult the Albunea Sibyl, who reportedly saw in one of the young emperor's dreams the onset of Christianity, thereby winning him an unusual special mention in the iconography of the Aracoeli church on Capitoline Hill in Rome.

Brutus and Cassius, Julius Caesar's assassins, had villas here, as did the poets Horace and Catullus. And it was to Tivoli that emperors such as Trajan and his successor, Hadrian, repaired to wait out the hot and sultry summer months, far from the heat of Rome. Even Totila, the Ostrogoth chieftain who briefly conquered Rome in the sixth century, made Tivoli the capital of his short-lived reign.

It was, however, Hadrian (A.D. 117–138) who really put Tibur on the map. His magnificent imperial villa (Villa Adriana) may well be the major architectural achievement of the philosopher-emperor from Spain to whom one must already feel grateful for the Pantheon and Castel Sant'Angelo.

The town's traditional appeal to the Roman elite may have reached its apex during the Renaissance, most notably after 1550, when Cardinal Ippolito II, a scion of the wealthy d'Este family, became governor and settled here. The d'Estes' architects turned an old monastery into a sumptuous palace, embellishing it with magnificently elaborate terraced gardens and a Mannerist complex of secluded grottoes, classical statuary, waterfalls, and cascading fountains. ■

Ostia Antica

Follow the Tiber River out of Rome, down to its mouth on the Mediterranean, and see the fascinating ruins of the ancient settlement of Ostia. A Roman military installation and a major commercial port, the once thriving city's second-century B.C. population exceeded 100,000.

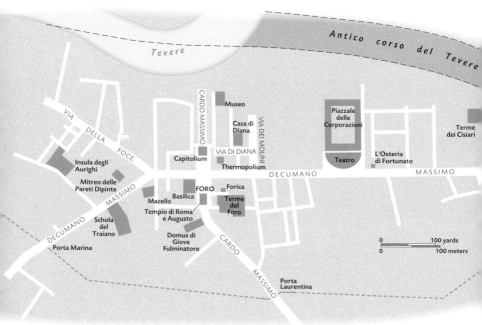

Located only 14 miles (23 km) from Rome, Ostia is easily reached by car or subway, and its limited size makes navigation simple. Unlike Pompeii, this hauntingly lovely site was not a resort for the rich and powerful; it was an urban complex made up for the most part of ordinary people. It had baths, temples, a civic center, and *insulae* (multistory apartment houses) similar to those in Rome.

History of Ostia

The name Ostia comes from *ostium*, the Latin word for "river mouth." It was probably Rome's first colony, and the oldest remains found date from the fourth century B.C. By late Republican times (the second century B.C.), it had become Rome's major port, as well as an important naval outpost.

Throughout the first two centuries of the Imperial period, Ostia flourished and acquired all the trappings—fora, basilicas, porticoes—of an important urban center. It maintained its primacy until Constantine's reign in the fourth century, when it gradually became more residential.

Ostia was home to shippers and shipbuilders, merchants and traders, tanners, ropemakers, tavern keepers, carters, prostitutes, and priests. The city's lower- and middle-class residents lived in rooms or apartment building that by law could climb as high as four stories (about 46 feet/14 m).

At its apex, Ostia had all the amenities of a leading Roman city including a lovely theater (still used in summer), scores of bathhouses, shops, temples, and taverns, as well as commercial offices, which were concentrated in the Piazzale delle Corporazioni, a sort of ancient mall or port authority.

Porta Romana

atua di inerva ttoria

Decumano Massimo

To get the best possible sense of this ancient coastal town you'll need several hours. Start at the beginning of the Decumano Massimo, the main drag, lined with shops, baths, theaters, and warehouses. This street was a continuation of the Via Ostiensis, which connected Ostia to Rome. It is crossed at midpoint by the Cardo Massimo.

Just inside the Porta Romana, the city's main gateway, is a large **Statua di Minerva Vittoria** (Statue of Victory) from the first century A.D. To the right, a path leads to the **Terme dei Cisiari,** Carter Guild's Bathhouse, with a black-and-white mosaic of a cart and driver that you really shouldn't miss.

Continue along the Decumano to the **Osteria di Fortunato,** or Tavern of Fortunatus. The mosaic inscription on the floor (an early advertisement?) reads, "Fortunatus says: Drink from this bowl to quench your thirst." Farther on is the **teatro,** or theater, built by Agrippa. It held 2,000 to 3,000 people. Originally, there were three tiers of seats (the top one has not survived) and, like today, there were snack stands in the alcoves between the external arches on the ground floor.

The pulse of second-century Ostia may have beat hardest, however, in the **Piazzale delle Corporazioni,** a huge portico behind the theater, where some 70 local guilds and foreign corporations had their offices. Their trademarks, which have supplied historians with invaluable information, are immortalized in the arcade's mosaic floors.

Via di Diana

Turn right onto the Via dei Molini and take the first street on the left, Via di Diana. The **Casa di Diana,** a large *insula,* had shops on the ground floor, apartments with windows on the first floor,

INSIDER TIP:

In a beautiful location in the countryside, Ostia Antica is a perfect place to imagine life in the times of the Roman Empire.

—CJ FAHEY
National Geographic International Channel

Ostia Antica

🅜 Map p. 227

✉ Viale dei Romagnoli 717, Ostia

☎ 06 5635 8003

🕐 Closed Mon. (museum also closed Sun. afternoon)

💲 $$. Audio guide: $

🚇 Metro Linea B to the Piramide stop; then take the train to the Ostia Antica stop. Boat service from Rome (Ponte Marconi) operates Fri.–Sun. Departure 10 a.m., arrival 12:30 p.m., 2-hr visit, return boat leaves 4:30 p.m. Round-trip €13, one-way ticket €12 (Online booking, tel 06 9774 5498, www.rexervation.com/crociere.asp)

www.itnw.roma.it/ostia/scavi

and balconies higher up. Next is the **Thermopolium,** a restaurant or snack bar with stone seats near the door (for waiting customers, perhaps?), an L-shaped counter, and holes in the wall, probably for coat hooks. Faded frescoes depict the day's fare. You can just make out eggs, fruits, and vegetables.

If you turn right at the next crossroads, you'll come to the **Museo Ostiense,** which displays artworks found during excavations. A snack bar and bookshop are behind it. Otherwise, turn left on the Cardo Massimo.

Cardo Massimo

The Cardo and Decumano intersect at the **Foro** or Forum. At one end of the square was the **Capitolium.** Ostia's major temple—dedicated to Jupiter, Juno, and Minerva—still has the broad staircase that leads up to the *cella.* Niches once held statues of the gods. At the opposite end of the Forum was a second temple, **Tempio di Roma e Augusto,** dedicated to Rome and Augustus. The terme, or baths, and the basilica, or law courts, flanked the area. Don't miss the forica (public latrine) near the baths.

"Newer" Ostia

If you continue along the Decumano, you will eventually leave the *castrum* (the earlier, fortified city) and enter the newer Ostia Antica. Take Via della Foce to the right, from which a pathway to the right leads to the **Domus di Amore e Psiche,** richly decorated with a polychrome marble pavement. Continue on to see the charioteer frescoes at the **Insula degli Aurighi.**

Find your way back to the Decumano, where there is a traders' guild, the **Schola di Traiano.** Back behind the Temple of Rome and Augustus, on the Cardo, are a number of elegant one-story houses. The **Domus di Giove Fulminatore** has an interesting welcome mat: a mosaic depicting a phallus. ∎

EXPERIENCE: Join Romans at the Beach

When in Rome, do as the Romans do and head for the closest beach. Located some 15.5 miles (25 km) west of Ostia on the Tyrrhenian shore, **Lido di Ostia** is a major destination for those seeking sun and surf. On an average summer day, as many as 55,000 people descend on this satellite city of 250,000 inhabitants to sun themselves and frolic in the sand.

You may find pockets of totally free beach, where bathers use their towels or bring their own beach chairs. But most Romans prefer to use *stabilimenti*, or beach clubs, where you can rent changing cabins, sun chairs and umbrellas, buy drinks or snacks, have a meal, play games, and possibly even get a massage.

You can drive to Ostia, or take the subway from the Ostiense station near the Piramide and get off at Stella Polare, Castel Fusano, or Cristoforo Colombo. (The stabilimenti toward the end of the line may be less crowded and the sand is whiter.) If you are a nudist, take the Castelporziano bus (number 07) outside the Cristoforo Colombo Lido metro stop; it will take you down the coast a few more miles to the **Capocotta** beach.

Tivoli

Green hills, rivers, and cascading waterfalls—for centuries, ancient Tibur (later Tivoli) was a well-known summer resort. If contemporary Tivoli unfortunately lost much of its charm under the onslaught of runaway postwar building construction, the historic center still retains much of the atmosphere of a medieval hill town.

The atmosphere of the villa of the Emperor Hadrian is conducive to study and reflection.

Throughout its history, Tivoli has been a favored resort destination among Romans, but its fame as a getaway was greatly heightened by Emperor Hadrian's decision to make it the site of his magnificent imperial villa. The inventiveness of his design enabled him to create a sprawling residence where intellectuals and friends could enjoy the pleasures of a contemplative life.

More than a thousand years later, a noble Renaissance churchman decided to make life in Tivoli bearable by turning a dilapidated Benedictine monastery into the lovely Villa d'Este. This was embellished by one of the most fascinating garden and fountain complexes in the world, recently listed by UNESCO as one of Italy's 31 major historical/artistic sites

The **Rocca Pia**, or Fortress, built over the ruins of a Roman amphitheater, dates back to the 15th century. There are some lovely churches. **Santa Maria Maggiore** *(closed p.m.)*, a fifth-century church next door to Villa d'Este, was rebuilt in the 13th century and has a Gothic portal set in a Romanesque facade. The church

Tivoli

◮ Map p. 225

Visitor information

✉ Largo Garibaldi

☎ 0774 334 522

🕐 Closed 1–3 Mon. & Fri., Sat. p.m.–Sun.

🚇 Metro: Linea B to Ponte Mammolo, then CoTral bus to Tivoli. Trains depart regularly from Tibertina Station (Roma-Pescara line) to Tivoli Station, then shuttle bus

Villa d'Este

◮ Map p. 225

✉ Piazza Trento 1

☎ 199 766 166 or 0774 332920 (call ahead to make sure fountains are working)

🕐 Closed Mon.

💲 $$. Audio guide: $. Guided tours in English: $$$$.

🚇 Metro: Linea B to Ponte Mammolo, then CoTral bus to Tivoli. Trains depart regularly from Tibertina Station (Roma-Pescara line) to Tivoli Station, then shuttle bus

www.villadeste tivoli.info

of **San Silvestro,** charmingly Romanesque except for a hideous, recently built glass front door and a couple of garish shrines, contains some extremely attractive 13th-century frescoes. Next door is an interesting fountainhead and nearby is the attractive Casa Gotica (Gothic House). **San Lorenzo,** the Duomo, unfortunately was rebuilt in the 17th century, but the 12th-century "Triptych of the Saviour," in wood with a 15th-century gold-and-silver cover, is definitely worth a look. The same goes for the disturbingly modern-looking 13th-century "Deposition" group.

Walk down Via Valerio and along Via della Sibilla to the Sibilla restaurant to see the remains of both the circular **Tempio di Vesta** and the rectangular **Tempio della Sibilla.** Not far from here, on Largo Sant'Angelo, is the entrance to the gardens of **Villa Gregoriana,** with its lovely waterfall.

Villa d'Este

Cardinal Ippolito II, a son of Lucrezia Borgia, wanted to be pope. But things didn't work out, so in around 1550 this scion of the wealthy d'Este family of Ferrara settled for the governorship of Tivoli and decided to make the best of it.

Money was not a problem for the cardinal, who wasted no time in engaging the services of major architects to transform an old monastery into a sumptuous palace, the Villa d'Este.

After dispossessing many small landowners, the architects embellished the new villa with magnificently extensive **terraced gardens** and an elaborate

Mannerist complex of secluded grottoes, classical statuary, and fountains. After the cardinal died, the villa fell into neglect. In the 1920s, it was restored and opened to the public.

Among the most bewitching of the villa's mossy **fountains** are the Fontana del Bicchierone (water pours out from a large shell-shaped basin), attributed by many art historians to Bernini; the Rometta fountain, which is a miniature Rome complete with Tiber,

Tiber Island, and a wolf-suckling Romulus and Remus; the Avenue of the Hundred Fountains, where animal heads, lilies, a small boat, basins, and so on all spurt water; the Fontana dell'Ovato, whose sibyl watches over naiads and river gods; the Water Organ fountain, which once played music; and the Owl and Bird fountain that made hooting and chirping sounds. You can also visit the rooms of the *appartamento nobile,* but make sure you don't miss the **Loggia dello Scalone,** that is the terrace, from which there is a lovely view.

Villa Adriana

Just a few miles outside of Tivoli lie the ruins of Emperor Hadrian's villa, or summer estate, undoubtedly the largest and most elaborate Roman imperial palace ever to have existed. As you can see from the model in the kiosk near the entrance, it extends over a broad area and includes the remains of an enormous villa, with baths, theaters, libraries, and extensive gardens. Below is a network of tunnels, some large enough for a horse and carriage. Choose a nice day and plan on spending several hours. It is best to buy a brochure in the bookstore adjacent to the café and follow the suggested itinerary.

After you enter, walk up the hill and pass through the high perimeter wall to find yourself at midpoint in the **Pecile,** a large square, said to have been modeled on the Stoa Pokile of Athens. The square was originally covered and surrounded by a portico. As you will see, it is also the upper story of a vast building with hundreds of rooms, probably for slaves and other palace staff.

Continuing on you come to the Small Baths and the Large Baths, much of which are still standing. Next is one of the complex's most mystical monuments, the **Canopus,** a 750-foot-long (228 m) reflecting pool. It is surrounded by columns and statues (don't miss the river god or the stone crocodile) and ends in a large *nymphaeum* that once held fountains and statues. The pool may have been inspired by the canal that linked Alexandria in Egypt to ancient Canopus. Along the west side stand six caryatids like those on the Erechtheum on the Acropolis in Athens.

Return via the Stadium and the Room with Three Exhedrae, or apses (probably a large outdoor dining room), to reach the remains of the **palace proper,** an enormous structure composed of pavilions built around peristyles, or courtyards. Don't miss the Fishpool Quadriportico, the Hall of the Doric Columns, the Heliocaminus Baths, which may have been heated by solar power, the circular Maritime Theater, and the Republican Villa, where you can see the remains of mosaic floors and vault decorations. ■

Villa Adriana

- Map p. 227
- Largo Marguerite Yourcenar s.n.c
- 0774 530203 or 06 3996 7900
- Open daily
- $$. Audio guide: $. Tours in English on request: $$$$$
- Metro: Linea B to Ponte Mammolo, then CoTral bus (direction Via Prenestina), which stops 300 m from site. Or train from the Stazione Tiburtina to Tivoli, then CAT bus No. 4, which also stops 300 m from site.

www.pierreci.it

Hadrian's Masterpiece

Hadrian ruled between A.D. 117 and 138. He began building Villa Adriana shortly after he ascended the throne and completed it in A.D. 133, although by that time he was ill and grief-stricken by the deaths of his wife and of Antinous, his young lover.

Much traveled and highly educated, Hadrian is known for other architectural achievements, such as the Pantheon and Castel Sant'Angelo in Rome, but the villa is his masterpiece. When he built the villa, Hadrian sought to re-create, or re-evoke, some of the world's architectural wonders. The vast sprawling site (almost 300 acres/121 ha) was designed both as a monument to man's achievements and as a place for study and reflection.

More Excursions from Rome

Italians love Sunday outings, and fortunately the regional bus company, CoTral, goes most places *(tel 06 7205 7205, www.cotralspa.it)*. If you have a car, so much the better, as all roads leading out of Rome go someplace interesting. Here are some suggestions.

Castelli Romani

Situated among the chestnut trees, olive groves, and vineyards that cover the slopes of extinct volcanoes, the Castelli Romani (Roman Castles) are small towns in the Alban Hills southeast of Rome best known for their white wine, *porchetta* (roast pork), and restaurants.

Founded in the Middle Ages, **Frascati**— home of the best-known Roman white wine— became a resort for the wealthy, who built luxurious villas (many of which, sadly, were damaged during World War II). The best preserved is Villa Aldobrandini, while the park attached to Villa Torlonia has wonderful fountains designed by Carlo Maderno. Nearby is the Etruscan settlement of **Tusculum.** The view from the ruins, which include a forum, a small theater, and an amphitheater, is wonderful.

Grottaferrata's beautiful fortified Greek-rite abbey was founded by St. Nilus in the 10th century and later incorporated into a castle. Don't miss the chapel of St. Nilus in the Church of Santa Maria, with Domenichino's wonderful frescoes. **Marino,** on Lake Castelgandolfo (or Albano), is known for its October wine festival, when the town fountains spew forth wine rather than water. There's a Guido Reni painting in the Trinità church and a Mithraeum with interesting frescoes. Medieval **Rocca di Papa** is the highest of the Castelli, whereas the most charming town is **Nemi,** with a Renaissance castle that overlooks a miniscule lake in a crater. The remains of two of the Emperor Caligula's pleasure boats (burned by the Germans in 1944) are housed in a small museum. Across Lake Nemi, **Genzano,** with its lovely lakeside restaurants and a 13th-century castle, is known for the June *"infiorata"* when

the streets are "paved" with pictures made out of flower petals.

Near Albano, once the Castra Albana, headquarters of Rome's Second Legion, is the Etruscan-style Roman tomb of the Horatii and Curiatii. And **Castel Gandolfo's** castle, the Pope's summer residence, was built by Carlo Maderno over an earlier fortress. The fountain in the piazza is by Bernini.

🅰 Map p. 227 ✉ Casteli Romani information: Piazza Marconi 1, Frascati ☎ 06 942 0331 (for Frascati and Grottaferrata) 🕐 Open 9 a.m.–1 p.m. 🚇 Metro: Linea A to Anagnina then CoTral bus to all Castelli Romani towns. Train: Termini Station to Frascati.

Palestrina

Some say ancient Praeneste was founded by Telegonus. In any event, this medieval-looking town outside Rome is built over the remains of the **Sanctuary of Fortuna Primigenia,** a Roman shrine that dates back to the second century B.C. This may have been the largest Hellenistic construction in Italy, a series of climbing terraces culminating in a (now) partially reconstructed temple. Its foundations are incorporated into the Palazzo Colonna-Barberini, currently the site of the **Museo Nazionale Archeologico Prenestino,** which houses numerous statues, artifacts, and reliefs. But its prize possession is the remarkable **Nile Mosaic,** discovered in the city's ancient Forum.

The **Cathedral of St. Agapitus** has a 12th-century campanile but was built over the remains of a pagan temple. A grill opens onto a small section of Roman Road. The Renaissance musician Giovanni Pierluigi da Palestrina, the creator of contrapuntal composition, was born here.

🅰 Map p. 227 ✉ Via Barberini 2 ☎ 06 957 3176 🕐 Closed 12:30 p.m.–3:30 p.m. Sat. & Sun. 🚇 Metro: Linea A to Anagnina then CoTral bus to Palestrina. Train: Termini Station to Zagarolo, then CoTral bus to Palestrina. ∎

Travelwise

Traffic policeman

TRAVELWISE

Rome is a very rewarding city to visit and, on the whole, it's also very welcoming. However, some aspects of life here are difficult to understand for those used to a more streamlined (and less idiosyncratic) way of doing things. Although tales of Italian inefficiency may well be exaggerated, there is no doubt that the pace of life (and of change) is slower here, and some of your transactions may take far longer, or be much more complicated, than you would have expected.

PLANNING YOUR TRIP

When to Go

See also sidebar p. 11.
From May through summer, Rome's social life takes place outdoors. Restaurants and bars move their tables onto streets and piazzas, and there is a plethora of open-air cinemas and arts festivals. Many stores and restaurants shut in August, but fewer do so than in previous years. Romans have learned that the city can be enjoyable in August, when traffic jams end and the thermometer drops a bit compared to July.

In recent years hotel prices have risen significantly, but discounts can sometimes be had in summer, as well as in January and February.

Climate

Rome has mild, damp winters; the temperature seldom drops below freezing and it rarely snows. Spring and fall tend to be rainy and warmish. Summer is hot—sometimes oppressively so in July and August—and, apart from the occasional dramatic thunderstorm, dry. The rainiest months are October, November, and December. It may, of course, rain at any time of the year—the average annual rainfall is 31 inches—but you're unlikely to have more than two or three days without seeing the sun, whatever the season.

What to Take

Casual clothes prevail except in banking or political circles, so you can pretty much wear what you like. However, if you are planning to visit any churches,

make sure not to wear shorts or a very short skirt, and cover your arms to at least the elbow or there is a chance you will not be allowed in. You'll also probably want to have one fairly elegant outfit for the evening. In spring and fall, it's a good idea to dress in layers because temperatures in the evenings can drop sharply. In winter, remember that interiors are heated less than in the United States—bring warm clothes.

Bring comfortable shoes because the cobblestoned streets can be hard on the feet. An umbrella is essential in the spring and fall wet seasons. Sunglasses are also advisable because even the winter sun can be dazzling. Binoculars will help you make the most of views and lavishly decorated interiors.

Other essentials are your passport, driver's license, credit cards, and insurance documentation. In Italy you're meant to carry identification at all times—although you're unlikely to need to produce it.

Insurance

Take out enough travel insurance to cover emergency medical treatment, repatriation, and loss or theft of money and possessions.

HOW TO GET TO ROME

Passports

U.S. and Canadian citizens do not need a visa for stays in Italy of up to three months. By law, however, all visitors are supposed to announce their presence to the local police. Hotels do this for you—leave your passport at reception when you check in and you'll

get it back the following morning. You have to do this every time you check into a hotel, even if it's just for one night. Independent travelers and anybody staying for more than three months should contact the central police station (La Questura), tel 064686, to find out what to do.

Airports

Rome now has two international airports, Leonardo da Vinci–Fiumicino, southwest of Rome, and the smaller Ciampino, southeast of the city, both run by Aeroporti di Roma (tel 0665951, www.adr.it). The website has transport information as well as real-time arrival and departure flight information. Ciampino currently services low-cost airlines such as Ryanair and easyJet, charters, and regional Italian airlines. The Aeroporti di Roma website has plenty of other useful information.

Getting to Rome center from Fiumicino airport

Two train services link the airport to central Rome. The "Leonardo Express" departs every 30 minutes from Rome (6:30 a.m.–11:30 p.m.) and from the airport (5:25 a.m.–10:50 p.m.). The nonstop trip costs €11 and takes about 30 minutes. The FR1 train to Trastevere, Ostiene, and Tiburtina costs €5 and departs every 15 minutes, from 5:57 a.m. to 11:36 p.m. For exact departure times, see www.ferroviedellostato.it (tip: to search, use "Roma" and "Fiumicino airport"). For transfers between 11:30 p.m. and 6 a.m., a bus runs between Fiumicino airport and Tiburtina station *(tel 800 150008, www.cotralspa.it)*.

Getting to Rome center from Ciampino airport

Several companies link the airport to the Termini station. You should allow at least three hours before your flight departure, especially for international flights. **Sitbus shuttle,** tel 06 591 7844, *www.sitbusshuttle.it*. First bus from Termini 4:30 a.m., last 9:15 p.m. From Ciampino, first departure 8:30 a.m., last 11:45 p.m. Cost €6. **Terravision,** tel 06 7934 1722, *www.terravision.eu*. Departures coincide with flights and are restricted to passengers flying on certain airlines. Cost €6. The **Cotral** bus company *(tel 800 150008, www.cotralspa.it)* runs a night service to and from the Termini station. Cost €5. The company also runs a shuttle service to the Anagnina station on the Metro A line, where you can catch trains to Termini station. **Schiaffini** *(tel 800700805, www .schiaffini.it)* runs a shuttle to the Anagnina station and Ciampino train station, as well as two buses a day to Fiumicino airport.

Taxi

A taxi from Fiumicino airport to central Rome should cost €40; Ciampino airport to central Rome should cost €30.

Limousine & shuttle service

Airport Connection Service *(tel 06 338 3221, www.airport connection.it)* offers limousine service to Rome's airports and other cities in Italy.
If you are alone with luggage, **Air Port Shuttle** *(tel 06 4201 3469, www.airportshuttle.it)* is a useful service.
Rome Airport Shuttle *(tel 06 9774 5497, www.rexervation .com/shuttleservice.asp)* runs

every 30–40 minutes from 7:45 a.m.–10:15 p.m.

GETTING AROUND
By Car
Car rentals
In Italy:
Avis, tel 199 100133
www.avisautonoleggio.it
Budget, tel 06 482 0966
www.budget.it
Europcar, tel 06 9670 9592
www.europcar.it
Maggiore, tel 199 15120
www.maggiore.it
Sixt, tel 199 100666
www.sixt.it

Unless you're planning on making a lot of trips out of the city, a car in central Rome is more of a hindrance than a help. Parking is nearly impossible, and the local driving style is daunting. If you do need to rent a car, check prices before leaving home. Rentals booked in the U.S. often cost less. Car rental in Italy is about the most expensive in Europe as, incidentally, is gas.

Driving regulations & conventions

An international driver's license is not required for short-term visitors. When driving, keep all relevant documents (including at least a photocopy of your passport) in the car. Driving regulations in Italy are not always strictly adhered to (although you should do so). See sidebar p. 42 for information on right-of-ways at street crossings.

Italian law makes the use of seatbelts obligatory and—although you never could tell—also prohibits driving while using a cell phone without a headset. Outside the city, headlights should be on even in daytime and most drivers use their parking lights in the city on rainy days. Remember that in Italy a car flashing its headlights at you

generally means the driver will be taking the right of way and not giving it to you.

Although speeding is a national pastime, there are official limits in Italy. The speed limit in built-up areas is 30 mph (50 kph); other normal roads, 70 mph (110 kph); and motorways, 80 mph (130 kph). The legal limit for drinking and driving works out to about two drinks.

If you are parked illegally or if your parked car is blocking somebody else's access, the police may tow it away. If you think this has happened, call the Polizia Municipale *(tel 06 676 9838)* to find out where it is, when to collect it, and how to pay the fine.

Car breakdown

Rental car companies have an emergency number for break-downs. Otherwise call the emergency number of the Automobile Club d'Italia *(tel 803116 and press "3" at the prompt to get an English-speaking operator)*. Emergency phones are located along the Autostrade toll roads.

Public Transportation

Buses, trams, the metro, and local rail services in Rome are all integrated into one transport system. Tickets can be bought at most tobacconists, some newsstands, train stations, and at machines placed at key locations (go to "tickets and passes" on the English-language version of *www.atac.roma.it* for a list). All new buses now have ticket-dispensing machines on board that work with a €1 coin. An ordinary ticket (BIT—*biglietto integrato a tempo*, €11) entitles you to 75 minutes of unlimited bus and/ or tram travel plus one journey by train or metro. A day pass (BIG—*biglietto integrato giornaliero*, €5) is valid until midnight. A BTI (*biglietto turistico integrato*, €11) is good until midnight of the third day after purchase. A CIS (*carta integrata settimanale,* €16) is a weekly pass.

All tickets must be validated at the beginning of your first ride and again if you switch to the metro or vice versa. Machines for doing this are on buses or at the entrance to metro and train stations. Keep the validated ticket until the end of your journey in case you are queried by an inspector. If you do not have a valid ticket, or if your ticket has not been validated, you are liable to pay a fine of at least €50.

Metropolitana

The Rome subway, where many stations have been spruced up with original mosaics by top contemporary artists, operates from 5:30 a.m. to 11:30 p.m. (Saturday until 1:30 a.m.). Rome has only two subway lines (A and B) which cross at Termini and only go to limited areas of the city. (See also "Charting Your Trip, p. 8.)

Buses & trams

ATAC has a vast bus and tram system, which can take you almost anywhere in the city (at peak hours travel times can be lengthy). On weekdays most lines run until midnight or 12:30 a.m; there are several nighttime, or *notturni,* lines as well. A series of small, electric buses navigate the historic center's narrow streets and are good for sightseers. The 119 runs every 10–15 minutes and will take you around the historic center; the 117 runs from S. Giovanni to Piazza del Popolo; the 116 from the Gianicolo and Piazza Farnese to near the Villa Borghese; the 115 from Viale Trastevere to the Janiculum park; and the 125 goes around Trastevere.

For information about bus routes call 06 57003 (*Mon.–Sat., 8 a.m.–8 p.m.*) or use the excellent ATAC website (*www.atac.roma.it*) in Italian or English. The Trovalinea box lets you see any bus line's exact route. Be wary of pickpockets, especially on the 64 and 40 lines which serve the Vatican and other tourist areas.

Buses to many towns in the Lazio region are operated by Cotral (*tel 800 150008, www.cotralspa .it*), departing from eight termini coinciding with railway and metro stations. Its website has no English translation but see *"Trasporto, capolinea"* for a list of destinations and *"Linee e Orari"* for the full schedule. People over 70 years of age travel free.

Taxis

Taxis are available at taxi stands, generally marked with blue-and-white or orange-and-black signs saying "Taxi." They can also be hailed in the street, although by law they are not allowed to pick you up within 100 meters (110 yds) of a stand. When a cab is free the "taxi" sign on the roof is lit up. Taxis run on meters, which start at €2.80 and increase every km or 20 seconds. On Sundays/holidays, the beginning fare is €4 and, at night (10 p.m.–7 a.m.), €5.80. The first piece of baggage is free; additional bags cost €1 each. Travelers who start their journey at the Termini station must pay an additional €2. For rides out of town, a second fare system kicks in once you're a certain distance out of town (outside the ring road). By law, fares must be clearly displayed inside the taxi. Tipping is optional but a good idea if you ask for added help with your baggage.

Radio-Dispatched Taxis

Rome's "Radiotaxi" system is surprisingly efficient, and increasingly you will find operators who speak English. However, hotels and restaurants will generally be happy to place the call for you. The two larger companies, **Radio Taxi 3570** (*tel 063570*) and **Capital** (*tel 064994*), have satellite telephone systems, so if you're speaking from a landline they don't need you to give the number or the address, but they may ask for your name. An automatic system will tell you if a taxi is available and give you its number and the estimated number of minutes you will have to wait. If you understand and accept, just hang up. Otherwise wait until an operator comes on the line. As well as the beginning fare, you must pay €2 for a wait time of up to 5 minutes, €4 if the wait is between 5 and 10 min., and €6 if it is more than 10 min. All radio-dispatched taxis in Rome accept reservations but only for trips to the airports or to Termini or Tiburtina train stations. If you reserve, you will receive a phone call 10 to 15 min. before pick-up telling you the number of your taxi. Other companies are **Prontotaxi** (*tel 066645*), **Tevere** (*tel 064157*), and **Cosmo** (*tel 068822*). Drivers prefer cash but most will take credit cards if necessary (many will not take Diners Club or American Express).

Traffic

Newcomers to Rome may find the city's undisciplined drivers and darting mopeds intimidating. For hints on crossing the street, see sidebar p. 42.

Trains

Trains to other cities in Lazio or the rest of Italy leave from either the Termini or Tiburtina stations. You can get a specific Roma–Viterbo line from the Ostiense and Trastevere stations, and a special metro line to Viterbo runs regularly from Piazzale Flaminio (near Piazza del Popolo). Tickets can also be bought from selected travel agencies or online at *www .trenitalia.it.* Call 06 6847 5475 for information and for Eurostar or Intercity bookings or purchases. You can choose the "ticketless" option, in which you pay by credit card and get a reservation number to give to the conductor. If you don't have your receipt or reservation code, you will be considered as being without a ticket. You can also pick up tickets from automatic teller machines at the station by inserting the same credit card. Eurostar and Intercity trains tickets can now be bought up to 10 minutes before departure if seats are available. Unless you're traveling by Eurostar, remember that before boarding you must punch your ticket in one of the yellow punch boxes scattered throughout the station.

Internal flights
Alitalia *(tel 062222, www.alitalia .com)* flies from Rome to most Italian cities, as do **Air One** *(tel 199 207080, www.flyairone.it/it)*, **Meridiana** *(tel 199 111333, www .meridiana.it)*, and a number of low-cost airlines such as **Wind Jet** *(w1.volawindjet.it)*; **Blu-Express** *(www.blu-express.com)*, and **Ryan Air** *(www.ryanair.com.)*

Tours & Sightseeing
Independent sightseeing
Unless you're short on time, Rome is easy to visit on your own. The key is flexibility. Sightseeing hours at major attractions are much longer than in the past, but because of staff shortages and strikes, official opening hours are not always reliable. In general, archaeological sites are open the whole day, closing an hour before sunset. Museums sell their last tickets an hour before closing. Churches generally close from noon to 3 p.m. and then for the night at around 7 p.m. The Rome Tourist Office *(tel 060608, www.060608.it)* can provide information, in English, about events, hours, and transport (press "2" for an English-speaking operator).

There are also a dozen information centers in green kiosks scattered throughout the city (see sidebar p. 11). The English-language version of the official tourism website *(www.romatur ismo.it)* has a lot of information— see "Rome Welcomes You" for important phone numbers, and "Discovering Rome" for other helpful information.

Reservations for most museums and archaeological sites can be made online at *www.pierreci.it* or by calling 06 3996 7700 *(Mon.–Fri. 9 a.m.–6 p.m., Sat. 9 a.m.–2 p.m. Small fee charged).*

In Rome Now *(www.inromenow .com)* is an excellent source for information on what is going on in Rome. *Wanted in Rome* magazine, available at newsstands, also has plenty of useful information, both in print and online at *www.wanted inrome.com.*

Bus tours
Trambus Open *(tel 800 281281),* run by the city of Rome, offers moderately priced stop-and-go bus tours equipped with audio guides that allow you to hop on and off at any of the stops all day. Tours start from Piazza dei Cinquecento (Termini station), and tickets can be bought on board, at the Trambus Open info box in Piazza dei Cinquecento, at Trambus Open authorized dealers, and online at *www.trambusopen .com.* In peak season, the company suggests you depart from Termini early in the morning, otherwise the wait could be very long.

The **110 Open** *www.trambus open.com* tourist line takes you to all the major historic and artistic sights in the city. It starts from Termini station and runs daily, every 10 minutes, 8 a.m.–8 p.m., lasting about 2 hours. Cost €16. Discounts for Rome Pass holders.

The **Archeobus** passes through the center of Rome and along the Park of Via Appia

Antica. It runs daily, every 20 min from 9 a.m. to 4 p.m. and lasts about 1.5 hours. Cost €13. Discount for Rome Pass holders.

Opera Romana Pellegrinaggi (Pilgrim Office) also runs two bus tours using the same stop-and-go formula called Roma Cristiana (Christian Rome), which go to the most important churches and holy places in Rome. They run daily from 8:30 a.m. to 7:30 p.m. and last about 2 hours each. Tickets can be bought directly on board, at ORP info points, and online at *www.terravision.eu.* Cost €19. ORP also offers a reasonably priced package that includes a tour of the Vatican museums (audio guide), with entrance through the "no wait" gate, plus the Christian Rome bus tour for €39. Make reservations at the website above.

Boat tours
Rome now has its own *bateaux-mouches* running up and down the Tiber. **Batelli di Roma** runs several different cruises (dinner, wine bar, night, guided tour, Ostia Antica), as well as a regularly scheduled navigation line that runs from Duca d'Aosta Bridge to the Tiber Island, stopping along the way. For further information and reservations, tel. 06 9774 5498, *www.rexervation.com.*

Walking tours in English
Our author Michael Brouse and his colleague Dennis Cigler conduct private walking tours in affiliation with **In Italy's Companions** *(tel in U.S. 877 655 9221, www .initaly.com).*

Scala Reale *(tel 06 482 0911, www.scalareale.org)* offers tours of the historic center, Vatican, and archaeological area.

Rome Revealed *(tel 06 324741, www.romerevealed.com)* offers walking and private tours of the Vatican, catacombs, fountains, and more.

Jogging tours

If you're the sporting type and want to combine a sprint around Rome with tourism, you might want to give sight jogging a try. A knowledgeable personal trainer will run you around the city's sights. Contact **Sight Jogging**: tel 347 33 53 185, *www.sightjogging.it.*

Carriage tours

If you are interested in seeing Rome by horse carriage and want to book in advance, see *www .romeguide.it.*

Night tram tours

These romantic night tours pass through the most attractive parts of the city on a tramway coach from the 1920s. The tour includes dinner overlooking the Colosseum and a live concert of opera arias performed on the tram. Tours leave from Porta Maggiore every Friday at 9 p.m. and last three hours. For reservations, tel. 33 9633 4700, trambelcanto@ yahoo.it, or *www.trambus.com.* Cost is €55–90 per person depending on the menu chosen.

Flying over Rome

Cityfly *(www.cityfly.com)* offers the opportunity to see Rome from a different point of view. Planes leave from Urbe Airport, just outside the city. Cost is €70 per person. For reservations (2-person minimum) call 06 88333 at least two days in advance. Cityfly also operates an air taxi service to all 150 airports in Italy.

Bicycle & Scooter Rental

Rome has about 100 miles (160 km) worth of dedicated bike paths. One runs along Viale Tiziano; another, barring floods from a rain-swollen Tiber, runs along the river's embankments for 18 miles (30 km). Many people brave the city's traffic on motorscooters, the quickest way to get anywhere

with almost no parking problems. For maps and bike rentals see *www.romainbici.it.*

Many companies rent bikes and scooters. Some are listed on *www. romeguide.it.* The most convenient are **Scooter Rent** at Termini Station *(to the right of Piazza dei Cinquecento, tel. 06 4890 5823, www.trenoescooter.com)* and **Bici & Baci** *(Via del Viminale 5, tel. 06 482 8443, www.bicibaci.com).*

PRACTICAL ADVICE
Communications
Post offices

The Italian post office, which has branches in every neighborhood, has been largely reorganized in recent years and is far more functional than in previous years. The main post office *(Piazza San Silvestro 19, Mon.–Sat. 8:30 a.m.–6:30 p.m),* has been totally revamped and has splendid service and a helpful, multilingual information desk. Most tourists' needs will involve mailings (mailing boxes and padded envelopes can be bought here along with stamps), so go straight to the line for *Prodotti postali* and avoid *Prodotti finanziari,* which is for paying bills, picking up pensions, and the like. Most smaller post offices *(Mon.– Fri. 8:30 a.m.–2 p.m., Sat. 8:30 a.m.–1 p.m.)* now have a number queuing system—but make sure you take a number for the proper sector. Still, unless you are sending a package, your best bet is to buy stamps from a tobacconist. Letters and postcards can be mailed from one of the red boxes you will find outside the tobacconist's or outside a post office. Get the *posta prioritaria* (priority mail) stamps, which will get your mail on its way quicker. Most mailboxes have two slots, one for the city *(per la città)* and one for everywhere else *(altre destinazioni).*

You can have mail sent to you at the post office by having it ad-

dressed *"Fermo Posta"* followed by your name, the branch name, and its address.

Vatican Post

The Vatican has its own postal system with two post offices *(Mon.–Fri. 8:30 a.m.–7 p.m., Sat. 8:30 a.m.–6 p.m.)* in Piazza San Pietro, one on either side of the basilica. Stamps (or *francobolli*) cost marginally more than they do for the Italian system. There are mailboxes at the post offices and at the Vatican offices on Piazza San Calisto in Trastevere.

Telephones

To call Italy from the United States, dial 011 39 (international and Italian country code) followed by the local number, which always includes the city area code, e.g. 06 for Rome, 055 for Florence, 02 for Milan, 081 for Naples, and 041 for Venice. This goes for in-city calls as well. Be aware that, not counting the area codes, Italian phone numbers can have from four digits (government offices, some embassies) to eight digits. 800 and 848 numbers are toll free. 199 numbers have a higher rate. To make an international call from Italy, dial the international country code (001 for the U.S. and Canada, 0044 for the U.K.) followed by the phone number. For directory assistance call 1254 or visit *www.info412.it.* To make a collect call, dial 170.

Public phones are now operated by phone cards, which can be bought from tobacconists, bars, and post offices. Most have clearly displayed instructions in English. To make a call, lift the receiver, then insert your card (first break off the perforated corner) in the slot. The amount of money available on your card will be shown on an LCD. Dial the number. You can watch how quickly you're using up the card on the LCD—just before it's about to expire, you'll hear a shrill sound.

Insert another card to continue the conversation. International phone cards are also available at tobacconists and often have very reasonable rates.

Internet Cafés

They may not be on every corner, but if you need an Internet point you can find it.

LidoNet *(Campo dei Fiore, Vicolo delle Grotte 26, tel 06 6813 4537, www.lidonet.it)* has an English-speaking staff and can help you with faxes, international calls, money transfers, and memory cards. .

Il Mastello *(Via San Francesco a Ripa 62, 7 a.m.–10:30 p.m.)* in Trastevere allows you to go online while doing your laundry or to make long-distance calls at cheap rates at the phone center.

Centrally located **Internet Train** *(Piazza Sant'Andrea della Valle 3, www.internettrain.it)*, an international chain, offers other services such as scanning, call center, courier, etc.

Navona Cyber Cafe *(Vicolo del Fico 17)* offers Internet access, printing, scanning, and coffee.

If you have your own laptop computer with a wireless card, you will be able to access the Internet from the many cafés and public places that now offer free WiFi connections. To find public places where you can access the Internet, see *www.romawireless.com.*

Crime

See sidebar p. 105

Electricity

Nearly all Italian circuits use 220 volts; American appliances need adapter plugs and those that operate on 110 volts will also need a transformer. These can be bought at a *ferramenta* (hardware store) or before you leave home.

Media
Newspapers
Most downtown newsstands

(edicole) have a selection of English-language papers and magazines; the *International Herald Tribune* is widely available. The major Italian dailies are the Milan-based *Corriere della Sera*, and the Rome-based *La Repubblica. Il Sole 24 Ore* is the country's leading business daily.

Television
The main national stations are the state-owned RAI 1, 2, and 3, Mediaset's Italia Uno, Rete Quattro, and Canale 5. La 7 is a privately owned station. All programs are in Italian (English-language imports are dubbed). Channels such as CNN, BBC, TV5, and CNBC are available via cable or satellite.

Radio
Vatican Radio (93.3 FM) broadcasts news and other programs in a wide range of languages including English. For 24-hour classical music without breaks, try Auditorium (100.3 FM). Radio Centro Suono (101.3 FM) plays a range of dance, reggae, ragga, Afro-Caribbean, and other music. The state-owned stations (RAI-1 on 89.7 FM, RAI-2 on 91.7 FM, and RAI-3 on 93.7 FM) broadcast a mixture of news and chat shows combined with (usually fairly middle-of-the-road) classical and light music.

Books
If you're interested in ancient Rome, read Suetonius' *The Twelve Caesars*, Livy's *History of Rome*, and Tacitus' *The Histories*. Also try Robert Graves' *I Claudius* and *Claudius the God*, Marguerite Yourcenar's *Memoirs of Hadrian*, or the works of Allan Massie—*Augustus, Caesar,* and *Tiberius*—which, although fiction, give a good idea of what life was once like. Literary works set in more recent times include: *Roman Fever* by Edith Wharton; *A Time in Rome* by Elizabeth Bowen;

History by Elsa Morante; *The Marble Faun* by Nathaniel Hawthorne; and the works of Roman author Alberto Moravia.

Money Matters
Banca Intesa, Via del Corso 226, tel 06 67121.
American Express, Piazza di Spagna 38, tel 06 67641.
Thomas Cook, Piazza Barberini 21/A, tel 06 4202 0150.
Banca Nazionale del Lavoro (BNL), Via Bissolati 2 (Piazza Barberini), tel 06 47031.

In 2002, the euro became the only legal tender in Italy as well as in eleven other European countries. There are 100 cents to the euro which is available, in bills, in denominations of 1, 2, 5, 10, 20, 100, and 500 as well as in coins worth 1, 2, 5, 10, 20, and 50 cents.

To change money, go to any of the financial offices listed above, a major bank, or a store-front exchange office (look for the *"cambio"* sign). For the best rate of exchange, however, use your debit or credit card at one of the hundreds of ATMs in the city. Called Bancomat machines, they generally give you a choice of operating languages. Travelers checks are accepted by many stores and hotels but seem to be falling out of use. The main post office will also change U.S. dollars, British pounds, Swiss francs, and Japanese Yen into euros.

National Holidays
Jan. 1, Jan. 6, Easter Sun., Easter Mon., April 25, May 1, June 2, June 29 (Rome only), Aug. 15, Nov. 1, Dec. 8, Dec. 25, Dec. 26.

Opening Times
Hours in Rome can be erratic, making sightseeing and shopping difficult. Many shops in downtown Rome now stay open all day, but they have no obligation

to do so. Those in other areas like Trastevere or Testaccio still tend to close at lunchtime (generally 1 or 1:30 p.m–3:30 or 4 p.m.) so be sure to phone first. Most Italian banks are open 8:30 or 8:45 a.m.–1:30 p.m. and 2:45–4:15 p.m. Mon.–Fri.; a very few are also open Saturday mornings. Many clothing stores are closed on Monday mornings, as are hairdressers. Supermarkets are now generally open on Sundays and, since it's optional, so are some other stores, although most shopkeepers prefer to take the day off.

Bars open in the early morning; some close at 8 p.m. but many in the center stay open until midnight or 2 a.m. Traditional restaurants generally serve between 12:30 and 3 p.m. and from 8 to 11 p.m, but some areas, such as Trastevere, have many restaurants catering to tourists that open at noon and stay open all day. Many businesses close for summer holidays in August.

Time Differences

Italy is six hours ahead of New York and nine hours ahead of Los Angeles. Europe changes to daylight saving time on the last Sunday of March and returns to standard time on the last Sunday in October.

Tipping

If service is not included on the bill (it appears as a separate charge under *"servizio"*), add about ten percent—depending on how satisfied you've been— which should be left in cash if you're paying with a credit card. Even when the tip is included, it's normal to leave some small change if the service has been good.

Toilets

Rome has few public toilets, but bars and cafés must let you use theirs if you ask. One toilet often serves both men and women.

Standards of hygiene vary dramatically but tend toward the lower end of the scale; it's a good idea to carry tissues, as toilet paper isn't guaranteed.

Travelers with Disabilities

Rome is not an easy city for people with disabilities. Most museums now have wheelchair-accessible bathrooms and stair lifts, but the entrances and exits of many museums, shops, restaurants, and hotels have not yet been made accessible. The Vatican Museums, which have ten wheelchairs available at its Guardaroba (cloakroom), is a notable exception. Many sidewalks in Rome lack curb cuts or ramps and those that exist are often steep. Stair lifts in museums and churches (even those that appear fairly new) tend to be narrower, shorter, and have a lower weight capacity than those in the U.S. There are elevators at all the metro stations on the B line except for Circo Massimo, Colosseo, and Cavour. Only Cipro (Vatican) and Valle Aurelia have elevators on the A line. (When necessary, Romans will help carry a disabled person up the stairs.)

A reliable but expensive private van service is **Fausta Trasporti** *(tel 06 503 6040 www.faustatransporti.it)*. Free guided tours for disabled persons (English-speaking as well as Italians) are available through **CO.IN,** but book early *(tel 06 570 6036 or 800 271027)*.

EMERGENCIES
Embassies & Consulates
British embassy and consulate, Via XX Settembre 80/A (Porte Pia), 00187, tel 06 4220 0001. Bus: 16, 36, 60, 61, 62, 84, 90, 492.

Canadian embassy, Via G.B. De Rossi 27, 00161, tel 06 445981. Bus:
36, 60, 62, 84, 90; Metro: Linea B (Bologna). **Canadian consulate,** Via Zara 30, tel 06 445981 (24-hour emergency service).

United States embassy, Palazzo Margherita, Via V. Veneto 119/A, 00187, tel 06 46 741. Metro: Barberini. **United States Consulate,** Via V. Veneto 121, tel 06 46 741.

Emergency Phone Numbers & Addresses
Police, tel 113
Carabinieri, tel 112
Fire, tel 115
Emergency medical assistance, tel 118
Italian Red Cross, tel 065510 (ambulance emergency)

Nighttime Pharmacies:
Piran, Via Nazionale 228, tel 06 488 0754
Farmacia Internazional, Piazza Barberini 49, tel 06 487 1195
The Vatican Pharmacy *(enter Vatican at the Porta Sant'Anna entrance, tel 06 686 4146, open Mon.–Fri. 8:30 a.m.–6 p.m. & Sat. 7:30 a.m.–1 p.m. Bus: 23, 49, 51)* has an English-speaking staff and a wide range of non-Italian pharmaceutical products.

Lost Property
Oggetti Rinvenuti, Via Nicolo Bettoni 1 (Trastevere train station), tel 06 581 6040 or 06 581 0583. Bus: H, 780; Tram: 3, 8. Open 8:30 a.m.–1 p.m. Mon.–Fri., also 3–5 p.m. Tues. & 1–5 p.m. Thurs.
Termini station at track 24, tel 06 4782 5543. Open 7 a.m.–midnight.

Lost Credit Cards
American Express, tel 06 72900 347 or 800 914 912
Diners Club, tel 800 864064
MasterCard, tel 800 870866
Visa, tel 800 819014
Cartasi, tel 800 151616

Hotels & Restaurants

While Rome Is not particularly known for its accommodations, both luxurious and charming places do exist, if you know where to look. The cuisine is a different story. It's very difficult to eat badly in Rome—even the humblest of fare in the smallest trattoria is usually lovingly prepared and tasty.

HOTELS

Accommodation in Rome for the most part is scarce and expensive: You should book as much in advance as possible. You'll probably be asked for a faxed confirmation and a deposit or credit card number. Many Rome hotels and restaurants do not take American Express or Diners Club so check if you are planning to pay your final bill with either of those cards.

Central Rome (especially Trastevere and the areas around Piazza Navona and Campo dei Fiori) is noisy until 2 or 3 a.m. every night. If you're booking in these areas ask for a quiet room—and consider ear plugs. Remember, too, that many of the older hotels in the city have fairly small rooms.

Few hotels have rooms that are specially adapted for disabled travelers, but many will do all they can to accommodate special needs, especially if you let them know in advance.

Street parking is extremely difficult to find in the historic center, but most hotels will help you and arrange for you to use a garage—for which you will usually have to pay an additional daily charge. It's a good idea to inquire in advance about parking if you know you're going to need it.

Grading System

Italian hotels are rated from one to five stars by the Government's Tourist Office according to such facilities as the number of rooms with private bathrooms, rooms with TV, etc., rather than style or comfort. However, this is not always a reliable measure as for tax reasons many hotels opt to stay in a lower category. Unless otherwise noted, all the hotels listed here have private bathrooms in all rooms (upper categories have bathtub and shower; lower, only shower). English is spoken at all the hotels listed; however, the amount spoken varies and may only be sufficient to take a booking and deal with the most basic visitor requests. Value-added tax and service are included in the prices, and so is breakfast, unless otherwise noted. Room price categories are given only for guidance and do not take account of seasonal variations.

Alternative Accommodations

Many Roman monasteries and convents have comfortable rooms to rent at reasonable prices. (See sidebar, p. 84.)

For short-term apartment rentals, check out www.VRBO.com, www.Vacationrentals.com, and www.romaclick.com/Roma.htm.

RESTAURANTS

Italians take eating seriously and tend to eat a lot when they go out. A traditional meal consists of antipasti and goes on to the primo (usually pasta, soup, or risotto) before hitting the main, or secondo, course (meat or fish) accompanied by salad or vegetable contorni. Desserts or fruit round off the meal, followed by an espresso. But most restaurants are now used to people only having one or two courses.

Dining Hours

Lunch is eaten between about 12:30 p.m. and 2:30 p.m. Dinner is seldom served before 8 p.m. and continues until about 10:30 p.m. or even later. In traditional restaurants, making reservations is often advisable, sometimes essential. Today, however, in areas like Trastevere and around Campo dei Fiori, there are more and more restaurants geared to tourists, which stay open all day and where you can always get a meal. Menus are often displayed outside and one orders à la carte. At some restaurants a menu di degustazione allows you to sample several specialities.

Trattorias

These are relatively simple restaurants that are often family run and were originally geared toward serving local people good, home-style cooking. Their clientele may have widened over the years (people will travel for miles to eat at a good trattoria), but their value for money has, in most cases, remained.

Smoking

Since January 1, 2005, Italy became one of Europe's growing number of nonsmoking countries. This means that smoking is banned in public offices and shops and permitted only in those very, very few bars and restaurants that have installed the powerful ventilation equipment required by law. However, restaurants or cafés with al fresco seating easily accommodate smokers.

Tipping

Some establishments add a place-setting charge to the bill and others don't. When it hasn't already been calculated, leave about ten percent; whether it's been added or not, a few coins left on the table shows that you've enjoyed your meal and service, and is a gesture that will be much appreciated.

One of the anachronisms of Italian dining is the charge for *pane e coperto* (bread and cover), which appears on nearly all restaurant bills and is usually a euro or two per head. It may seem odd that you should effectively be charged for using the cutlery and table linen, but it's standard practice and not an optional extra that depends on whether or not you've eaten any bread.

Organization & Abbreviations

All sites are listed first by price, then in alphabetical order.

The abbreviations used are:
L = lunch
D = dinner

AE = American Express
DC = Diners Club
MC = MasterCard
V = Visa

■ ANCIENT ROME

Until a few years ago, the Monti area (which straddles the lower end of Via Cavour) was busy during the day but relatively quiet in the evening. That has all changed. Monti, now full of bars, pubs, and restaurants, has become a nighttime destination, so the late-night Friday and Saturday traffic on Via Cavour is often at a standstill. Bus: 60, 75, 84, 85, 87 Metro: Linea B (Colosseo or Cavour).

FORUM
$$$$ ★★★★
VIA TOR DE' CONTI 25
TEL 06 679 2446
FAX 06 678 6479
www.hotelforumrome.com
Tucked in a comparatively quiet corner behind the Imperial Forums, the atmosphere and decor of this grand hotel

are reminiscent of an English gentlemen's club. Rooms vary in size, but all are well furnished, and there's a wonderful roof garden restaurant.
⊙ 80 ⓟ ⊜ ⓢ
⊠ All major cards

INN AT THE FORUM
$$$$ ★★★★★
VIA DEGLI IBERNESI 30
TEL 06 6919 0970
FAX 06 4543 8802
www.theinnattheroman forum.com
Located just a few steps from the Forum, this luxury hotel actually houses Roman ruins. Three of the rooms offer terraces with delightful views of a little garden with palm and fig trees, which is also a lovely spot for a drink in the evening.
⊙ 12 ⊜ ⓢ ⊠ All major cards

NERVA
$$ ★★★
VIA TOR DE' CONTI 3
TEL 06 679 3764
FAX 06 6992 2204
www.hotelnerva.com
This friendly hotel, situated just steps from the Roman Forum, underwent a recent renovation. The public areas are pleasingly decorated and the rooms comfortable and sound-proofed.
⊙ 18 ⓟ ⊜ ⓢ ⓢ V, DC

RICHMOND
$$ ★★★
LARGO C. RICCI 36
TEL 06 6994 1256
FAX 06 6994 1454
www.hotelrichmondroma .com.
A small, family-run hotel strategically placed for sightseeing. The rooms are simple and well equipped. In summer breakfast is served on a splendid terrace with magnificent views over the Imperial Forums.
⊙ 13 ⓟ ⊜ ⓢ
⊠ All major cards

PRICES

HOTELS
An indication of the cost of a double room in the high season is given by $ signs.

$$$$$	Over $450
$$$$	$350-450
$$$	$250-350
$$	$120-250
$	Under $120

RESTAURANTS
An indication of the cost of a three-course meal without drinks is given by $ signs.

$$$$$	Over $80
$$$$	$55-80
$$$	$40-55
$$	$25-40
$	Under $25

CAVOUR 313
$$
VIA CAVOUR 313
TEL 06 678 5496
This wood-lined wine bar has more than a thousand different wines from all over the world and serves an interesting range of cheeses, salamis, and freshly prepared salads.
🪑 60 🕐 Closed L Sun. & D Sun. June–Sept.
⊠ All major cards

■ COLOSSEO TO SAN CLEMENTE

The streets around the Colosseum, particularly Via Capo di Africa, have undergone a renaissance. New hotels have opened, restaurants serving innovative food thrive, and bars stay open until the early hours of the morning. Bus: C3, 60, 75, 81, 85, 87, 175, 673 Tram: 3. Metro: Linea B (Colosseo)

🏨 HOTEL DEI GLADIATORI
$$$$ ★★★
VIA LABICANA 125
TEL 06 7759 1380
FAX 06 700 5638
gladiatori.hotelinroma.com
An elegant hotel facing the
Colosseum and next door
to the ancient gladiators'
training ground. The rooms
are tastefully decorated. The
roof terrace offers spectacular
views, particularly at sunset,
and at night when the monuments are lit.
🛏 17 🅿 (extra) 🔲 🔳
🔳 All major cards

🏨 CAPO D'AFRICA
$$$ ★★★★
VIA CAPO D'AFRICA 54
TEL 06 772801
FAX 06 7728 0801
www.hotelcapodafrica.com
Located in the shadow of the
Colosseum, this four-star hotel
is a fusion of contemporary
and classic styles. The rooms
have been furnished with
great attention to detail. There
is a wonderful view of the
Colosseum from the terrace.
Breakfast extra.
🛏 64 🅿 (extra) 🔲 🔳 🔳
🔳 All major cards

🏨 CELIO
$$$ ★★★
VIA DEI SANTI QUATTRO 35/C
TEL 06 7049 5333
FAX 06 709 6377
www.hotelcelio.com
Located on a quiet street near
the Colosseum, this family-run
hotel is one of Rome's most
pleasant, featuring bedrooms
frescoed with reproductions of
Renaissance and baroque artists.
🛏 19 🅿 (extra) 🔲 🔳 🔳
🔳 All major cards

🍴 IL BOCCONINO
$$
VIA OSTILIA 23
TEL 06 7707 9175
In this local trattoria you can
find typical Roman dishes such

as spaghetti carbonara, tripe
(on Sat.), and roast lamb with
potatoes. Outdoor seating.
🍴 60 🕐 Closed Wed. & Aug.
🔳 🔳 All major cards

🍴 PAPAGIO'
$$$
VIA CAPO D'AFRICA 26
TEL 06 700 9800
A blend of traditional and
innovative cuisine plus efficient
service makes this restaurant
a popular choice. Fish is their
specialty. Outdoor seating.
🍴 55 🕐 Closed Sun. & 2
weeks in Aug. 🔳
🔳 All major cards

■ LATERANO TO TERME DI DIOCLEZIANO

Although the area immediately
around Termini, the central
train station, is probably
best avoided at night, the
atmosphere changes quickly
as you venture slightly farther
out. Here you will find hotels
and restaurants ranging from
the simple to the most luxurious. For public transport, see
individual listings.

🏨 GRAND ST. REGIS
🍴 $$$$$ ★★★★★
VIA V.E. ORLANDO 3
TEL 06 47 091
FAX 06 474 7307
www.stregis.com
A traditional luxury hotel
with public rooms that are
awe-inspiringly decorated
with marble columns and
richly patterned Oriental
carpets. The spacious and
comfortable guest rooms
are furnished with valuable
antiques, and bathrooms
are well-equipped. Its highly
recommended restaurant,
Vivendo, serves traditionally
innovative dishes in an exclusive ambience.
🛏 161 🅿 Garage 🕐 Closed
Sat. L & Sun. 🔲 🔳 🔳 All
major cards 🚌 Bus: 60, 61, 62,

84, 175, 492, 590, 910 Metro:
Linea A (Repubblica)

🏨 RADISSON SAS
$$$$$ ★★★★
VIA FILIPPO TURATI 171
TEL 06 444841
FAX 06 4434 1396
www.radisson.com/romeit
Though not in the nicest part
of town, this minimalist-style
hotel is conveniently located
close to the central train station. It has individually designed guest rooms on seven
floors, two restaurants, and a
roof terrace with swimming
pool. Breakfast extra.
🛏 262 🅿 (extra) 🔲 🔳 🔳
🔳 All major cards 🚌 Bus:
70, 71 Metro: Linea A (Vittorio
Emanuele)

🍴 AGATA E ROMEO
$$$$$
VIA CARLO ALBERTO 45
TEL 06 446 6115
This family-run restaurant is
one of six Rome restaurants
to have earned a Michelin star.
The menu offers exquisite
versions of traditional dishes
(such as spaghettini all' amatriciana, pasta with broccoli, and
beef filet in balsamic vinegar)
and menu di degustazione with
suitable wines to accompany
each dish. No outdoor dining.
🍴 40 🕐 Closed Sat.–Sun. &
Aug. 🔳 🔳 All major cards
🚌 Bus: 70, 71 Metro: Linea A
(Vittorio Emanuele)

🍴 DANILO
$$
VIA PETRARCA 13
TEL 06 7720 0111
A small, family-run restaurant,
Danilo serves the tables while
his mother looks after the
kitchen.
🍴 44 🕐 Closed Mon. L &
Sun. 🔳 🔳 Visa

🍴 F.I.S.H.
$$$$
VIA DEI SERPENTI 16
TEL 06 4782 4962

The restaurant's name, an acronym for Fine International Seafood House, aptly describes the fare. The very modern interior is divided into a sushi bar and a restaurant with a view of the kitchen. The menu ranges from Italian Mediterranean to Pan-Asian. Try the clam soup with ginger.

🔹 42 🕐 Closed Mon. & Aug. 🔹 🔹 All major cards 🚍 Bus: H, 40, 60, 64, 70, 75, 84, 170

🍴 TRATTORIA MONTI
$$

VIA DI S. VITO 13/A
TEL 06 446 6573

A warm welcome is guaranteed at this elegant yet cozy, family-run trattoria serving traditional seasonal dishes from the Marche region—lamb with artichokes, mushrooms, and truffles or thick winter soups.

🔹 45 🕐 Closed D Sun., Mon. & Aug. 🔹 All major cards 🚍 Bus: 71, 590, 649 Metro: Linea A (Vittorio Emanuele)

🍴 EST! EST! EST!
$

VIA GENOVA 32
TEL 06 488 1107

This well-loved pizzeria has been here since 1905, and you may have to wait in line to get in. It serves both thin-crust (Roman) and thick-crust (Neapolitan) pizza and the usual range of fried *supplì*, cod fillets, and zucchini flowers.

🔹 120 🕐 Closed Mon. & Aug. 🔹 MC, V 🚍 Bus: H, 40, 60, 64, 70, 170

■ FONTANA DI TREVI TO VIA VENETO

Many of Rome's luxury hotels can be found on the Via Veneto, made famous by Fellini's film *La Dolce Vita*. Although the glamor of the 1950s is gone, there are plans to revitalize the area. 🚍 Bus: 52, 60, 61, 62, 63, 80, 95, 116, 175, 492, 590 Metro: Linea A (Barberini)

🏨 ALEPH
$$$$$ *****

VIA SAN BASILIO 15
TEL 06 422901
FAX 06 4229 0000
www.aleph.boscolo
hotels.com

This luxury hotel, of the Boscolo chain, was created by the Israeli architect Adam Tihany. In public spaces the theme is paradise to purgatory, while the guest rooms are decorated in an elegant but contemporary style. The Seventh Heaven roof terrace is ideal for relaxing after a hard day's shopping or sightseeing. The Paradise Spa is also open to the general public. Breakfast extra.

🚹 96 🅿 (extra) 🔹 🔹 🔹 All major cards

🏨 EDEN
$$$$$ *****

VIA LUDOVISI 49
TEL 06 478121
FAX 06 482 1584
www.hotel-eden.it

This luxury hotel is a favorite among international celebrities. Every detail has been thought of, from the antique furnishings to the imaginative welcome baskets when you arrive. Stunning views from the famous roof terrace. Breakfast extra.

🚹 121, including some suites 🅿 Garage 🔹 🔹 🔹 All major cards

🏨 EXCELSIOR
$$$$$ *****

VIA VITTORIO VENETO 125
TEL 06 47081
FAX 06 482 6205

A dramatically grand hotel, opulently decorated with swaths of rich fabric and antique and reproduction furniture. All the more-or-less uniformly decorated rooms are luxurious, while the suites look like stage sets. Breakfast extra.

🚹 316, including some suites 🅿 (extra) 🔹 🔹 🔹 All major cards

🏨 FONTANA
$$$ ***

PIAZZA DI TREVI 96
TEL 06 678 6113
FAX 06 679 0024
www. hotelfontane-trevi.com

The view over the Trevi Fountain from this quirky little hotel is breathtaking (also sleep-depriving—in summer the noise can go on all night). Rooms come in all shapes and sizes in this rambling old building.

🚹 25 🔹 🔹 🔹 AE, MC, V

🏨 LA RESIDENZA
$$ ****

VIA EMILIA 22–24
TEL 06 488 0789
FAX 06 485 721
www.hotel-la-residenza
.com

At this converted town house conveniently situated near Via Veneto, the service is attentive and the rooms comfortable. But the real charm of this hotel is found in the bar, terrace, and warmly decorated lobbies.

🚹 29, including some junior suites 🅿 Garage 🔹 🔹 🔹 All major cards

🍴 GIRARROSTO FIORENTINO
$$$

VIA SICILIA 46
TEL 06 4288 0660

This classic Roman restaurant has been making clients happy for the last 50 years. Known for its open-fire grilled beef, it also has excellent appetizers that are piled onto your table, a large selection of fish and other meat dishes, and a good wine list.

🔹 75 🕐 Closed Dec. 24–26 🔹 🔹 All major cards

🍴 TRATTORIA TRITONE
$$$

VIA DEI MARONITI 1
TEL 06 679 8181
Here you're guaranteed not

just excellent Roman cuisine, but courteous, attentive (English-speaking) service and a warm welcome—non-Italian eating habits are courteously accommodated. Underneath the elegant extension are some carefully preserved ancient remains. Il Tritone's popularity with journalists from the nearby *Il Messaggero* proves its appeal with discerning locals.

🛏 180 🕐 Closed Dec. 25–26 🅂 🅒 All major cards

🍴 TULLIO
$$$
VIA SAN NICOLA DA
TOLENTINO 26
TEL 06 474 5560
A Tuscan restaurant particularly famous for its *bistecca fiorentina* (T-bone steak) and other grilled meats, Tullio also has an extensive selection of Tuscan wines.

🪑 80 🕐 Closed Sun. & Aug. 🅂 🅒 All major cards

🍴 PICCOLO ARANCIO
$$
VICOLO SCANDERBEG 112
TEL 06 678 6139
A popular and thus packed little restaurant that extends over several rooms on a tiny, steep alleyway near the Trevi Fountain. The food offers a good, rather than exceptional, range of Roman standards slightly adapted for international tastes.

🪑 50 🕐 Closed Mon. & 3 weeks in Aug. 🅂 🅒 All major cards

■ PIAZZA DI SPAGNA TO VILLA BORGHESE

Rome's main shopping district also boasts a variety of interesting and original hotels and restaurants. 🚌 Bus: 81, 117, 119, 628, 590, 926 Metro: Linea A (Spagna)

🏨 ART BY THE SPANISH STEPS
$$$$$ ★★★★
VIA MARGUTTA 56
TEL 06 328711
FAX 06 3600 3995
www.hotelart.it
Color is the theme of this hotel. Previously part of an exclusive private school, the new space incorporates elements of the old with modern minimalism. The guest rooms are reasonably large and highly styled.

ⓘ 44 🖨 🅂 🅒 All major cards

SOMETHING SPECIAL

🏨 DE RUSSIE
🍴 $$$ ★★★★★
VIA BABUINO 9
TEL 06 328881
FAX 06 3288 8888
www.hotelderussie.it
In the heart of the city, between the Spanish Steps and Piazza del Popolo, this hotel is the ultimate in luxury. The guest rooms are spacious and exquisitely decorated. A stunning feature of the hotel is its extensive, terraced gardens, which provide a tranquil oasis amidst the bustle of central Rome. Nestled in the garden, the hotel's restaurant Le Jardin du Russie is a perfect place for a drink or a meal. The menu is devoted to classic Italian cooking with an emphasis on Mediterranean flavors based on olive oil, tomatoes, and garlic.

ⓘ 65 🅿 (extra) 🖨 🅂 🅒 All major cards

SOMETHING SPECIAL

🏨 HASSLER VILLA MEDICI
🍴 $$$$$ ★★★★★
PIAZZA TRINITÀ DEI MONTI 6
TEL 06 699340
FAX 06 678 9991
www.hotelhasslerroma.com
The hotel's enviable location at the top of the Spanish Steps is matched by elaborate interior design (marble columns and

well-upholstered seating) and bustlingly attentive service. The good-sized rooms are comfortably furnished and have traces of their more than 100-year history as a hotel. Breakfast extra. The hotel's panoramic restaurant, Imàgo, has a spectacular view over Rome and serves fine Italian cuisine in elegant surroundings.

ⓘ 65 🅿 🖨 🅂 All major cards

🏨 D'INGHILTERRA
$$$$ ★★★★
VIA BOCCA DI LEONE 14
TEL 06 69981
FAX 06 6992 2243
www.royaldemeure.com
Famous for well over a century as one of the best in Rome, this hotel can list Oscar Wilde among its VIP guests. Antique furnishings tend toward the lugubrious but make for an appropriately historic atmosphere. It's also perfectly placed for the city's most exclusive shopping streets. Breakfast extra.

ⓘ 98 🖨 🅂 🅒 All major cards

🏨 INN AT THE SPANISH STEPS
$$$$ ★★★★★
VIA DEI CONDOTTI 85
TEL 06 6992 5657
FAX 06 678 6470
www.atspanishsteps.com
This new, small, family-run luxury residence sits on Rome's famed shopping street, Via dei Condotti. Quality and style in a discreetly refined atmosphere, with a lovely rooftop terrace for breakfast and aperitifs.

ⓘ 24 🖨 🅂 🅒 All major cards

🏨 LOCARNO
$$$ ★★★
VIA DELLA PENNA 22
TEL 06 361 0841
FAX 06 321 5249
www.hotellocarno.com
This intriguing art deco hotel is just off Piazza del Popolo. Both

the lobbies and guest rooms are tastefully decorated, and in winter there is an open fire in the bar area. It also boasts a lovely roof garden.

🛏 63 🅿 (extra) 🔼 🔄
🔄 All major cards

🏨 FORTE
$$ ✱✱✱
VIA MARGUTTA 61
TEL 06 320 0408
FAX 06 6799 5433
www.hotelforte.com
Located in one of Rome's most charming streets, this recently renovated hotel offers stylishly decorated rooms.

🛏 19 🔼 🔄 🔄 All major cards

🏨 MARGUTTA
$$ ✱✱
VIA LAURINA 34
TEL 06 322 3674
FAX 06 320 0395
www.hotelmargutta.it
Excellent value in an expensive part of town. The rooms are simply and traditionally furnished in wood with iron bedsteads. Bath and shower rooms are small but adequate.

🛏 24 🅿 Garage 🔼 🔄
🔄 All major cards

🏨 PARLAMENTO
$$ ✱✱
VIA DELLE CONVERTITE 5
TEL/FAX 06 6992 1000
www.hotelparlamento.it
A simple, well-run, and spotlessly clean pensione where not all rooms have air-conditioning. Double-glazing reduces outside noise. Breakfast is served in the little roof garden in summer.

🛏 23 🅿 Garage 🔼
🔄 Extra fee 🔄 All major cards

SOMETHING SPECIAL

🍴 BABY DELL' ALDROVANDI PALACE
$$$$$
VIA ULISSE ALDOVANDI 15
TEL 06 322 3993

The Michelin guide has given a well-deserved star to Baby and its well-known chef, Alfonso Iaccarino. This elegant, contemporary restaurant has views onto both Villa Borghese park and the Aldrovandi Palace Hotel's pool. Outdoor seating.

🪑 60 🕐 D only; closed Mon.
🔄 🔄 All major cards
✉ Bus: 52, 926

🍴 DAL BOLOGNESE
$$$$
PIAZZA DEL POPOLO 1/2
TEL 06 361 1426
This chic restaurant is where the in-crowd gathers to enjoy the time-honored cuisine of Bologna. Try the *bollito* (steamed meats). Outdoor seating.

🪑 160 🕐 Closed Mon. 🔄
🔄 All major cards

🍴 CAFFÉ DELLE ARTE
$$$
VIA A. GRAMSCI 73
TEL 06 3265 1236
This restaurant is located on the opposite side of the Villa Borghese from the Via Veneto. Unlike many other beautifully situated restaurants, here you don't have to make any compromises on the food, which is good, especially the fish dishes served with olives, aniseed, and a host of other compatible flavors. Reservations essential.

🪑 130 🅿 🕐 Closed D Mon.
🔄 All major cards 🚇 Bus: 3, 19

🍴 'GUSTO
$$–$$$
PIAZZA AUGUSTO IMPERATORE 9
TEL 06 6819 3032
www.gusto.it
Occupying an entire block, this amazing gastronomic center contains three restaurants, a wine bar, a cookware emporium, a cheese shop, and an enoteca. The informal street-level pizzeria ($$) also serves homemade pasta, salads, and grilled dishes. The upscale

restaurant upstairs serves a fusion of Italian and Pacific Rim cuisine. The Osteria (Via della Frezza 16, tel 06 3211 1482, $$) around the corner serves traditional Mediterranean cuisine. Attached to the Osteria is the cheese shop, where you can select cheeses either to eat on the spot or take with you (open 10 a.m.–2 a.m.).

🪑 250 🔄 All major cards

🍴 MARGUTTA VEGETARIANO
$$$
VIA MARGUTTA 118
TEL 06 3265 0577
This most elegant of Rome's vegetarian restaurants serves varied and tempting dishes. Contemporary art lines the walls of the large dining area.

🪑 150 🔄 🔄 All major cards

🍴 NINO
$$$
VIA BORGOGNONA 11
TEL 06 678 6752
A classic restaurant serving excellent Tuscan cuisine. With its cozy, old-fashioned interior, this restaurant is a favorite of politicians, journalists, and film stars.

🪑 95 🕐 Closed Mon. & Aug.
🔄 🔄 All major cards

🍴 PALATIUM ENOTECA REGIONALE
$$
VIA FRATTINA 94
TEL 06 6920 2132
A few steps from Piazza di Spagna, this wine bar/restaurant run by the Legion of Lazio (the region that surrounds Rome) specializes in showcasing the products of the region, including wines, olive oils, cheeses, and cured meats. The simple, modern decor makes a nice atmosphere in which to enjoy a glass of wine while sampling traditional local dishes.

🪑 90 🕐 Closed Sun. 🔄
🔄 All major cards

🏨 Hotel 🍴 Restaurant 🛏 No. of Guest Rooms 🪑 No. of Seats 🅿 Parking 🚇 Metro 🕐 Closed 🔼 Elevator

SOMETHING SPECIAL

🍴 INTERNATIONAL WINE ACADEMY TERRACE
$$

VICOLO DEL BOTTINO 8
TEL 06 699 34 1000
For a special treat on a sunny day, sip an *aperitivo* on the rooftop terrace of the International Wine Academy overlooking the Spanish Steps. Spectacular setting, excellent wines. The Academy also has its own excellent restaurant, Aroma de Il Palazzetto ($$$$), managed by the staff of the Hotel Hassler, and four boutique hotel rooms.
🍴 22 🕐 L only; closed Sun.– Mon.

■ PANTHEON TO PIAZZA VENEZIA

The true heart of Rome includes the parliament and senate buildings, some of the city's oldest monuments, as well as a labyrinth of narrow streets and alleys. It is also home to some of the city's most established restaurants and hotels.
🚌 Bus: 40, 46, 62, 63, 64, 70, 81, 87, 116, 119, 492, 628

🏨 GRAND HOTEL DE LA MINERVE
$$$$$ *****

PIAZZA DELLA MINERVA 69
TEL 06 695 201
FAX 06 679 4165
www.grandhoteldela minerva.it
Renovated by postmodernist architect Paolo Portoghesi, this 17th-century building has all the comforts of a luxury hotel, including a beautiful roof garden (closed in winter), where you can enjoy a superb view of the "Eternal City." Guest rooms are elegantly furnished and of varying size. Breakfast extra.

[i] 134 🅿 (extra) 🔵 🔵 🔻
🔵 All major cards

🏨 SANTA CHIARA
$$$ ***

VIA DI SANTA CHIARA 21
TEL 06 687 2979
FAX 06 687 3144
www.albergosantachiara.com
Located behind the Pantheon, this hotel is known for its pleasant, calm atmosphere and efficient service. Bright rooms combine function with comfort.
[i] 100 🅿 (extra) 🔵 🔵 🔵 All major cards

🍴 LA ROSETTA
$$$$$

VIA DELLA ROSETTA 8
TEL 06 686 1002
Fresh seafood delivered daily from Sicily and simply prepared makes the Michelin-starred La Rosetta one of the best seafood eateries in Rome. Good selection of wines and efficient service. Small outdoor garden for spring and summer dining.
🍴 50 🕐 Closed Sun. & Aug.
🔵 🔵 All major cards

SOMETHING SPECIAL

🍴 CASA BLEVE
$$$

VIA DEL TEATRO VALLE 48/49
TEL 06 686 5970
A refined, elegant wine bar with stained-glass and stucco ceilings and marble columns. Offers an exceptional selection of wines, an excellent choice of cold dishes, and knowledgeable and efficient service.
🍴 40 🕐 Closed Sun.–Mon., L Wed.–Fri, & Aug. 🔵
🔵 All major cards

🍴 SANT'EUSTACHIO
$$$

PIAZZA DEI CAPRETTARI 63
TEL 06 686 1616
Restrained, polite atmosphere with pleasant outdoor dining in summer. The menu features

Roman and more elaborate dishes—*saltimbocca* (veal with ham), fried artichokes, salmon *carpaccio*, and satisfying homemade tarts for dessert.
🍴 100 🕐 Closed Sun. & 2 weeks in Aug.
🔵 All major cards

🍴 VINI E BUFFET
$

VICOLO DELLA TORETTA 60
TEL 06 687 1445
Previously a wine and oil outlet (you can still see the sign outside), this friendly restaurant offers crepes and a huge range of salads. Perfect for a light lunch.
🍴 50 🕐 Closed Sun.

🍴 OBIKA
$$

VIA DEI PREFETTI 26A
TEL 06 683 2630
If you love mozzarella don't miss this place. A number of varieties of fresh and smoked mozzarella are served with a large range of delicious salads. A good choice for lunch. Outdoor seating available.
🍴 140 🔵 🔵 All major cards

🍴 ENOTECA CORSI
$

VIA DEL GESÙ 87
TEL 06 679 0821
This trattoria has managed to maintain its original wine-and-olive-oil shop feel. Here you can order simple tasty Roman food. Order the house wine, or choose from a large selection of bottled wines.
🍴 100 🕐 L only. Closed Sun. & Aug. 🔵 All major cards

■ CAMPO MARZIO

This area, central Rome at its most charming and typical, is one of the city's busiest areas both day and night. The range of hotels and restaurants offers something to suit all pockets. For public transport, see individual listings.

🔵 Nonsmoking 🔵 Air-conditioning 🔵 Indoor Pool 🔵 Outdoor Pool 🔻 Health Club 🔵 Credit Cards

🏨 RAPHAEL
$$$$ ★★★★
LARGO FEBO 2
TEL 06 682831
FAX 06 687 8993
www.raphaelhotel.com
Just a step away from Piazza
Navona, this hotel is known
for its quiet, luxurious charm
and stunning terrace (closed
in winter) with bar and
restaurant. Guest rooms,
though small, are attractively
decorated. Breakfast extra.
🛏 58 🅿 (extra) 🔵 🔲 🔲
🔲 All major cards 🚍 Bus: 70,
81, 87, 116, 280, 492, 628

🏨 DUE TORRI
$$$ ★★★
VICOLO DEL LEONETTO 23
TEL 06 687 6983
FAX 06 686 5442
www.hotelduetorriroma.com
Elegant furnishings and a
warm welcome combine with
a romantic atmosphere to
make this one of the most
attractive hotels in its price
category. The 19th-century
building, on a quiet street near
Piazza Navona, used to be the
home of bishops and cardinals.
🛏 26 🅿 🔵 🔲 🔲 All major
cards 🚍 Bus: 70, 81, 87, 116,
280, 492, 628

🏨 RESIDENZA IN FARNESE
$$ ★★★★
VIA DEL MASCHERONE 59
TEL 06 6889 1388
FAX 06 6821 0980
www.residenzafarnese
rome.com
Housed in a converted
14th-century monastery near
Campo dei Fiori, this quiet
comfortable hotel has pleasant
rooms, some with frescoed
ceilings, overlooking either the
gardens of Palazzo Farnese or
Palazzo Spada.
🛏 31 🔵 🔲 🔲 All major cards
🚍 Bus: 23, 116, 280

🏨 TEATRO DI POMPEO
$$ ★★★
LARGO DEL PALLARO 8

TEL 06 6830 0170
FAX 06 6880 5531
www.hotelteatrodipompeo.it
A small hotel built over the
ruins of a Roman theater,
some of which is still visible.
The rooms are not large but
are tastefully decorated. Street
noise can be a problem.
🛏 13 🔲 🔲 All major cards
🚍 Bus: 116

🏨 TEATROPACE 33
$$ ★★★
VIA DEL TEATRO PACE 33, 00186
TEL 06 687 9075
FAX 06 6819 2364
www.hotelteatropace.com
Opened in 2004, this 17th-
century cardinal's former
residence offers tastefully
appointed bedrooms equipped
with modern comforts.
Conveniently located only 20
yards from Piazza Navona.
🛏 23 🔲 🔲 All major cards
🚍 Bus: 70, 81, 87, 116, 492, 628

SOMETHING SPECIAL

🍴 L'ALTRO MASTAI
$$$$$
VIA G. GIRAUD 53
TEL 06 6830 1296
Opened in 2003, this elegant
restaurant near Piazza Navona
quickly became very fashionable and won itself a Michelin
star. The interior combines
classical elements with rich
colors and abstract art. The
dishes are inspired by the
Mediterranean tradition, with
extra care for detail. It also offers more than 1,200 wines.
🪑 50 🕐 D only. Closed Sun.–
Mon. & Aug. 🔲 🔲 All major
cards 🚍 Bus: 40, 46, 62, 64

SOMETHING SPECIAL

🍴 IL CONVIVIO TROIANI
$$$$$
VICOLO DEI SOLDATI 31
TEL 06 686 9432
Three brothers run one of the
best and nicest restaurants in
Rome. Service is cordial and
informative and the food is

PRICES

HOTELS
An indication of the cost of
a double room in the high
season is given by **$** signs.

$$$$$	Over $450
$$$$	$350-450
$$$	$250-350
$$	$120-250
$	Under $120

RESTAURANTS
An indication of the cost of
a three-course meal without
drinks is given by **$** signs.

$$$$$	Over $80
$$$$	$55-80
$$$	$40-55
$$	$25-40
$	Under $25

ambrosial—basically Italian
with some touches of creative
genius from the chef (one of
the brothers). Every dish is a
beautifully presented work
of art but the desserts are
masterpieces.
🕐 D only. Closed Sun. 🔲
🔲 All major cards 🚍 Bus: 30,
70, 87, 186, 492 (Corso del
Rinascimento)

🍴 CAFFE BERNINI
$$$
PIAZZA NAVONA 44
TEL 06 6819 2998
This restaurant/bar serves qual-
ity food in a magnificent setting.
🪑 45 🕐 Open 9:30 a.m.–2
a.m. 🔲 🔲 All major cards

🍴 PIERLUIGI
$$$
PIAZZA DE'RICCI 144
TEL 06 686 8717
Although a mecca for visitors
in the know (prices have
risen and it's always full), this

establishment is still a very agreeable place to sample deliciously fresh dishes—pasta with zucchini flowers, fish cooked in various ways, and tasty desserts. A good first experience of a real Italian restaurant that's used to coping with non-Italians.
🍴 120 🕐 Closed Mon. 🚭 All major cards 🚌 Bus: 23, 40, 62, 64, 116, 280

🍴 RISTORANTE ROSCIOLI
$$$
VIA DEI GIUBBONARI 21/23
TEL 06 687 5287
The Roscioli brothers have transformed the family grocery, on Via dei Giubbonari, into Ristorante Roscioli, a fashionable wine bar where you can eat high-quality food and buy specialized food products.
🍴 42 🕐 Closed Sun. 🚭 All major cards

🍴 DITIRAMBO
$$
PIAZZA DELLA CANCELLERIA 74
TEL 06 687 1626
Charming staff and attractive decor make for a pleasantly busy atmosphere that is matched by the standard of the ever-changing menu. Innovative versions of Italian regional dishes include a potato and broad-bean soup and lamb with lentils. Tasty homemade bread and pasta. Good value for money. Reservations are essential.
🍴 55 🕐 Closed L Mon. & Aug. 🚭 MC, V 🚌 Bus: 40, 46, 62, 64, 116

🍴 LA CAMPANA
$$
VICOLO DELLA CAMPANA 18/20
TEL 06 686 7820
This trattoria is one of the oldest in the city and is well known for its traditional Roman cooking. The menu offers a wide choice, but don't miss the spaghetti alla carbonara.

🍴 130 🕐 Closed Mon. & Aug. 🚭 All major cards 🚌 Bus: 70, 81, 87, 116, 492, 628

🍴 CUL DE SAC
$$
PIAZZA PASQUINO 73
TEL 06 6880 1094
A lively wine bar with a good reputation for food. The Cul de Sac offers a variety of light dishes and has a vast selection of wines. Outside tables.
🍴 60 🚭 MC, V 🚌 Bus: 46, 62, 64, 70, 81, 87, 116, 492, 628

🍴 ANTICO FORNO ROSCIOLI
$
VIA DEI CHIAVARI 34
TEL 06 686 4045
The Roscioli brothers have opened a tavola calda (the Italian version of a fast food counter) in their bakery, where you can get cheap delicious ready-made dishes to take away or eat on the premises. You can also buy a roll and have a sandwich made at the tavola calda.
🍴 34 🕐 Closed D & Sun. 🚭 All major cards

🍴 TRATTORIA DA LUIGI
$$
PIAZZA SFORZA CESARINI 24
TEL 06 686 5946
This friendly, large trattoria offers an enormous menu that includes the best of Italian cuisine and then some. The dark, wood-panelled interior is pleasant but the best thing about da Luigi is the outdoor dining in a lovely, tree-shaded square that seems more Parisian than Roman.
🍴 240 🕐 Closed Mon. & Dec. 25–26 🚭 Upstairs only 🚭 All major cards 🚌 Bus: 40, 46, 62, 64, 116

🍴 IL BAFFETTO
$
VIA DEL GOVERNO VECCHIO 114

TEL 06 686 1617
One of Rome's most popular and best pizzerias, lingering is not possible here. Unless you come early or late, you'll have to wait for a table and then possibly share it when you are seated.
🍴 100 🕐 Closed L & Aug. 🚭 Cash only 🚌 Bus: 40, 46, 62, 64, 116

■ VATICANO

Much of the solidly respectable residential area around the Vatican dates from the late 19th and early 20th centuries. There are a few unflashy but high-quality hotels. With few exceptions, most of the touristy eating places close to the Vatican are best avoided. For public transport, see individual listings.

🏨 COLUMBUS
$$$ ★★★★
VIA DELLA CONCILIAZIONE 33
TEL 06 686 5435
FAX 06 686 4874
www.hotelcolumbus rome.com
A 15th-century building right in front of St. Peter's is the setting for this aristocratically austere hotel. Guest rooms and bathrooms are functional, but public areas make up with a surfeit of carved stone and frescoed walls.
🛏 92 🅿 🚭 🚭 🚭 All major cards 🚌 Bus: 23, 34, 40, 62, 982

🏨 FARNESE
$$$ ★★★★
VIA A. FARNESE 30
TEL 06 321 2553
FAX 06 321 5129
www.hotelfarnese.com
A charming choice (and value for money) in the residential Prati area near St. Peter's, connected to the center by metro. Tranquil atmosphere with 17th-century decor and comfortable rooms.

(1) 23 [P] [⊟] [⊡] [⬈] All major cards [⬈] Bus: 70, 224, 280, 590. Metro: Linea A (Lepanto)

ST. ANNA
$$$ ★★★
BORGO PIO 133/134
TEL 06 6880 1602
FAX 06 6830 8717
www.hotelsantanna.com
Located in the shadow of St. Peter's, this small family-run hotel offers tastefully decorated, comfortable rooms and caring service. Breakfast is served in a pleasant, inside garden in the summer.
(1) 20 [P] (extra) [⊟] [⊡]
[⬈] All major cards [⬈] Bus: 23, 34, 40, 62, 280, 982

DA BENITO E GILBERTO
$$$
VIA DEL FALCO 19
TEL 06 686 7769
This small, crowded trattoria has a well-deserved reputation for its high-quality seafood. Reservations recommended.
[⊞] 30 [⊡] D only. Closed Sun.–Mon. & Aug. [⬈] All major cards [⬈] Bus: 23, 34, 40, 62, 982

TAVERNA ANGELICA
$$$
PIAZZA A. CAPPONI 6
TEL 06 687 4514
Reservations are essential for this romantic little corner restaurant serving delicate, flavorful, and innovative Italian cuisine, like *tagliatelle* with nettles and curry, duck breast in balsamic vinegar, and chocolate crêpes. All are accompanied by a carefully selected wine list.
[⊞] 45 [⊡] Closed L & 2 weeks in Aug. [⊡] [⬈] AE, MC, V [⬈] Bus: 19, 23, 40, 62

DA ROMOLO ALLA MOLE ADRIANA
$$
VIA FOSSE DI CASTELLO 19
TEL 06 686 1603
A trattoria with friendly service and a menu featuring primarily Roman dishes—from delicious pizza to a wide choice of pasta and meats. Romolo observes the tradition of the daily specialty, e.g. gnocchi on Thursdays, tripe on Fridays, etc.
[⊞] 100 inside. Some outdoor tables [⊡] Closed Mon. & most of Aug. [⬈] All major cards [⬈] Bus: 23, 34, 40, 62, 982

DAL TOSCANO
$$
VIA GERMANICO 58
TEL 06 3972 5717
Located conveniently close to the Vatican Museums, this well-established restaurant specializes in traditional Tuscan cuisine. Outdoor seating.
[⊞] 120 [⊡] Closed Mon. & Aug. [⊡] [⬈] All major cards [⬈] Bus: 32, 81, 590, 982

IL MOZZICONE
$$
VIA BORGO PIO 180
TEL 06 686 1500
A simple family-style trattoria said to serve one of the best *spaghetti alla carbonara* in the city. In nice weather, you can eat lunch or dinner outside, resting up from your hours in the Vatican Museums and St. Peter's.
[⊞] 40 [⊡] Closed Sun. & Aug. [⬈] Cash only [⬈] Bus: 23, 34, 40, 62, 982

■ TRASTEVERE TO GIANICOLO

Visitors and Romans alike come nightly in search of a good time in this lively area "across the Tiber." It has always been packed with bars and restaurants, but recently a number of appealing hotels have also opened. [⬈] Bus: H, 23, 75, 115, 125, 280, 780 Tram: 3, 8

HOTEL SANTA MARIA
$$$ ★★★
VICOLO DEL PIEDE 2
TEL 06 589 4626
FAX 06 589 4815
www.htlsantamaria.com
A charming, ground-floor hotel set in the tranquil garden of a 16th-century cloister, only a few minutes from Piazza Santa Maria in Trastevere.
(1) 18 [P] [⊡] [⬈] All major cards

DONNA CAMILLA SAVELLI
$$$$ ★★★★
VIA GARIBALDI 27
TEL 06 588 8861
FAX 06 588 2101
www.hotelsavelli.com
After a remarkable restoration, this 17th-century convent in the heart of Trastevere now operates as a refined hotel. Broadband access to the Internet is available.
(1) 78 [P] [⊟] [⊡]
[⬈] All major cards

SAN FRANCESCO
$$ ★★★
VIA JACOPA DE SETTESOLI 7
TEL 06 5830 0051
FAX 06 5833 3413
www.hotelsanfrancesco.net
A recently inaugurated hotel, the San Francesco offers pleasant guest rooms, a breakfast area facing a 15th-century cloister, and a terrace with a 360-degree panoramic view over Rome.
(1) 24 [P] (extra) [⊟] [⊡]
[⬈] All major cards

DOMUS TIBERINA
$$ ★★
VIA IN PISCINULA 37
TEL 06 580 3033
www.ggromehotels.it
This hotel is located in the heart of Trastevere, not far from both Santa Cecilia and Tiber Island. The rooms are comfortable and attractively decorated.
(1) 10 [⊡] [⬈] All major cards

VILLA DELLA FONTE
$$

VIA DELLA FONTE D'OLIO 8
TEL 06 580 3797
FAX 06 580 3796
www.villafonte.com
A tiny, welcoming hotel a few yards from Piazza Santa Maria in Trastevere. Guest rooms are comfortable and well-equipped, and a lovely terrace allows guests to relax after a busy day. Breakfast extra.
[i] 5 [S] [A] All major cards

[H] ORSA MAGGIORE WOMEN'S HOSTEL
$
VIA DELLA LUNGARA 19
TEL 06 6840 1724
FAX 06 6840 1725
www.casainternazionale delledonne.org/foresteria.htm
Housed in a 16th-century former convent in Trastevere, the Orsa Maggiore offers accommodations for women only. Completely refurbished but maintaining the building's antique style, the rooms are simple and look onto a peaceful courtyard. Both singles and dormitory accommodations are available. Restaurant on the premises.
[i] 10 [↔] [S] [A] All major cards
[B] Bus: H, 23, 75, 115, 125, 271, 280, 780

[H] ENOTECA FERRARA
$$$$
VIA DEL MORO 1
TEL 06 5833 3920
Two sisters run this excellent and popular wine bar, which has an impressive list of wines and after-dinner drinks to accompany a constantly changing menu. The soups are particularly recommended. The decor is original and pleasing, with touches such as glass panels in the floor allowing you to look down into the all-important cellars.
[↔] 100 [S] DC, MC, V

[H] PARIS
$$$$
PIAZZA SAN CALISTO 7/A

TEL 06 581 5378
Civilized surroundings and friendly service at this Jewish-Roman restaurant, whose dishes include elegant versions of such favorites as skate-wing soup, pasta and chickpeas, oxtail, and roast fish and meats with potatoes.
[↔] 90 [clock] Closed Mon., Aug., & D Sun. [S] [A] All major cards

[H] SABATINI
$$$$
PIAZZA SANTA MARIA 13
TEL 06 581 2026
Tourists love the stunning setting and archetypal Italian restaurant ambience (complete with serenaders) of this Trastevere locale. The good (sometimes exceptional) mainly fish-based cuisine also draws locals. Super-fresh ingredients.
[↔] 120 [S] [A] All major cards

[H] BOTTICELLA
$$
VICOLO DEL LEOPARDO 39/A
TEL 06 581 4738
Tucked away in a small Trastevere alley, this characteristic trattoria serves typical Roman and Roman-Jewish dishes, such as *carciofi alla giudea* (fried artichokes) and *coda alla vaccinara* (ox-tail). Outdoor dining.
[↔] 40 [clock] Closed Wed. [S] [A] All major cards

[H] DA LUCIA
$$
VICOLO DEL MATTONATO 2B
TEL 06 580 3601
The same family has run this no-frills trattoria for more than 60 years. In summer tables fill the alley outside. The interior is lined with wooden slats. The unchanging menu includes some standard *primi* followed by dishes such as rabbit *alla cacciatora* and cuttlefish with peas.

[↔] 40 [clock] Closed Mon., 3 weeks in Aug., & Christmas
[S] Cash only

[H] LE MANI IN PASTA
$$
VIA DE'GENOVESI 37
TEL 06 581 6017
This inexpensive trattoria, small with a simple interior and a view of the kitchen, offers a wide selection of delicious pastas, fish, and grilled meats. There is a separate dining room for smokers.
[↔] 70 [clock] Closed Mon. & Aug. [S] [A] All major cards

[H] RISTORANTE LA SCALA
$$
PIAZZA DELLA SCALA 60
TEL 06 580 3763
A former, low-end *birreria* (beer and food joint), this warmly decorated restaurant offers very friendly service, good and abundant food, and low to moderate prices. It also has uninterrupted service to the wee hours of the morning. For those who just want a drink, an adjacent entrance leads to a cozy, wood-panelled bar. Outdoor seating.
[↔] 120 [A] All major cards

[H] BIR & FUD
$$
VIA BENEDETTA 23
TEL 06 589 4016
This pizzeria combines the best ingredients in unusual but delicious ways. It also offers Italian artisanal beer, perfect for hot summer nights.
[↔] 60 [clock] Closed L., Mon., & Aug. [S] [A] DC, Visa

[H] DAR POETA
$
VICOLO DI BOLOGNA 45/46
TEL 06 588 0516
A lively Trastevere pizzeria offering a wide selection of pizzas and *bruschette* (toasted breads). Arrive very early to get a seat. A few outdoor tables.

🛏 80 🕒 D only 🔶
🔷 All major cards

🍴 PANATTONI
$

VIALE TRASTEVERE 53/57
TEL 06 580 0919
Also known as the "mortuary" (obitorio) because of its marble tabletops, this place is an institution for both its pizza and the typical Trastevere atmosphere. Outdoor seating.
🛏 100 🕒 D only. Closed Wed.
🔷 Cash only

■ FORUM BOARIUM TO AVENTINO

This green, leafy hill just outside the center has been one of Rome's most sought after residential areas since ancient times; it now contains some excellent, tranquil hotels. Many of the nearest restaurants are in the popular Testaccio area or the Ghetto. For public transport, see individual listings.

🏨 RESIDENCE PALAZZO AL VELABRO
$$$ ★★★★

VIA DEL VELABRO 16
TEL 06 679 2758
FAX 06 679 3790
www.velabro.it
If you are planing to stay a week or more this could be a good choice. Centrally located near the Palatine Hill, it offers quiet, comfortable studio apartments with kitchenettes for 2 to 4 people, some with wonderful views.
🚪 35 🔁 🔶 🔷 All major cards
🚇 Bus: C3, 81, 95, 170, 715, 716, 628

🏨 FORTY SEVEN
$$$ ★★★★

VIA LUIGI PETROSELLI 47
TEL 06 678 7816
FAX 06 6919 0726
www.fortysevenhotel.com
Each floor of this new, centrally located hotel is dedicated to a 20th-century Italian artist: Mastroianni, Greco, Modigliani, Quagliata, or Guccione. The guest rooms are large and luminous, many overlooking the surrounding monuments. Roof terrace with views.
🚪 80 🔶 🔷 Visa

🏨 SANT'ANSELMO
$$$ ★★★★

PIAZZA DI SANT'ANSELMO 2
TEL 06 570057
FAX 06 578 3604
www.aventinohotels.com
Sant'Anselmo's lush garden shaded with orange trees on the Aventine Hill makes the perfect setting for relaxing after sightseeing. And you can wake to the singing of birds yet be at the Roman Forum in minutes. The lobbies and guest rooms are attractively decorated.
🚪 46 🅿 🔁 🔶 🔷 All major cards 🚇 Bus: 175, 715

🍴 GIGGETTO AL PORTICO D'OTTAVIA
$$$$

VIA DEL PORTICO D'OTTAVIA 21A
TEL 06 686 1105
The main street of the Jewish Ghetto is the perfect setting for sampling traditional Jewish-Roman cuisine—starting with fried cod, anchovies, zucchini flowers, and artichokes and finishing with cheesecake and blueberry sauce.
🛏 200 🕒 Closed Mon. & last 2 weeks in July 🔶 🔷 All major cards 🚇 Bus: 23, 46, 62, 63, 64, 70, 87, 119, 280, 492, 780

🍴 PIPERNO
$$$

MONTE DEI CENCI 9
TEL 06 6880 6629
In the heart of the Jewish Ghetto, this longtime favorite has changed little over the years. Here carciofi alla giudea (fried Jerusalem artichokes) are at their best, or try the fritto misto vegetariano (lightly fried artichokes, cheese-and-rice croquettes, mozzarella, and stuffed zucchini blossoms). Outdoor seating available.
🛏 75 🕒 Closed D Sun., Mon., & Aug. 🔶 🔷 All major cards 🚇 Bus: 23, 46, 62, 63, 64, 70, 87, 119, 492, 280, 780

🍴 IL SANPIETRINO
$$$

PIAZZA COSTAGUTI 15
TEL 06 6880 6471
Named after the cobblestones of Rome, this stylish restaurant offers high-quality food and service. Good selection of wines.
🛏 53 🕒 Closed Sun., L Mon.–Tues., & Aug. 🔶 🔷 All major cards 🚇 Bus: 23, 46, 62, 63, 64, 70, 87, 119, 492, 280, 780

🍴 DA FELICE
$$

VIA MASTRO GIORGIO 29
TEL 06 574 6800
This popular restaurant in the Testaccio area is home to cucina romana (Roman cuisine), based on the "fifth quarter" or the cheaper cuts of meat and innards that were once partial payment for the workers at the nearby slaughterhouse.
🛏 90 🕒 Closed Wed. & Aug. 🔶 🔷 All major cards 🚇 Bus: 3, 23, 30, 75, 280

🍴 VOLPETTI
$

VIA ALESSANDRO VOLTA 8
TEL 06 574 4306
Around the corner from the famous Volpetti deli (see Taste Treats p. 258) the Volpetti brothers have opened a "tavola calda." The selection includes both hard-to-find and classic cheeses and cold cuts, as well as freshly baked pizza, excellent breads, and prepared dishes.
🛏 35 🕒 Closed Sun.
🔷 All major cards

🍴 REMO

$

PIAZZA SANTA MARIA
LIBERATRICE 44

TEL 06 574 6270

Here you can find the traditional Roman pizza—thin and crusty. Arrive early if you don't want to wait for a table.

🔟 85 🕒 D only. Closed Sun.
🔵 🔷 Cash only 🚌 Bus: 23, 75, 95, 170, 280, 716

■ FUORI LE MURA (OUTSIDE THE WALLS)

Itallans love the *gita fuori città*, the trip outside the city, and the Castelli Romani area as well as Tivoli and Palestrina have many unpretentious but enjoyable eating spots. Outside the Roman walls, but still in the vicinity of the city, you can also find a variety of hotels and restaurants. For public transport, see individual listings.

🏨 CAVALIERI HILTON

$$$$$ *****

VIA A. CADLOLO 101

TEL 06 35091

FAX 06 3509 2241

www.cavalieri-hilton.it

A shuttle service transports guests to and from central Rome, leaving you free to enjoy the peace of this country location. The well-equipped rooms have balconies, and tennis courts and a jogging track are among the many features typical of this top-of-the-market chain. Breakfast extra.

🔟 347 and 25 suites 🅿️ 🔶
🔵 🏊 📺 🔷 All major cards
🚌 Bus: 90

🏨 SHANGRI LA CORSETTI

$$$ ****

VIALE ALGERIA 141

TEL 06 591 6441

FAX 06 541 3813

www.shangrilacorsetti.it

A peaceful setting, the hotel is surrounded by greenery in the geometrically planned EUR district, which was based on designs commissioned by Mussolini. Excellent service and facilities.

🔟 52 🅿️ 🔵 🏊 🔷 All major cards 🚌 Bus: 714

🏨 HILTON ROME AIRPORT

$$$ ****

VIA ARTURO FERRARIN, FIUMICINO

TEL 06 65258

FAX 06 6525 6525

www.hilton.com

Finally, Rome has an airport hotel. Just 200 yards from Fiumicino, the Hilton's bedrooms are functional and fully equipped. There is a restaurant and snack bar, plus a complimentary shuttle service into central Rome eight times a day. Breakfast extra.

🔟 517 🅿️ 🔶 🔵 📺 🏊
🔷 All major cards 🚌 See page 236 Fiumicino-Leonardo da Vinci Airport

🏨 TURNER

$$ ***

VIA NOMENTANA 29

TEL 06 4425 0077

FAX 06 4425 0165

www.hotelturner.it

A superb combination of historic charm (in a late 19th-century palazzo) and modern comfort. Decor is elegant and welcoming and the staff is efficient and friendly.

🔟 47 including 2 suites
🅿️ Garage 🔶 🔵 🔷 All major cards 🚌 Bus: 60, 62, 84, 90

SOMETHING SPECIAL

🍴 LA PERGOLA DE L'HOTEL ROME CAVALIERI HILTON

$$$$$

VIA A. CADLOLO 101

TEL 06 3509 2211

Recognized as Rome's best and, innovative restaurant, La Pergola's reputation has rocketed since the arrival of Heinz Beck, as of 2005 the only chef in the city awarded three Michelin stars. His dishes show strong Italian influences. The attentive service is superb, the wine list fantastic, and the view of Rome near unmatched.

🔟 75 🕒 Closed Sun., Mon., & L 🅿️ 🔵 🔷 All major cards 🚌 Bus: 990

🍴 ARCHEOLOGICA

$$$

APPIA ANTICA 139

TEL 06 788 0494

A perfect lunch stop when sightseeing along the Via Appia Antica. In winter, the dining areas have open fires, and in summer there is a lovely outdoor seating area studded with Roman statues.

🔟 300 (inside and out)
🕒 Closed Tues. 🅿️ 🔵
🔷 All major cards
🚌 Bus: 118, 218

🍴 TRAM TRAM

$$

VIA DEI RETI 44

TEL 06 490 416

The frequently changing menu at this popular trattoria is oriented toward Pugliese cuisine but makes the most of what's available—for example, spaghetti with octopus, anchovy and endive tart, and bean and chicory purée. Good service but a bit chaotic when it gets busy. Reservations are essential.

🔟 50 🕒 Closed Mon. & 1 week in Aug. 🅿️ 🔵
🔷 All major cards
🚌 Bus: 71, 492

Shopping in Rome

Combining shopping and sightseeing is one of the delights of Rome. Each shopping district in Rome has its own particular characteristics. Generally, however, most shops are small and specialized, department stores are few and far between, and large shopping malls are situated outside the city.

Main Shopping Areas

Piazza di Spagna: In the grid of streets around Piazza di Spagna you will find the top names in Italian fashion and design, as well as, on and around Via del Babuino, quality antiques and prints. Less invitingly, Via del Corso is crowded and frenetic, offering many of the same clothes and prices as Via Cola di Rienzo and Via Nazionale (see below).

Piazza Navona/Campo Dei Fiori: Narrow, bustling Via del Governo Vecchio boasts the highest density of independent designer shops in Rome, as well as classy secondhand garment stores and accessory shops. Via Giubbonari offers reasonably priced clothes, mostly for the younger generation. Top-quality antiques or prints can be found on Via dei Coronari and Via Giulia.

Trastevere: In this labyrinth of narrow streets you will find any number of small shops and street vendors selling unique pieces.

Via Cola di Rienzo: Close to the Vatican Museums, this street offers shops selling mid-range clothes and accessories similar to those in Via Nazionale (see below), department stores, and gourmet food shops. For religious souvenirs, head for the shops around St. Peter's.

Via Nazionale/Monti: Located between Piazza Venezia and Termini station, Via Nazionale is the place to go for affordable fashion. Monti, squeezed in between Via Nazionale and the Roman Forum, is home to some delightful boutiques selling a mix of high-end clothing, shoes, accessories, and home furnishings.

Opening Hours

See pp. 241–242

Tax-Free Shopping

Non-EU tourists can apply for a tax refund on purchases. Refunds are slightly less than sales tax percentages and work out to be around 16 percent. The minimum purchase to qualify is €154.94, spent in one store. Merchant participation is voluntary, and smaller shops may feel that refunds aren't worth the hassle. Ask the shop assistant for the appropriate tax-free forms. You will need your passport. When leaving the country, have your purchases available for inspection when you present your Tax-Free Shopping Cheques or refund forms to be stamped.

Sales (Saldi)

Winter sales start after the 6th of January and go through the end of the month; summer sales start in early July. These are the best times to pick up a bargain: Prices are discounted by 50 percent or more. Make sure the original price is on the tag, along with the discounted sale price.

Malls & Department Stores

Although not nearly as the size and scope of their North American cousins, some malls do exist in central Rome. They are open daily, usually until 10 p.m. The **Galleria Alberto Sordi** at Piazza Colonna, on central Via del Corso, not far from Piazza di Spagna, is a small, recently refurbished art nouveau mall. With its 50 or more shops, the **Forum Termini** mall located at Termini, the central train station, Piazza dei Cinquecento, is an excellent place for one-stop and last-minute shopping needs.

There are two notable department stores in Rome, both selling clothing, leather goods, accessories, cosmetics, and housewares: **Rinascente** (Via del Corso 189, tel 06 679 7691; Piazza Fuime 1, tel 06 884 1231) and **Coin** (Via Cola di Rienzo 179; Piazzale Appio 7, tel 06 708 0020).

Clothing

Italy leads the world when it comes to designer fashion. Although most major houses have their headquarters in Milan, all have branches here.

Tip: Always try on clothing and measure gifts, as sizes in Italy are not always uniform. Remember Italian shops rarely make refunds and the smaller shops are often even reluctant to exchange items.

Piazza di Spagna Area

Albertelli, Via dei Prefetti 11, tel 687 3793. Classy menswear including wonderful (and expensive) custom-made men's shirts. **Armani Boutique,** Via dei Condotti 77, tel 06 699 1460. The king of understated elegance for men and women. **Brioni,** Via Barberini 79, tel 06 484517. Internationally famous and the preferred tailor of celebrities. Fine line of suits both off-the-rack and tailor-made. There is also a small women's collection. **Davide Cenci,** Via del Campo Marzio 1-7, tel 06 699 0681. Top quality, elegantly conservative men and women's wear and outerwear.

Dolce e Gabbana, Via dei Condotti 51, tel 06 6992 4999. D&G Line, Piazza di Spagna 93, tel 06 6938 0870. Very "in" and stylish clothes for women.

Emporio Armani, Via Babuino 140, tel 06 322 1581. More casual and affordable clothes.

Ermenegildo Zegna, Via Borgognona 7E, tel 06 678 9143. Three floors of classic men's fashion.

Fendi, (Men) Via Borgognona 36, tel 06 696 661; (Women) Largo Goldoni 419. These impressive stores sell everything from furs to gifts.

Gianni Versace, (Women) Via Bocca di Leone 27, tel 06 678 0521; (Men) Via Borgognona 24, tel 06 679 5037; (Jeans) Via Frattina 116, tel 06 678 7681. Flamboyant color schemes and styles beloved of Hollywood stars and the glamor set.

Max Mara, Via dei Condotti 19, tel 06 6992 2104. Wearable, classic styles for women.

La Perla, Via dei Condotti 79, tel 06 6994 1934. Luxury lingerie for women.

Prada, Via dei Condotti 88–92, tel 06 679 0897; cutting-edge clothes and accessories.

Tad Concept Store, Via del Babuino 155/A, tel 06 3269 5131. State of the art fashion, accessories, and home furnishings. There is also a beauty salon, as well as a flower shop and a café.

Trussardi, Via dei Condotti 49, tel 06 678 0280. Beautifully tailored suits, and more, for men and women. For casual wear, try the **T'Store,** Via del Corso 478, tel 06 322 6055.

Valentino, (Women) Via dei Condotti 13, tel 06 679 5862; (Men) Via Bocca di Leone 15, tel 06 678 3656. Chic elegance from Rome's most famous home-grown fashion house.

Piazza Navona/ Campo Dei Fiori Area

Arsenale, Via Governo Vecchio 64, tel 06 686 1380. Quirky fashions using swaths of luxurious and unusual fabric.

Best Seller, Via dei Giubbonari 96, tel 06 6813 6040. For the younger generation. Discount section at the back of the store.

Degli Effetti, Piazza Capranica 75, 79, and 93, tel 06 679 0202. Major Italian, Japanese, and French designers can be found here.

Josephine de Huertas and Co., Via di Parione 19, Via del Governo Vecchio 68 & 59, tel 06 6830 0156. These three boutique stores sell carefully selected collections that include Missoni, Paul Smith, Michael Kors, and others.

Nuyorica, Piazza Pollarola 36, tel 06 6889 1243 & Via de Pellegrino 15, tel 06 6821 5494. Chic shops with a growing range of clothes, shoes, and accessories. Carries Chloé, Marc Jacobs, and other designer lines.

Regola 71, Via dei Cappellari 71, tel 06 683 2169. Stylish shop catering to women who are looking for something modern but not overly trendy.

L'una & L'altra, Piazza Pasquino 75, tel 06 6880 4995. Clothes for feminine sophisticates. Exclusive franchise for Dries Van Noten.

Trastevere Area

Scala Quattordieci, Via della Scala 14, tel 06 588 3580. Very original but still wearable custom-made women's clothes.

Shoes & Bags

The Italian leather industry's worldwide reputation is well-deserved. Don't leave Rome without a bag, a pair of shoes, or one of the leather accessories available for all tastes and pockets.

Piazza di Spagna Area

Dal Co', Via Vittorio Veneto 64, tel 06 678 6536. Highest quality made-to-measure shoes for women.

Fausto Santini, Via Frattina 120, tel 06 678 4114. Trend-setting styles ranging from everyday to eccentric.

Ferragamo, Via Condotti 65 & 73, tel 06 678 1130. World-famous designer shoes and apparel.

Furla, Via dei Condotti 55, tel 06 679 1973. Smart bags and accessories at accessible prices.

Gucci, Via dei Condotti 8, tel 06 679 0405. The ultimate in elegance, top quality shoes and accessories. Like Ferragamo, a Japanese favorite.

Modi di Campagna, Via dei Prefetti 42, tel 06 6880 2631. Stunningly beautiful leather goods and clothes.

Tod's, Via Fontanella di Borghese 56/57, tel 06 6821 0066; Via Condotti 52/53, tel 06 699 1089. Attractive shoes and bags for men and women.

Jewelry & Other Accessories

Alessandra, Via Monserrato 122a (Campo dei Fiori), tel 06 686 9405. Jewelry using precious and semi-precious stones.

Bulgari, Via dei Condotti 10 (Spagna), tel 06 679 3876. The ultimate in jewelry design.

La Coppola Storta, Via del Piè di Marmo 4 (Pantheon), tel 06 679 5801. A vast collection of the famous Sicilian "coppola" caps.

Fabio Piccone, Via del Boschetto 140 (Nazionale), tel 06 485 511. A real find for costume or vintage jewelry.

Massimo Maria Melis, Via del Orso 57 (Navona), tel 06 686 9188. Beautifully crafted gold jewelry.

Materie, Via del Gesù 29, tel 06 679 3199. Unique jewelry made from a wide variety of materials. Also carries scarves, handbags, and other accessories.

Mondello Ottica, Via del Pellegrino 98 (Campo dei Fiori), tel 06 686 1955. Your best bet if you are looking for a very special pair of glasses.

Sermoneta, Piazza di Spagna 61, tel 06 196 0679. Gloves in all colors and styles.

Tempi Moderni, Via Governo Vecchio 108 (Piazza Navona), tel 06 687 7007. Art Deco necklaces and Bakelite brooches.

Troncanelli, Via della Cuccagna 15 (Piazza Navona), tel 06 687 9320. High-quality versions of many hat styles.

Kids Clothing

Children's clothes don't come cheap in Italy, but they do have that inimitable touch of style.

La Cicogna, Via Frattina 138 (Spagna), tel 06 679 1912. Maternity, baby, and children's wear. Carries designer labels such as Armani and Trussardi.

Mettimi Giù, Via Due Macelli 59e (Spagna), tel 06 678 9761. Stylish clothing, accessories, and shoes for 0-14s.

Al Sogno, Piazza Navona 53, tel 06 686 4198. Gorgeous, cuddly toys, some of them life-size. Collectors models, miniature Ferraris, and dolls.

Città del Sole, Via della Scrofa 65 (Navona), tel 06 6880 3805. Educational and environment-friendly toys, books, games, and puzzles for children and adults.

Specialty Shops

Alinari, Via Alibert 16 a/b (Spagna), tel 06 679 2923. Fratelli Alinari is the oldest firm in the world working in the field of photography. In their shop in Rome you can find books and a vast number of photographs of Rome and Italy as they used to be.

Casali, Via dei Coronari 115 (Navona); Piazza della Rotonda 82, tel 06 678 3515. A wide range of beautiful prints.

Cesari, Via del Babuino 195 (Spagna), tel 06 361 3456. Lovely household fabrics and linens.

Crocianelli, Via dei Prefetti 37/40 (Spagna), tel 06 687 3592.

Rome's oldest haberdashery sells an amazing variety of tassels, fringes, edgings, and bows in every imaginable color.

Fabriano, Via del Babuino 173 (Spagna), tel 06 3260 0361. Stylish store selling luxury stationery. Leather and cloth photo albums, guest or address books, and fountain pens all make great gifts.

Officina Profumo Farmaceutica di Santa Maria Novella, Corso di Rinascimento 47, tel 06 687 9608. Products from the ancient Florentine pharmacy made with natural ingredients and the monks' traditional methods.

L'Olfattorio: Bar à Parfums, Via di Ripetta 34 (Spagna), tel 06 361 2325. Expert assistants at this elegant perfumery will help you find the perfect scent. Call to arrange a *passeggiata olfattoria*–an olfactory tour of the shop. Closed Sun., Mon., & until 3:30 p.m.

Polvere di Tempo, Via del Moro 59 (Trastevere), tel 06 588 0704. Everything for measuring time and space.

Spazio Sette, Via dei Barbieri 7 (Navona), tel 06 686 9746. This converted 17th-century frescoed palazzo houses one of the best stocked houseware and design stores in Rome.

Stilo Fatti, Via degli Orfani 82 (Pantheon), tel 06 678 9662. A wide range of pens, briefcases, and stationery.

Gifts & Souvenirs

Gift and souvenir shops surround Piazza Navona and Campo dei Fiore. Along Corso di Rinascimento you will find Murano glass, ceramics, Roman reproductions, and stationery. Shops selling religious items cluster in the Via dei Cestari area and around St. Peter's.

Tip: Most Roman museums, galleries, and archaeological sites have excellent gift shops offering a large range of souvenirs at reasonable prices.

Taste Treats

Antica Norceria Viola, Piazza Campo dei Fiori 42, tel 06 6880 6114. An impressive selection of salamis, hams, and other pork products, many vacuum-packed for easy transport.

Ai Monasteri, Piazza delle Cinque Lune (Navona), tel 06 6880 2783. This attractive shop sells gourmet goodies, cosmetics, and health products prepared by the monks and nuns of several monasteries and convents.

Bar Sant'Eustachio, Piazza Sant'Eustachio 82 (Navona), tel 06 686 1309. This café, selling what is considered the best coffee in central Rome also sells beans or ready ground in a variety of gift packs.

Dely Chef, Via dell' Oca 34 (Piazza del Popolo). A small shop offering high quality Italian food products from the Naples region.

La Fabbrica dei Marron Glacés, Via P. Emilio 67 (Prati), tel 06 324 3548. The best place in Rome to try and buy marron glacés, Giovanni Giuliani has been producing them in his laboratory for the last 50 years and uses only the best quality products. The specialty is chocolate-covered marron glacés.

Franchi, Via Cola di Rienzo 200 tel 06 686 4576. Love to eat? Head for Franchi, the city's best gourmet take-out. Imported cheeses and wines, too.

Moriondo e Gariglio, Via del Piè di Marmo 21 (Pantheon), tel 06 699 0856. Fantastic, home- and custom-made chocolates.

Pastateca, Via della Vite 44/45, tel 06 4549 1431. This shop offers around 500 varieties of pasta for all tastes and occasions. Other than the classics, there are flavored, diet-friendly, gluten-free, and biologically grown pastas, all produced traditionally and in a plethora of different shapes.

La Peonia Cose di Sardegna, Via delle Carrozze 85 (Spagna), tel 06 678 8432. A wide range of

products from Sardinia.
Quetzalcoatl Chocolat Passion,
Via delle Carrozze 26, tel 06 6920
2191. Quality chocolates beautifully presented.
Trimani, Via Goito 20 (Nazionale), tel 06 446 9661. Considered
the best-stocked wine cellar in
Rome. Worldwide shipping.
Volpetti, Via Marmorata 47, tel
06 574 2352. This Testaccio area
shop is a must for any foodie. It
sells and ships the highest quality
produce and specializes in aged
cheeses.
Boccione, Via del Portico
d'Ottavia 1 (Ghetto), tel 06 687
8637. Closed on Saturdays, this
bakery is known for its traditional
Roman-Jewish cakes, particularly
the *torta di ricotta* (cheesecake)
with berries *(visciole)* or chocolate.

Books & Music

There are some excellent English-
language bookshops in Rome,
with a wide range of books.
Several Italian stores also carry
selections of English books.
The Almost Corner Bookshop,
Via del Moro 45 (Trastevere),
tel 06 583 6942. A welcoming
treasure trove of fiction, poetry,
history, biography, and a wide
range of other categories.
Anglo American Bookshop, Via
delle Vite 102 (Spagna), tel 06 679
5222. Open Mon. p.m.–Sat. Particularly good for nonfiction titles,
catering to a wide range of special
interests. At No. 27, a second
branch (tel 06 678 9657) specializes in science and technology.
Borri Libreria Termini, atrium
of the central train station, tel
06 481 7940. Open daily until 11
p.m. A good selection of foreign
language fiction and some guides.
Feltrinelli, Largo Torre Argentina
11 (Navona), tel 06 6866 3001.
Open daily. This branch of a major
national bookshop chain features
an extensive selection of Italian
books, a large music section, and
some English-language fiction and

guidebooks. There is a café and
a ticket office where you can buy
tickets for events in Rome.
Feltrinelli International, Via V.E.
Orlando 84 (Nazionale), tel 06
482 7878. Wide range of books in
English and other languages.
Libreria del Viaggiatore, Via del
Pellegrino 78 (Campo dei Fiori),
tel 06 6880 1048. Open Mon.
p.m.–Sat. English-language travel
books, guides, and maps.
Ricordi Media Stores, Via del
Corso 506, tel 06 361 2370. One
of several branches in Rome, it
has a good selection of CDs.

Markets

**Fruits & Vegetables: See
sidebar p. 155**

Flea Markets & Antiques:
See sidebar p. 195

Sunday Markets
1st Sunday of the month: **Ponte
Milvio, Ludovisi Garage** (Via
Ludovisi), 06 3600 5345; 2nd Sunday: **Piazza Mazzini,** tel. 338/965
7690; 3rd Sunday: **Piazza Augusto
Imperatore,** tel 06 3600 5345
and **Piazza Medaglia D'Oro,** tel
338 965 7690; 4th Sunday: **Piazza
Verdi,** tel 06 855 2773

A number of smaller clothes, print,
bric-a-brac, and antiques markets
are scattered throughout Rome:

Book & Print Market, Piazza
Fontanella Borghese (Spagna).
You can find old books, prints,
postcards, and music scores in this
small market. Open Mon.–Sat.
9:30–sunset.
Piazza Mazzini (Prati), tel 06 904
4263. Sells antiques, handicrafts,
paintings, and collectibles. Held
every first Sunday of the month.
Ponte Milvio (Flamino), tel 06
907 7312. This market stretches
along the Tiber from Ponte Milvio
to Ponte Duc d' Aosta and takes
place on the first weekend of the

month. The choice ranges from
furniture to costume jewelry.
Soffitto Sotto i Portici, Piazza
Augusto Imperatore (Spagna), tel.
06 3600 5345. Small collectibles
can be found here every first and
third Sunday of the month.
Villa Gloria, Viale Maresciallo
Pilsudski (Parioli), tel. 06 854
1461. Shop for collectibles, antiques, handicrafts, and clothes
every second Sunday
of the month.
Piazza Verdi (Parioli), tel 06 855
2773. Held on the fourth Sunday
of the month, this market has a
huge selection of small antiques.

Discount Outlets

Discount outlets are rare in central
Rome and their stock is often limited; however, it is possible to pick
up a designer item at a bargain
price if you are prepared to look.

De Carlis Outlet, Vicolo delle
Orsoline 30 (Spagna), tel. 06 323
0165. An outlet for women.
Il Discount dell'Alta Moda, Via
Gesù e Maria 16/a, tel 06 322
5006. This small, popular outlet
sells many famous designer labels.
Fausto Santini Outlet, Via Cavour
106 (Nazionale), tel. 06 488 0934.
This outlet sells the designer's
previous season's collection at a
fraction of the price.
Firma Stock, Via delle Carozze
18 (Spagna), tel. 06 6920 0371.
Check this place out for discounted designer labels.
Mercatino Michela, Piazza
Pitagora 7, tel 06 8069 0510. This
store in residential Parioli has
rooms of designer label cast-offs.
Quadrofoglio Outlet Under 12,
Via delle Colonnelle 10 (Spagna),
tel. 06 678 4917. Outlet for
children's clothes.
Regola 33, Via San Paolo alla
Regola 33, tel 06 6813 6245. A
small outlet near Piazza Navona
that sells designer labels, including
Dolce e Gabbana, Versace,
and Fendi.

Entertainment

Rome has developed into a lively entertainment center. Nightlife has become increasingly active and varied. The opening of the Parco della Musica has added a valuable performance space, the Casa del Jazz is a focal point for jazz enthusiasts, while the new Casa del Cinema is a must for film buffs. Other than movie houses, the vast majority of places listed here are closed Monday.

Details of what's on and where for the following week are published in the weekly *Roma C'è* (out on Wednesday, also online at *www.romace.it*) and Thursday's *TrovaRoma* (an insert in the daily *La Repubblica*). For clubs and live music, the online *2night* (*www.2night.it*) has good, reliable information on nightlife, as do *In Rome Now* (*www.inromenow.com*) and *Wanted in Rome* (available at newsstands and online at *www.wantedinrome.com*). Entertainment listings and a booking service are available at *www.0606008.it*, or tel 060608.

Vivaticket (*www.vivaticket.it*) and **Hello Ticket** (*tel. 06 4807 8400 or 800 907 080, www.helloticket.it*) offer online booking services as well as call centers.

Ticket agencies also exist throughout the city: **Orbis** (*Piazza dell'Esquilino 37, tel 06 474476*), which also sells tickets for sports events; **Messaggerie Musicali** (*Via del Corso 472, tel 06 6819 2349*); and **Feltrinelli** (*Largo di Torre Argentina 5/a, tel 06 6830 8596*) are just a few. A commission is charged.

Rome has a number of festivals that take place throughout the year, although most of them are concentrated in the summer months when many of the permanent cultural venues and social Rome pack up. Rome's film festival, RomeFilmFest, takes place in October and is enormously popular, both for its choice of films and events. For information see *www.romacinemafest.it*. **Estate Romana** (*www.estate romana.comune.roma.it*), held June

through September at venues throughout Rome, is a mind-boggling array of outdoor cinema, theater, opera, music, and dance performances from some of the world's best artists. **Romaeuropa Festival** (*www.romaeuropa.net*), an international cultural event held in November, features a program of dance, theater, and music, with a focus on classical music.

Theater & Dance

Nearly all theater is in Italian unless specifically noted. Check *Wanted in Rome, InRomeNow*, and with the theaters themselves for details of any English-language drama. Most theaters offer online booking. The Miracle Players, an English-speaking theater troupe based in Rome, perform original texts and comic adaptations of classics in various historical locations. See *www.miracleplayers.org* for details.

Argentina–Teatro di Roma, Largo Argentina 52, tel 06 6840 00311, *www.teatrodiroma.net*. The repertoire presented at this beautiful, well-restored 18th-century theater includes Italian classics, international contemporary, dance, and festivals. **Colosseo,** Via Capo D'Africa 29/A, tel 06 700 4932. Many big names in Italian theater and cinema cut their teeth at this long-established home of experimental productions. It also stages concerts, short films, and dance. **Eliseo and Piccolo Eliseo,** Via Nazionale 183, tel 06 488721, *www.teatroeliseo.it*. The Eliseo puts on well-loved classics from Italy and elsewhere. The Piccolo

next door concentrates on more contemporary theater. **Quirino Vittorio Gassman,** Via delle Vergini 7, tel 06 679 4585, *www.teatroquirino.it*. Home to the Italian National Theater Company, it stages top-quality productions of classics and the best of contemporary theater. **Sistina,** Via Sistina 129, tel 06 420 0711, *www.ilsistina.com*. This spacious venue specializes in dramatic productions and musicals. **Valle,** Via del Teatro Valle 21, tel 06 6880 3794, *www.teatrovalle.it*. One of the oldest theater buildings in Rome (built in 1726), the Valle features Italian and international contemporary drama, as well as the occasional non-Italian play in original language. **Vascello,** Via G. Carini 72, tel 06 588 1021, *www.teatrovascello.it*. There is a bit of everything in this popular venue, although it tends to focus on contemporary dance.

Opera, Music, & Dance

As well as the places listed below, look for posters or check *www.inromenow.com* for details of free classical concerts held in historic churches. (See sidebar p. 149) **Auditorium Parco della Musica,** Viale Pietro de Coubertin 15/30, tel 06 8024 1281 or 199 109783, *www.auditorium.com*. This complex includes three concert halls offering a wide-ranging program of classical, jazz, and contemporary music, dance, an outdoor amphitheater, restaurants, art gallery, bookstore, and an archaeological area and museum. Home to the Santa Cecilia orchestra, the Parco della Musica offers a rich program of classical music. (See also p. 224.)

Auditorium Conciliazione, Via della Conciliazione 4, tel 800 913518, *www.auditoriumconciliazi one.it.* Programs feature classical and contemporary music as well as some dance and film events. **Oratorio del Gonfalone,** Via del Gonfalone 32/a, tel 06 8530 1758. This glorious, 16th-century setting is perfect for programs of chamber and choral music, with emphasis on the baroque. **Teatro Ghione,** Via delle Fornaci 37, tel 06 637 2294, *www.ghione .it.* It stages concerts of up-and-coming and big-name soloists, as well as theater productions. **Teatro Nazionale,** Via del Viminale 51, tel 06 4816 0255. A prime venue for ballet company performances and other productions of the Teatro dell'Opera. **Teatro Olimpico,** Piazza Gentile da Fabriano 17, tel 06 326 5991, *www.teatroolimpico.it.* Home of the Accademia Filarmonica Romana, the program includes music, theatre, and dance, with many visiting international artists. **Teatro dell'Opera,** Piazza B. Gigli 8, tel 06 481 7003 or 800 016665, *www.operaroma.it.* The home of Rome's Opera and Ballet Company, this theater is host to classical productions as well as some more contemporary ones. In summer, opera and ballet are performed outdoors in the impressive surroundings of the Terme di Caracalla. **Il Tempietto,** tel 06 8713 1590, *www.tempietto.it.* This classical-music association performs concerts throughout the winter at Sala Baldini (Piazza di Campitelli 9) and Villa Torlonia (Via Nomentana 7). In summer, it stages nightly outdoor concerts, each in the atmospheric Teatro di Marcello (Via Luigi Petroselli) and at Villa Torlonia.

Contemporary Live Music

Rome has a dynamic live-music scene, with a number of venues offering jazz, soul, rock, and ethnic music. The soccer stadium, race track, and other unusual locations are often settings for concerts and festivals, particularly in the summer months. **Alexanderplatz,** Via Ostia 9, tel 06 3975 1877, *www.alexanderplatz .it.* Plastered with photos and signatures of visiting performers, Alexanderplatz is one of Italy's most important and well-known jazz clubs. Reservations advised. In summer, the club moves to the outdoor setting of Villa Celimontana, where one can also enjoy light meals and/or a drink in the evening breeze. **Big Mama,** Vicolo San Francesco a Ripa 18, tel 06 581 2551, *www .bigmama.it.* The self-styled "home of the blues in Rome" offers an interesting selection of international and Italian musicians with the great names of the past and present. Reservations advised. **Caffè Latino,** Via di Monte Testaccio 96 (Testaccio), tel 06 5728 8556. One of the first to open in an area now packed with clubs, this is still popular, especially among the not so young. It offers live jazz, blues, rock, and funk. A little down the street, **Caffè de Oriente** (Via di Monte Testaccio 36, tel 06 574 5019) is the hotspot for live Latin American music and DJ sets. **Casa del Jazz,** Viale di Porta Ardeatina 55, tel 06 704731, *www .casajazz.it.* Villa Osio and its 2,500-square-meter park are the site of this center hosting top names in jazz. Facilities include a multi-media library, a book- and record store, bar, and restaurant. **Fonclea,** Via Crescenzio 82a, tel 06 689 6302, *www.fonclea.it.* This cozy music venue features live jazz, soul, and rock. Nourishment can be had in a good selection of beers and whiskeys and a range of light supper dishes. **Villaggio Globale,** Lungotevere

Testaccio 1, tel 06 575 7233. An architecturally interesting, 19th-century slaughterhouse makes an exotic venue for open-air world music concerts in summer and a variety of year-round cultural events.

Several bookshops in Trastevere hold concerts and other live events and are worth checking out if you are looking for something a little different. **Daseia Music Bookshop,** Via di San Francesco a Ripa 60, tel. 06 454 2211. This music bookshop and bar holds concerts, performances, and events on Sat. nights. **Bibli,** Via dei Fienaroli 28, tel. 06 581 4534. More like a cultural center than a bookstore, holds concerts, readings, lectures. In addition to a bar, it also serves a buffet lunch and a wonderful Sunday brunch.

Exhibition & Art Galleries

Le Scuderie (*Via XXIV Maggio 16, tel. 06 3996 7500, english. scuderiequirinale.it*), **Palazzo delle Esposizioni** (*Via Nazionale 194, tel. 06 3996 7500, www. palazzoespo sizioni.it*), and **Complesso dello Vittoriano** (*Via di San Pietro in Carcere*) all host temporary art exhibitions of international standards. **MACRO** (*Via Reggio Emilia 54, tel 06 6710 70400, en.macro .roma.museum*), **Future** (*Piazza Orazio Giustiniani 4 [Testaccio], tel 06 6710 70400, open 4 p.m.–midnight, closed Mon.*), and **MAXXI** (*Via Guido Reni 2, tel 06 3210 1829, www.darc.beniculturali.it*) are all dedicated to contemporary art.

Nightlife

Rome may not be the hippest of capitals, but it is still possible to party all night if you are young and know where to go. Discos and clubs start around midnight and go to the early hours of the morning. Wine bars tend to close around 1 a.m. In summer, clubs usually close or transfer to outside areas in Rome or to the nearby beaches of Ostia or Fregene. The greatest concentration of nightclubs and ristro-bars (places where you can eat, drink, and dance) are in the Testaccio (Via di Monte Testaccio) and Ostiense (Via G. Libetta) districts. The cocktail and wine bars are mainly gathered around Trastevere, Piazza Navona, and Campo dei Fiori, which changes from a fruit and vegetable market during the day into a lively bar and meeting spot at night.

Alibi, Via Monte Testaccio 40 (Testaccio), tel 06 574 3448. One of Rome's earliest gay bars/disco, and also one of its most popular regardless of sexual preference. A little down the street at **Radio Londra** *(Via di Monte Testaccio 67, tel 06 574 0044)* the music is vibrant (house, techno, and deep) and the crowd outlandish.

Anima, Via Santa Maria dell'Anima 57 (Navona), tel 06 686 4021. A focal point for those who like good music and drinks. Dancing until 5 a.m., with expert DJs spnning nonstop funk, soul, house, and jungle. Unlike most club-bars in Rome, entrance is free.

Gilda, Via Mario dei Fiori 97 (Spagna), tel 06 678 4838. *www .midra.it.* This well-established disco used to be the place to ogle at the VIPs of Italian politics, culture, and society. A younger crowd patronizes it during the week.

Goa, Via G. Libetta 13 (Ostiense), tel 06 574 8277. The music at this one-room chic club (with corners for dancing) tends to be avant-garde, with some of the best DJs in town at the console.

Micca Club, Via Monte Testaccio 95 (Termini), tel 06 8744 0079, *www.miccaclub.com.* A labyrinthine structure defined by a spectacular spiral staircase. Music ranges from jazz and funk to soul. There is a program of DJs, visual arts, and

even a market on Sundays. **Saponeria,** Via degli Argonauti 20 (Ostiense), tel 06 574 6999. Expect the best in this former soap factory, one of the cult places in Rome. Depending on the evening, nu-house, hip-hop, electronica, and nu-funk rattle the walls.

Bars

Bars range from the classic *enoteca,* serving wine by the glass or by the bottle, to cool cocktail venues open until late and often serving light meals. In summer many spill onto the street, particularly in Campo dei Fiori, which is transformed from a fruit-and-vegetable market during the day to a lively bar and meeting spot at night.

Ristro-Bars (Eat, Drink, & Dance)

Classico Villaggio, Via G. Libetta 3 (Ostiense), tel 06 5728 8857, *www.classico.it.* Located in the trendy Ostiense district, this former factory has two dance floors and a restaurant, as well as good rock and jazz concerts.

Distillerie Clandestine, Via G. Libetta 7 (Ostiense), tel 06 5730 5102, *www.distillerieclandestine.com.* Glamorous 1930s-themed club, considered one of the coolest places in the capital. Early in the evening, the restaurant serves Mediterranean dishes; later, dance and music range from live acts to DJs.

Nottinsolite, Via di Monte Testaccio 65 (Testaccio), tel 389 649 1785, *www.nottinsolite. it.* A new club in the Testaccio district. Cozy with cool design and elegant decor. At 11:30 p.m, the restaurant turns into a disco where you can dance to house, disco, Latin, and R&B into the early morning hours.

Le Rune, Via di Monte Testaccio 46 (Testaccio), tel 06 5730 1015. Le Rune is a restaurant, cocktail bar, and dance club rolled into

one. Doors open for dinner, and the kitchen doesn't shut down until 5 a.m. The decorations highlight the traditional *cocci* (earthenware) found in this particular area of Rome.

Supperclub, Via dei Narni 14 (Navona), tel 06 6880 7207. For something different, try this chic club located between the Pantheon and Piazza Navona. Eat lying down and expect all your senses to be titillated in the combo restaurant, club, performance venue, and bar.

Bars/Cocktail Bars

Le Coppolle, Piazza delle Coppelle 52 (Navona). Red is the dominant color in this bar where the cool and trendy gather. Perfect for a pre-dinner drink or nightcap.

Doppiozero, Via Ostiense 68 (Ostiense), tel 06 5730 1961. Smart and fashionable, with sleek decor and a relaxed atmosphere. A popular spot at all times of day, it is great for brunch and a cool place to hang out in the evening.

Freni e Frizoni, Via del Politeama 4/6 (Trastevere), tel 06 5833 4210. A former car workshop on the edge of Trastevere, this fun place is perfect for brunch-lunch, cocktails, and nightcaps.

Jonathan's Angels, Via della Fossa 16 (Navona), tel 06 689 3426. This chaotic, packed cocktail bar is not the place for shrinking violets: You may be pulled into one of the semi-impromptu evening floor shows that sometimes take place. The decorations—wall paintings, statuettes—must be seen to be believed, especially the gorgeous bathroom.

La Mescita, Piazza Trilussa 41 (Trastevere), tel 06 5833 3920. The Enoteca Ferrara has recently opened this small elegant bar in the heart of Trastevere. Seating is limited so drinks are taken at the bar. Delicious snacks included in the price of the drink.

Nazca, Via del Gazometro 42

(Ostiense), tel 06 4544 7372. This cocktail music bar and restaurant is an extremely elegant destination. Sip some of the best cocktails in town while listening to electronica and house music. **Salotto 42,** Piazza di Pietra 42, tel 06 678 5804. Trendy bar located in front of the Tempio di Adriano. Open from morning until 2 a.m. A great place to savor a coffee or aperitif. **Stairs,** Via della Scala 43 (Trastevere), tel 06 9727 7421, *www .stairsclub.it.* This bar, made up of two floors, has become the trendy place in Trastevere. Warm and welcoming during the week and fun on the weekends.

Bars/Wine Bars

Antico Enoteca di Via della Croce, Via della Croce 76b, tel 06 679 0896. Near Piazza di Spagna, this attractive wine bar offers a vast selection of wines and a buffet lunch. **Buccone,** Via di Ripetta 19, tel 06 361 2154. Established in 1870, this traditional wine bar showcases an excellent selection of wines. Also offers light lunch and dinner (except in summer). Closed Sun. **Il Cantiniere di Santa Dorotea,** Via di S. Dorotea 9 (Trastevere), tel 06 581 9025. Open 5 p.m.–2 a.m. Closed Tues. This unpretentious but extremely cozy *enoteca* features a good selection of Italian and French wines. Light fare is also offered. **Costantini,** Piazza Cavour 16, tel 06 321 3210. One of the better-known cellars of Rome, Costantini also has a pleasant bar serving wine by the glass. Closed Sun. **Divino Amore,** Via dei Balestrari 12/14 (Campo dei Fiore), tel 06 686 4413. Originally a wine shop, now transformed into a well-stocked wine bar. Small and friendly, it is a popular meeting place for wine buffs. Closed Sun. & Mon. L.

Enoteca Ferrara, Piazza Trilussa 41, tel 06 5833 3920. Wine tasting (more than 600 varieties of wine are available) begins at 6 p.m. every day—snacks are available. The accompanying restaurant is interesting, but somewhat pricey. **Il Goccetto,** Via dei Banchi Vecchi 14, tel 06 686 4268. This cozy wine cellar specializes in wines from small Italian vineyards. The English-speaking owner can guide you in your choice. Closed Sun. **Trimani,** Via Cernaia 37b (Termini station), tel 06 446 9630. This elegant wine bar is an excellent place for enjoying good wine and food in a casual, fun atmosphere. Closed Sun. **Vineria Reggio,** Piazza Campo dei Fiori 15, tel 06 6880 3268. Expats, tourists, and Romans flock here to quaff reasonably priced wines and other drinks at the bar or outside on the pavement. **Vinoteca Novecento,** Piazza della Copelle 47 (Pantheon), tel 06 683 3078. Small, cozy wine bar with outdoor seating and romantic torchlight. Head inside for salami and cheese tastings. Closed Mon.–Wed. L.

Cinema

Most films in Italy are dubbed into Italian. There are, however, several cinemas that screen films in original language (listed as VO), either one day a week (usually Monday) or every day. **Alcazar,** Via Cardinale Merry del Val 14, tel 06 588 0099. Shows the latest releases in their original languages on Mondays. **Casa del Cinema** (at the entrance to the Villa Borghese at the top of Via Veneto; then proceed to Largo Marcello Mastroianni. Tel 06 423 601, *www.casadelcinema. it.*) Screenings in Italian and occasionally VO, as well as debates and exhibitions. The Cine Caffe, open from 9 a.m. to 7 p.m., serves drinks and light meals in the

beautiful surroundings of Villa Borghese. **Cinema Farnese,** Campo dei Fiori 56, tel 06 686 4395. Shows films in VO on Mon. & Thurs. **Cinema Trevi,** Vicolo del Puttarello 25, tel 06 678 1206 or 06 7229 4301, *www.csc-cinematografia.it.* The cinema of the National Film School and Archives. Shows quality films in their original languages. **Metropolitan,** Via del Corso 7, tel 06 320 0933. One of the four screens here always shows a recently released film in its original language. **Nuovo Olimpia,** Via in Lucina 16, tel 06 686 1068. A two-screen venue where the latest international releases are shown in their original languages. **Nuovo Sacher,** Largo Ascianghi 1, tel 06 581 8116. A mecca for cinema fans, the Nuovo Sacher shows recent releases in their original languages on Mondays.

Soccer

See sidebar p. 219

Ice Cream

In Italy ice cream isn't just for kids. Taste it and you'll soon understand why. It's especially delightful on an after-dinner summer stroll through the historic center. See sidebar p. 97 for several excellent options, in addition to: **Café du Park,** Piazza Porta San Paolo (across the street from Porta San Paolo), tel 06 574 3363. Open daily. This place specializes in *cremolato*—a creation similar to ice cream, but without milk products. Serving all sorts of fruit flavors (fig, raspberry, blackberry, melon, etc.), Café du Park is one of the best taste treats in town. **Duse,** Via Duse 1, tel 06 807 9300. Family-run, Duse serves some of the best ice cream in town. Try the *zabaione* or the *zuppa inglese.*

LANGUAGE GUIDE

Yes *Si*
No *No*
Excuse me (in a crowd or asking for permission) *Permesso*
Excuse me (asking for attention) *Mi scusi*
Hello (before lunch) *Buon giorno*, (after lunch) *Buona sera*
Hi or Bye *Ciao*
Please *Per favore*
Thank you *Grazie*
You're welcome *Prego*
Have a good day! *Buona giornata!*
OK *Va bene*
Goodbye *Arrivederci*
Good night *Buona notte*
Sorry *Mi scusi* or *Mi dispiace*
here *qui*
there *lì*
today *oggi*
yesterday *ieri*
tomorrow *domani*
now *adesso/ora*
later *più tardi/dopo*
right away *subito*
this morning *stamattina*
this afternoon *questo pomeriggio*
this evening *stasera*
open *aperto*
closed *chiuso*
Do you have? *Avrebbe?*
Do you speak English? *Parla inglese?*
I'm American (man) *Sono americano*, (woman) *Sono americana*
I don't understand *Non capisco*
Please speak more slowly *Potrebbe parlare più lentamente?*
Where is...? *Dov' è...?*
I don't know *Non so*
No problem *Niente*
That's it *Ecco*
Here/there it is (masculine) *Eccolo*, (feminine) *Eccola*
What is your name? *Come si chiama?*
My name is... *Mi chiamo...*
Let's go *Andiamo*
At what time? *A che ora?*
When? *Quando?*
What time is it? *Che ora è?*
Can you help me? *Mi può aiutare?*
I'd like... *Vorrei...*
How much is it? *Quanto costa?*

MENU READER

breakfast *la (prima) colazione*
lunch *il pranzo*
dinner *la cena*
appetizer *l'antipasto*
first course *il primo*
main course *il secondo*
vegetable, side dish *il contorno*
dessert *il dessert*
wine list *la lista dei vini*
the bill *il conto*
I'd like to order *Vorrei ordinare*
Is service included? *Il servizio è incluso?*

Pasta sauces

See Food, p. 36

Meat

l'abbacchio lamb
l'anatra duck
la bistecca beefsteak
ben cotta well-done
non troppo cotta medium
appena cotta rare
al sangue very rare
il filetto filet steak
il carpaccio finely sliced raw cured beef
il cinghiale wild boar
il coniglio rabbit
il fegato liver
le lumache snails
il maiale pork
il manzo beef
misto di carne mixed grill
il pollo chicken
le polpette meatballs
la porchetta cold roast pork with herbs
il prosciutto ham, *crudo* raw, *cotto* cooked
i rognoni kidneys
la salsiccia fresh, spicy (usually pork) sausage
saltimbocca allo Romano veal and ham in a wine and sage sauce
straccetti pan-fried strips of beef or veal
lo stufato stew or casserole
il tacchino turkey
la trippa tripe
il vitello veal

Fish

L'alici/acciughe anchovies
l'aragosta/astice lobster
il calamaro squid
le cozze mussels
i gamberi prawns
i gamberetti shrimp
il granchio crab
le ostriche oysters
il polipo octopus
il salmone salmon
le sarde sardines
la sogliola sole
la spigola bass
il tonno tuna
la trota trout

Vegetables

l'aglio garlic
gli asparagi asparagus
il carciofo artichoke
la carota carrot
il cavolfiore cauliflower
la cipolla onion
i fagioli dried beans, usually haricot or borlotti
i fagiolini fresh green beans
i funghi (porcini) mushrooms
l'insalata mista/verde mixed/green salad
le melanzane eggplant
le patate potatoes
le patate fritte french fries
le patatine potato chips
il peperone bell pepper
i piselli peas
i pomodori tomatoes
il radicchio bitter reddish lettuce
il riso rice
gli spinaci spinach
il tartufo truffle
le zucchine zucchini

Fruit

l'albicocca apricot
l'ananas pineapple
l'arancia orange
le cilegie cherries
le fragole strawberries
la mela apple
la pera pear
la pesca peach
la pescanoce nectarine
il pompelmo grapefruit
l'uva grapes

INDEX

ILLUSTRATIONS CREDITS

National Geographic
TRAVELER
Rome

Published by the National Geographic Society
John M. Fahey, Jr., *President
and Chief Executive Officer*
Gilbert M. Grosvenor, *Chairman of the Board*
Tim T. Kelly, *President, Global Media Group*
John Q. Griffin, *President, Publishing*
Nina D. Hoffman, *Executive Vice President;
President, Book Publishing Group*

Prepared by the Book Division
Kevin Mulroy, *Senior Vice President and Publisher*
Leah Bendavid-Val, *Director of Photography Publishing
and Illustrations*
Marianne R. Koszorus, *Director of Design*
Barbara Brownell Grogan, *Executive Editor*
Elizabeth Newhouse, *Director of Travel Publishing*
Carl Mehler, *Director of Maps*
Barbara A. Noe, *Series Editor*
Cinda Rose, *Series Art Director*

Staff for this Book
Lawrence M. Porges, *Project Editor*
Kay Kabor Hankins, *Art Director*
Al Morrow, *Designer*
Mary Stephanos, *Text Editor*
Connie D. Binder, *Indexer*
Michael McNey, Nicholas P. Rosenbach, and Mapping
Specialists, *Map Production*
Bridget A. English, Christine Georgeff, Susan Hannan,
Maura Walsh, Meredith Wilcox, *Contributors*
Richard Wain, *Production Project Manager*
Rob Waymouth, *Illustrations Specialist*

Jennifer A. Thornton, *Managing Editor*
R. Gary Colbert, *Production Director*

Manufacturing and Quality Management
Christopher A. Liedel, *Chief Financial Officer*
Phillip L. Schlosser, *Vice President*
Chris Brown, *Technical Director*
Nicole Elliott, *Manager*
Monika D. Lynde, *Manager*
Rachel Faulise, *Manager*

**National Geographic Traveler: Rome (Third Edition)
ISBN: 978-1-4262-0407-4**

First edition: Edited and designed by AA Publishing
(a trading name of Automobile Association Develop-
ments Limited, whose registered office is Norfolk House,
Priestley Road, Basingstoke, Hampshire, England RG24
9NY. Registered number: 1878835).

Area map illustrations drawn by Chris Orr Associates,
Southampton, England
Cutaway illustrations drawn by Maltings Partnership,
Derby, England

Founded in 1888, the National Geographic Society is
one of the largest nonprofit scientific and educational
organizations in the world. It reaches more than 285
million people worldwide each month through its
official journal, *National Geographic,* and its four other
magazines; the National Geographic Channel; television documentaries; radio programs, films; books; vid-
eos and DVDs; maps; and interactive media. National
Geographic has funded more than 8,000 scientific
research projects and supports an education program
combating geographic illiteracy.

For more information, please call 1-800-NGS LINE
(647-5463) or write to the following address:

National Geographic Society
1145 17th Street N.W.
Washington, D.C. 20036-4688 U.S.A.

Visit us online at www.nationalgeographic.com/books

For information about special discounts for bulk
purchases, please contact National Geographic
Books Special Sales: ngspecsales@ngs.org

For rights or permissions inquiries, please contact
National Geographic Books Subsidiary Rights:
ngbookrights@ngs.org

Printed in China

The Library of Congress catalogued the first edition as
follows:
Gilbert, Sari.
   The National Geographic Traveler : Rome / Sari Gilbert and
Michael Brouse.
      p. cm.
   Includes index.
   ISBN 0-7922-7566-7
   1. Rome (Italy)--Guidebooks. I. Brouse, Michael. II.
Title.

   DG804 .G55 2000
   914.5'63204929--dc21

00-021915
                                              CIP

The information in this book has been carefully
checked and to the best of our knowledge is accurate.
However, details are subject to change, and the
National Geographic Society cannot be responsible for
such changes, or for errors or omissions. Assessments
of sites, hotels, and restaurants are based on the
author's subjective opinions, which do not necessarily
reflect the publisher's opinion.

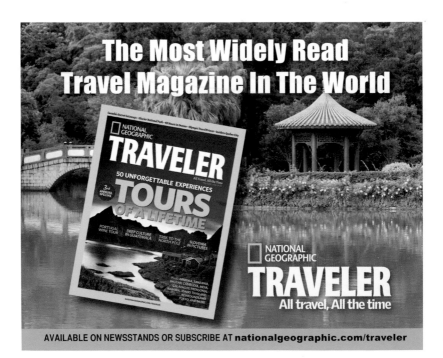